AMERICAN FOLKTALES

AMERICAN FOLKTALES

FROM THE COLLECTIONS OF THE LIBRARY OF CONGRESS

FOREWORD BY
PEGGY A. BULGER

EDITED BY
CARL LINDAHL

BASED ON THE COLLECTIONS
OF THE AMERICAN FOLKLIFE CENTER

M.E.Sharpe, Armonk, New York; London, England
IN ASSOCIATION WITH THE LIBRARY OF CONGRESS, WASHINGTON, D.C.

CONTENTS

VOLUME 1

Maud Long   44

Ray Hicks   131

2. SARA CLEVELAND: IRISH AMERICAN TALES FROM BRANT LAKE, NEW YORK

3. J.D. SUGGS: ITINERANT MASTER 183

4. JOSHUA ALLEY: DOWN-EAST TALES FROM JONESPORT, MAINE 219

VOLUME 2

8. LEGENDARY AMERICA

9. TALL TALE AMERICA 461

11. PASSING IT ON: STORIES FOR CHILDREN   539

12. VOICING THE PAST: TALES TRACING THE PATHS OF AMERICAN HISTORY   581

Native American Visions   581

AMERICAN FOLKTALES

7

THE NATION'S MOST CELEBRATED FOLKLORE COLLECTORS

JOHN A. AND ALAN LOMAX

If any two people bear responsibility for shaping the Archive of American Folk Song (AAFS) into the preeminent storehouse of the nation's folkloric memory, they are John Avery Lomax (1867–1948) and his son Alan (1915–2002), whose feats in collecting folklore are nearly as legend evoking as the names of the great folk artists they recorded: Texas Gladden, Woody Guthrie, Aunt Molly Jackson, Huddie (Leadbelly) Ledbetter, Blind Willie McTell, Jelly Roll Morton, Henry Truvillion, and innumerable others.

Working with cumbersome and faulty equipment (including a mis-wired recording machine that weighed over 300 pounds) mounted on overburdened cars, they traveled barely navigable mountain, desert, and marshland roads in search of singers whose voices they would ultimately share with the nation. Particularly when attempting to cross the color barrier in the segregated South of the 1930s, they encountered social troubles as tough as the country they traversed. Having sent ahead word to a South Carolina prison that they were coming to collect music from the inmates, they were met by an angry warden who told them to leave immediately; the prisoners, believing the Lomaxes to be federal agents coming to save them from their jailors, threatening to riot. In order to collect folksongs from French-speaking blacks in Louisiana, Alan traveled in secret, avoiding the disapproving eyes of the whites. In preparation for one journey, he lay down with his 300-pound machine in a truckbed. Man and machine were then concealed under a pile of sugarcane stalks so they could be driven to a remote location where recording could proceed in safety.

In spite of many such technological and social adversities, the Lomaxes laid the foundation of the AAFS virtually by themselves. Of the first 3,000 recordings

Uncle Billie McCrea (right) with John A. Lomax (center), collector of stories 85–91, 98–101, and 111–113. (Library of Congress)

in the American Folklife Center's current catalogue, more than 2,000 were made by John and Alan, sometimes working separately, sometimes together, and often in the company of John's wife, Ruby Terrell, or Alan's wife, Elizabeth. These recordings comprise twenty-five collections created in a period of just over five years. All the more remarkable, John was nearing age 67 when he undertook the first of these expeditions and was 71 when he completed the last. After 1939, John and Alan, working separately, added thousands of additional recordings to the holdings of the Library of Congress.

The Lomaxes' long and intense travels were largely self-subsidized. In September 1933, when he was named "Honorary Curator of the Archive of American Folk-Song," John agreed to draw a salary of one dollar a month—an arrangement that gave him "the biggest title and the smallest pay in the government," as he would later put it. Yet it was in many ways an ideal arrangement for both the Library of Congress and for the Lomaxes. Nolan Porterfield, John's biographer, writes, "For essentially nothing, the Library got not only Lomax's expertise and labor but copies of everything he recorded—and felt it had gotten the best of the bargain. Lomax, in return for a nebulous title, the loan of a recording machine, and office help, was able to go on with his work of preserving rare and vanishing elements of American culture while retaining control of his original recordings, to do with as he pleased."

The Lomaxes are known primarily, and justly, as the nation's foremost collectors, preservers, and popularizers of folksong. Through their archival recordings and such books as *American Ballads and Folk Songs* (1934), they established a national folksong repertoire. Nolan Porterfield has called *American Ballads and Folk Songs* "one of the first truly great collections of American song, in its rough, robust, distinctly American character as well as in the range of titles that have become national classics: 'Casey Jones,' 'Frankie and Albert (Johnny),' 'Jesse James,' 'Down in the Valley,' 'Rye Whiskey,' 'Little Brown Jug,' 'Shortenin' Bread,' 'Cotton-eyed Joe,' . . . 'Swing Low, Sweet Chariot,' and dozens more whose place in our culture was established by the work of John Lomax."

Their inestimable contribution to folk music has long obscured the fact that the Lomaxes were also important pioneers in the collection and presentation of folktales, particularly in their work with the autobiographical and oral historical narratives of folk artists. John and Alan's *Negro Folk Songs as Sung by Lead Belly* (1936) and Alan's *Mr. Jelly Roll* (1950) stand among the earliest and most important attempts at collaborative ethnography, in which these musicians speak largely of, and for, themselves.

The twenty-eight stories that follow offer only a fraction of the sum collected by the Lomaxes and merely hint at the diversity and depth of the narrative store that John and Alan accumulated for the Library of Congress.

Out West with John A. Lomax

Although John Avery Lomax was born in Mississippi, his name is inevitably associated with Texas. John was not yet 2 years old in 1869, when his family settled on a farm outside Meridien, some thirty-five miles northwest of Waco, on the eastern fringe of the southwestern frontier that he was to celebrate in his first book, *Cowboy Ballads* (1910). John came of age as a farmer, and he spent most of the early decades of his life too busy practicing folklife to be able to study it. He would be 39 years old and a student at Harvard University before he began his academic work on cowboy ballads.

Geographically and chronologically, Lomax just barely missed the frontier.

The boys of the LS Ranch lingering near the chuck wagon after the day's work is done, listening to the range boss telling stories, LS Ranch, near Tascosa, Texas, 1907. (The Erwin E. Smith Collection of the Library of Congress on deposit at the Amon Carter Museum, Ft. Worth, Texas)

His father's farm lay near a fork of the Chisholm Trail, and as a young boy working that farm he would watch the cowboys ride by in the distance, but just close enough for him to hear their songs. In his autobiography he recalled having heard, at age 4, the voice of a cowboy in the night calming his cattle with the song "Git Along, Little Dogies."

John Lomax's last seven major collecting expeditions for the Library of Congress took place, in whole or in part, in Texas. He was 75 years old by the time he completed the last of these, but he was still haunted by what he had missed as a boy more than seven decades back. He continually asked his sources for true-life accounts of the old West. What was it really like?

Lomax was so interested in getting specific information about the old days that he often cut in on his sources' stories. But the collector's zeal has less to do with the brevity of the following tales than does the narrators' laconic style. Each of the tellers speaks in a deadpan monotone, without raising pitch or volume, no matter how dramatic or humorous the events he or she relates. Most speak in short sentences, and most make every word count.

86. I Don't Know How to Run

JOSEPH GRAHAM
Pecos and Odessa, Texas
Recorded by John A. Lomax and
Ruby Terrill Lomax,
July 2, 1942

Joseph Graham, aged 73, was just a year younger than John Lomax when this recording was made in Odessa, Texas. Graham recalled his life in Pecos (some seventy miles southwest of Odessa) during the last decades of the nineteenth century and the beginning of the twentieth. Lomax asked him, "Well, did you carry a gun when you rode?" Graham's answer was uncharacteristically long: "Why, no. I've had one in my bed if I wanted one. . . . Of course, some boys had one hid in the bed. They didn't carry a gun. . . . It was dangerous then to have a gun around. Somebody'd make you use it. It was dangerous. T'ain't like it is now. . . . That's all picture show, like Roy Bean . . . and all of that stuff. This real stuff, there ain't much of it. It's just a thing of the past."

John Lomax: Well, now, the Wild West stories tell lots about the rowdy cowboys and how they went to town and drank a lot of liquor and wore guns and shot up the saloons and shot the lights out. How much of that kind of life have you seen?]

There wasn't a bit to that. That's all moving picture show outfit. . . .

Got a friend I'll tell you about. Do you know of him, Jim Miller? He was a great friend of mine. That was the bravest man I ever seen. You know him? . . .

[John Lomax: Know *of* him. Well, tell us about Jim Miller.]

Well, he used to run a hotel at Pecos. He was a deputy sheriff there when I first knew him, under Bud Frazier. Frazier was sheriff. Well, they had some kind of difficulty. I don't know what it's over, nor does nobody else. And old Bud tried to kill him. Met him one morning and jerked his gun and shot him a time or two and broke his arm. And Jim whipped around and run him around the corner.

Well that went on. Didn't kill Jim. Went on some few months, till one morning, I think it was Christmas Eve morning, Jim come down to the black-smith shop for something and Bud hid. . . . Shot him again. That time Jim run him off. So they went on and at last, Jim found out through friends, I guess, that he was up at Toyah. You know Toyah. Says he was going there. He was in there playing poker in an old house one day about daylight, and old Jim just pushed open the door and shot Bud's head off.

Well, Bud had two old maid sisters. One of em . . . , she come out and commenced shooting at Jim. Jim asked em, "Gentlemen, take somebody and do something with that woman. I don't want to hurt her, and I don't know how to run."

That's just the kind of men that didn't know how to.

. . . But that's the worst man I ever seed that was a good fella. I was afraid to be around him.

87. You Can Cook Breakfast, Too

W.D. (BILL) CASEY
Deming, New Mexico, and Pecos, Texas
Recorded by John A. and Ruby Terrill Lomax,
July 3, 1942

W.D. Casey was 83 when he shared this tale with John Lomax. Son of a Union soldier who migrated from Massachusetts to Texas after the Civil War, Bill was 9 years old when his father once more pulled up stakes and led the family on a grueling and often dangerous journey to New Mexico. The following account begins with recollections of that trip.

My father . . . left Liberty County at about the age of fifteen on account of his health. He had poor health—chills and fever—he said, on account of eating a lot of persimmons before they got ripe. He, he moved into this Angelo country, which is quite a distance west. At that time the Indians hadn't been whipped out but some two or three years before, and he wasn't satisfied with that country, that consisted of sheep herding, and naturally that didn't suit a cowboy. So he moved on into New Mexico, but on his way across there, he and a friend had to ride some ninety-six miles without water, which is quite a distance.

There were no brush in this country at that time, and you had no sense of direction any more than just the way the man pointed when he started you out. That night as they camped, well, they drew an arrow pointing toward the North Star, which was the best they had, because in the trail herds, we always pointed our wagon tongues north, but being horseback, you're horse would turn around if you pointed him north.

They got to the Pecos River some—quite a while after they'd started, of course, and when they got there, that was gyppy water, very gyppy. Stock would hardly drink it. But being a long time without water, he said it was very wet when they got there, and tasted good. . . .

He moved on from there, went on to New Mexico, and those people had moved out to an open country where's there's no law. The town of Deming, New Mexico, at that time was a population of about two thousand, had neither a preacher nor a doctor in it. No law at all. Each man, if he wasn't big enough to take care of hisself, somebody else did it for him.

He said he was working in a hay camp, camped out thirty, forty miles from town. There's a fellow had killed a man up in the mountains there, and they'd been after him several days, not giving him time to eat nor sleep. He found my father's camp, and my father being the only one in camp, sleeping by himself, he got in bed with him. After feeding his horse and finding something to eat in the pots himself.

Next morning, as my father woke up, to arouse the other man, said, "Well, I'll get up and build a fire."

This fellow jabbed a six-shooter in my father's ribs and said, "Just lay still, my friend," said, "I'll build a fire."

My father says, "Hell, yes. You can cook breakfast too if you wish."

The feller went on into Old Mexico and was captured and hung later for this offense. [My father] said that there was still a cold place in his ribs where the six-shooter jabbed him.

88. My Brother's Last Ride	**SLOAN MATTHEWS** **Alpine, Texas** **Recorded by John A. and Ruby** **Terrill Lomax,** **July 3, 1942**

The third paragraph of the following tale repeats some of the information from the previous paragraph, probably because the story was interrupted to allow the collectors to turn over the recording disk; it is likely that John Lomax then asked Sloan Matthews to backtrack a bit in the story to guarantee that all of it was successfully recorded.

When I was eleven years old, there were four of us holding a roundup, and I was on the south side and the cattle, the one that was trying to get away, was trying to go south, and one maverick, about a year old, started out. I was circling around the roundup, and I heard somebody say something, and I looked back and my brother was coming. No doubt he realized I'd soon need help.

And just about that time, I was riding full speed by the side of this maverick, and my brother went behind my horse. On account of being only eleven years old, I allowed that to happen, of course, and he went behind my horse, and his horse hit it with his knees. I was looking back and saw it all. I'd never seen such a fall, only when a horse jumped the fence or something of that kind. . . . I could see the horse's head, it didn't touch the ground at all. While I was looking back, I saw . . . his four feet stuck straight up, and my brother still in the saddle with his head on the ground.

. . . I saw him turn over, with all four of his feet off the ground. He didn't leave the saddle. As I was looking back, I saw all four feet straight up, and my brother's head on the ground. They came down straight together. The horse rolled over one time, but he stayed in the saddle. The horse started to get up, and he stayed in the saddle till the horse was half up, and fell off on the right hand side with his neck broken. He never spoke a word.

89. Getting Stuck on a Pony

SAM HILL
Odessa, Texas
Recorded by John A. and Ruby
Terrill Lomax,
July 2, 1942

The Lomaxes described Hill as "a bachelor of 73, . . . a 'cowhand' all his life. . . . He boasts that he never wore a pair of shoes in his life, always boots." A master of understatement, he told his most outrageous adventures in an almost bored tone.

When I moved to the place I'm staying right now and camped with the man I'm working for, they was two horses, bay horses that he had raised. One of em died at twenty-six and the other one, the last count I had of him was twenty-one, twenty-one years old. And those two old ponies was, well I don't hardly know how to explain it, they couldn't read and write English, but they could *very near.* They'd help an ordinary man do, you know, just nearly most anything, from cowpunching to windmilling. And . . . the boss man decided one spring that he was going to set em free, and he told me that . . . he'd furnish the feed if I'd feed em, or he'd furnish the cartridges if I'd kill em.

I said, "No, just get the feed out. I'll feed em."

But springtime come, I done turned em out. They wintered, and in the spring I kept a-watching for em. And eventually I found one of em where I suppose lightning had killed him. He never made no sign, but passed away. And the other one, I have never yet known what become of it. So those two ponies there, were the last ones I ever allowed myself to get stuck on.

[John A. Lomax: Well, what were their names?]

I called one of em Powder River and the other one Chunky. . . .

90. Shooting a Wife

SAM HILL
Odessa, Texas
Recorded by John A. and Ruby
Terrill Lomax,
July 2, 1942

Up here in the Davis Mountains, they have a big summer resort, a big lodge there, and myself and the housekeeper one evening, we framed up on a big company there to entertain that night. He asked me to, rather, and I went over to the lodge where they were that night. He said, "Mr. Hill," he said, "if you don't mind," he said, "I wish you'd tell us your past just for entertainment." And I said, "Well, I don't much like to talk about it. It's pretty sad."

He said, "I know it." He said, "You talked to me about it, but I want you to tell the company here to help me entertain tonight."

And I said, "Well, in my younger days . . . I went to Arizona, and went to work for a cattle company and later on I got out to myself and had a little bunch of cattle and a good bunch of horses eighty miles from the railroad, or trading point, I went about twice a year in a wagon and," I said, "I got acquainted with a girl down there and didn't make but a few trips before she and I are married. And there come a drought. The cattle was poor and the horses was poor, and I run out of oats and it didn't look I was going to get by hardly, but at that I was getting along pretty good, just taking everything into consideration, and I went in one evening and the girl had fell off the porch and broke her leg—and I had to kill her."

[A man in the audience] said, "Well, I'll declare." He was a Frenchman. Kind of dropped his head.

And I said, "Yeah, it was pretty bad."

He said, "Couldn't you have got her to the railroad?"

I said, "Eighty miles from my doctor, in a wagon? Rough roads, mountain roads?" I said, "The poor thing would've died before I could a got her there."

And he said, "Well, I declare."

I looked over, and the congregation has tears in every eye. And people gray-headed, older than I am today, with tears running, plumb, you know, off their chin. And I broke down and about to go to cry myself, so I got up and walked out.

. . . Next day, and I was about uneasy, afraid they was going to mob me. And that's a fact if ever I told it so.

91. Hard Times in the Toyah Country

ANNIE AGNES KINGSTON
Toyahvale, Texas
Recorded by John A. Lomax and
Ruby Terrill Lomax,
September 1942

Why, the young folks wish they could live like we did. I tell them they don't know what a good time they're having. I tell my experience one time. My husband went to court. And he left me with a neighbor. I had a two-months-old baby and a four-year-old child. And he'd taken, we thought, diphtheria.

So I started out with the hired man, a-horseback, and had to ride about eight miles horseback on a man's saddle and carry him with a pillow and a blanket, met my husband a-horseback, and we had to go to a ranch, and . . . borrow another horse and take his saddle horse and go into Fort Davis and carry that baby in my arms, and no wagon seat, with nothing in the world of a seat to it, . . . and we got there. And when I—

[John Lomax: How far was it to Fort Davis?]

About forty miles. And I said, "Doctor," I said, when he had examined my baby—I said, boy, I says, "what's the matter with it?" I says, "Has he got diphtheria?"

He says, "No, I wish to God he did."

Well, . . . my heart just came right up in my throat. I says, "Well, what's the matter with him?"

He says, "He's got membranous croup."

Well, we stayed there till daylight in that army doctor's home. And he doctored him. And I says, "Doctor, I've got a little baby two months old, I want to go to." And he says, "You'd better stay with this one, because," he says, "he's more dangerous." Then I had to go back and be taking that wagon, and I had to ride back about eight miles a-horseback, and carry that four-year-old child in my arms. But I went.

And I saw the man coming from the ranch—the boss's ranch. And I says, "Oh, I'm afraid my baby's dead." And he was riding one of these choice saddle horses.

And I says, "Oh, Mr. Morris, how's my baby?"

And he says, "All right." So we got home all right. And the little boy got all right. And the baby was all right. But that was my worst experience, since I've been married, in my family.

[John Lomax: Well, how long did it take for you to make those two forty-mile trips?]

Well, I don't know. We had to go horseback and in a wagon. We . . . left there about four o'clock, the ranch. And we got to Fort Davis eleven o'clock that night. . . . We stayed at Fort Davis till next day about four o'clock, and then went back to this ranch, part of the way by wagon and part of the way horseback.

Down in the Delta with Alan Lomax

At the same time that John Lomax was collecting tales in west Texas, his son Alan was a thousand miles away, engaged in a month-long survey of the traditional culture of Coahoma County, Mississippi, cradle of the Delta Blues. The expedition was co-sponsored by Fisk University, a pioneering African American educational center in Nashville, Tennessee.

Alan, now 27 years old, had been recording songs and stories for the Library of Congress since he was 18. Among the seventy-one disks emerging from this summer survey were recordings of magnificent blues and gospel performances, many of which have been commercially released through the American Folklife Center. There were also some masterfully crafted traditional tales, some told by the same people who performed blues for Lomax's recorder, but the stories have not been previously published.

92. John Loses the Race

"BUCK ASA" ULISSES JEFFERSON
Clarksdale, Mississippi
Recorded by Alan Lomax, July 1942

This tale belongs to the African American tradition of jokes based on the relationship between slaves and their masters. Such narratives are often called "John and Old Marster tales," after the two central characters. Elsewhere in this book, African American artists John Davis (stories 169–171), Son House (stories 147, 148, and 150), and J.D. Suggs (story 51) apply their arts to the same theme.

Old Master back in slavery time, you know. He had, he had a nigger called John. And another [master] had one called Jack. So they wanted to put on a big race. So one bet the other [master] five hundred dollars that John could outrun Jack. John was a little old fellow and Jack was long and tall.

So John's Old Master asked him, said, "Hey, John. Do you reckon you can outrun Jack?"

So John say, "Yes, sir, yes, sir, boss. [Laughs] I sure can outrun him."

"I don't know." Says, "Jack mighty tall."

"Yes, sir, but I can outrun him though. I know I can outrun him."

Alan Lomax playing guitar on stage at the Mountain Music Festival, Asheville, North Carolina. (Library of Congress)

He says, "I'm going to put up five hundred dollars on you."

"All right," he said. "Put it up." Said, "I'm going to win you five hundred dollars, Old Master."

All right, the Old Master said he had to go off. He said, "Well, John, I can't be here . . . for the race. And now you have to tell me when I come back how the race come out."

"Don't you worry, Master, I sure will tell you. I'll going to tell you all about how it come out."

So that Saturday the race come off. John—little old fellow—got out there and rolled his britches up above his knee. Jack, he's long and tall, slim. He rolled his britches up.

All right. They got up there, and they braced themselves right good, and they counted em off: "One, two, three. Go!"

And they lit out, Jack and John. Jack got in front of John. Beat John to the mark [at the halfway point]. They turn around and come back. Jack still in front of John. John running, sweating and panting—and scared too. And lost Old Master's five hundred dollars. He told Old Master he was going to win it.

So John went home and wouldn't eat no supper. The cook called and said, "John, come up and eat your supper."

He said, "I ain't hungry."

So, Old Mistus want to know what's the matter with John. Says, "What's the matter with John? He won't eat."

"I don't know."

Said, "John." Said, "John." Said, "Why don't you come on and eat your supper? Why don't you come on eat your supper?"

"No, ma'am, Mistus, I ain't hungry."

And she worried and worried. Wondered what's the matter with John. Said, "I'll buy his supper all the time."

. . . Next thing, Old Master come in. Got in the yard and he commenced to hollering at John. "Oh, John, where—where's John?" Said, "Where's John?"

Say, "Hey, he out there."

Say, "Tell him to come in."

John come on in. "Hey, Old Marse."

"Hey, John." He say, "Tell me about the race, old boy." Say, "I know you win the race," he say. "Tell me about the race. Tell me about how it come out."

"Well, Old Master, I tell you, I'm going to tell you just like it was."

"All right," he said, "come on. I know you win."

"Well, Marse, we—we started off. I'm going say, when I started off Jack was a-fore and I was behind. Jack before and I behind."

"John," said Master, "come on, come on, I know you win that race."

"Well, we run. Jack's a-fore and I'm behind. Jack before and I behind. Jack before and I behind." Said, "Finally the thing changed around, Old Master: I behind and Jack before, I behind and Jack before. Well, it changed around again, Old Master, after awhile: Jack before and I behind, he before and I behind, he before and I behind. Then I behind and he before, then I behind and he before." [Laughing]

Then Old Master, you know, begin to get wise to John, you see. He said, "Now, John, say, I don't ever see where you say you was before no time."

"No, sir, Old Master, I was always behind." Say, "I was never before." Says, "Jack was always before. I, I was always behind." [Laughs]

Say, "Well. You lost my five hundred dollars, didn't you?"

"Yes, Old Master, I sure did. Sure did lose it, but . . . I couldn't help it, Old Master. Jack is too tall. His legs is too long."

Say, "All right." Say, "That breaks me and you up." Says, "I'm through with you. [Laughs] And you told me you would win that race."

And that's, that's all.

93. Jack Guesses What Is Under the Pot

"BUCK ASA" ULISSES JEFFERSON
Clarksdale, Mississippi
Recorded by Alan Lomax,
July 1942

"Buck Asa" was holding forth in the back room of the Nelson Funeral Home in Clarksdale, Mississippi, when Alan Lomax recorded the following story. This is a version of a tale often called "The Old Coon," one of the most popular African American slavery-days tales; another version, collected by Zora Neale Hurston, appears later in this book (story 171). The opening words of Buck Asa's tale were not recorded.

Jack had a smart way of guessing, you know. He always sneak around and find out what [his master and the white folks] was going to do, you see, before, before they do it, and when they do it, then he already know what's going to happen, and he just hem and haw around and everything, till he get a chance— and he just come on in there and tell em what it was.

So he got . . . his Old Master really believing in him, believing that he was knowing what he was doing. And, so [Old Master] bet five hundred dollars on him that time, . . . that he could put anything under that wash pot that they wanted, and Jack could tell em exactly what it was.

All right, so . . . him and another Old Master, they got this bet. So his Old Master went and got a coon, and put it under the wash pot. Put the coon under the wash pot and then they went and got Jack. They didn't tell Jack nothing about it. Didn't let him know nothing about the deal at all. Just went and got him.

"Jack," said, "we want you to tell us what's under that wash pot. I got five hundred dollars betted on you that you can tell us exactly what's under that wash pot."

Well, Jack sat there and scratched his head and wiggled his feet.

They say, "Come on, now. Come on, now. Come on, now."

He walked up there and to touch the pot—

"No, no, no, no! Keep your hands off of it now. You can't look under it now. Now, I know you can tell us. I know you can tell us. Don't, don't, don't touch that pot."

So Jack knowed he didn't know what was under there. *Knowed* he didn't know. And knowed they done caught up with him, right there. See? Jack said, "Well, Old Master, I tell you." Said, "You all done caught the old coon at last."

They say, "Ah, hah!" Say, "I told you! I told you! That's the thing!"

[Laughter]

| **94. The Preacher and His Hogs** | **"BUCK ASA" ULISSES JEFFERSON** Clarksdale, Mississippi Recorded by Alan Lomax, July 1942 |

There was a preacher and he raised a lot of hogs. So his deacon (one of his main deacon of the church, you know) took over there every once in a while at night, you know, would steal one of the preacher's hog.

And he had [a] little boy that he never did carry to church. Make the little boy stay home. Didn't buy him no clothes or nothing to go to church in. So the little boy found out that his daddy was stealing the preacher's hogs.

One Sunday—the preacher was coming over one Sunday evening to take dinner with the deacon and leave from there and to go back to church. Little boy sat out in the yard playing, looked up and seen the preacher coming, and he started to singing:

> Papa stole the preacher's hog
> And we got a plenty pork now

> Papa stole the preacher's hog
> And we got a plenty pork now

So preacher's stopping and listening. He thought he caught it at first, you know, but he want to make sure. He walked on a little further and the boy watched him.

So preacher got a little closer; he started singing again—

> Papa stole the preacher's hog
> And we got a plenty pork now

So the preacher walked on a little closer. Little boy continued to sing:

> Papa stole the preacher's hog
> And we got a plenty pork now

Preacher walked up. [Clearing his throat:] "Uh-mmh. Hi, son."

"All right. How are you, Reverend?"

"Say, what's that song that you're singing?"

"Ain't anything. Little old song I sing."

He said, "Well, would you promise me if you'd come to church tonight and sing that song?"

Say, "Yes, sir, I can come out there and sing it," say, "but I ain't, I ain't got no shoes to wear."

"So I'll buy you some shoes."

He say, "I ain't got no suit."

"I'll buy you a suit."

So, "I ain't got no, I ain't got no hat."

"I'll get you a little hat."

Say, "I ain't got no money to put in my pocket."

"I'll give you some money to put in your pocket."

The old preacher, he went back to town—turned around right there and went back to town and got the little boy a suit and some shoes. Hat. Come back there at dinnertime and give him fifty cents from his pocket.

Little boy come on out to church that night. Old reverend got up and seen the little boy come in church and got up, said, "Now. Come up, son. Come up. Come right on up here. I'm going to stop till you come right on up here."

His daddy said he didn't know why he come to church for.

The little boy kept on over to where the preacher was.

He said, "Now, my Christian friends." Said, "I have a little boy here, just a lad of a boy, who's going to sing you a song, and I want everybody to pay strict attention to this song that this little lad's going to sing." Saying, "Every word of this song is just as true as you see me standing in this pulpit."

The little boy's daddy sitting there looking at him, you know, and wondering what it was he was going to sing. He didn't know he even knowed no songs. He knowed he hadn't never been to church.

So, the old preacher, he told him, he said, "Now, now don't be afraid. Don't be afraid. Brace yourself up. Be strong. And I want you to sing with uplifted voice."

Little boy cut his eye over at his daddy.

"Okay now. You may proceed. Everybody keep quiet now. Listen to this song that this kid's going to sing."

Little boy pulled the little coat up on him tight, you know, and cut his eye at his daddy. Started off to singing:

> Passed by the preacher's gate one day
> He was playing a game of cards
> Old preacher begin to bug his eyes
> Then he give me this little coat that fits so well
> And this half a dollar to not to tell [laughter]

And the old preacher, he jumped out the window [laughter], back window of the church.

95. The Preacher Who Could Always Be Trapped by Women

"BUCK ASA" ULISSES JEFFERSON
Clarksdale, Mississippi
Recorded by Alan Lomax, July 1942

There was a preacher. And he had a youngster, you know, that he'd always put up with. [That young man] had a right young wife. Nice looking woman, he was crazy about her, this preacher was, you know.

And every time this boy would go out, you know, during any time the preacher was there, any time the boy would go out, to cut wood or catch a chicken or something, well, this girl would pass the preacher's door, he'd beg for her to come in.

"Come in, honey. Come in."

"No, go on, Reverend. If you don't go on, I'm going to tell my husband on you."

"Oh, No, no, no. Don't do that, don't do that, don't do that. Be a shame to tell."

Well, the preacher kept a-whining and kept a-whining and whining, you know, and whining, but she did tell her husband. . . . "Well, you just got to do something about it, then. I get tired of the reverend wooing me all the time. I can't stand it."

"All right." So this boy sent her off to her mother's and told the preacher that he had to go off that Sunday night. (The preacher would say a service that time of night.)

"Say, Reverend," said, "I'm about to go off tonight and I can't be at service. Will you, will you come over here and stay with my wife? Will you get yourself a nightie and come stay with my wife until I come back? Because she's scared to stay in there."

"Why, sure, young man, I believe that I'd be glad to. Say, you know I would. Hey, we're colored brothers, me and you. Say, don't you know, I couldn't afford to turn you down. Say, if you got to go off on business, something like that, I'd be glad to omit service tonight and come back and stay with your wife."

So the old preacher hurried and went to church. He got up and all the people's there. "And now," he says, "I got something to tell you all, I had happen to me today." Said, "I didn't know that I stood that high in this community. I didn't know I was trusted that well. I didn't know I was that much of a gentleman. So, now, our young brother in here, whom I always put up with, says he's got to go off tonight, on some special business, and his wife's at home by herself, and he asked me to come back and stay with her until he come back. And if you all will excuse me tonight, I would like to go back and keep the girl company, because I know she's afraid down there by herself."

"All right," they say. "Yeah, Reverend. Go right ahead. Go right ahead."

He grabbed his grip and pack and headed for the house. And the girl's in bed.

The old preacher went on up there and knocked on the door.

"Come on in, now." (The boy done put on his wife's gown and nightcap.)

Went on in. "Now, your [husband] with you?"

"No, no, no, no, no, no. . . ."

Pulled his clothes off, you know, and he crawled over into bed. Crawled over into the bed, take the boy in his arms, pulled him over, and say, "My little honey, can I have a feel down there?"

Felt down, and felt the wrong thing.

The preacher didn't say nothing, but turned her over and got out, got out on the same side he got in on. Got his pants. Walked right on out the door, putting his pants on.

Boy say, "Come back, Reverend."

Say, "No. Uh, uh. I know that wasn't nothing but a trap." Say, "I felt that was a trap." Said, "Any time you got a trap like that and bait it with pork," said, "you catch me."

[Laughter]

96. The Woman Who Couldn't Count	M.C. ORR Clarksdale, Mississippi Recorded by Alan Lomax, July 1942

There's a feller come out saying, saying he want to make a date with this girl. He's saying, he's going to pay this girl, just to the amount they could count to. He's going to pay em for that.

"All right," the old lady said, "that's a chance to get rich, young children." She called em.

"All right."

One got up, said, "I'm the oldest."

"All right. Start to count."

"One, two, three." Far as she could count. [Laughter]

The lady, that made her mad. "You ain't worth nothing. Didn't make but three dollars. You get out of here. Let the other gal come in."

All right, he got the other gal.

"One, two." All right, two is far as she could count.

So he called the youngest one in there. Old lady's having a fit at that end, boy. Hadn't made but five dollars, there.

So they called the youngest in there, and he got it in her and got it in her, and she couldn't count to but one.

The old lady said, ". . . Let me show you how to make some money."

So the old guy got her down, and put it on that side of the old lady. "That ain't it."

Put it over on that side. "That ain't it."

So he put it back over here. "That ain't it."

So all at once, he's hauling sugar. She says, "Na na, na, na, na—that's it!" [Laughing]

She didn't make nothing.

"Na na, na, na, na—that's it."

97. The Lady and Her Three Daughters

M.C. ORR
Clarksdale, Mississippi
Recorded by Alan Lomax,
July 1942

Yeah. Once, once a lady had three daughters and . . . [this man came by and told her he had a way for them to] make some money.

"My daughters ain't never done did nothing like that."

"Well, I'll prove they done did something like that."

"All right-y, if you can prove it, let me see you prove it. They ain't never did something like that."

"All right, call em in here."

She called the oldest daughter in.

Said, "Lay down on your back now."

He put a stick through her legs. The stick said, "*Boom, boom*, hello, cunt."

"Hello, stick."

"You ever been fucked?"

"Ooh, lord, a many and a many old times."

"Get up and get out of here, you nasty—now call my next oldest daughter in here."

Called the next oldest daughter in there.

"All right, lay down flat on your back."

She laid down flat on her back. The stick goes, "*Boom, boom*, hello, cunt."

"Hello, stick."

"You ever been fucked?"

"Oh, Lord, a many, a many old times."

"You get up and get out of here. Call my youngest daughter here. She's a good girl. She goes to Sunday school every Sunday and all that kind of stuff. She ain't never did nothing like this."

"All right," the old man says. "Lay down, daughter; lay down flat on your back."

She lay down flat on her back. He puts the stick down there. Bumped it, "*Boom, boom*, hello, cunt."

"Hello, stick."

"You ever been fucked?"

"Oh, Lord, a many, a many old times."

Old woman say, "Get up and get out of here." Then told the fellow, said, "Wait a minute, I bet you can't make mine say nothing like that."

All right, "Lay down there."

"Wait till I go in here." She went on in there and got a quilt and put it in, and a sheet . . . , ripped out a pillow and [stuffed it in]. She went on back in and said, "All right, I'm ready."

Said, "Lay down." Put the stick down and "*Boom, boom*, hello, cunt."

[Muffled tones:] "Mmm, mmm."

"Hello, cunt."

[Muffled voice:] "Mmm, mmm."

Say, "All right, turn her on her back."

"*Boom, boom*, hello, ass."

"Hello, stick."

"You ever been fucked?"

Says, "No, sir."

"What's a matter with cock?"

"She filled it full of rags."

Old lady looks back and she says, "Uh, you son of a bitch, if I knowed you was going to say anything I'd a stuffed you full of rags too."

In Prison and at Home with "Clear Rock"

Mose "Clear Rock" Platt seems to have been the first narrator to record a tale for the Lomax Library of Congress collections. John and Alan visited "Clear Rock" in July 1933, on the first of their many celebrated prison farm expeditions,

Mose "Clear Rock" Platt (teller of stories 98–101) in a mule-drawn wagon, Sugar Land State Prison Farm, Sugar Land, Texas. (Library of Congress)

and John and his wife, Ruby, revisited him in the spring of 1939, after he had been released from prison.

"Clear Rock" was one of the oldest inmates of the Imperial Prison Farm near Sugar Land, Texas. He was a magnificent and prolific singer whose repertoire, according to John Lomax, could "fill a volume of 500 pages."

Most of Platt's tales are tall ones, told in the first person and delivered in a deadpan voice. "Clear Rock" is the dupe in nearly all of them, and they typically end with him in flight from a specter or a corpse or the law.

98. Watermelon Story

MOSE "CLEAR ROCK" PLATT
Sugar Land, Texas
Recorded by John A. and Alan Lomax,
July 1933

You know one time me and some boys decided we'd go out and steal our neighbors' watermelons. And when we went out, you know, a-walking, we found, going down the lane, we going down the lane, and going down the lane, we saw a nice watermelon patch.

And I said, "Let's go out and get some melons. Steal some of em."

Why, old Jake, he says, "All right. Rock, we'll go get some of em."

So we cross over the old rail fence out there in the nigger quarters, and when we get over there we see such good watermelons we commenced to eating and eating. And the boy dropped so much juice out of the watermelon, he taken his Waterbury watch out of his pocket and laid it on a stump. So we all busted three big ones. That was all we could eat. And so we went away then, found a lane on our way home.

And when we crossed a branch about three miles and a half from there, this boy says, "Oh, Clear Rock, I done lost, left my watch over yonder on the stump." He says, "You all come, go back with me. I can't go back that far. I may meet something that'll scare me."

"Well," I says, "all right, we'll go back over there with you." And walking back, we got hungry again, wanted some more watermelons. And so, when we got there to the patch, why, quite natural, we had come in the corner of the fence then. We didn't get over the side lane, like we did first, but over in a new place, in the corner. And so we found a lot of striped watermelons laying around in the moonshine. And so we begin to try to break the watermelons with our fists. We couldn't. And so I says, "Wait, hand it here, Jake. I'll bust it." And walked over to a man sitting on a stump, which I thought was a stump, and bust this watermelon over this old nigger's head. And he got up and said, "What's up."

I said, "I don't know what's up. I'm just gone," and, boy, I run until I get back to the . . . town and I meet a ranger, and he told me, "hold on," he says. "You're going too fast there. You must have got into something."

I said, "No, sir, I'm just getting out of something."

99. Cat Story

MOSE "CLEAR ROCK" PLATT
Taylor, Texas
Recorded by John A. and Ruby
Terrill Lomax,
May 10, 1939

Six years after first visiting Clear Rock in prison, John Lomax, this time accompanied by his wife, Ruby Terrill, went looking for him again. Mose Platt, known to his neighbors as "Wyandotte," was now a free man and a practicing preacher in Taylor, Texas.

The Lomax log of their visit uses eye dialect to attempt to capture Platt's speaking style. "Asked about this release from the penitentiary, he explained: 'One day some o' my white friends in Taylor heard dat Miss Ferguson (Gov. Miriam Ferguson) was goin' to be down at Central a-visitin; and they sont a car down there wid a letter signed by thirty thousand peoples; they was de name o' all de prominent lawyers an' officers an' all the other whichocrats around Taylor, and Miss Ferguson let me go free.' " John and Ruby Lomax also observed that "Clear Rock himself was ready and willing to do anything the 'boss' asked, except to stop talking." Apparently, John solicited the tales that follow as icebreakers: "To unwind him somewhat, Mr. Lomax let him record some stories first" and then asked for the songs that were the collector's primary interest. But the log goes on to state that "Clear Rock's 'off the record' stories are rich in themselves."

Now we went down, me and a bunch of boys, to pick some cotton out here for a farmer, and it's an old log cabin set right on the side of the hill down on the edge of his field.

So he said, "You boys might go down there and stay in that old house."

So I went down there, and it had an old hearth in it, an old log chimley, and I built me up a fire out of some cotton sticks and some old pieces of rotten wood along the bank of the creek.

And along about one o'clock that night, the boys said, "Let's cook some supper and make some coffee."

I said, "I believe I will."

I put the coffee pot on the fire, and so we begin to have a little coffee, and so all at once on this little shelf, sitting back on the west end of the room, just a old-fashioned shelf built into the wall, and I looked up there, and it was a great big old black cat standing on there, and his eyes begin to turn around just like millstones, looking at me.

And I told em to look at that strange cat yonder. And the more we fellas would look at this cat, why the larger it would grow.

And so finally the cat says, "We're all here together."

I says, "Yes, we here now. But we won't be here long," and out the window we went.

[John A. Lomax: What about his spitting in the fire?]

And so we had fire burning. Fire was burning good. We was fixing to cook some eggs, and that thing just sent to spit in the fire and put it out. Now, I just couldn't stand it no longer, so Luke and John and Clear Rock, all of us, we just went out the window. And left there.

100. Music for Me to Run By	**MOSE "CLEAR ROCK" PLATT**
	Taylor, Texas
	Recorded by John A. and Ruby
	Terrill Lomax,
	May 10, 1939

So we had a sick man in our county. It happened here in Taylor, here, a night or two ago, and he finally laid down and died. And so the man had pronounced that he's dead, at least the doctor pronounced he's dead, and they had him laying out on . . . what you call a cooling board. It's a white cloth, bandages wrapped around his jaws, and he's laid out really for dead.

And so we—all of us was sitting up. There was a house full of lady folks and lots of boys sitting around. And so a lady told me, said, "Clear Rock, we just dug potatoes today." Says, "Look back there in that bathroom there, and get a basket of them taters and put em in that fire up there," And said, "They'll roast and when they get done," says, "we ain't gonna cook. You all'll have that for your meal."

I said, "Yes, ma'am, it'd be a good idea." So I poured half a basket of potatoes in there and roasted em in that old nigger's fireplace. And so this old man was dead, least we thought he was, and he's laying out there. And finally I take one of them potatoes off and was blowing em, patting em that-a-way, getting the ashes off, to eat em, and the dead man raised up on his cooling board and looked *strictly* straight at me, and asked me, says, "Is they *done?*"

I said, "I don't know whether them taters're done or not, but I'm done with this place." And out the window I went.

And niggers was jumping out of the windows and running there and tore the old man's clean fence down. Tore his picket fence down. . . .

And I run way down the side stairs where some boys was rehearsing with some horns upstairs with the bugles and cornets and all other trombones and things that they was trying to learn, and when I run by there, one fella said [tune of "Taps"], *Da-da-DA, da-da-DA, da-DA,* and when it blowed that a-way, I thought that was music for me to run by, I only run but more.

I lean over and when I raised up I was clean in another town they call Fort Worth. To take a look at Fort Worth.

101. The Leaky House

MOSE "CLEAR ROCK" PLATT
Taylor, Texas
Recorded by John A. and Ruby Terrill Lomax,
May 10, 1939

John A. Lomax: Now tell me a story and begin at the beginning.]
The same one I was talking about?

[John A. Lomax: About the house leaking.]

Oh, yeah.

Other day a neighbor come to us, it was a man and his wife, and he says, "Mr. Clear Rock," say, "why don't you all get your house fixed?"

I said, "Well," I say, "we don't need it fixed." I say, 'It ain't been raining here lately." He says, "Well, why don't you get it fixed," he said, "when it's not raining?"

I said, "When it don't rain, it don't leak."

And he says, "Other words, the lumber, buying the lumber for this house," says, "I see that you bought some pieces that's short lumber and you've bought long lumber, and you've bought wide lumber and you bought narrow lumber. And what's your idea for buying so many different kinds of lumber?"

I says, "Well," I says, "the land is so high here you can't buy a big acre. You have to buy a small acre. And if you got little lumber, you can make you a little house."

Aunt Molly Jackson: Playing, Courting, Witches, Ghosts, and Lies

Aunt Molly Jackson (born Mary Magdalene Garland) was best known as a fiery folksinger and labor activist who used her music as a weapon for social justice, particularly on behalf of coal miners. Born in Clay County, Kentucky, in 1880, Aunt Molly began composing songs in traditional mountain styles while still a child. At age 7, she fashioned a song in memory of her mother, who had died the year before. At age 10, after being "jailed" in the home of the sheriff for playing a Christmas prank, she wrote a song appealing to the sheriff to let her go back home. The sheriff refused, but he was so impressed by her song that he had her sing it repeatedly for visitors, thus providing an unlikely start for Molly's career as a public performer.

Molly grew up to marry a man who, like her father, worked the coal mines and served the unions. Her first attempt to use music in the cause of the mineworkers incited a powerful, but undesired response: in 1910, she wrote and circulated a song protesting the conditions at the Ely Branch mine, where her husband worked; when the owner discovered that Molly had written the song, Molly's husband lost his job.

For the first half century of her life, Molly's reputation as a performer was strictly local, and even in her home region, she was far better known for her skills as a midwife than for her songs. This was to change in 1931, when novelist Theodore Dreiser led a committee of celebrated writers into Harlan County to investigate the plight of the miners and their families. Molly came forward to testify and soon shifted from speech into song, performing a version of "Ragged Hungry Blues" that so electrified her distinguished audience that they immediately came to look upon Molly as "Kentucky herself."

An instant celebrity, Molly left the Kentucky mountains forever at the end of 1931, when she traveled to New York to begin a career as a stage performer and activist for labor causes. Her name was a household word in 1939, when 24-year-old Alan Lomax sat down with her in New York to record her rich repertoire of songs. Between songs, Molly told a number of tales illustrating late-nineteenth-century lifestyles, folk belief, and humor.

Scholars have noted that the details of Aunt Molly's stories would change from telling to telling, and that she was often unreliable as a source of historical information. Nevertheless, even Aunt Molly's wildest tales embody a sort of social and environmental truth. Her family was noted for its tall tales, and Molly's tales follow faithfully in the family tradition of artful verbal embroidery. Her autobiographical accounts and her anecdotes involving family members are imbued with the content and flavors of Appalachian joke and tall tale traditions. Or, as John Greenway, who worked extensively with Aunt Molly, expressed in a remembrance of her, "The good informant is above all things else an imaginative creator who molds the traditional material inherited by his group into a unique expression of the best things in himself and in his people, and in so doing is willing to sacrifice a small fact for a greater truth. . . . Aunt Molly Jackson was a great informant."

The AFC recordings provide ample testimony that Aunt Molly greatly enjoyed performing her tales and songs for Alan Lomax. She frequently punctuates her tales and rhymes with laughter. Yet, when Lomax wrote her requesting her permission to incorporate her stories and songs into a book, Molly answered with a terse letter explaining that she intended to write her own autobiography:

Mr. Alin [*sic*] Lomax

In ancer to your letter i am not interested in your using eny of my storys or songs as I am writing a book of my own I want to use all of my songs an storys in my own book, so do not use eny of my songs or stories whatever you do

If you do I am shure you will be sorry

Despite the sour relations that developed between them, Alan Lomax held Aunt Molly Jackson in deep esteem; in an obituary tribute, he remembered her as "a tigress, a great talker and a great bard" whose "songs of protest can only be matched by those of Woody Guthrie, but they were more passionate than his, and they cut deeper." Of her tales, Lomax said, "The shame of it is, that Aunt Molly did not have the training that would have allowed her to write, because her talent, which amounted to genius in the field of story-telling, was far greater than that of many successful writers. . . . She knew folk tales, and could make up her own endlessly."

Aunt Molly died in 1960 without having published an autobiography. She left behind only a few manuscript fragments to suggest the shape that her book might take. The following tales, then, are offered as a very belated effort to help Molly tell the story that she was never able to publish herself.

102. My First Dance

AUNT MOLLY JACKSON
Clay County, Kentucky
Recorded by Alan Lomax,
New York City, May 1939

Molly's father, Oliver Garland, practiced many skills, including farming, coal mining, and union organizing. But he was also a preacher, a strict Baptist who believed that dancing was one of the Devil's arts. He forbade his daughter Molly to dance. But one Christmas Eve, when Molly was 9, a neighbor family lured her to a dance simply by not telling her that she would be dancing.

When I was nine years old, we lived at a little coal mining camp. . . . And these Spivey children, George Spivey's children, they wanted me to come and stay all night with em on Christmas Eve night one night, because that they was going to have a dance. And John Spivey, Uncle Jules Spivey's boy, he was the oldest one. He was about fifteen. And he played a banjo. So they was a-going to get enough together to have a set for a square dance, just children, and have a party. So Charlie Spivey, he come out to the house and said to my stepmother, he said, "Aunt Lizabeth," he says, "can't Molly go and stay all night with us tonight . . . ? It's Christmas Eve night."

And she said, "You'll have to go out to the commissary and ask her father." So he went and asked my father, and my father said, "No," I can't go. And they come back and told a story, and said my father said yes, I could go.

So I dressed up and went to stay all night with the Spivey children, and when my father come from the commissary home to go to bed that night, I was missing, and the dance was on and I was a-dancing in the dance, but I didn't know that I was a-dancing. I thought that . . . it was a play that we was a-playing, called "Swing Your Partner." . . . It was a square dance. But then, they knowed if they told me that it was a dance they was a-dancing, that I'd be so afraid that I wouldn't dance it.

[Alan Lomax: You really didn't know?]

No, I didn't. But it was actually a square dance, and I was nine years old. So John Spivey, he was a-picking the banjo. He was the oldest one. He was fourteen. He was a-picking on the banjo and singing, calling the sets. And, in the square dance, back them days, why they said,

"Flies in the buttermilk shoo fly shoo—
Gone again, skip to my lou."

And just as my father come in to the door, why they called that part of the set, and he reached in and got me, right by the back of the neck . . . and went pecking me in the head with his fists, and he said,

"Gone again, skip to my lou, my darling."

He took me home and I jumped in the bed with my shoes and dress and all on, and he, he kept a-pecking me in the head, saying,

"Gone again, skip to my lou, my darling."

So then all of the kids, every time that . . . they'd seeing me come out in the yard, out of the house, why they'd kid me and scream,

"Gone again, skip to my lou, my darling."

And then he kept me housed up for a month or more, in the house, to keep them other children, you know, my neighbors' children a-hollering.

"Gone again, skip to my lou, my darling"

—and teasing me because my old man come and drug me out away from the first dance that I was ever at, and I didn't even know that it was dancing. And then I never went to another dance in my life until I was a married woman.

103. How We Entertained Ourselves: Song, Rhymes, Toasts

AUNT MOLLY JACKSON
Clay County, Kentucky
Recorded by Alan Lomax,
New York City, May 1939

Alan Lomax was fascinated by Molly's reports that she had composed songs at such a young age.

Alan Lomax: You'd learn a song, . . . when would you get an opportunity to sing that song? Nobody would listen to you when you were so little, would they?]

And I wasn't that interested to sing it, either. I was more interested at them years in playing around with my dolls or kittens or anything that I had to play with—

[Alan Lomax: How would you remember those songs if you didn't practice those songs?]

Well, the reason that I remembered . . . a lot of these songs was because my mother sung em, and then I lost my mother at a very young age, and then, in memory of her—like most any child is, you can remember every little thing that your mother said or done or anything, after you once lose your mother.

[Aunt Molly went on to describe other forms of rhyming and singing entertainments practiced during her childhood:]

Well, the larger children—my father's youngest sister and my father's youngest brother— . . . they would sing these little funny songs, and us smaller children, we heared em, and then we'd get together and sing em and laugh and make a big laugh out of it. And that Sunday, particular Sunday, well, we was all down under a shade tree, a-swinging on the limbs, and a-singing:

Teed up, teed up my blue britches
Teed up, teed up my cod itches
Sambo, Sambo sitting on a clod
Along come a bumblebee and stung him on the cod
Sambo, Sambo sitting on the grass
Along come a bumblebee and stung him in the ass
Teed up, teed up my blue britches
Teed up, teed up my cod itches

[Hearing obscene verses on the lips of his grandchildren, Molly's grandfather cast blame on Molly's father, Oliver Garland. Oliver countered by pointing out that it wasn't his children, but his "sibs" (Molly's grandfather's own children) who were making up the rhymes; Molly and the younger children were merely repeating what they'd heard from the older children.]

Well, my father, he hollered back over to my grandfather and told him, he said, "Is that all that you've got to do," he says, "is to be out," he says, "a-paying attention to what babies and children says?" Says, "If you don't want these little children to sing these things and do these things, correct your children, that's much larger and older than them, and stop them from singing these songs before em, and I assure you that my baby and Vance Rollins's babies won't be a-singing these songs that they learned from the bigger kids."

. . . Well, I just remember that particular song that we was a-singing that day . . . but there's many funny little verses like that. Like I always thought that song . . . one of Uncle Wilts Garland's songs, that he used to sing an awful lot when he was a boy a-growing up, was the "Greasy String" [Molly laughs through much of the following performance]:

Greasy string, greasy string
Now pull down heavy on your greasy string
Take your ladies and let me pass
Hear I come with a greasy ass
A greasy ass, a greasy ass
Here I come with a greasy ass
O Doc Sunday, don't get scared
I need your grease for to grease my beard

Goose chew tobacco and a duck drinks wine
And a hog plays the fiddle on a pumpkin vine
A pumpkin vine, a pumpkin vine
A hog plays the fiddle on a pumpkin vine

Old Granny Hare, what you done there
Setting on a cat turd, picking out a hair
Picking out a hair, picking out a hair
Setting on a cat turd, picking out a hair

[Alan Lomax asks Molly about ways in which toasts were performed.]

Well, they'd be a group of people a-drinking and . . . they called it a drinking toast. It's who could make the roughest rhyme . . . before they all drink, you know. And they took it by turn, around, you know. Like they'd start here. Everybody'll have their glass in their hand, and like, John stands here first. And all in a circle around, or John sits here at the head of the table. And then it goes all around, you know, everyone's supposed to say a toast, and, like John, he should start—

> God bless the mast that fell last fall
> And set the fowls to boarding
> God bless the bee that stung old Adam in the ass
> And set the pretty women to whoring

Next one to him—Dick, Tom, or Harry, whatever he may be—maybe he'd say,

> Of all the beasts I ever saw
> I'd rather be a boar
> Every jig I'd get a pig
> And sometimes three and four

Next one'd maybe say,

> Of all the fowls that flew through the air
> I'd rather be a martin
> I'd spread my wings and flop my tail
> And leave this wide world a-shittin and fartin

And maybe the next one would say . . . I just thought of that,

> Here's to those that wears old clothes and has no wife to mend em
> Here's to the boys that has but a few dimes but a damn free heart to
> spend em

And, oh, so many like that. . . .

This here is John Garland's memory lesson he said at school one time, and run out of the house and was afraid to go back. [John's teacher] told him, says, "John, . . . all the rest of the children has to have a memory lesson, and you've got to get a memory lessen." So John got up and . . . made a nice bow, and he said,

Come ladies, come quick
Here's a big Irishman a-fixing to show his prick
As long as my arm, and as big as my wrist
And a knot on the head of it as big as my fist
Jack Frost!

He grabbed his hat and run out. [Laughing]

[Alan Lomax: Did he know what he was saying, Molly?]

Sure. He made it up. That's all the kind of poetry that boy'd make. He was a good poet, but he made up just funny poetry like that, and rough poetry.

And he stayed away from school then two or three days, and he went back, and . . . the schoolteacher come to see my father about him a-staying out of school, and told him to tell John he wouldn't whip him for saying that rough speech if he'd come back to school.

104. An Unreasonable Lie: The Land of the Yeahoes	**AUNT MOLLY JACKSON** **Clay County, Kentucky** **Recorded by Alan Lomax,** **New York City, May 1939**

My family, the generations all the way around, on the father's and mother's side, they are noted for great storytellers. And, if fact, quite a few of em have won prizes. Especially my youngest brother, Jim Garland, he won a prize for telling the biggest lie in the coal mine one time, at a picnic in the coal mine. So they're real good storytellers, and this story about the land of Yeahoe is a story that . . . my father's youngest brother, he just composed it hisself and told it hisself. That's a kind of what he called an unreasonable lie. [Laughter]

He said when he was a young man, him and his father had a falling out and they disagreed, and he decided to leave the country. And he left the country and he crossed over, he caught a ship and he sailed across, on the other side, of what he called the other side of the pond. And the boat landed right in the land of Yeahoe.

In this land of Yeahoe, my Uncle Wilts Garland said that there was the beautifullest women in that land that he ever saw in his life. But they had no heads at all.

And he married one of these beautiful women without any heads, and he had one son. And when this little boy was seven years old, they had to carry shillelaghs to keep the flying serpents from stinging em and killing em when they went out a-hunting. So him and his little boy went out a-hunting and the little boy laid down his shillelagh to pick a briar out of his toe, and one of these flying serpents stung him right on the top of the head and killed him.

My Uncle Wilts Garland said that that made him awful bad dissatisfied, although he loved his beautiful wife very much, but he decided then how could he get back across on the other side of the pond. So he knowed where there's an old rockaloa a-setting, he said, and she had to fly on this side for her food. He went and crawled up on her back, and she flew on this side and let him down right into a snag of young bears.

And he had always heared the story told, he said, that . . . the old she-bear would come down a-carrying her food to the young bears, and she'd come down backwards. So my uncle said, he grabbed the bear by the tail, and she pulled him out of the holler snag of the tree and let him down right by the roots of a big tree that was five thousand million feet around. And he heard a roar and he said that roaring begin, and he found out that it was bees. And this was a big bee tree. And he went to his neighbor's house and cut this bee tree down in twenty minutes. Although it was five thousand million feet around he cut it down in twenty minutes, and it rolled in the sea and made some of the healthiest, nicest, best mathiglum that he ever tasted. He said he stayed and used that mathiglum six months for his health.

105. Courting Hungry

AUNT MOLLY JACKSON
Clay County, Kentucky
Recorded by Alan Lomax,
New York City, May 1939

One interesting story, my father's brother, Uncle Wilts Garland, used to tell, we always liked to hear him tell so much, was an experience that he had . . . when he was a young man a-going a courting. He said that they was seven of the brothers, and their mother made a rule that if they wasn't in at mealtime then they didn't get anything to eat at the next meal. So Uncle Wilts he went to church and . . . he got back late, and he didn't get any dinner.

Then he went to church that night, and he went home with his girl to stay all night without any supper. They put him in the hall of an old log cabin to sleep and they was a large crack in the house. So he was afraid a cat, he said, would crawl in on him or something. And he stuffed his pants in the crack in the log house, and that night an old cow come along and drug his pants out and chewed his pants up. When he waked up the next morning and looked up to get up to put his pants on and he was so hungry he wanted to get up and eat breakfast, well, he missed his pants. And, uh, so, when the old man come in and said, "Get up, young man, to breakfast," he said he couldn't think of nothing else only to tell the old man that he was sick that morning. And they was a bench in the hall and it was all full of buckets of milk.

So he decided when the old man went back to breakfast he was so hungry that he'd just get up and stand there and drink a bucket of that milk. And just as he got the lid off, he said, and went to drinking the milk in a big way, he heard someone a-coming and he started to set the bucket down and the bucket bell hung over his neck [laughter] and he took right out at the door, he run right out of the door with a bucket a-hanging around his neck and they set the dog on him and he run down through a sawbriar field where it's full of sawbriars and said he scratched his legs all to pieces and you can imagine, he says, what else was scratched to pieces. And, uh, that girl give him the name of the Bell Calf, and he never did [laughing] go back to see her no more, he said.

106. Churning Up the Devil

AUNT MOLLY JACKSON
Clay County, Kentucky
Recorded by Alan Lomax,
New York City, May 1939

My father's brother, Uncle Wilts Garland, he told another story about going to Tennessee and getting him a job of work on the farm. And he got acquainted with a preacher's daughter and he, him being strange in that country, well, the preacher didn't want him, he said, to keep company with the girl. So he had to slip around and see the girl unbeknownst to . . . her parents. One Sunday he knowed of the father and mother of his sweetheart a-going to church, so he went over to spend the morning with her, and figured that he'd leave before they got back from church, which was around twelve o'clock. And they got so interested in talking that the old man and woman was right at the gate ready to open the gate and come in when they saw him. So Uncle Wilts Garland asked his sweetheart what, what to do and she said, "Jump in the big churn and I'll put the lid over you." The big churn held fifty gallons. The old preacher, he run a milk dairy, in Tennessee. So the old lady, they went around looking at all the milk that'd been strained away and what expect to be churned the next time, and she, she found that there had to be churning done in the big churn that day. So the girl, she begged him to churn in the little churn, that she was afraid they'd churn up the devil if they churned in the big churn that day.

And the old man said if the ox was in the ditch on Sunday, why we had to pull him out.

So Uncle Wilts said, here come the old lady, the girl's mother a-pouring one bucket full of milk and crock full of milk, right after another, in on him. And he begin to stretch his neck up and finally the milk got right up around up his ears, and it was a running in his ears and in his mouth and a-strangling him so that he give a big leap and a yell and jumped right out of the churn into the floor and run out of the house. The old preacher's wife, she said, she begin to scream that she had poured up the devil and Uncle Wilts said that he was awful sorry, that that's the first, that's the first, as he called it, store-bought suit of clothes that he ever had in his life. All the other suits he had up till then was made out of . . . jeans cloth, and his mother made em at home by hand. And so he said that he never did go back to see that girl no more.

But the preacher's wife believed that he was really the devil, and the girl never did have to churn no more on Sunday.

107. Becoming a Witch and Undoing Spells

AUNT MOLLY JACKSON
Clay County, Kentucky
Recorded by Alan Lomax,
New York City, May 1939

How you come to be a witch: you go on the top of a mountain before sunrise, and as the sun comes up, you turn your face to the sun, and cuss God and give yourself over to the devil.

A witch story that was told to me—that it was told by a neighbor woman of mine—that they was a woman by the name of Jane, that everybody was afraid of her, afraid she . . . would cause em to have some kind of spells, or bewitch their cows and have em to die or bewitch their children or something like that.

So Lula Paine she had a cow that, every time that she was turned out of the barn lot, she'd go straight and jump into Old Aunt Jane's corn. And Old Aunt Jane, she come over and told her, "If you don't keep that cow out of my corn, the next time that I have to drive her over here, when I drive her inside of the barn lot, she'll fall and she'll never get up no more."

So the next time she turned the cow out, she went straight back to the field and jumped in. Old Aunt Jane, she brought her and turned her into the lot and just waved her hands over the cow's back three times, and the cow fell down and straightened out and just laid like she was dead. And Lulu Paine said that she went and told her, said, "Aunt Jane, some of the children turned the cow out of the barn lot, and I didn't know it," and said, ". . . my little children will starve without milk. If you'll break the spell from off the cow, well, then, I'll see that she's not turned out no more." And she just walked up, Lulu Paine said, and kicked the cow with her foot and told her to get up, and she just jumped up.

[Alan Lomax: . . . Didn't the people ever prosecute any of these witches, Molly, in the courts, or any . . . other way? Didn't they ever beat em, or do anything to the witches when they found out. . . ?]

Oh, yes. They claimed that if you made a silver ball, and then made . . . a picture and named this picture the witch, and made the picture of a heart, and shot that silver ball through the heart, that wherever that witch was, why she'd . . . fall dead of that. And that was one way they had of killing the witches, to get rid of em.

[Alan Lomax: Well, how . . . did witch doctors learn their trade? How did they learn their secrets?]

. . . All I know is just what they claim. They claim that they had power from the Lord. The Lord give them power to break these witchcrafts, as the devil give the witches power to put the spells on the people, is what the witch doctors claimed.

[Alan Lomax: Are there still witch doctors and witches in Kentucky?]

Yes, a few, but not so many as they used to be, but they's still a few, said to be. . . . Rache, which is the daughter-in-law of this old woman Jane, everybody that believes in witches at all, they're afraid of her until this day. She's about eighty years old now, and all the people in the neighborhood and country that believes at all in witches, or even thinks that there *might* be something in witches, they're afraid to insult old Aunt Rache about anything, afraid that she'll put some kind of spells on their children, or them.

[Alan Lomax: Did the witches ever go to church, Molly?]

Oh, yes. They're the biggest hypocrites that we have. The ones that they claim to be witches, well they pretend to be the best people, the very best people.

[Alan Lomax: Do they ever actually kill anybody, these witches?]

Well, it's *said* that people dies with spells, . . . some kind of sudden death, and they believe that, it's caused by witches, by what they call the witchcraft, put on em, by these witches, the witchery.

108. The Witch and the Witch Doctor

AUNT MOLLY JACKSON
Clay County, Kentucky
Recorded by Alan Lomax,
New York City, May 1939

This witch story was told to me by my husband, Jim Stewart. His brother, youngest brother, Albert Stewart, he told me, begin to have some kind of strange fits. His father, Ike Stewart, he went and called the doctor in, and when the doctor come and looked at the child, he said there was nothing he could do for the child because that he was bewitched. And advised him to get a witch doctor. So they called in a witch doctor. This witch doctor told the mother of the child there would be someone in that house to borrow something, or to try to get away with a little, just a little thread or a rag or something out of the house—and not to let anybody have anything out of the house. And first and all, the old lady neighbor that lived near them, she came for a half a pint of cornmeal, and Mrs. Stewart refused her the cornmeal. Then she come back for a needle full of sewing thread, and she refused her. And when she refused her of the sewing thread, when she started out of the house, she grabbed up a string in the floor and tried to get away with it. And Mrs. Stewart, the mother of the child, struck her in the back with a broom and knocked the string out of her hands and she run down the pathway about fifteen feet from the house and fell in the road and begin to take the same kinds of fits that the child was taking—and died in the road.

But before she come, when this witch doctor was a-working with this child, why his elbows would fly out of joint and his knees would fly out of joint just like the child's and he was all in a perspiration of sweat.

And as soon as this old woman fell dead in the path with a fit, well that was the last fit that the child had and the spell was broken. He never did have another spell like that in his life.

My husband told me this story to be the truth. Jim Stewart.

[Alan Lomax: It happened to his brother?]

Yes, his youngest brother, Albert Stewart.

[Alan Lomax: Were there still any witch doctors around when you were growing up in Kentucky?]

Oh, yes, they was witch doctors and also they was said to be plenty of witches.

[Alan Lomax: Well, what were the witch doctors, what did they do? Did they ever give people these spells too?]

Oh, no, the witch doctors . . . was the ones that broke the craft, the witchcraft. Like I say, if anybody would witch your cow till the milk wouldn't turn, then you'd send for the witch doctor to know what was wrong, and they would advise you to put a piece of silver in the churn and churn on . . . a silver half a dollar, for so many times.

And . . . if your cow began to give lumpy milk, or something like that, you're supposed then to milk the cow and set the milk down.

109. Ridden by a Witch

AUNT MOLLY JACKSON
Clay County, Kentucky
Recorded by Alan Lomax,
New York City, May 1939

This man—Newt Payne—said that he would swear this, about this same old woman, that she turned him—he said that she turned him into a horse one night—

[Alan Lomax: Let's tell it all. We can turn over the record.]

Newt Payne said that Old Aunt Jane turned him into a horse one night and rode him through a briar field and . . . got his hands, the palms of his hands, and his feet was all full of, of a thorns from the briars—and tied him up then, turned him into a horse and rode him, and then tied him up to a poplar hitching post and he stood there and gnawed that post almost in two. And another time he said then that she turned him into a dog and when he come to himself he was in a smokehouse with his head hung in a soap gourd, eating soap grease and trying to get the gourd from off of his head. And another time, he said, that she, that she turned him into a cat, and that he got into a bunch of other cats, and got into a terrible fight with the other cats and . . . the next morning he said that his face was literally scratched to pieces.

[Alan Lomax: Well do you know that any of this is true or do you think that. . . .]

Well, I always had my opinion about these things, of course everybody has their opinions, and my opinion was that Newt Payne . . . dreamed these things. He had these terrible dreams, and he was really afraid of Jane a-witching him, and he went to sleep and he had these bad dreams, and, and he actually thought the dreams was so plain.

110. Living in a Haunted House

AUNT MOLLY JACKSON
Clay County, Kentucky
Recorded by Alan Lomax,
New York City, May 1939

The story . . . about ghosts, that puzzled me the most, and I don't until this day understand what the noises was, nor nothing at all about it. But anyhow, they was a man by the name of Pres Hendricks. He . . . was a whiskey maker and had his own saloon and sold whiskey at his own, in his own house for quite a few years, and he raised his family at this place. And him and his wife was said to have killed quite a few people when they was drunk, and then the Cumberland River was near the house and they'd always . . . put the people they killed up in the attic till dark and then take and throw em into the river. So, when Pres Hendricks died, my—everybody was so afraid of the ghosts at this place, the place was said to be so hainted that nobody wouldn't even stay and wait on him in his sickness, but my father. And my father always said that there was no such a thing as the spirit of a dead person a-coming back. If they went to rest, they didn't want to come back, and if they went to hell, why, they couldn't *get* back. And so he wasn't afraid. And my father, he nursed this Pres Hendricks day and night for three weeks before he died. And after he died, it was a beautiful big, eight-room house . . . a big rock wall cellar down underneath—what they call a basement here. And that's where he made his whiskey and sold it and kept it.

So when he died, none of his children wouldn't move in the house, . . . nor none of the neighbors, and everybody, so they said, "Brother, Garland, if you will live at this house, you can have the house," the heirs told him, "free of charge." And my father moved to that house. And my brother—then he was ten years old, my full brother, and he was so fraid of ghosts, the little feller, he left home and never would stay at home. But *I stayed* at that place, and you *could* hear all kinds of noises. And whether it was . . . what we called wharf rats, as large as half-grown cats in the cellar and all everywhere—and whether it was them or something else, I don't know, but you could hear a lot of noises at that place. And nobody wouldn't live at that place at all.

[Alan Lomax: Did you all finally move out?]

We, we stayed there till finally . . . when the Cumberland River, whenever—in the spring of the year, when the backwater got to coming up, raising, why it'd raise right up into this house and we had to move out. But . . . my father lived in that house for many, many years free.

On the Range with J. Frank Dobie

111. My Father Prays

J. FRANK DOBIE
Live Oak County and Austin, Texas
Recorded by John A. Lomax, Austin, Texas, November 1941

When John Lomax sat down in an Austin hotel room to record the reminiscences of J. Frank Dobie, he was facing the one man in Texas whose reputation as a folklorist could rival his own. Dobie had served for two decades as secretary-treasurer of the Texas Folklore Society, had edited some fifteen of its more-or-less annual books, and had worked intimately with Lomax after John assumed the presidency in 1940. Dobie had also written several folklore-centered books of his own, including *Coronado's Children* (1930), a collection of treasure legends, and *Tongues of the Monte* (1935), a fictionalized account of his youthful adventures in Mexico.

To Lomax, Dobie was both folklorist and folk: He had grown up on a ranch and actually lived the cowboy life that his older friend could only fantasize about. The one occasion upon which Lomax recorded Dobie's words was, not surprisingly, devoted to the latter's memories of a childhood spent on a cattle ranch. Dobie sang trail songs, performed cattle calls, spoke of the dangers of the trail ride, and distinguished his real-life experiences from Wild West fictions. Most often and feelingly, he spoke about his father, R.J. Dobie. The elder Dobie had grown up in Houston, one of Texas's largest cities at the time, but in the 1860s, even Houston was not far from the Wild West: "Papa used to tell me that when he was a boy in Harris County, the bad fellers would come into Houston and yell out: 'Whoopie! Born in the canebrake. Suckled by a she-bear. The farther up the creek they get, the worse they are, and I come from the head of it.' "

At one point during the interview, Dobie strayed briefly from the focus on his father to mention some details of his own life. He then abruptly corrected himself, saying, "I don't want to talk about myself, I'm just telling about what Papa did, and the kind of man he was. I never have been as good a man as he was, and I'm sorry."

This is Frank Dobie talking, now of the University of Texas, and formerly of Live Oak County, where I got more than I've ever got from any Ph.D.

*J. Frank Dobie, folklorist and narrator of stories 111–113, at barbecue given by Austin writer and publisher Joe Small,
ca. 1957. (Center for American History, UT-Austin, CN 03130, Lee [Russell] Photograph Collection, 1935–1977)*

professors. I want to talk about my father, and about the little ranchers. Most of the books you read and most of the talks you hear, it's the *big* ranch, and the big rancher that occupies the center of the stage. I was born and reared on a ranch of about seven thousand acres. We thought it was a mighty little ranch. My father used to hesitate to call it a ranch. He said it was just a place. It wasn't exactly a farm either, although we had several Mexican renters on it.

He was born back in the days of the open range, and had worked cattle and horses when the whole country was open. He'd driven up the trail, driven horses, he and Uncle Jim Dobie and Uncle Neville Dobie and Uncle Robert Dobie, and about the same time also that my mother's brothers were going up the trail, Frank Biler, and our half-brothers Ed DuBose and Judd DuBose, and our step-father, Friendly DuBose. They were all ranch people and trail drivers, on both sides of the "half."

Well, Papa was a little rancher. He used to buy yearlings in the spring and summer, and hold em through the fall and sell em next spring when they're two-year-olds. Of course, he had some cows and bulls and other cattle too. Sometimes he pastured cattle with other people. Sometimes he had other pastures leased. But was what—he considered himself—and what everybody else consider, a small ranch man. Not a big operator. And such is the salt of the earth, I want to tell you. He was a good man. You hear a great deal about *tough* cowboys and tough cowmen. My father was a good man. When he was young, he used to dance and play the fiddle. They called him Dancing Dick of Sore-toe. (His name was Richard, or Dick.)

After he married and got religion, he quit playing the fiddle, and quit dancing, but he was still a mighty cheerful man, and he used to sing half the time and whistle the other half of the time, while he was awake, and particularly while he was riding.

I was the first child in the family—there were six of us—and of course I was favored as being the oldest. When he went off to receive cattle, sometimes gone three or four days, why, he'd take me with him. Almost before I quit sucking—well, not quite that soon either. But I can remember getting so tired that I'd cry of sleepiness, coming back at night. And he and the Mexicans—all the hands were Mexicans—would be driving those cattle along. Maybe Pop'd be behind the herd, singing to em, and whistling. Perhaps he'd be singing "Kitty Wells." I think it's about the sweetest song that ever was. . . . And, you know, I believe those yearlings walked better, for hearing that song. Maybe he'd be singing "The Old-Time Religion":

It was the old-time religion
It was the old-time religion
It was the old-time religion
And it's good enough for me.

Or maybe he'd be singing about the "Rock of Ages." Or "Over There, on the Golden Shore." Or maybe he'd be singing about some character that he heard of when he was a boy, about a fellow that looked like me. If he wasn't singing, as I said, he was whistling, and those yearlings seemed to walk better because of it.

My father believed in education. He didn't have much education himself. He could read, write, and recollect all right, as Grandpa DuBose said. We took the semi-weekly *Houston Post*, the semi-weekly *San Antonio Express*. He read some books. He didn't like the *Arabian Nights*, said it was a pack of lies. But he liked stories that we children liked. He used to read us *Black Beauty* and *Beautiful Joe*, and a little book about an owl that was a hero to me. And he'd read Scott to us too, when Mama couldn't read to us. He believed in education. He and two other men . . . built a schoolhouse on our ranch for us children. About eight or ten of us children went to that schoolhouse, besides three or four Mexican children.

He was sincerely religious. He helped build two churches. Of course, they weren't big churches. They were the kind of churches where people came just once a month to hear the preacher preach and to eat dinner together. They had lots of pies and chicken and other good—and potato salads and pumpkin pies and other good things to eat.

Well, one time when I was a child, I heard Mama and some men talking about a trip that my father had had with some vaqueros off for a bunch of cattle he had to receive. And I got it that when they got to the Ram Rainy Creek, it was on a *rise*. It'd been a great rain, what Papa used to call a "gully washer and fence lifter." It . . . rained pitchforks and heifer yearlings—bobtailed heifer yearlings—three or four hours. This creek was on a terrible rise.

Well, I'll tell you right now, when a dry creek is on a big rise, it's dangerous to cross, it brings lots of driftwood. The water brings lots of driftwood down. And they said, when Papa got to that creek and had to cross, before he took his men in, he got down off his horse and kneeled in the ground, and *prayed*, prayed to God they'd all get over safely. You people that know cow people, that know ranch people, only through Zane Gray fiction and Wild West picture shows, think all the ranch people were tough hombres. That they feared neither God, man, nor devil. Well, my father feared God. He didn't fear the devil because he had nothing to fear from him, and I don't think he ever let the sun go down on his anger toward another man.

112. *Hilo!*

J. FRANK DOBIE
Live Oak County and Austin, Texas
Recorded by John A. Lomax, Austin, Texas, November 1941

J. Frank Dobie's father, R.J., left Houston early in life to settle in the Nueces River valley of south Texas, in the heart of the Mexican American culture area. As a boy, J. Frank Dobie was surrounded by Spanish-speaking cowboys, or—as he explains—vaqueros: "I must have been about grown before I came to know that 'cowboy' is not a literary word. Most of the cowhands I knew were Mexicans, and all of them were called vaqueros. My father was a stockman, having driven horses up the trail to Kansas with Mexican vaqueros, then turning to cattle. All that country used to be grazed by herds of wild horses. My father also rented fields to Mexicans, and several families lived on the ranch."

In response to John Lomax's request for cattle calls, Dobie recited several in Spanish. A commonly recurring word was *hilo*—"string out"—a reference to driving the cattle in a more or less straight and orderly line along the trail. Dobie paused to deliver a brief story about the word.

*H*ilo means "string out." I can tell you a little story about *hilo*. One time, there was a peon, an *arreoro*, a man that drives burros, loaded burros, or loaded mules—went hunting. He never had been able to kill a deer. He'd been out hunting lots and lots of times. Never had killed a deer. Had a fairly good gun. One day, came up on an old buck asleep, right in front of him. Pointed his gun at him, and knew he could shoot him, and his mind flashed out with pictures. Why, he said to himself, before he pulled the trigger, he said to himself, "Just look at that great big buck. I'm going to kill him, gonna skin him, gonna make *tewas*—moccasins—out of his hide. And then I'm gonna sell these moccasins and buy a cow with a calf. I'm gonna milk the cow. Gonna make cheese out of the milk. And when I get enough cheese sold, I'm gonna buy a mare.

And I'm gonna breed this mare to a jack. And the mare's gonna have a mule. And that'll be the first mule that I can pack, and load with goods, travel across the mountains. And then she'll have another mule, and another mule, and another mule, and maybe she'll have a filly for a colt. And then she'll grow up, and *she'll* have a mule. Why, *por dios,* I'll have fifteen or twenty mules, strung out, loaded, going over the mountains." And this fellow, thinking about the mules there, saw em going over the mountains all loaded up, and he yelled up, "*HILO*"—string out. And soon as he said that, why the buck jumped away, and he didn't even get a shot. [Laughter]

113. Beef and Tallow	**J. FRANK DOBIE** **Live Oak County and Austin, Texas** **Recorded by John A. Lomax, Austin, Texas, November 1941**

One of the most valuable parts of the cow was the tallow—the "hard fat" used in candle- and soap-making, leather dressing, and food preparation. Cattlemen expended great effort in keeping their cows fat: "I've never seen anything much in Wild West fiction and picture shows but *lies,* about cattle. You'd think that the cowboys were always trying to make em run. You'd think that the cattle were always running. And the cowboys were always jumping. The object of any sort of a good cowboy, or any sort of a cowman, was to keep em going slow. If they ran, they'd run the tallow off of themselves. If they went slow, why, they would make more time in the end than if they were running part of the time, and then sulling [stopped] the rest of the time."

To Dobie's family and fellow ranchers, it was inconceivable to waste a cow's tallow and equally inconceivable to waste its beef, as these brief recollections about ranching life and a character named Isom Like reveal.

As Dobie told these tales to John A. Lomax in an Austin hotel room, a budding folklorist named John Henry Faulk and a cowboy-singer named Frank Goodwyn were also present. In the course of recording, Lomax's wife, Ruby, passed in and out of the room. Forty-seven years after the session, Goodwyn explained to Lomax's biographer Nolan Porterfield that John was sneaking nips from a flask of whiskey when his wife was out of sight. Dobie's voice hints that he may have been helping Lomax with the whiskey.

Well, Grandpa DuBose used to buy cattle from Martin Culliver. Martin Culliver owned a hide and tallow factory down on the coast. They called em hide and tallow factories because the hides and the tallow was all that was utilized of the animals butchered. They'd take the hide off and send it to Boston to get shoes and boots with, and they'd melt out the tallow but the meat, good old beef, they'd throw to the fish in the bay, or they'd drop it out on the land for buzzards and coyotes to eat.

Of course, these people were all beef eaters themselves. But they couldn't eat up the beef that was butchered at these hide and tallow factories. Grandpa DuBose used to take his saddle pockets full of twenty dollar gold pieces and go out for Martin Culliver right after the Civil War and pay in gold coin for the cattle that were being taken to the factories.

You know, talking about beef makes me think of a story that old Jack Potter tells about beef-eating Texans. He said that, along in the seventies or eighties, maybe it was, he knew a feller named Isom Like that went out from Texas to New Mexico in the Apache and Comanche time. Well, he fought his way out there, and established a horse ranch up in northern New Mexico. Jack Potter said when old Isom Like was seventy-six years old, he got to his horse ranch one day, and they were having a contest, riding contest. People call em rodeos now, or ro-DAY-os. And old Isom and his four boys were riding wild horses, pitching horses in the pen. And Mrs. Like was sitting up on the fence judging the contest. Well, at the end of it, she declared old Isom was the best rider of the bunch and gave him the prize.

Horses got cheap, and old Isom had to drive them away to the town. People didn't come any more to his ranch. Jack Potter said that along in the nineties, he was in Trinidad, Colorado, at a hotel, when he saw old Isom. About the first time old Isom had been in town, for a long, long time at least. They were having supper together. And a waitress brought around a bowl of pudding for dessert. And Isom pushed it aside, and says, "That's for children."

Well, next morning, they got down to breakfast before daylight, and the waitress brought them some toast. Old Isom pushed it back, and said, "I ain't sick." And went on with his horses.

Well, finally, Isom Like moved to town. Jack Potter said he went there to seem him on his hundredth birthday. Heard he's celebrating. And he asked him, said, "Mr. Like," said, "have you got any sort of *remedio* [here, "prescription"] for long life?"

"Yes," Mr. Like says, "I have." Says, "Eat moderately and drink moderately. And get your steak three times a day. [Yelling] *Fried in tallow!* There's nothing like tallow to keep your stomach greased up." [Laughter]

8

LEGENDARY AMERICA

114. The Wolf Boy

LULA DAVIS
Southern Missouri and
Fayetteville, Arkansas
Recorded by Sandy Paton,
Fayetteville, Arkansas, November
1962

Lula Davis, a native of the Ozark Mountains and a celebrated folksinger, told the following three legends to Sandy Paton, a tireless folksong performer and collector, and an executive of Folk Legacy Records. Lula's tales, like her music, were part of her family heritage: she learned all three from her father.

All of Lula's legends take us to the border of the supernatural without ever quite crossing over. Tales of humans raised by animals are among the oldest in existence: according to ancient legend, Romulus and Remus, like the boy featured in the following tale, were raised by wolves. Today, tales of feral children are not as common in the United States as in South Asia, Africa, and other areas in which wolves, bears, and other large wild mammals are more abundant.

My father used to tell me a story of the Wolf Boy. He said that a young couple would take their baby with them into the field to work and leave it at the end of the row while they were working, and it disappeared. And they never did find it.

Well, about nine or ten years later, there was raids on the chicken houses and disturbances around farmyards and various places. So the neighbors ganged up and they went through the woods. They was going to hunt it down. And

Ghost stories at Jonesborough Cemetery, National Storytelling Festival, ca. 1980. (Tom Raymond)

they went up the hillside and searched, and trailed this thing down, and they came to a cave, a big cave. And they looked in and were really surprised to see a human, a boy of about that age, with no clothing on. And he was sitting beside a wolf that was old and almost completely helpless.

And they captured the boy and this young couple supposed that perhaps it was their son, that had been lost since they lost him in the field. . . . This was in Missouri, in I suppose about the central, west central portion of Missouri. It's pretty—lots of trees and things—foresty. There's not very . . . many houses. Not very well settled. . . .

This child was taking care of this mother wolf that had taken care of him. Perhaps. They supposed all this. But it was logical. He couldn't speak a word, and he was very savage, and they called him the Wolf Boy.

115. The Orphan Girl That Died

LULA DAVIS
Southern Missouri and
Fayetteville, Arkansas
Recorded by Sandy Paton,
Fayetteville, Arkansas, November
1962

In the days before embalming became standard practice in rural communities, the fear of being buried alive was rampant, and it often found expression in such stories as the following.

The orphan girl that died. Oh, yes. My father told this one too. There was an orphan girl that had no folks whatsoever living. She died of a disease that was unknown to the doctors at this time. And they buried her. Well, there was an old doctor living there that was studying diseases and their cures, and he had a young doctor was studying under him. They were studying together in other words. And so they didn't have to get permission to get this orphan girl from the grave and dissect to see what she died of—because she had no folks to go to to obtain the permission, so they just went and got her and had her laid out in the laboratory, and the old doctor was going to let the younger doctor study the case first, you know, and do the operation, and he went in the other room.

And the young doctor picked up the knife, and he started to cut on her, and he thought he saw her eyelid move. And he stood there a little while, almost petrified, and it twitched again. So he laid the knife down, and he walked in the other room, and called the old doctor to come in. Said he was just almost sure that he saw this girl's eyelid move. And the old doctor thought maybe that he was just getting kind of squeamish, and so he come in and said, "Oh, you're just getting afraid," or something. Walked up there, and he stood and watched her awhile, and her eyelid *did* move.

So they got a mirror and held it down there, and it showed that she was breathing a little. So they quickly revived her, and she got well, and she married the young doctor.

. . . This happened in Missouri. She'd been buried I think at least a day, and maybe over. I don't know just how long, but she had already been buried and covered up and everything.

[Child's voice: Is it true?]

Supposed to be true.

116. The Child and the Snake

LULA DAVIS
Southern Missouri and
Fayetteville, Arkansas
Recorded by Sandy Paton,
Fayetteville, Arkansas, November
1962

This is one of the most common American legends, well known in both European American and African American communities throughout the country. Most narrators express the belief that some sort of supernatural bond links the snake and the human baby, but Lula Davis's father, from whom she learned the tale, had his own medical explanation for why the child's death followed so quickly upon the snake's.

Oh, yes. My father knew another one, of a small child that always had a habit of eating bread and milk every day, in between meals. And regularly—at regular hours, he'd come in and ask his mother for a cup full of bread and milk. His mother give it to him. Instead of stopping there in the house or sitting on the doorstep or on the porch to eat it, he'd go off somewhere, and his mother got curious to know where he went with it.

So she followed him one day. And he went out behind the little henhouse—or building of some kind—and she went, she followed him around there, and, when she came around the corner, she was real shocked to see a rattlesnake coiled up beside him. And this boy was feeding the rattlesnake, you know, from the spoon. And taking a bite, alternating, the snake a bite and him a bite, eating together. And she was real shocked for a moment, and then she turned around and got a ax, and she killed the snake. And took the baby in the house, and the baby lived a few days—he just refused to eat anymore—and pined away and died.

My father supposed that perhaps he had been accustomed to a certain amount of this snake poison in his system, and deprived of it this way, well, he died.

[Interviewer: You mean, he was getting some of the poison?]

Yeah, some of the poison, by alternating with the snake. And deprived of this poison, he died.

117. A Haunted House

LAURIE HANCE
Newport, Tennessee
Recorded by Joseph S. Hall,
July 31, 1956

The following five tales were collected by Joseph S. Hall (1906–1992), a linguist who journeyed to the Tennessee–North Carolina border during the Great Depression to study local dialects. The federal government was then in the process of creating the Great Smoky Mountains National Park and had begun evicting the mountaineers whose homes lay within the boundaries of the future park. Many of the dispossessed had occupied their homes for well over a century.

Hall was hired by the government to document the folk speech of the people who were being relocated. Understandably, many of the women and men who spoke to him, noting that he was working for the same government that was evicting them, were slow to warm to him. For his part, Hall began his work in rather reserved and removed fashion, asking the mountaineers to read such dialect exercises as "Arthur the Rat" rather than to loosen up, share their thoughts, and tell him stories. Nevertheless, as Hall's work continued he became engaged not merely with the language but also, increasingly, with the folk traditions of the mountaineers. Hall's government project was done by 1940, but he kept returning to the region over the next two decades, and by the time the following five tales were recorded he had known Laurie Hance for nearly twenty years and they were friends.

Laurie Hance appears on several of Hall's recordings, where she relatess a number of supernatural belief traditions, including this witch belief: "My mother said if you was ever bothered by a witch, or thought a witch was a-messing around with you, just sprinkle a little salt across the door, or lay the broom down. If she sees the broom, laying across the door, . . . you could ask her in, but she wouldn't come in over that broom."

The following tale—of a man who is rewarded for his bravery in daring to spend the night in a haunted house—is just one example of one of the most widespread plots in American folktale tradition. The haunted house plot often appears in fictional tales, but in the Appalachians and elsewhere in the United States it most often takes on the form of a legend, presented as a true account of past happenings.

One time a man come to a feller's house, and he asked to stay all night, and the man said, "My wife's sick," said, "I couldn't keep you," he said, but said, "they's an empty house . . . down the road there, already furnished," and said, "if you can go down there and stay all night, I guess they'll give it to you."

[The traveler] said, "Well, my wife's kindly nervous, if you let her stay up here," he said, "I'll go down there and stay all night."

Well, he said, he went on down there and got him a chair and sit down and went to reading a Bible and said he heared something a-coming down out of the loft—like chains. And said, when he looked, it was a man standing there in front of him.

And he said, "If, if you'll look in under that hearth there," he said, "they's a lot of money there." He said, "They killed me to get my money, but they didn't get it, and," he said, "they buried me out here in the woods . . . right out there." he said, "You dig down and you can find my bones." . . .

And [the traveler] lifted at the rock, and it wouldn't hardly raise up, [but he] said all at once the rock just raised up just pretty. And there laid all that money.

And he said to the [ghost] when he was talking to him, he said, "In the name of the Father and the Son and the Holy Ghost, what do you want?"

And said, he told him then. He said, "If you take this to court, you can have this house and all this money." And said, "I'll help you out in court." Said, "I'll come down there," and said, "I'll tell em that what you tell em is so."

And said he told it, and they all fainted in the courthouse.

And the man got the house and money and all.

118. Lights That Listen

ELLIS OGLE
Pigeon Forge, Tennessee
Recorded by Joseph S. Hall,
Gatlinburg, Tennessee, August 4,
1956

Ellis Ogle was born in the Great Smoky Mountains near Pigeon Forge, Tennessee, some eighty years before the town became famous as the home-place of country music star Dolly Parton. In the years just before and after 1900, he lived in wild isolation among the mountains: there were just three houses and a country schoolhouse in the hollow inhabited by his family.

From his youngest years, Ellis was captivated by the "haint" ("haunt," or ghost) stories exchanged by his neighbors, Granny Shields and Granny

Ferryman, after the children had gone to bed. The old women argued about the nature of the ghostly lights and strange sounds that stalked their mountains after dark. Granny Shields always found rational explanations for the hauntings: the lights were caused by "minerals" (probably methane gas released from the ground in the form of luminous shapes, a phenomenon that has been used to explain the appearance of the traveling lights identified as "will o the wisp" throughout the English-speaking world), and the sounds were made by "painters" (panthers), the large mountain cats that preyed in the surrounding forests. But Granny Ferryman believed that witches and black magic lay at the root of these eerie happenings. Ellis would "possum" ("play possum"), pretending to sleep while the old folks talked, and he heard their every word.

The haint tales both frightened and fascinated Ellis. Eventually, the stories infected his dreams. He began to roam the mountains at night, regularly encountering terrifying sights and sounds, and once grew so frightened that, he says, his hair stood on end and pushed the hat off his head. Ellis eventually heard natural explanations for nearly all of these strange encounters, but he was so affected by the supernatural explanations of Granny Ferryman that, for him, even the earthly phenomena took on unearthly properties: at one point in his narration, he uses the oxymoron "natural haint" to describe a panther that he had mistaken for a ghost. The natural explanations did not fully satisfy Ellis, who often interpreted the ghostly lights as punishments for foul language, and who once saw a fireball in the exact place where he had dreamed that his neighbors had built a scarecrow to scare him.

Ellis Ogle's storytelling style is remarkably eloquent, even if his vocabulary and phrasing are difficult for most modern-day readers to follow.

Granny Shields lived in above us, and Granny Ferryman lived right over in sight of us. And that was the only three families in there. Well, we bought part of Granny Shields's place, you know, and that made three homes in there together. Three homes and the school. That's all we had. Our own [community], we might say, in a five- or six-mile circle. Well, they'd visit our home regular. And, they got this haint tale started; why, they just talked it to the old folks, altogether through the old folks. Us children didn't hear none of it, or wasn't *supposed* to hear any of it.

[Joseph S. Hall: Your mother sent you to bed?]

She'd send us to bed. . . . And, when I caught what they was a-using for a pastime—why, they'd put us to bed, and they'd watch us all off to sleep . . . — well, they'd say, "Ellis is asleep now." And the other children, some of em were snoring, and directly [Granny Shields and Granny Ferryman would] start up. Well, I'd be a-hearing all the time. I was just snoring with my eyes shut, you know, to get to hear what was gonna go on.

[Joseph S. Hall: You were a-possuming on em.]

Possuming, that's right, and they'd start this haint tale up. Old Granny, Granny Shields she'd say, "There's something to be seen. . . . Minerals. I don't think it's dangerous."

Well, Granny Ferryman say, "No, I believe in . . . these black witch tales. . . ." She'd say, "I believe something's gonna happen to me or Tiny. Been too much of it seen around." Well, that'd be interesting me, you know. I'd be laying there a-catching it all. Well, they'd tell about that noise, that's been heared at the schoolhouse, or . . . the schoolhouse a-burning down so many times, you know.

Bill Ferryman, he was out a-fox hunting one night, and he says, "The school's a-burning down, look what a light!" Well he saw the light, and he sat on the mountain right up over it and watched it burn down, later come in and he . . . called the old folks, and he says, "The school burnt down last night. I saw the light, saw the fire of it." Well, they went and looked, and the school was sitting right there, and nothing's burnt, . . . and, well, I got to wondering what it was, you know, and I possumed them. Every time one of them was by, I'd lay and listen to see what they talked about. Well, they talked about those haints.

So when they dug this new road, why I knew I had to go right by the school and graveyard. It went right out by the graveyard and schoolhouse both. Well I, every time I went through late at night or . . . early of the morning, I'd hunt for a booger [bogey man, or ghost], I'd look for one of those boogers. Just, not exactly afraid, but imagin[ing] I'd see some of it later. [After] we dug [the] new road . . . , why, it [be]come handy for me to go after a mule, or borrow a mule to make a Knoxville trip. And I was taught not to use no bad language. [Walking along the road at night to borrow a mule], I bumped my toe, and I cut a nail off of it, and I grabbed my foot up and I said, "God damn! I've ruined my foot!" and about the time I said that, this light sprung up over me. And I looked up at it. And it looked just exactly like a fish, only it was a light. Now, it was a dark, rainy, foggy, drizzly night, and when this light sprung it was right straight up over me. And when I said that by-word, that was right when it flashed up—it was just like the bat of your eye—and I looked up at it, and I think I turned around and looked back towards the house, and . . . I was just about a hundred yards [from the] house when I saw this light. And it just looked like I could make a hop and a jump back to the house. Well, I looked back, and I think to myself, "I'll just look down at the ground, and just go on. If it's gonna kill me, it'll kill me anyhow."

And it followed me about a mile like that. And I looked away on the mountain, way beyond the way I was traveling, looking down, trying not to see up to see it, and I could see my shadow over there just exactly like the sun was shining on me. But when this bursted and come down, why the shock of it or something or other numbed me, numbed my body till I couldn't walk. Well I got up in an old field, out of the road, in case [live]stock or something would come along, and I laid down and I went to sleep, after the light disappeared. When it disappeared, it disappeared in sparks, and the sparks come down all around me: just covered me up within them. And, I went to sleep there, and when I woke up, why, the sun was a-shining.

My daddy expected me back again [at] three o'clock in the morning. And the sun was shining everywhere when I woke. Well, I went on and got the mule and about eight o'clock, why, I rode him in home. My daddy was awful angry. He says, "What on earth have *you* been a-doing?"

I says (he taught me never lie to him about nothing), I says, "I'd just as well tell you all about it," I says, "I couldn't get to old man George" (George Lemon was the man I was borrowing the mule off of) "and he wouldn't let me bring him off there to eat!" Well, that was the way I fixed up my tale. Well, we . . . made this Knoxville trip. And when we come back, why my, one of my cousins were there. . . . She was a big young woman, and awful scary [easily scared]. I was telling her what I'd seen. My daddy was out and I held by him a-being out, that I'd [talk to] Mother, about using the by-word. I told her what I had said and what I saw and—Lord!—she just drawed up, and she says, "Lord, Tiny," she says, "I thought we'd see something or another like that. If that'd happened to us, what would we do?"

I says, "You just do like I did, you just die, or run, or fall, or do something or other." She says, "I'd just *die* away." Well, just as she says "I'd just die away," why I looked on the mountain, right at this mineral hill, graveyard hill: I saw one a-coming, but it wasn't as big as the one I'd saw, by a good deal. And Maude, she just spread out in the yard, her chair just kicked over. And Mother grabbed her. Well, I made a grab for an old bucket or two, there where I thought I'd saw it before it got dark, and I missed all those buckets, and I just grabbed my hat, and just got a hat full of mud and water and I just pitched [it] on her and we finally got her in and got her on the bed. And just as we started up the steps with Maude, why this here light that I saw coming fell right in the yard and bursted right where we was sitting.

119. Sounds That Listen

ELLIS OGLE
Pigeon Forge, Tennessee
Recorded by Joseph S. Hall,
Gatlinburg, Tennessee, August 4,
1956

After this here one . . . all happened and everything, why I'd got older, you know. And I got big enough to go off to schools. . . . Well, I got big enough to want to look at the . . . girls a little. So, Old Man Jim Lemmons had moved in there by then, and he had two daughters, getting about grown. And I'd got my eye on one of em, and Bate King, that's my right-hand buddy, he'd got his eye on the other one. So we'd sit with these girls during school hours, and we told them, if they'd slip off, that we'd get away, and we'd go to [the school] to a spelling. Well they says, "We don't know whether we can get away or not." Says, "We'll try." And me and Bate, we got away that evening before dark. . . .

We went to Beecher Pate and Sam Lemmon, . . . and we went back to the schoolhouse, we's to meet the girls at the schoolhouse, in case they got away. Well, we got there, why, one of these old fashioned charts is what they had up [on the wall], to teach the first grade school. Bate says, "What'll we build a fire with?" He says, "I'll tell you, by God" (he was awful bad to use bad language). He says, "By God, I'll just tear this chart up."

Well I says, "I won't have no part of that!" Well, he got on the wall, and he got to taking the chart down off the wall, and I heared something *in* the wall a-making a racket . . . like it was on the outside. Well, I think to myself, "I'll not mention this racket without Bate hearing it," and he's a-making a good deal of racket taking the chart down, and he never mentioned it either, till after he got the chart tore up and got the fire started.

He says, "By God!" he says, "What kind of a noise is that am I hearing?"

I says, "It's Beecher and Sam on the outside a-scratching on the wall. We told them we's aiming to go to this spelling. It has to be them," I says, "that noise couldn't be out there with nothing else, nobody knows we're here but them." And, we went around, and I says, "Bate, you go that-a-way, and I'll go this-a-way, and we'll whoop them birds, trying to scare up this-a-way." We wasn't near as big as them, or old as Sam and Beecher, but we thought we was big

416

enough to whoop them and we was gonna try it. So Bate went that-a-way, and I went *that*-a-way. Well, I met him and I says, "Did you see anybody?"

"No," he says, "I didn't see nobody."

Well, I says . . . , "No, I didn't see anybody." But I thought Bate was a-playing with them [i.e., was on their side], you know, I thought he let them by him. I says, "You go my way, and I'll go yours," and I just turned the corner and looked, one corner, and I just wheeled and took after him to see if he was letting them by again. Nobody didn't come by and, well, by then the noise is getting awful . . . and it sounded on the outside like it was on the *in*. Well we went in, and we turned every bench over and looked under every bench, turned the stage over and looked under it, and we couldn't find nothing nowhere. By then it was just [sounding] exactly like carpenters working around there, best I could tell you: saw work, hammer work, and everything else. But . . . when you was *in*, it [sounded] like it was on the *out*, and when you was on the out, it went like it was on the in.

I says, "You can stay and wait on the girls, Bate, if you want to," but I says, "I'm going home," and I started right then. Bate says, "Wait a minute, wait a minute," he says, "I'm a-going too!" And Bate's home was . . . close [to] my home, but he was afeared to go home after I got to the road with him. He went in and stayed all night [with] me, and when we had gone out of sight, that was the awfullest noise that I've ever heared in my life, and not by nothing.

Now this here was at the same place that this mineral work was, but we *seen* nothing, just *heared* that time. Well, I found out Granny Shields and Granny Ferrryman naturally knowed what they's talking about, about something a-being there to be seen and heared, but I couldn't tell you what it was yet. It was either mineral or something to be heared. . . .

[Listener: Well, you know it was a haint.]

Oh yeah, and it . . . naturally wasn't nobody, for I sufficiently, before I got scared or excited, I sufficiently hunted, and I thought it was Beecher and Sam *all* the time. It was not nothing—to be *found*.

[Joseph S. Hall: What about that mineral, could you explain that a little?]

That mineral—the old man, Bob, said, "In rainy weather," he said, "that mineral explode and throwed these here lights."

Some of them looked like moons, and some of them looked like babies, and some of them looked like fish. Well, the way they called it, and this one special light that I saw, looked exactly and fine-like like a baby, taped off like a fish's tail. It look like it was flying with its tail, and it absolutely shined brighter than the sun or moon either. For I seen my shadow way on the back mountain, and it look brighter and stronger by that than the sun ever give it. And this here one that fell on Maude [was] just exactly in the shape of a half moon.

120. Natural Haints

ELLIS OGLE
Pigeon Forge, Tennessee
Recorded by Joseph S. Hall,
Gatlinburg, Tennessee, August 4,
1956

In the two following brief tales, Ellis finds natural explanations for other-worldly lights and sounds, but these explanations do little to diminish the sense of eerie dread he feels when alone in the mountains at night.

Well, what happened here, you know, I was peeling stakes, I was setting stakes there one evening and forgot myself, you know, and I'd left three stakes setting against one. Peeled stakes, and I'd a-went fox hunting that night. And I come back in. Why, my uncle lived there first, before I moved there. Well, he'd seen, he'd claimed he'd seen a woman dressed in white with a sheet over her head, running up and down through the field there. Well, I's thinking about that as I come in, about my uncle saying he'd seen this here woman with a sheet over her head, and I looked down there where I had quit building the fence there that night, and it looked exactly . . . like a woman dressed in, sort of white or yellow, you know, and her arms shaped up in every way, the way I set those three field stakes up. Well my hair just pushed up, just went up, just—I'd felt that I had to pull my hat . . . on my head to keep it on. My head—my hair pushed my hat up, it scared me so bad. Me a-thinking about what my uncle had said, you know, and well I was twenty or thirty steps from those stakes. Well, they was betwixt me and that door. And I's, I was out of the house. Well, I looked back up through the field and think to myself, "Will I run plumb up yonder and around through the back of the bottom and go in? Or will I just venture up and see if that naturally is a woman with her head cut off? And it looked exactly and fine-like like a dressed woman with no head. Now, that's what it put me in the mind of. Well, I think to myself, "I'll shut my eyes, and slip up on it, and feel of it, to see if it is a natural woman." Well, I slipped up and got to feeling, just before I got to those stakes, and I opened my eyes to see how close I was to getting on it, and I'll be doggoned if my hair didn't go up again, and I had to grab my hat and pull it down on my head. It just looked exactly like a woman standing there propped up against the fence, with her head off. And I could naturally see the blood running down her shoulders, the way I'd crossed them [stakes] up there. Well, I went on and felt of the stakes, and I was the worst surprised man you ever seen in your life, and the shock and everything that it give me, by Ned I, I was just numb, all over!

Yeah, this here natural haint—they got to know . . . there's a haint loose down there, a painter, or whatever you might call it, and it jumped on a [mule] with Jack Starkie on it. . . . And he had to go up to . . . Laurel Lick, about two miles off of the road. He was riding this mule up there, and this thing—painter, or whatever this was—jumped on the mule at this road, and rode *with* him, nigh two miles. And he just fell in the forge, and his mule run off with the painter on it, the way he told it. And he found his mule on top of the mountain in an *old* stable, with the saddle torn off of it, plumb off of it, next morning, when he got out to hunting for his mule. And the mule was cut very bad, where this [thing] jumped on his back behind him and rode.

Well, I didn't *see* none of this. So one evening, my uncle and one of my cousins was sitting there, and it was raining, one Sunday, and I herded my cattle in the woods. Well, it rained so hard, I didn't mention to the children to go get the cattle till after my uncle and cousin left. And they waited for the rain to quit until dark. What we call "dark": dusk-dark. Well, they says, "We got to go. It ain't gonna quit raining."

Well, I says, "I got to hunt my cows. It's past milk time now." And I got an old overcoat and just hung it over my head, and as they started, I started in the woods to hunt the cattle. Well, I heard something holler on the hill. I holler at the cow. I said, "Sook, Susie!" Heared her bell up on the hill, and I say's "Sook, Susie." And that thing says, "Whaa." About the time that I said, "Sook, Susie," well, it started right up the hill a-hollering and making that noise, and it come right over to me. Well, I looked the best I could see in, out in the brake, and it looked like a big dog.

[Joseph S. Hall: But it wasn't a haint, it wasn't something in human form, was it?]

No, it was a panther. I learned later how come it was there and all about it. But it was a natural panther, you know. And it drove this mule. Well, I thought Jack had told a tale like that, to scare somebody. And it come off with the cow, the cow come running down off the hill. And it come down with the cow, or following after the cow, but it was making this hollering noise all the way down. Continual hollering.

121. The Scarecrow Dream

ELLIS OGLE
Pigeon Forge, Tennessee
Recorded by Joseph S. Hall,
Gatlinburg, Tennessee, August 4,
1956

In this nightmare-come-true, the ghostly lights of Pigeon Forge seem to know not only what Ellis says but also what he dreams. They seem to know exactly what scares him.

. . . I'd got big enough to get out and go to play cards at night. And I had a dream one night. I was going to play [cards with Bate] regular, that was this same boy now that we'd got in this wreck with over here at the school. Well, we took up together and we both married, and had a home of our own, and we get to playing Five Up, and we'd get our wives in with us, you know, a little family Five Up game, after supper. So, well I got to going to Bate's regular for that. Every Friday, why, he'd do his day's work, and I'd do mine, why I'd meet at his house and have a Five Up game. . . . Just a card game, you know, playing Five Up. . . . So the old woman got sort of jealous, Bate's old lady, on the last, and she got to trying to keep me away.

She said, "Something'll happen to you and Bate if you don't quit going over there directly."

"No," I said, "not a bit of danger to that."

She says, "Bate'll fall out over you and Rhody some of these days. And you'll have to kill him, or him you."

"No," I says, "I don't think so."

Well, a night or two after she said this to me, why, I had a dream that the old lady and my sister and her man put me up a scarecrow up in this same field. Out of my clothes. Put my hat, my shirt, and my overalls up on a stick, you know, for a scarecrow for me to pass down by. And, well, this dream got [to] me. I got to studying: maybe me and Bate might happen to fall out or something or other and something'd happen to us, just like she said. And I got afraid to go through this field. I'd go down and around the road. I went several more trips up over to have Five Up games, but I'd go around, I wouldn't come down this same field, for a *long* time, afraid something would happen.

. . . I come to the fence one night, way in the night, and hung my head over the fence where I had to climb over the fence and come down this holler field where I dreamt that they put the scarecrow up for me. ([In my dream], I

Scarecrow, photographed by John Vachon. In story 121, Ellis Ogle is haunted by a dream in which his family fashions a scarecrow from his own clothes. (Courtesy Library of Congress)

could see them putting that scarecrow up. And I dreamt it so plain that they used my lantern, my hunting lantern and everything for it. I think that's just an idea I had got.) I hung my head over the fence a few minutes and I finally decided I'd venture over and see if that was going to happen. Well, I got on top of the hill and looked right down in the field where they had put the scarecrow up ([in] the dream I had). There was a light, a big old light. I just think to myself, "Well, I'll just wait till they get it put up. They're doing just what I dreamt they was going to."

This light come *right* up the holler and had to turn a little by-path to come up to me on the top of the hill where I [was standing] and look[ing] down the holler. I had to run down to the main holler and go down the road. Well, I was on top of the hill where I had to run a little by-path down there. This light turned *right* up the holler and where the scarecrow should be put up, and turned and come *right up* by me. Well, I got my gun, and I got behind a tree. I was aiming to shoot at ever-who that was carrying it—or ever-*what* that was carrying it. And that light was rolling on the ground. And I looked and seen there wasn't a thing in the world but a light a-rolling. And I just stood behind that tree, let it pass . . . on over the hill out of sight. And I just turned and went on down the holler. And that was the end of my dream. . . . That was a light, and nothing was carrying it at all. I even stooped down and looked under it. It just looked like a light about as big as a bush a-rolling on the ground.

122. The Yankee and Marcum

BURL HAMMONS
Pocahontas County, West Virginia
Recorded by Carl Fleischhauer
and Alan Jabbour,
April 24, 1972

In 1969, Alan Jabbour began working in the Library of Congress as head of the Archive of Folk Song; in 1976, he became the first director of the newly named American Folklife Center, a position that he held until 1999. A specialist in fiddle tunes, Jabbour worked extensively with the Center's musical holdings, but his life-long interest in verbal lore came into play when he teamed with Carl Fleischhauer to explore the folklore of the Hammons family of West Virginia. Over a period of three years, Jabbour and Fleischhauer repeatedly visited the family and made copious recordings of their singing, instrumental music, riddles, family history narratives, and belief legends. In 1973, the Library of Congress released a two-record set, *The Hammons Family: A Study of a West Virginia Family's Traditions*, on which many of these musical and narratives performances are recorded.

Burl Hammons's tale of "The Yankee and Marcum" has recently been released in an expanded Hammons Family double CD. In his notes to that CD, Alan Jabbour speaks about the content of the tale and assesses the style of Burl Hammons's performance: "Witch stories of all sorts are current in the Hammons family repertory and throughout the region. Male witches are mentioned at least as often as female witches, perhaps more. The formula of climbing a mountain and shooting a gun at the sun to gain magical powers is particularly characteristic of the Allegheny region. . . .

"Burl's story is a good sample of his story-telling style—and, to a great extent, the style of the whole [Hammons] family. The pace of the story's progress is leisurely, whether the words come fast or slow; the tellers are fond of repetition for rhetorical emphasis and pacing; the telling style frequently uses fragmented phrases instead of complete sentences, conveying

Burl Hammons, teller of "The Yankee and Marcum" (story 122). Photo shows him playing the banjo, 1972. (Photo by Carl Fleischhauer)

The forebears of Burl Hammons, teller of "The Yankee and Marcum" (story 122). Burl's father, Paris Hammons, is flanked by brothers Pete (left) and Neal. (Hammons Family photograph, copy by Carl Fleischhauer)

a sequence of images rolling rhythmically by; and there is a good deal of dialogue."

They was a Marcum, a feller by the name of Marcum, and they was a Yankee there. . . . They didn't know where he'd come from. And this feller got talking about building a mill, you know, a grist mill, and [Marcum] told him he could build one. And he got this feller, this stranger to build his mill for him. He told him he'd just hire him to build the mill for him. And he went to work at the mill.

And it, it kindly got scarce, you know, directly: meat. You know, they killed the bigger part of their meat, and so, he asked this feller, he said to Marcum, he said, "Why don't you get out," he said, "and . . . kill us a deer?" he said.

"Well," Marcum said, "that's kindy hard," he said, "but," he said, "they're plenty of sign," he said, "I just didn't happen to see ary one."

And he said, "Well, I'll go with you in the morning."

And he said they took out, and he said they didn't go but a little piece till here'd went a deer. And he said he looked at the track, and he said . . . ,

"Now that deer's a long ways from here," he said. "But," he said, "we can kill it."

"Oh," Marcum said, "it ain't no use to track that deer, follow after that deer, just no telling how far it is," said. "It's no use to follow after it," he said.

And he said—told Marcum, the Yankee did, he said, "Just," he said, "just get up there," he said, "and sit down."

"Oh," Marcum said, "it ain't no use to set here," he says, "no telling where," he says, "that deer is, they ain't no use to set here," he said.

And, "Well," he said, "now, no," he said, "we might kill that deer."

And, "No," he said, "ain't no use."

And [the Yankee] said, "Sit down there."

And Marcum just sat down, just setting there, and he said he got right down over the track, this fellow did. . . . And he said, "Don't you speak," he told him, he said, "don't you speak," he said.

And Marcum said he just set there a little while, he said he thought that was one of the biggest, craziest men setting there over that deer track. And he said he set there right smart while, he said. And after a while he said he heard something a-coming the way the deer'd went, he said he heared something a-coming. And he said he looked, he said directly and he saw that deer a-coming, he said it was just a-coming, and he said its hair was all buzzed up and its tongue was out of its mouth, he said, that far, just like it had run to death. And he said he just set there, he said, and he . . . said the deer just, he said, come up in about, oh, he said, twenty steps to him, and he said, he said, "Well all right now, kill it."

And he just took the gun and killed it. "And now," he said, "now," he said, "I can't eat a bit of that deer myself." Said, "You can eat all you want," he said, "I won't eat a bite of it."

"Well," he said, "I don't know why."

"Well," he said, "I won't. But," he said, "that deer's just as good as any deer."

"Well," he said, "now I'll tell you one thing," said, "if you'll tell me how you done that," he said, "I'll just give you anything that I ever seen," he said. I think he had two or three cows that he said he'd give him, a cow or something: "Just give you anything if you just tell me."

"Now," he said, "it ain't no use to tell me," he said, "I don't want anything. But," he said, "it wouldn't be no use for me to tell you because," he said, "you wouldn't do it if I'd tell you."

"Oh, yes," he said, "I will," he said, "I'd do anything just if I can just do a thing like that."

"Now, well now," he said, "it wouldn't be no use, to tell you because," he said, . . . "you will," and he just kept on. . . .

And he says, "Besides, if I'd tell you," he said, "you'd aim to kill me, and," he said, "that'll you'll not do; I can tell you before it." "No I won't," he said, "now you know a friend like you," he said.

"Yes," he said, "but . . . it ain't no use to tell you."

Then he just kept on.

"All right," he said, "I'll tell you." He said, "You go on that high mountain, and," he said, ". . . when you see the sun . . . a-getting up of a morn, just as it's hit the hill," he said. "You shoot at that sunball, nine mornings. And," he said, "the ninth morning there'll be a drop of blood on your gun barrel. And," he said, "you take a piece of paper and," he said, ". . . cut a little place on your arm, and write it on it how long you want to be sold to the devil and give it to him when he comes to get it."

"All right," he said, he'd do that.

And he'd go every morning up there and, and the ninth morning, he said, when he shot that time, he said he looked onto the gun barrel and there was a drop of blood. And he just cut a little place on his arm and writ, I think it was, a year he wanted, just. And he said the gun never quit roaring: he said the gun never quit roaring, he said it just kept on roaring, he said the longer the worse, and the longer the worse, and after a while he said the whole earth just seemed like it got to jarring with him just up and down. And he said directly he looked a-coming through the treetops, and he said there come some kind of a thing that they was balls of fire coming out of its mouth. And he just dropped and away he went to the house and told em what he'd seen and all about this. He told them all about it and he said, "I'm a-going down to kill the Yankee just as quick as I can go down. Man telling me such stuff as that, I'm a-going down to kill him."

They tried to beg him not to go.

"Yes, sir, I'm a-going down," he said, "to kill the Yankee." And he just took his gun and started down where he was a-working on the mill and the Yankee seen him a-coming. He knowed just exactly what he'd done.

And, "Well," he said, "I've come to kill you." He said, "Just as I expected. But," he said, "you ain't a-yet." And . . . the Yankee just picked up his gun, and just took and shot him, and they said that he just jumped up and just crowed like a rooster and just fell over dead.

The Yankee just quit and they never did hear tell of him no more, he just quit right there and . . . went right on. They was no way they could get trace of him. They had no phones, they had no way to trace him. . . . That was the last of him; never heared tell of him again.

123. The Thing on the Bridge

NEWTON DOWNEY
Rock Hall, Maryland
Recorded by Gerald E. and
Margaret Parsons,
June 15, 1974

Gerald E. Parsons worked at the American Folklife Center from its inception in 1976 until his death in 1995. A specialist in material culture and the folklife of hunting and fishing, he also recorded a substantial amount of verbal lore, including personal experience stories, family sagas, and legends. When visitors came to the AFC reading room in search of information concerning a song or a story that their parents or grandparents had performed, Parsons would not only help the visitors find similar performances in the AFC collections but also sit them down and record their stories, songs, and reminiscences to add to the archive.

The following two tales were recorded during a visit paid by Gerald and his wife, Margaret, to the home of Newton and Hazel Downey in Rock Hall, Maryland. Downey, a devout Seventh-Day Adventist, interpreted many strange and seemingly supernatural events according to his understanding of the Bible. He told the Parsonses during their visit that ghosts may be the tricks of the devil: "It says in Second Corinthians 11:14, . . . 'And marvel not, for Satan has transformed himself into an angel of light.' That's what I say about these things. About these things. You can't tell. It can be the devil himself. He can come back."

Gerald E. Parsons: Tell me about that one you saw that you said that you thought was the devil—along the road there? . . .]

I was going with my first wife—she was my girlfriend. And those days, when we went to see girls, you didn't stay till twelve and one o'clock. You. . . . left her house nine, half past nine. . . . So I went there one night, and I came out, and it was a dark night, . . . just some starlight. And when I came over this bridge, I looked. There was a man going along the road with me. And I looked again— and he was that quick, he was gone. And these were the very words I said, "Well, I've got to see you . . . a third time before I believe, and I know you's the devil."

Well, I went by there again another night. . . . I see a man stand on the side of the road just like this. About that much of his cuffs were showing. And he was a little taller than I was. And I say, "Well, I got to see you another time."

So this night, it was blowing a gale . . . in the northwest, and I left my girlfriend's house, and the . . . moon was shining as bright as day. Not a cloud to be seen. In those days, what they did . . . on these dirt roads, they used to put wooden struts across to put a bridge in over a ditch. . . . These struts would go down when the ground's soft and then they would stay put. And the dirt was about that much higher than the bridge.

But anyhow, when I got part of the way past the woods, I saw a man standing on the north side of the road. He was dressed in a black suit. It's been so long, I can't exactly—I don't know if it was an oilskin hat or slouch hat, he had on. So, when I got down the road a little farther, he went to work, and I crossed— started to get on the other side of the road. And I did. And when *I* got on the other side of the road, why, . . . he come across on the bridge and I stopped. And I says to myself, "Now, that don't look like that's very good to me." I said, "Looks like I'm looking for trouble."

We always used to carry a gun in those days. I never shot nobody in my life. So I reached around, I said, "No, I don't have it." So I said, "Well, I'm pretty fast." And what I expect, I'm gonna pull my hat tight down, my derby hat down on top of my head, and button my coat up, and I says, when I get close enough, if he shows any resentment, I'm gonna dive for his feet. I said, "I'll have him. My word." I said, "Then I'll kick the breath out of him, and then I'll go on."

So when I got almost to him, he didn't look at me one bit. Of course, I couldn't tell whether he was looking this way or that way, and he was standing there, just this erect, just like this. And I don't know whether he turned or not, but anyhow, I went to make that grab for him, make that dive for him. And when I made that dive for him, that bridge being that much lower than the road, both feet slipped out from under me, and I went down . . . and quick as I could have my guard up, he was gone. I looked every way that I could look, and I never, I never seen anything whatsoever.

And I said, "If you're a human being, show yourself."

. . . And you know, though, I never seen that thing no more.

[Gerald Parsons: Just three times?]

Just three times. That was the third time I saw him.

[Gerald Parsons: . . . You say you think that might have been the devil?]

And nobody else.

Gerald E. Parsons (collector of stories 123 and 124) boating on the marshes of the Delmarva Peninsula. Parsons was also present when stories 129, 130, 172–175, and 189 were recorded. (Photo by Paula Johnson, American Folklife Center, Library of Congress)

124. The Vanishing Hitchhiker

NEWTON DOWNEY
Rock Hall, Maryland
Recorded by Gerald E. and
Margaret Parsons,
June 15, 1974

The tale of a mysterious young woman dressed in white who wanders desolate roadsides is one of the most widespread legends in the United States. The story persists in innumerable variations.

People who tell and comment on "The Vanishing Hitchhiker" typically interpret the mysterious woman as a ghost, but Newton Downey has a more negative interpretation, based upon his understanding of the Bible.

Big restaurant and bar . . . Bud's Place. . . . Well, that's my nephew runs that. B . . . But, yeah, I worked there, and this fellow, he was a tobacco salesman. And I was fooling around there. I always cleaned up every night, and when there wasn't nothing to do, I'd go to work and scrub the walls and things like that, just to make time go by. Rainy nights, you know, and all. But anyhow, after a while this fellow walked in and he acted like he was scared to death. He come in there, trembling, just like, and he sat down in a chair.

And he says, "Do you have any coffee?"

"I have plenty of it."

He says, "I'm scared pretty near to death."

I said, "Now, you haven't hurt nobody? Have you killed nobody? Run over em?"

And he said, "Oh, no." He said, "Give me a cup of coffee."

I said, "Well, if you can use some."

"My nerves is shot."

I say, "Well, I'll [pay] your bill. Don't put no cream and sugar in it." [Laughter] And he drank that, and I gave him another one.

I said, "Now, tell me your story." I wouldn't charge him nothing. [Laughter]

He said, "Well." (You won't pass that-a-way, but . . . it's the road that goes to Beddleton, and then, when you're coming from around Elkton, it makes a curve like this. A little ways down below that is a house, and it's a story-and-a-half house, and it's about three hundred yards from the road.)

And he said, "When I got just about two miles above that road," he said, "there was a girl on the side of the road dressed in pure white." And he said, "I went to work," and he said, "I drove up to the curve. I said, . . . 'you mind me taking you?' Said, 'I'll take you down if you get in the car with me.' "

She got in with him, and he says, "Where do you want to get out?"

She says, "I'll tell you when I get down to where I want to turn." Well, he said, she never said a word to him all the way down the road, whatsoever.

And she says, "Turn right here."

Well, when he turned, there was that house, *all lit up*. Now he got to the station about two o'clock. This house was all lit up. And when he went up in the lane, a man come out. And he says, "What are you doing up here?" . . .

"Well," he says, "I picked up a girl about two miles up the road," and says, "she said she was coming down, and she'd tell me where to turn. She told me to turn here. And when I stopped my car, she wasn't even in there with me."

He says, "Well, come on in the house."

He says, "No you don't." Says, "I'm going to leave this place, soon as I tell you."

"Well, don't worry about it." Says, "You's the third man brought her here *tonight.*"

[Gerald Parsons: For heaven's sake.]

And I believe the man was scared. I *know* he was scared. . . .

[Gerald Parsons: Isn't that something. What, what do you suppose—why were there three—why did it happen three times that one night? Do you have any idea why that should be?]

No, I couldn't tell you that. But *I* know the devil can do that. . . . The devil does have a lot of power. I'm going to tell you that. Because he's the one . . . that causes all of our distresses, our troubles, and everything.

[Gerald Parsons: Well, you think that this girl was some sort of a manifestation of the devil?]

Well, yes, I—it had to be. Now, that man, I saw him just as plain as I'm looking at you, and I was as close to him as I am to you. . . .

I tell you. You'll find out that things happen in mysterious ways. And yet, people, people today who do not follow after Christ, . . . what do they have to live for?

[Gerald Parsons: Money, I guess.]

Money.

125. The Three Knocks; A Grandmother's Ghost

LILLIAN DOANE
Jasper, Indiana
Recorded by Carl Lindahl,
Jasper Public Library, August 16,
1977

Lillian Doane was born in Dubois County, Indiana, in a German American farming region. Her forebears had emigrated from Germany about 1840, but they did not assimilate into the dominant Anglo culture. As she was growing up nearly a century later, German remained the first language of her parents and her nine "sibs." The supernatural traditions circulating in her community were also heavily influenced by Old World beliefs.

Mrs. Doane and her mother considered themselves much less susceptible to supernatural beliefs than most of their neighbors, yet the whole community was apparently steeped in certain types of witch lore. When Mrs. Doane was a child, a host of legends circulated around *The Seventh Book of Moses,* a magic manual that was supposed to instruct its readers on means of making contracts with the devil to obtain supernatural powers. Mrs. Doane herself knew a man who kept a copy of *The Seventh Book.* The sorcerer's wife, a friend of Mrs. Doane's, claimed that this man "would have such an *awful, terrible* odor when he woke up in the morning," presumably as the result of his nocturnal dealings with the devil. But then "he would go out—and he always had rags outside in the yard—and he would wash himself with his rags. . . . And then the odor would leave." When this cruel neighbor died, his widow found his copy of *The Seventh Book*. She brought it to Mrs. Doane and asked her what to do with it. "And I said, 'Oh, . . . go burn it up.' She took it down to some old maid friends of hers. They put it in their kitchen range, and it *blew the stove lids off* of the range and the pipe out of the wall and soot and everything all over the kitchen. . . ."

Apparently, the sorcerer had gotten his copy of *The Seventh Book* from an in-law in Louisville. "And when this relative died—I remember my mother talking about it—my mother was still living and she kept saying, all [this evil woman's] communions were spilling out of her mouth. Now, whether it did physically, or whether she thought they did, I don't know. I was young."

Mrs. Doane's tales of her sorcerer-neighbor were necessarily circumspect, as she did not want innocent members of his family to suffer on account of the man's evil reputation. But she spoke at some length about her own and her mother's unsolicited visits from supernatural forces. Present to hear these tales was Mrs. Doane's neighbor, Mrs. Norbert Krapf, who contributed a few supernatural beliefs of her own.

Now, I must tell you one thing. This is not superstition. This is something that absolutely happened. And when my family got together, last year, year before (they're scattered all over now), but my sisters and brothers, we talked about this again.

One of these bachelors that I mentioned lived across the fields from us. And one night my sister (who's about three years older than I) and I were doing dishes. And there was snow on the ground. It was cold, and the rest of em were in the dining room, right off of the kitchen.

And we heard three knocks on the door. And it went like this [raps fist on table three times]. And the kitchen door was like so, and the table here. And Ella and I had been fighting over doing the dishes, because we didn't like to do them. We . . . run to the door to answer it, and we thought the neighbor had come. There was no one there. Bright moonlight, that night.

And they heard it in the dining room too. And mother hollered out, "Who's there?"

And I said, "Nobody." And my brother said, "Oh, some, one of the neighbor boys is trying to play a trick on us."

Well, we kind of looked out the window, and we didn't see anybody, and we went on washing dishes, in a hurry now to get finished in case we got company.

It wasn't long, and it knocked again, three times, like that.

Well, I didn't go to the door. But my brother came out and went to the kitchen door and there was nobody there. And he said, "There's nobody there."

And one of the others—and there was no footprints, later on, when they checked, there were no footprints that came up to the door.

And one of the others then went, looked out the dining room door, which was to the front of this room. Nobody there. Well, when the second knock came, we were just a little frightened, and we run on in to the dining room. And there was nobody.

So then my brother[s]: one, went out around the house this way [making a clockwise circle with her arm], and the other, *this* way [a counterclockwise circle]. Nobody there.

Well, mother made us go back out and do the dishes, finish the dishes. And we had a lot of em, because there were ten children in the family at that time. So . . . it knocked again. Same way.

Well, by that time, my sister and I both *run* for that dining room door. We knocked each other down, and we crawled to the door on our hands and knees. And each one—my brother, though, at that time, had gotten the gun. And they went around. And there was absolutely no sign of anybody. No footsteps coming up to the house. There had been a new snow. And we decided we weren't going to finish the dishes, so one of em came out and sat in the kitchen with us while we finished the dishes.

And it wasn't long, when that dog got on the front porch and bayed at the moon. And he *never* did that. And he bayed at the moon. I can still hear him. I can get goose bumps when I think about it. And, well that was the end of it. We all went to bed. And the next morning, we got a telephone call saying that one of these bachelors had died that night.

And now this may be superstition, I don't know. But the whole family heard the knocks on the door. They heard the . . . dog bay at the moon. And they used to say, if your dog bays at the moon, somebody's going to die. And I remember my mother saying, "Somebody's going to die tonight."

But we talked about it [just last year] when my family got together. And they all heard it. They all remembered it, and so on. . . .

I do not think my mother was a superstitious woman at all. And I know she wasn't, because she would never, she didn't teach us some of the things that I know some of the neighbors believed, that I don't even remember. But I remember that one time—she would go around and take care of mothers when they had babies, after my father died and she had to help earn some money, although we had the farm. But my brother had married, and they were living on the farm, so she could leave, and she was a very motherly, very wonderful person, really, and this was before hospital days and so on. And she was taking care of a baby, and the baby had cried a lot, and she had been up with it and the mother was restless. And she said she had just lay down. My mother was a tall woman, but she was also heavy, and she had a large abdomen. And she would lay these babies over her warm stomach and pat em. And she said it seemed to relieve their colic. And she—this baby had just quit crying. Then it had gone to sleep, and she had just laid down.

And they had said this house was haunted. She didn't believe it. She always made fun of that type of thing. In fact, she even made fun of these knocks on the doors, you know. But, anyway, she said she hadn't dozed off or anything, cause she had just laid down. And *something white* came, reached over her, for this baby. And she looked up, and she recognized the picture of this mother's mother, the grandmother to this baby.

And she pushed it back. She said she reached up and she pushed it back. And she, she didn't feel anything, but it pushed back. And then it reached over again. And she said, "What do you want, in the name of Jesus?" And it disappeared. So. Whatever it is, whatever it was, she said she had just lay down, so she knows she wasn't asleep. And when she mentioned the name of Jesus, that was the end.

126. The Visions of Lloyd Chandler

GARRETT CHANDLER
Marshall, North Carolina
Recorded by Carl Lindahl,
October 15, 2002

Lloyd Chandler (1896–1978) was a Free Will Baptist preacher well remembered in the Southern Appalachians for his faith, his visions, and his songs. Born in Madison County, North Carolina, in one of the most precipitous and least accessible pockets of the Blue Ridge Mountains, he grew up in a culture that has since become world renowned for its folk traditions. As a young man, Lloyd lived ten miles from the celebrated ballad singer Maud

Gentry Long (teller of stories 13–23) and a short walk from his brother-in-law, singer and musician Lee Wallin (teller of story 191). In 1916, when Lloyd was 20 years old, the English folklorist Cecil Sharp, touring the Appalachians in search of songs that had originated in Britain, found Madison County to be the richest site for traditional ballads of all the places he visited in America. Sharp called Madison a "nest of singing birds," a place where "singing was as common and almost as universal a practice as speaking." Ultimately, thirty-nine residents of that county, including Maud Long's mother, Jane Gentry, and Lloyd Chandler himself, contributed to Sharp's collection. Manly Wade Wellman chronicles the moment on August 29, 1916, when the young mountain man met the English scholar:

[Sharp] was listening to songs, probably by William Riley Shelton. A boy named [L]loyd Chandler came to the door saying, "I always like to go where there is sweet music." Sharp invited him in. Shelton was slow in remembering a version of "Young Hunting," and the boy sang it himself "and in a way which would have shamed many a professional vocalist."

Lloyd Chandler never lost his vocal artistry or his love of music. Forty-nine years later, at age 69, when his voice was captured for the first time on state-of-the-art audio equipment, he sang "Conversation with Death" with such power that the man who made the recording was moved to write: "Although Lloyd had suffered a stroke he sang this so strongly that I could hear it echo off the surrounding hills. . . . Recording cannot represent adequately the great range of volume given by this performance."

Lloyd sang numberless songs, but "Conversation with Death" was the one that affected both the singer and his listeners most profoundly. The song had come to him in a vision in 1916, the same year that Cecil Sharp had come to the mountains looking for folksongs. Before that time Lloyd had been a wild young man, a heavy drinker who astonished and often terrified his neighbors with grotesquely improbable feats. Standing, he would bend over from the hip, clench a hundred-pound feed sack in his teeth, and then jerk his back straight to heave the sack off the ground. He pulled his own teeth with pliers. In drunken delight, he'd try to milk mares and pull open the mouths of mules while they kicked at him. One day, after downing a jug of moonshine, he declared war on a swarm of yellow jackets nested in a hollow log. As his son Garrett recalls, "He set down a-straddle that log and took his old gray derby hat and smacked that log with

Garrett Chandler (narrator of story 126) at his home near Marshall, North Carolina, October 2002. (Photo by Carl Lindahl)

it and said, 'Now, come on, let's see who's going to run.'" The yellow jackets circled and stung repeatedly as Lloyd crushed them in bunches between his hands until he'd killed them all.

But in 1916, Lloyd had a vision in which Death, personified, confronted him; the experience transformed his life and set him on a new path. He translated his vision into the song, "Conversation with Death," and then took to the road preaching. Though severely crippled, he would walk, dozens of miles at a time, to find a place to sermonize and to sing his "Conversation with Death." When he had the money, he rode buses and trains across the highest peaks of the Blue Ridge to Newport, Tennessee, or south and west hundreds of miles, into Alabama, Georgia, and South Carolina. Once he reached a place where his preaching was welcome, he'd spend weeks at a time in the homes of relations, friends, and strangers, staying as long as he felt there was even one soul nearby who still needed his preaching. In a time when black and white did not often mix either in the mountains or anywhere else in America, Lloyd would stay in the houses of African Americans and preach in their churches.

Lloyd Chandler had been dead for twenty-two years when the motion picture *O Brother, Where Art Thou?* debuted, featuring the song "O Death," in a version that incorporates twenty lines of the song that Lloyd had learned from his vision. *O Brother* became enormously popular and Ralph Stanley, who sang "O Death" on the soundtrack, won a Grammy Award for his performance. But Lloyd Chandler's children and grandchildren were deeply upset by the way in which the song is used in the film: in the midst of a KKK meeting, "O Death" emerges from the mouth of the Klan leader presiding over the torture of an African American captive. Lloyd's son Garrett will never forget the day he first saw that scene: "Here's what broke my heart about it: . . . Ku Klux Klan . . . hanging a black man, and Ralph Stanley a-singing 'O Death.' That song wasn't meant for that purpose. No." Garrett Chandler believes that the true purpose of his father's song is the opposite of that depicted in the film: to draw people to God by making them consider what it would be like to confront death unsaved.

Lloyd frequently told his vision and sang his song in church services as part of his personal testimony. Some listeners would be so shaken by the song that they had to leave the church—even, in one case, by jumping out a window. But others responded exactly as Lloyd wished them to, by crowding the altar and begging for salvation. Reverend James Beaver, who often heard Lloyd preach, attests: Lloyd "explained in his singing, how it would be to meet death and go out of this world without God. And it would have such a bearing upon the congregation, and so much power, that people would fall in the altar. He would testify that God give him the song that others might make it right with God. That song went so far, and done so much good, that I'm sure that God give it to him, because God used it in such a way, and I'm thinking, when it's all over and we all stand before God, that it's really going to shine out in the Other World."

Born in 1944, Garrett Chandler is Lloyd's youngest child. Like his father, Garrett is a preacher. Throughout his life he has heard stories told by and about his visionary father. In the first of the narratives below, Garrett recalls the day (ca. 1950) when his father first told him about his conversation with Death.

Carl Lindahl: Garrett, could you tell me . . . what your dad told you about the vision?]

Yes, sir. Just as well as it was yesterday. . . . When he told me, I had more than likely (as mischievous as I was and as many whippings as I got) done something I shouldn't have, and he was correcting me. He was talking to me about the Other World. That's what he was talking about, about doing right: if I done wrong, that I would have to pay.

And he was talking. He said, when he was a young man, that he drank a lot. (Which I'd heared that story before, you know, that he had drank and was a pretty mean feller. Actually now, I want to tell you this: that that influences a boy, if he's got a rough daddy, a daddy that used to be mean. . . .)

And he told me that he had had a vision. And he was talking to me about dying. Mainly what he was talking to me about was to always do the right thing, you know, and put my trust in the Lord and give my soul to him. That then I didn't have to worry about anything.

And he told me that he had a vision. That he had been drunk, him and another fellow. And that he had a vision about death, that he talked *to* Death. And I can tell you what he said he looked like. And I was very interested in knowing, but I'll tell you this: it won't be as shocking as you think it is.

It was a shadow. (And to me it was sort of like, maybe, Moses: nobody could see God, but it was a burning bush, and He was talking to his mind. Now, I couldn't see that then, but I can now, knowing what I know.)

But he said it was a dark shadow, a black ghostly-looking thing, and it talked to him. And he said it laid hold on him and it was icy cold, and it told him that it was Death. And he had a conversation with it.

. . . The point that he was trying to get over to me as a little boy, . . . the main thing he wanted me to know, is that one day after a while I would meet Death. And he wanted me to know, when I met Death, that it was the end. And how I was [at the moment I met Death], was exactly the way I would stand in judgment, on the Day of Judgment. He believed that—and I believe that—there's a day a-coming when, the Bible says, that every knee would bow and every tongue would confess. And we'll all appear in front of the Judgment Seat of Christ. Now, he was telling me this, this young, and he believed this way: to train a child in this way, so when it gets old it won't depart from it.

So the story of the "Conversation with Death," he told me, and he wanted me to realize above all things that he wasn't bragging about being a mean man or about drinking, that that was no good. And [he] tried to steer me away from that, that I wouldn't have to go through the heartaches and troubles and stuff that he did on account of that. That it was no good. That it was the devil's drink. And he said that beared on his mind: he couldn't get it off. That if he died, where he was going. So he wrote a song about it:

"Oh what is this I cannot see
With icy hands gets a hold on me?"
"Oh I am Death, none can excel
I open the doors of heaven and hell."

"O Death, O Death, how can it be
That I must come and go with thee?
O Death, O Death, how can it be?
I'm unprepared for eternity."

"Yes, I have come for to get your soul,
To leave your body and leave it cold,
To drop the flesh from off your frame;
The earth and worm both have their claim."

"O Death, O Death, if this be true,
Please give me time to reason with you."
"From time to time you heard and saw,
I'll close your eyes, I'll lock your jaw.

"I'll lock your jaw so you can't talk.
I'll fix your feet so you can't walk.
I'll close your eyes so you can't see.
This very hour come and go with me."

"O Death, O Death, consider my age
And do not take me at this stage.
My wealth is all at your command
If you will move your icy hand."

"The old, the young, the rich, the poor
Alike with me will have to go.
No age, no wealth, no silver nor gold:
Nothing satisfies me but your poor soul."

"O Death, O Death, please let me see
If Christ has turned his back on me."
"When you were called and asked to bow
You wouldn't take heed and it's too late now."

"O Death, O Death, please give me time,
To fix my heart and change my mind."
"Your heart is fixed, your mind is bound
I have the shackles to drag you down.

"Too late, too late, to all farewell
Your soul is doomed, you're summonsed to hell;
As long as God in heaven shall dwell
Your soul, your soul shall scream in hell."

[About 1950, some thirty-five years after Lloyd Chandler held his "Conversation with Death," he experienced another uncanny vision, this one involving a lowly pest, the mole. The dream occurred soon after Lloyd had killed some moles, and it affected him so powerfully that he never killed another one. Lloyd dictated his vision to his daughter Barbara, and the family cherished the written account after their father died and they could no longer hear him tell it. Eventually, all but two pages of Lloyd's long narrative were lost.

Garrett Chandler was a young boy when Lloyd's vision occurred, and he vividly recalls how his father responded to the dream by taking pains to spare the lives of the moles invading his garden.]

My dad, he raised a garden, you know. He raised a garden, and if you know anything at all about a mole, you know that they plow and they'll take up your beans and corn and stuff and eat em. Well, naturally, you can see a mole in the ground when it's moving. And he'd stomp em out and kill em, because they were destroying his garden and he'd kill many, many of em.

So he had a dream or a vision one night of going into a molehill. And he was captured by a bunch of moles. And he was able to understand their language. And they had put him in something like a holding cell, and moles would come by with little moles and say, tell their children, "Look. This is the man that killed your father," or "your mother." And he said that they were very, very *ill* with him, you know . . . and that they kept him there for a certain length of time. And that they would feed him, you know, but they were very ill with him. And he said that they had sort-of-like meetings, and those moles would sing, and he said it was some of the prettiest songs, that he would try his best to remember . . . them songs—how pretty a tune and stuff—but he just couldn't do that.

And then, one morning, he said, that they came and got him and took him into like a big room, sort of like a courtroom, but in there, they had like a queen or a king mole, a-sitting up on a pedestal in a big chair, with a crown on. And they were going to try him for the murders that he had committed against them: all the moles that he had killed in his time. And they were all a-wanting to just dispose of him. Do away with him, in other words. Like we would be in a trial, and they would want to kill us. But the queen mole, somehow or another, had got—Dad said they had got together and she had talked to them, and he could see their little hands a-moving, and they'd look at him, and they'd look at her, and he said that when that was over, she asked him, said, "If we would let you go, would you promise that you would never kill another mole?"

And he said he promised that he never would kill another mole as long as he lived.

[Garrett then alludes to the only part of the story that still survives the account dictated by his father. The two extant pages of "The Mole" describe how, after Lloyd's vision, a mole appeared in a certain part of Lloyd's garden. True to his word, Lloyd did not kill it, but rather carried it to a spot about two miles away from his house and let it go. But soon Lloyd found another mole, and then a third, in the same spot where he had captured the first; these, too, he carried away. But, Lloyd writes, "By this time I began to wonder if it was the same mole that I had caught the first time to start with and was getting back somehow the same way. I thought that if I caught another one, then I would mark it and see if it was the first mole coming back all the time or new ones." Soon Lloyd found a fourth mole: "I caught it and brought it to the house and I cut out a line of fur down its back and then I took it to the same place that I had took all the three moles." The next time that Lloyd captured a mole at the same spot in his garden, its back was marked by a strip of shorn fur. It was the same mole that Lloyd had captured before.]

He would never kill another mole. He never did as long as he lived, that I know anything about, and that's how he become to find out that that mole was such a smart thing that he just couldn't believe that he would take a mole two miles away through the mountains, and turn it loose and watch it dig out of sight, and then a couple of days later, another mole—or a mole would be in the same place where he had caught that. And so he did that three different times, and on the fourth occasion, *I, myself,* remember him bringing it to the house and cutting a line of hair right up its back, and taking it back to the same place in the mountain and turning it loose.

And about a week later a mole was rooting and a-plowing, and he got it, dug it out, and it was the *same* mole. So, therefore, that gave him to believe that that same mole was traveling back to that same spot.

But there is a whole lot more, and it was either a dream or a vision that he had. That I wish that I could remember, but I know there was six or seven pages of it, and we got about four pages missing, full pages, so you can kindly imagine. It was a great story.

. . . I do know that he kept his promise. He never did kill another mole. He'd get em out, away, but he never would—and he never would let us kill one. I've never killed another mole. I have killed em in my time, you know, stomp em out, but I've never killed another one either.

I could even take you to this day, even though the barn's gone, and put my foot on the spot where he was getting the moles out. . . . Many years have gone by, but I believe I could almost find the route where he walked to his praying ground. That's where he turned em loose at; he had a praying ground, a path, just hewed out, beat down with a stick through the woods, that he'd travel to. It was smooth for two miles, go around under rock cliffs up over ridges and down through the hollers, and he had one certain little tree around there, about two inches in diameter, I guess, and it was a dogwood tree, and where he would kneel down—he was crippled—where he would kneel down and hold to that dogwood tree . . . with one hand and pray. . . . I can see it just like it was yesterday. But I can probably just about mark the spot, even though it's been that many years, but I been there so many times.

My dad had a heart of gold. It would melt at anything. And I guess it probably, maybe bothered him or something, killing those moles. And he had this dream. I just wish the world could see and really know the story, but there's four pages been lost. . . . And it would just amaze you, of how he could remember and write that down. He had a remembrance. . . . He would take the Bible— he wasn't no educated man—but he read it through twelve times and studied it, and he could quote it without a book. Anywhere. It didn't make no difference. He had that kind of remembrance. . . .

127. Witches

QUINCY HIGGINS
Sparta, North Carolina
Recorded by Patrick B. Mullen,
September 9, 1978

Born in 1900, Quincy Higgins had been a lay preacher in the Regular Baptist Church for forty-eight years when folklorist Patrick B. Mullen interviewed him as part of the Blue Ridge Folklife survey mounted by the American Folklife Center in 1978. Mullen spent a great deal of time with Higgins, who demonstrated great artistry in many forms of verbal expression: "Mr. Higgins interspersed pranks and tall tales with his telling of historical legends, family stories, witch and ghost tales, jokes, and personal experience narratives." In 1992, Mullen published a book, *Listening to Old Voices*, in which the voice of Quincy Higgins plays a prominent part. In that book Mullen focused upon Higgins's autobiographical accounts of preaching.

Mullen wrote of Quincy Higgins, "He has a self-consciousness and a strong identity as a performer, which has been with him all his life and has become even more important in his old age." Before Higgins became an accomplished storyteller, he was an avid listener to stories. Even the stories that he disliked stuck with him for decades. He listened in terror to such tales as "Witching a Cow" because as a boy he thought that these stories were true. "I hated [that the old people] ever told em to me, because I was so sure that they was all so factual, you know. That they was facts." As a result of the fear that these legends instilled in him, Quincy Higgins never retold them to his own children.

Mary Holecheck and Ethel Smith, Higgins's daughters, were surprised to find out that their father knew or told witch stories, because he spent so much time sharing religious teachings with them. Mary Holecheck writes, "Our dad and mother were God-fearing people, and my very first memory of life was me sitting in my daddy's lap reading the family bible, and Dad having to tell me every word as I had not learned to read yet. I never knew or met any person that knew the Bible as well as our dad."

The first of the following two accounts draws upon the belief that witches can use magic to make cows go dry, perhaps the most widespread witch belief reported by residents of the rural United States in the nineteenth and early twentieth centuries. The second narrative, like Ellis Ogle's tale of an encounter with a panther [story 120], plays upon the eerie, ghostly sounds produced by panthers in the dark forests of the Appalachian Mountains. In Ogle's tale, however, a panther sounds like a demon, while in Higgins's, the wailing creature is a demon that sounds like a panther. Like Ogle, Higgins describes the big cat as a "painter" (also sometimes "panter"), a variant pronunciation widespread in the Appalachians.

Pat Mullen: What about witches? Did you ever hear about witches?]
. . . I heared my mammy tell this, [about a woman who] was so hateful and hard to get along with. One time there was a cow, milk cow, that she just drawed up in a knot and it went dry, almost dry. And they got talking to some of the neighbors about it, says that old lady were kind of a witch. Got to put a spell on her. . . . Don't speak to nobody. But go in the morning and milk that cow and bring it to the house. And put you a skillet on the fire. And put nine new pins, new straight pins, in there. Nine new straight pins in there, and pour that milk in on that. And just as it begin to bubble, to boil, take a reap hook and "cut" that milk, in that skillet [i.e., pass a sickle through the boiling milk]. . . . And the cow'll get better.

Cow got better, and the old lady, she got worse. She come to—try to get my mammy to kill it. And she come to our house. And Mama baked some rye bread. And the cow got better, and she churned, and the old lady [came by and ate] the rye bread and butter. And got better.

But they had to come and dine with you before they could ever get better. They'd go over in that state of agony and things before they'd die—maybe they'd just [waste] away and die. But if they ever get to eat with you and lodge with you, . . . they'd [get better]. . . .

And they was a lot of that stuff what was believed. . . .

They was a fellow, Wes Brown, that I was telling about. One time he was out over some place and he started home. He stayed with his mother. And his daddy was dead. He got over there about halfway home and said something come right down in the road and *scre-ee-ee-amed*, just like a painter. And went back a-way back up and almost to the treetops. And he had one of those hog rifles, and he load it a couple times, and if it came down, he could shoot at it. And it'd just go back up and screamed. And said that he had . . . bullet molds, and everything with him. Bullets, and he could . . . mold him some more bullets if he wanted to.

Had his powder horn. And he got his little molds out there. He had a ten-cent, *dime*, in his pocket, from eighteen hundred or something. . . .

He loaded . . . muzzle of the gun, putting his powder in. . . . And he fired away at this thing as it come down, and he said it went, *wee-eee-oo-www*, run off over a cliff and went into the woods. And he said he run every step of the way home, and he fell in the front door. And he couldn't talk.

And his mama heard him, you know, and she said, "Wes, what's happened? Wes, what's happening?"

Wes couldn't say a thing. He was just scared to death. He had about a mile and a half to run, on this crooked path. . . . But he finally made it. . . . She tried to revive him, but it took hours. She put vinegar and . . . hold his nose in camphor or stuff. And sometime about daylight, he sort of recuperated, told em, he was coming down . . . and something got in his path and he went to shooting at it. He couldn't hit it until he rolled up this dime, this silver. And he blazed away with it. Said it went off over a cliff, into them thickets, screaming. And he was ready to go raise the rest of em. You know, they'd run up there and get him before he'd get anywhere. He took off for home before the rest of em get waked up.

[Pat Mullen: What was it?]

Never did know. He never did know. He told me that he never did know what it was. It was just something, just one of them haints or something, that we're talking about.

[Mrs. Higgins: No, it was probably a bobcat or a wildcat.]

Oh, it had the appearance of having wings or some sort of a flying purpose.

[Mrs. Higgins: Oh.]

It'd go up in the air and just right up out of the path, just like a hawk going up, you know. And he'd screamed from about treetop-high. And it come right back down, just like it was on a rope or something. And scream there, and when it come down, he'd be ready—after the old cap-lock gun, you know. He never believed in it, but he was shaking. He told me he fired on it twice, with lead bullets. It didn't persevere nor offer any comfort.

Then he rolled up that dime, so it'd go in the muzzle of his gun—

[Pat Mullen: Silver?]

Silver. And he'd heard, you know, to shoot a witch with silver, you would puncture his hide, you know. And he just knowed good and well if he'd get that thing, run that silver dime through him, with that hog rifle, that he could take his hide home with him. But [that thing] went off over a cliff into deep briars and stuff, and he never got the pelt off of him.

[Pat Mullen: Who'd you hear that from?]

Wes Brown. That man it happened to, he was the man that told it.

[Pat Mullen: How'd you happen to hear it?]

Well, we was just talking—we was with him a whole lot and he was a gunsmith, a blacksmith, and lived out close.

128. The Spider Witch

LEOZIE SMITH
Tupelo, Mississippi, and Calvin, Michigan
Recorded by Richard M. Dorson, ca. 1952

Leozie Smith was a young girl living in Mississippi around 1900 when she experienced the events narrated here. In 1917, she moved to Chicago. It was there that she met E.L. Smith (narrator of stories 188, 195, and 196), and in 1935 they moved to the rural, predominantly African American town of Calvin, Michigan. In 1952, folklorist Richard Dorson visited the Smith home and, with Mr. Smith, Dorson, and neighbor Mary Richardson listening, she narrated this fifty-year-old memory in sincere and dramatic tones.

But I'll tell you one, what I started to tell a while ago. When I was, oh, well I guess I was about ten or eleven years old, I was working for some white people, and this man, he just liked to tell so much, about a nice a white man as I'd ever want to see.

Near as I can remember (I was only a child), [he] was telling me there was witches riding him. He used to call me Zee. He would tell me, "Zee" (his girl, named Vera, he called her "Vee" and me "Zee"). Said, "Did you know that a witch rode me last night?" Said, "Look here how I got my hair turned." He was redheaded. We was always taught that redheaded people was the meanest men that was, you see. And I said, "Maybe it's cause you're so mean." But he said, "You know, a witch just rode me last night." Said, "Just rode me, rode me, rode me, rode me, until I just couldn't sleep."

Well, I had heard my mother say, you know, way back then, you had those sifters, great, big, round sifters—you know, do this-a-way—to sift out your flour meal. And I said, "Mr. Sparks," I said (I was a little talker, you know, to anybody that liked me, you know). I said, "Mother said if you take this sifter and put some salt on it, handful of salt, and turn it bottom side upwards, said you'll catch that witch—said, the next morning, when you wake up, the witch'd be there."

(Oh, he used to just laugh, you know, take me up on his lap, he just like thought an awful lot of me.)

He said, he told me, . . . "Zee. Come early in the morning. Cause we going to have that witch, because I'm . . . going to leave that sifter down tonight." You know, he was always after teasing me about this here, about me telling him what mother said.

Say, "All right." Say, "I'm going to get me a handful of salt." This white maid. Miss Jose, he called her Miss Jose. Said, "Miss Jose, I want you to get me a big handful of salt and put [it] down at my bed and bring that sifter and turn it down."

So she did. She put a big handful of that kind of coarse, heavy salt down. And then they take that big old sifter and turned it down, he said, when they got it, he . . . got into bed.

The next morning I woke up early. "I must just go down to Mr. Sparks early this morning, and go catch the witch." And, you know, when I got down there, they had barely woke up, you see. I knocked on the door, and there was a boy that sleep in the other room, one of the boys. And he opened the door. He was about, along about my age. And they was always so tickled when I come, you know. We'd have a row.

I say [whispering], "Let's go and see if Daddy catched the witch." So we eased in there and looked and there—you know, we seed a spider about as big as my hand. And I said, "Hi, Mr. Sparks." And he said, "What's the matter."

I said, "You just caught the witch" [laughs]. He hopped up and looked. And you know that old spider's legs had got up in the wire of that sifter and had swole underneath and on top, and he couldn't pull it out. And he was the biggest spider you ever see in your life. And it had a big wide mouth, about a inch wide. And just doing that mouth like that, your know. And it looked like he had two lips. . . . Sure. Big as, big as my hand, and the biggest old legs, that caught in that sifter. Now that is just as true as we look at each other. And if Mr. Sparks was living, he could tell you. I don't know whether any of his family is living, see, or not, because it's been a long time since I seed em. Can't tell. But we caught that big old spider over there. So I said I guess that witch had turned into it, and that's the last thing he could turn to.

129. Nightmare Ridden

JOHN JACKSON
Rappahannock County and
Fairfax, Virginia
Recorded by Charles L. Perdue Jr.
and Nancy J. Martin-Perdue,
November 11, 1967

John Jackson's career as a major performer of old-time acoustic blues began when he met folklorist Charles L. Perdue Jr. As Perdue recalls, "On a crisp October afternoon in 1964, I stopped for gas at a service station in Fairfax, Virginia, . . . and noticed a black man with a guitar standing in the station. Given my interests [in folk music], it was natural to walk in and ask him, 'Do you play that thing?' His reply was that he 'hit a couple of chords' and I asked him to hit a couple. . . . In that chance encounter I met John Jackson, a very skilled and creative musician, who grew up deeply rooted in the traditional music and culture of his area. . . . For several years subsequent to this discovery [my wife, Nancy J. Martin-Perdue] and I traveled with John, took him to festivals and clubs to play, and generally served as his managers by default. But we were never comfortable in the role of managers and progressively, we chose the role of friends and advisors." The Perdues remained close friends with John Jackson until his death on January 20, 2002.

John Jackson's musical artistry brought him worldwide recognition and a Heritage Award from the National Endowment for the Arts (1986), but it did not bring him great wealth. Throughout most of this musical career, his principal income came from his day job as a gravedigger.

Jackson was known to mix a tale or two—including a lengthy tall tale about a lucky hunter (similar to story 20 in this collection)—into his frequent stage performances. The narratives that he told at home, however, differed considerably from these public stories. Many of the private tales involved his personal supernatural experiences and those of his family members.

The following tale concerns a "nightmare," as that term was traditionally understood by past generations. The old-time nightmare was not merely a dream but a supernatural being that would mount its sleeping victim and ride the sleeper to exhaustion, and in some accounts, even to the point of death. Tales of victims attacked and worn weary by witches at night are pervasive in both African American and European American traditions.

John Jackson's nightmare narrative emerged in the course of a lengthy tale-swapping session that took place in Philadelphia in 1968. Charles L. Perdue Jr., then a folklore student at the University of Pennsylvania, and his wife Nancy J. Martin-Perdue were joined by Gerald Parsons (collector of stories 123 and 124) and folksinger Bryan Sutton as they sat down with their friends, John and his wife, Cora Jackson. By the end of the evening, John and Cora had shared more than eighty narratives, principally legends and jokes. Two of John's supernatural accounts and five of Cora's fictional tales appear in the present volume.

John's personal experience and the reports of his relatives made him certain that such beings existed. As John told Gerald Parsons shortly after the following story was recorded, "Well, I've heared tell of people talking about nightmares getting on em, beating em, and going on. And there's no doubt there is such a thing. There certainly is."

Charles Perdue: Tell me about the, that little man that beat you up that time too.]

About the time when we first moved to Fairfax? . . . That's right. When we first moved to Fairfax. I had did a hard day's work that day, come on in, and went to bed that night, and I'm just as wide awake as I am sitting here talking to y'all. And I heared this thing when it come down in the yard when it walked up on the porch with these shoes on, just a-hitting, just a-walking, and it come on in. And I swear to goodness this is the truth. I swear I ain't never believed nothing else. And it come on in and I tried to jump up and I couldn't, and it just paralyzed me. I couldn't move, and he rolled on me and like to beat me to death. I was sore for two or three days, that's the truth, all on up in my back and ribs, just like to stomped me to death.

And about the time I did get my strength to get up, and jumped up to get him, and he run. Never did, never could get a hold of him. Was a little bitty man, wasn't much higher than that. That's the truth. Had on shoes and he like to beat me to death. That's the truth.

[Charles Perdue: How'd he get out of the house?]

I don't know how he got out, but he went out of the room when I jumped up. And Cora asked me what in the devil was the matter with me. Has I gone crazy or what? And I told her this thing had nearly beat me to death, and she said, "Was nothing but the devil after you." And so when I run out of the bedroom and into that little other room where you first come out of the door, and that's the last time I ever seen it. Never did open the door or anything.

[Charles Perdue: You think it was the devil, or what do you think it was?]

449

John Jackson (teller of stories 129 and 130) prepares to play as Charles L. Perdue Jr. (collector of stories 129 and 130) adjusts the microphone, Bellegrove plantation, Virginia, ca. 1973. (Courtesy of Charles L. Perdue Jr. and Nancy J. Martin-Perdue)

I don't know. I believe it was a nightmare, what I think it was.

[Charles Perdue: . . . did you remember what his clothes looked like or anything?]

No, I don't remember what his clothes or anything looked like.

[Charles Perdue: Did he have on a hat?]

I know he had on these high heel shoes. I could see these shoes like cowboy boots, with real keen heels.

[Gerald Parsons: On both feet?]

Yeah, sir, and he kicked me in the ribs with em. Like to stomp me to death.

[Charles Perdue: You'd say he's about what? Eighteen inches high?]

At least eighteen inches high. Just come right in, and I mean he really gave me a mauling. There's no doubt about that.

130. The Preachers and the Spooks

**JOHN JACKSON
Rappahannock County and
Fairfax, Virginia
Recorded by Charles L. Perdue Jr.
and Nancy J. Martin-Perdue,
Philadelphia, November 11, 1967**

In this haunted house tale, as in Laurie Hance's (story 117), the haunting is caused by a murder victim. Immediately after the bodies of the victims receive posthumous justice, the ghostly happenings cease.

The first word of John Jackson's tale is "Mama." Here, and continually as the tale progresses, John underscores the fact that he learned it from his mother. He begins nearly every sentence with the verb "said"; in nearly every case, the unstated subject is John's mother, and John seems to be stressing throughout his narration that even when he tells it, this tale belongs more to her than to him.

Mama told a tale one time about this haunted house, about nobody couldn't stay at it. Said they hired this preacher to go there and stay. Said he was gonna stay and find out what this ghost was. Said he got there and made him a good fire in the fireplace, and sat back smoking his pipe. Said, finally, said a little cat come whining. Said he let him in and commenced to playing with him. Said the cat laid by the fire ever so long, and got warm, and stretched out, and said after he laid there a few minutes, said, he sort of dozed off to sleep, this preacher did. And said he happened to think about the cat, and looked over and was a great big, spotted dog with the biggest red eyes and red tongue looking at him. Said the preacher commenced to batting his eyes and looking. Says he commenced to getting bigger, said all at once, said the preacher just rolled up and went right out the window and left. Said it wasn't long, said the spook was too much for him.

He went and told what he saw, and there was another preacher come in and said he was going there and gonna stay. Said he went on in and made him up a good fire and sat there. Said finally after he sat there a while and the fire got to going good, said all at once something rolled down the fireplace there. Said after a while they turned in and got bigger and bigger. Said the old preacher setting there kept a-looking at em smoking his pipe and singing a hymn: "Nearer My God to Thee." Said, finally, said, it finally formed into two little boys and then they formed into two men. Said the preacher asked em, said, "What in the name of the Lord do you want?"

And said, "The people (the first people that was there) killed us, and buried us here, and buried us down underneath the floor." Said, "If you'll dig us up and tell everybody where we're at, we'll go away and never come back no more."

And said the next day, he went and told the people what he found, and said sure enough, they did. They dug up and found two dead bodies down underneath there, and the house never was spooky no more after that.

131. Fairy Forms

MARGARET SULLIVAN
Springfield, Vermont
Recorded by Alan Lomax,
November 10, 1939

Margaret Sullivan spent her childhood in Ireland, where she learned scores of songs centered on tragic and supernatural events. Many of these were ballads, songs that told stories, and, in Margaret's community, such songs were regarded as accurate reports of actual happenings. "They supposed that all the songs that they sang were founded on facts," she told folklorist Alan Lomax in 1939.

It was folksong collector Helen Hartness Flanders of the Vermont Folk Song Archive who alerted Lomax to Mrs. Sullivan's extraordinary repertoire.

In the course of singing ballads to Lomax, Margaret Sullivan made it known that she knew not only supernatural songs but also supernatural tales. She may have considered the songs true, but she did not volunteer that she was similarly impressed with the stories. In narrating two tales centered on fairy "forms"—spirits that appear in human guise—Mrs. Sullivan repeatedly stated that not everyone believed such stories, and at one point she asked Lomax if he believed them. At the same time, however, Mrs. Sullivan appeared unwilling to believe that the people who first told her these eerie legends had lied. Whether or not she herself believed them, she related the legends in persuasive and powerful language laden with memorable images: the baby who "lost her countenance" and "snarled like a monkey," and the rooster that she associated with the cock that crowed to signal that "Peter gave away our Lord."

The first of these two brief tales draws upon the Irish belief in changelings, otherworldly beings that fairies substitute for human children (see Sara Cleveland's "Baby's Gone," story 39); the second alludes to the banshee, a female fairy who visits mortals to foretell their deaths (see "The Kiln Is Burning," story 38, and "Banshees and Ghosts," story 132).

This is true. I never knew the foundation of it either. Why, I don't know if *they* did. But Mother, Margaret, was the oldest. And she was two years old [at the time of this occurrence]. Mary . . . was nine months old. . . .

Well, [Mary] slept, it was, the baby slept with my father and mother. And she was a little thing, you know; she wasn't walking or nothing. And their bed was high, with posts right to the ceiling, and curtains on them. They have em now, probably. . . . Down here, right where the school is, they had one when I come over here from Ireland. And all the curtains, you know. . . .

And so when Mother waked up in the night—after Dad come home, he fell asleep and she waked up, and she missed—she missed the baby. She wanted to nurse it, you know. And [the baby] slept between the two of em. She put her hand out and the baby was gone.

Well, she got scared blue. And, course, she waked my father up. She waked my father up and they got up. And they didn't have candles. . . .

And they found her in a big room. In a very big room. There was two beds in it, because we slept in one. The other children slept in one bed, and they had another one. A big, big room. And they found that little nine-months' baby over in the corner. And when they went over to take her, she began to snarl like a monkey. And she had lost her countenance. And she lived nineteen days, and died. And she never got her own features back. What become of her?

[Alan Lomax: You mean she looked like a monkey then?]

No. She snarled like a monkey, I said. No, she had the human features, but she wasn't Mary at all. Now what was the cause of it?

Well, there was an old woman . . . came into the house a day or two after that, and she said that she [had passed by the house a few days earlier]. She was coming home and she said as she was passing the house, she saw the form at the window and take something out the window, just as if somebody inside, a fairy, took the baby. . . . The baby wasn't there. . . .

[Alan Lomax: She had seen it that night?]

Yeah, when she was coming.

[Alan Lomax: What kind of a form was it, did she say?]

It was the form of a woman, but she couldn't tell what it was.

[Alan Lomax: And Mary died right after that?]

Yeah. She died in nineteen days.

[Alan Lomax: And the old woman thought it was a fairy?]

A fairy go and took it away.

[Alan Lomax: And left a—]

And left there something. But that's a story. Ireland's a funny place, anyway.

[Alan Lomax: Yeah. But did they tell just tales about fairies?]

Yes, and things like that, you know. I heard another one about this sea captain, was sailing up the channel, and they had to stop, they stopped in the channel. There was a cabin on the seashore, a little ways away. And as they, as they stopped there, the captain was up on deck, and they saw a light come toward that cabin. And a woman rapped at the door—was at the door. And she didn't go in, would she. And just then, the cock crew. And the woman, whatever it was, turned away, and was gone.

Well, the next night, he saw it again. And he saw it a third night. The same acts—and each night the cock crew. And the next day, he told the story, I suppose, and I suppose—I don't know whether he lied or not, but I suppose he didn't.

He went to that cabin, and he bought that rooster. That cock. And there was a young man in the house, and he was very, very sick.

And [the captain] bought the cock, and he put it on board the vessel.

Well, *that* night, he went up on deck, and he saw the form going towards the house. And it entered. And the next day, the boy was dead.

Would you believe that story?

[Alan Lomax: Why, I don't know.]

But he told that story for gospel. Well, you know, there's something about the rooster.

[Alan Lomax: Yeah.]

The cock. You know, you know that the cock crowed three times before Peter gave away our Lord, you know?

132. Banshees and Ghosts

FATHER SARSFIELD O'SULLIVAN
Butte, Montana
Recorded by Paula Johnson, Gary Stanton, and J. Barre Toelken, Butte, Montana, September 1, 1979

To hear Father O'Sullivan speak, one would swear he was born in Ireland. In reality, however, he is a native of Butte, Montana, one of the most Irish-influenced towns in the United States. During the second half of the nineteenth century, young Irish men sought their fortunes in the copper mines surrounding Butte, and the influx of Irish became so great that Irish became the dominant culture. As Father O'Sullivan explained, even the Serbs spoke English with Irish accents when he was a boy, and in the 1970s Mexican Americans of the Butte area referred to all English speakers—even if Slavic or German in background—as "Paddies."

Fieldworkers Barre Toelken, Gary Stanton, and Paula Johnson met Sarsfield O'Sullivan in the course of the Montana Folklife Project, a major cooperative venture involving the participation of the American Folklife Center. Father O'Sullivan demonstrated great familiarity with traditional Irish song and verse traditions, as well as extensive knowledge of the mining culture of Western Montana. He attributed his intellectual curiosity to his father: "You see, when Dad came here [to Butte] he had virtually no formal education. He had about maybe two months out of a year for a few years in his childhood. And he came here and just haunted the public library. And whoever was the librarian at the time, I'd like to look up the name, because I feel very grateful to a man whose name I don't even know. He took an interest in the young greenhorn trying to teach himself things, and he used to give my father any book he wanted that was being condemned. If somebody left a book out in the rain, or the spine was broken or it was being replaced, he'd just mark it with a big purple stamp, so they'd know it wasn't stolen, CONDEMNED, BUTTE PUBLIC LIBRARY and the date. When I was a kid in grade school, maybe about fifth or sixth grade, and heard about condemned books, I thought 'My God, if the nuns visit our house, they'd see all my father's books are condemned.' "

The fieldworkers sensed that Father O'Sullivan might prove a rich source of Irish supernatural tales, but the Father's first response was that he knew no such lore. He sought to explain this fact in terms of the influence of his father's teachings: "Whatever [such tales] my father knew, he would not be that interested in. I don't think he'd have that high a regard for them. Whereas he did have a high regard for little fragments of the epic poetry for people like Cuchulain, and Oisin, the Irish Homer, and even our dogs would be named after mythological [figures] like Bran." Father O'Sullivan believed his father may have "censored out" the tales of fairies, "not because he thought it would be harmful to us, but he thought it might be useless, since I know my dad regarded novels as completely useless. . . .

"And then too, maybe some of them I censor out in my own mind. I might have heard as a child or probably heard, and then just, maybe I didn't get the point, maybe it didn't stay in my mind at all. Which is kind of a pity, just thinking from it in the point of view of the priesthood. I wish I were just ordained, cause I think more and more, praise God, we're moving from the very analytical theology, and that was of presenting the truths of faith and service and so on, and get back more to storytelling. . . . It's sort of coming full circle for me, going to the extent of demythologizing, now we're going to have to remythologize."

When, after some reflection, Father O'Sullivan did recall some tales of the supernatural, he made it immediately clear that no matter what his opinion of and experience with legends, he had no trouble telling them. His tales were well wrought, even if they were not typical legends. Father O'Sullivan's narratives proved to be anti-legends, tales in which the humor rather than the horror of the supernatural prevails, tales that emphasize natural, common-sense explanations and tend to convert supernatural fears to hearty laughter. This brief narrative, also told by Father O'Sullivan during the day's recording session, serves to illustrate: "It was a young mother" who had just died, "and the tension is all the more powerful at a sad wake, and Jersey Mary came in. . . . They were still having the wakes at home in those days, and she knelt at the kneeler next to the coffin, and the wreath came just beautiful just right over her head. You know, those that were just perched all over the coffin. And she said (you know, the Irish for Jesus Christ is Yeasu Chrest), and she said, 'Yeasu Chrest, I'm next!' She took it as a sign from God."

The following two brief tales may not assert the existence of banshees and fairies, but Father O'Sullivan uses them as an opportunity to present brief and brilliantly wrought character sketches of the tales' tellers and the figures in them. For other Irish American banshee tales, see Sara Cleveland's "The Kiln Is Burning" (story 38) and Margaret Sullivan's "Fairy Forms" (story 131).

You know, the story you were asking me about the banshee. There was one priest from County Kerry, was a great friend of my dad's: a little, little fellow, Father Clifford, and he was always with another Irish priest, who was a great big husky man. Father Delane was like a big Saint Bernard, you know, with this little fellow, Father Clifford, turned to him. Father Delane would see him and hug him, and Father Delane used to wear his glasses down on the tip of his nose. . . . [Delane was also hard of hearing; he described one soft-spoken friend by saying,] "You have to hug him to hear him." He was terrible deaf. Father Delane was practically spitting on your nose all the time, he'd get so close to you. He'd get . . . Father Clifford most uncomfortable, under the crook of the arm of Delane, walking around, and Delane would be very friendly.

But Clifford said his family was followed by the banshee, and that they would—if any member of the family was going to die, then they'd hear the wailing of the woman. And he said when he was a high school student, he was cycling home, and going past the churchyard, he heard this groan and he thought, "This must be it," and he thought, "No, it's got to have some natural explanation, and I'm going to find out."

And he worked up all of his courage and he stopped his bicycle and he leaned it against the building. This was, of course, late at night, and he came closer, it was coming from the churchyard, and he heard the repeated groan, and he walked into the churchyard, past all the headstones, and there at the back of the churchyard, it looked like the figure of Christ on the cross, and he continued to hear this moan, and he said, "I'll go through my whole life wondering what that was, and thinking of some kind of an apparition and a vision unless I find out." And he just worked up all his courage and he got closer, and a sheep— the back of the churchyard, in this little village in Kerry, it was surrounded by this iron fence. A sheep had come down this hill and tried to get over it. It had got, not really impaled, but strung up on the iron fence and was bleating. And that was it. And he said that was his only experience with, quote, the banshee.

But I do remember hearing my mother talk about someone in our area: that this young man was at a fair in Castletown there, and heard this wailing, and said to his friends that he was going to go home. Somebody in his family was dying. And they said that [later] they found him dead. And the story went that that's who the wailing was for, was for him.

But I suppose that it'd be almost maybe a test tube of stories [for measuring] my dad's [attitude toward the supernatural]—on this island, some one of the men was building a boat and died. And the other people on the island said, after his death that they could hear hammering. And my dad said his father and his grandfather had two very different reactions to it. His father, my dad's father's, reaction to it was, "Let's not talk about it." In other words, let the dead alone, this is sort of sacred territory, let's not talk about it. His grandfather was exactly the opposite: if any someone was hammering late at night on the island, he was going to find out damn well who was doing it and who would stop it. Dad's grandfather left no room for this—for any supernatural and preternatural interpretations. He wasn't interested in that.

133. Raising the Dead; The Nephite on the Road

DR. AND MRS. NORMAN FREESTONE
Los Angeles, California
Recorded by Austin E. Fife, February 1947

Austin Fife, one of the great pioneer collectors of the folk music of the American West, amassed an especially rich collection of Mormon lore, including a few narratives. The following two brief legends, told by a husband and wife, exemplify two of the most common themes of Mormon folk tradition. The first tale, told by Mrs. Freestone, recounts a church service during which one of the congregants stood and delivered a testimonial about God's power to raise the dead. Such testimonials—and the tales they spawn—are common legend themes in many religious traditions.

The second tale, told by Norman Freestone, has a uniquely Mormon subject: the Nephites. As folklorist Richard M. Dorson explains, "One supreme legend arose soon after the establishment of the Church of Latter-Day Saints in Utah, which came to symbolize the whole Mormon experience. In time of distress, physical or spiritual, one, two, or three elderly strangers appeared at a Mormon home, or by the roadside, or even in the desert, proffering aid." Often it was only after the mysterious bearded man or men disappeared that their beneficiaries would realize that supernatural helpers had come to their aid.

There's something that you don't hear these days anymore. I used to, and I know you did too, about people who had these kind of experiences. But this man was a medical doctor from Hawaii. He—well he took quite a long time to tell his story, did it very dramatically too. But he was over here in Los Angeles, for a medical convention of some kind. And he visited the Glendale East ward. But he told his experience of how he had—I've forgotten what church—well, he was going to study to be a minister for either a Methodist or a Baptist church, or some other, some Protestant church, and he got to know a Mormon missionary over there. And he was all set to be sent from Hawaii over here to the United States to . . . this church school that he was going to study for.

And then he met this Mormon missionary, and became interested in Mormonism. In the meantime he had married a Catholic girl. And so he was all mixed in with his religious experiences and he became very interested in the Mormon Church and finally decided that he wouldn't continue with this work that he had started with the Methodist Church (if that was the Church that he was interested in) and became a Mormon. In the meantime, his family was *very* unhappy about it. Well, he went on with all these long experiences he had of converting them. Himself first, and then he was so happy about it . . . that he wanted to get his wife converted. But she was a very strict Catholic and wasn't at all interested.

But, just the same, he finally got his father and mother interested, and then I think he had quite a large family, he came from a large family. Then, this experience that he told about that was so—that he told with such enthusiasm. . . .

Well, his sister was gravely ill. In fact she was—she died, really. The doctors gave her up and said she was dead. And he *really* told us—he cried when he was telling it—how that he wouldn't give her up, and he brought in some Mormon missionaries. And here he was, a medical doctor himself. No, he wasn't a medical doctor yet, I guess, he got to become that later.

Anyway, . . . she was dead, and they said that she was dead. And he had these people come in and administer to her, and she came, became alive again. And that was really a very interesting thing to hear. You hear . . . I mean you can remember, people telling those things, a long while ago, that used to happen. But you don't hear them get up and tell them in church anymore.

[Interviewer: Norman, will you tell your story while we're still running this disk?]

This is a Nephite story. Well this is just a very short incident. It was told to me, you remember, in northern Arizona, where the roads go up over one hill and down another, which makes a very good story for something of this type.

It was a very hot day, and the car came over. And here was this bearded man, as you say, dressed in black, and perspiring profusely. So they stop and ask him if he wants a ride. And they say "no" and so forth, that he doesn't want a ride. So this car drives off and leaves this old man.

And then, after they get up over the hill, why then they get feeling sorry for this man in the heat of the day, you know, and so they turn around and come back over the hill to really try to really talk him into picking him up, to give him a ride, because it really is hot. And after they come back, go over the hill, why the poor man has vanished, and so the logical consequence, or the Mormon interpretation is, that here was a Nephite who just went [his] way, and in this particular episode or instance when they came back to find him, why he had vanished.

9

TALL TALE AMERICA

134. Paul Bunyan on Round River	**PERRY ALLEN** **Shepherd, Michigan** **Recorded by Alan Lomax,** **Mount Pleasant, Michigan, 1938**

Thanks largely to Disney cartoons and innumerable giant statues and theme parks spread across the northern Great Lakes states and the Pacific Northwest, Paul Bunyan's is the best-known name in American tall tale tradition. The massive lumberjack and his pet blue ox have so saturated the media that some folklorists see Paul as the creature of the advertising industry rather than as a subject for storytellers. After finding Paul far more popular in newsprint and children's books than in oral tradition, folklorist Richard Dorson labeled him "the pseudo-hero of American lumberjacks" and ascribed his popularity to one of the most successful ad campaigns of the early twentieth century. In 1914, W.B. Laughead, an advertising executive for the Red River Lumber Company of Minneapolis, began contributing anecdotes and pictures of Paul Bunyan to the company's sales brochures. The features on Paul grew to be at least as popular as any of Red River's products, and by the late 1940s Laughead's books were being sold independently in substantial numbers even after the lumber company had ceased to exist.

Tracking media accounts of Paul Bunyan, Dorson became convinced that there was no more than "a slender trickle of oral tradition" behind "the torrent of printed matter" about Paul and his blue ox. Dorson came to view Paul Bunyan as the defining example of "fakelore," "the presentation of spurious and synthetic writings under the claim that they are authentic folklore."

Paul Bunyan Monument, Bemidji, Minnesota, 1939. (Library of Congress)

Yet Paul's towering presence in the American media cannot negate the fact that he was a major subject of folktales told in and around lumber camps in Maine, Wisconsin, Michigan, Minnesota, Wisconsin, northern California, Oregon, and Washington during the late nineteenth and early twentieth centuries. Long before Stith Thompson became known as America's most distinguished folktale scholar, he was listening to Paul Bunyan tales while lumberjacking in Washington state.

In the all-male working communities of the northern forests, Paul Bunyan took on special and localized roles. In some camps, seasoned lumberjacks would test and tease greenhorns by attempting to pass off some of Paul's more modestly outrageous adventures as if they were the actions of a flesh-and-blood human being. Clearly, such stories were more subtle and small scale than the inflated accounts of Paul's size and acts best known in today's media, which have ballooned him into a figure of fantasy impossible to mistake for an actual person.

Although it is easy for children to see Paul Bunyan as just another intriguing giant capable of acts beyond the reach of ordinary mortals, the lumberjacks' tales feature another force, a force even more powerful than Paul. In the tale of Round River, as in many other camp stories, nature is not only larger than, but smarter than Paul, and he and his men become the dupes of their environment. Such tales must have resonated for men who spent months at a time in the wilderness, dwarfed by giant trees, exposed to treacherous storms, and—when breaking log jams or felling trees—assigned the humbling and sometimes fatal work of fighting nature one on one.

Perry Allen, narrator of the following tale, was a bit of a natural force himself. Folklorist E.C. Beck, who spent considerable time with Allen and often accompanied him to folk festivals, describes him as an all-around talent, "a clever teller of tall tales as well as a master entertainer with song and dance." Allen's skills at spinning yarns were so prolific and second-nature that "he once won a liar's contest at Traverse City [Michigan] without knowing he was competing."

Beck offers further evidence of Allen's skills as a deadpan comic, extemporizer, and comeback artist: "I first learned the veteran entertainer could tell stories as well as play the spoons and dance a jig when we were waiting our turn to go on the stage at Constitution Hall, Washington, D.C. I was growing restless with long hanging about, so when a woman reporter approached for a story I pointed to old Perry and said, 'Interview him.' Perry began to tell that reporter some tall tales with a sincerity that kept her puzzled. When she finally decided that she was the butt of the shanty boy's fun, she tried to turn the subject with 'What do you think of politics?' Without taking a long breath or changing his even tone the old storyteller answered, 'Poly ticks? What's that? We had cattle ticks and wood ticks, but not poly ticks.' The reporter retreated in haste."

We was getting on a pile of logs one winter on Round River, and we cut our logs and we banked em on the river and in the spring when the ice and snow was off we started to spring drive the logs. Well, we drove those logs downstream for a couple of weeks and we come to a set of camps that looked just like old Paul's camps, so we drove for a couple weeks more and we come to a set that looked just like old Paul's—and we started the third week, and we began to think there might be something wrong, so when . . . two weeks were up, we come to the set of camps again and we went ashore, and sure enough they was old Paul's camps. And there we'd been driving those logs right around and around, around and around, all around Round River all that time, never knowed no difference, didn't know that that river didn't have no beginning, no end. It flowed in a circle.

So we was up against it, we had to save our logs, so we hitched up old Babe, the big blue ox, [and dragged those logs] from Round River into the Manistee, floated the logs down the river, down the Fir into the Manistee, and saved our logs.

That was the winter, the cold winter, that we had such a big crew that the cooks couldn't keep the salt and pepper shakers full. They was all fagged out from running back and forth trying to keep the shakers full. And you know how a lumberjack likes salt for his beans. Well, Paul made up the idea of getting a team of iron grays on the salt and pepper wagon, so I drove that team on the salt and pepper wagon up and down the table in the cooks' shack all the rest of that winter except Sundays. Sundays we'd have prunes for breakfast, and it'd take me all day to haul the prune pits out.

135. Paul Bunyan Moves in Circles Again

BILL MCBRIDE
Isabella City,
Michigan
Recorded by Alan Lomax,
August 1938

In the midst of collecting the folksongs of fishermen and lumberjacks in Michigan and Wisconsin, folklorist Alan Lomax ran into a number of Paul Bunyan tales. Bill McBride, locally known as a singer and composer of lumberjack ballads, sang numerous songs for Lomax. Described by folklorist E.C. Beck as "a wiry old river hog," McBride possessed a prodigious memory: "Bill learned many songs . . . along the rivers, and he seems to have remembered all of them. I rode with him once for twenty-four waking hours, during twenty of which he sang and recited with almost no repetitions. . . . Most of the material was printable. He must know as much more . . . that is not printable." McBride was clearly a verbal artist even when he wasn't singing. The following account provides interesting insights into how various lumberjacks viewed Paul Bunyan and how they used his tales to play tricks on each other. Speaking into a microphone in the presence of a stranger, McBride immediately states that Paul Bunyan is simply a "made up" character. But as Lomax presses him for more details, McBride reveals how various lumberjacks passed on Paul Bunyan stories as true tales to gullible rookies. Novices would be treated to stories of how Paul could carry massive loads, how the sparks that flew from his ax when he was sharpening it could set fire to a river, and how he could spend a whole spring going in circles.

Alan Lomax: Did you ever know anybody like Paul Bunyan?]
Oh, no. Not just like him. . . . That's just a story made up, you know, about Paul Bunyan. That's just a story. Everything is made up like that. The older fellow that they used to—feller by the name of Old Jim. . . . He was a lumberman. . . . He was a great feller to start out and do something Paul Bunyan, taking all of this and that and tell you about this thing and that thing and . . . tell you about what he had done [while working] on Round River [with Paul Bunyan] and all these things like that until you'd be shocked at things—and how . . . [Paul Bunyan] carried five hundred pounds of shot right over there in the new pavement they was putting in there. He took five hundred pounds in each hand of [rock] and put it in a sack and walked right across that new pavement, and he sunk clear to his knees. . . . [Laughing] They'd tell lots of stories when they'd get up about Paul Bunyan, or different things. . . .

This fellow [could really go] to work [telling Paul Bunyan tales]. He was pretty young; he'd get up and just tell you so you'll think it's just so. He'd say, "I used to work for Paul, quite a good bit. . . . I used to work for Paul. And one time," he says, "Paul got him a big tract of timber and went up and looked this here tract over and seed this . . . water here that didn't go down." And he bought this timber here and the reason why that this here timber stayed in here, is that it was such a long ways in them days to get it out to a stream.

Well, Paul, he . . . bought this timber quite cheap at that time. He [and his men] made a mess of camps, and everything, and they worked there all winter . . . in this river. . . .

And had lots of teams and put in all this work and was there all winter, and when it come to . . . spring, well, they had broke the roadways—and kept breaking the roadways, and had some of the men keep the logs going, going a little bit, and when they had the roadways all broke, why then they started their drive to go, you see. To drive these logs out.

Well, they started to ride these logs out. They go two weeks. And finally, they came right straight back with the jammers or the head fellows running the head logs. . . .

They go through and they run on to some camps—that looked like where they'd worked all winter, these boys, you see. And Paul did too. And they said, . . . "Them camps resembled our camps. Your camps." And then they drove two weeks more . . . went right around and come back to that same place again. There was these camps again. Well, then they got out and discovered and found out that, hell, they'd been driving around for four week with seventy or eighty or a hundred men, on that drive, . . . working like that, and Fahey said he was one of the fellers working on it for four weeks.

"Well," Paul says, "well, now, we're in an awful fix," he says. "We'll investigate this." So they went around and around and they couldn't find no inlet or outlet of that lake. It was a lake. Instead of a river, it was a lake.

136. A Liars' Contest	**JERRY PHILIPS** **Oklahoma and Visalia, California;** **L.A. LEDFORD** **Texas and Visalia, California;** **ERNEST ARNOLD** **Oklahoma and Visalia, California;** **"LUCKY JAKE"** **Oklahoma and Visalia, California** **ROY TURNER** **Louisiana and Visalia, California** **Recorded by Charles Todd and** **Robert Sonkin,** **Tulare Farm Security** **Administration Camp,** **Visalia, California, September 1,** **1941**

The great majority of storytellers featured in this book typically performed for small, intimate audiences, among whom tales would emerge naturally from the context of conversation. Such genres as legends and märchen were very seldom told in large public gatherings. One of the few exceptions to this rule is the tall tale, which (though often cropping up in the give-and-take of daily talk) has long been used for large-group entertainment in public settings. Many American communities feature stage presentations of liars' contests. It is not surprising to find such entertainments being practiced on a large scale in the California migrant camps at the end of the Depression. As discussed in the Dust Bowl section of this book (stories 209–211), droughts and dust storms in the Great Plains created a major ecological and social disaster in the late 1930s, forcing millions of the region's inhabitants to relocate. California became the major destination of these "Dust Bowl refugees" (see story 209), and by 1940 the numbers of "Okies" (Oklahomans) and other groups displaced from the plains grew so great that the federal government's Farm Security Administration (FSA) had established several residential "tent cities" in California to house the impoverished and often unemployed masses that had migrated from the east. It was in these makeshift living quarters that the following tall tales were recorded.

Charles Todd and Robert Sonkin recorded this stage performance at the Visalia FSA Camp. The event was large and formal enough to require an emcee (S.C. Loop), and the background noise indicates a large, often restless crowd. The performance featured four acts by five storytellers (Ernest Arnold and "Lucky Jake" collaborated in a tall tale dialogue). The recording ends before the winner is announced.

[S.C. Loop:] All right, we're going to have now a famous liar from the Tulare Farm Worker's Community. Mr. Jerry Philips is going to tell you a lie. Mr. Philips.

[Jerry Philips:] He told that a little bit wrong. Now, I can't lie. I'm just going to tell you the truth about it. It's kind of hard for me to lead this contest off because these guys have kind of ganged up on me [framed me] in the first place. Down in Oklahoma one time, I started to go a-fishing. I got a little bit tired and take me a half gallon of White Mule along and I went down to the river and found a nice shady place to fish and got me a fishing pole and I take me a few drinks of the White Mule and I got started fishing. After awhile I got kind of tired of fishing and I stuck my pole out on the bank, set there and drink this White Mule, and I got to feeling pretty good.

So I noticed a little trout with a little white spot on his head. He come a-swimming along next to the edge of the bank. I kept a-noticing that he'd come up there and open his mouth, and I started to take another drink, and so I just poured a little over in *his* mouth.

So he went away and in a few minutes he come back and stuck his head out again. And I give him another drink.

I didn't pay any attention to him. I kept drinking along there and got to feeling pretty good. So directly I heard a fuss down below [the bank] and I looked around and I see this minnow bringing me a eight-pound bass. . . .

[S.C. Loop:] That's Mr. Jerry Philips from Tulare. Now, then, we're going to have one from—well, let's see, where you from? . . . Well, looks like Tulare is

Photo from the Shafter Camps. Charles Todd, collector of stories 136–139 and 209, recording music performances at the Shafter FSA Camp, 1941. (Library of Congress, photo by Robert Hemmig)

the only one that's represented up here. What's the matter? Haven't they got any liars any place else? All right. We'll have Mr. Ledford tell his tall tale. Mr. Ledford.

[L.A. Ledford:] Ladies and gentlemen, I don't whether I can compete with these Okies or not. I'm from Texas, and I was in Texas, and people from Texas don't lie. I was down there in Texas in nineteen and seventeen when the World War started off. And during my childhood, why, my father died, he left me a little gray horse. And when they drafted me, I told em I wouldn't go to the army unless they'd take my little horse with me. He weighed about five hundred pounds.

Well, they decided to take me. They needed some horses anyhow. And this little horse was so tough they carried him along. Well, they put me and this little horse with seven more horses and an ammunition wagon. And we started to carry some ammunition across to the front. And there's a bomb hit this wagon and blowed everything all to pieces except the little horse and myself. It blowed me off the wagon and broke my leg, and it blowed the little horse out of the harness and didn't even hurt him. Well, we had to have some ammunition along the front right away. I hopped over on the side of the hill and got some more harness, I put on this little horse. I took him out and I hooked him to the end of a boxcar that was off a piece from where this happened. And the track was all blowed away in front of this car. So I started the little horse, and he started it rolling. And he pulled so hard going up this hill that he bogged up, up to his knees in solid rock. Well, we got it over to the front and went all through the war and the little horse didn't get a scratch, and they discharged us both and sent us back to Texas.

Well, I got me a little wagon, made me a little wagon out of an old car. I hooked him to it, and I got to selling chicken powder around there. I sold insect powders. . . . I sold it for sixty cents a box.

Well, chickens went high, and people didn't have no money, and I'd trade a box for a hen. Well, a lot of these women said that their hens were worth more than sixty cents. They wouldn't take less than a dollar for em, but when I got . . . these wrappers all used up, I had me some wrappers made and had the price of a dollar put on it so the women would think they was getting more for their chickens.

Well, I made pretty good, but finally my health got bad and I had to move out into New Mexico. Went out there on account of my health and the high climate out there. I lived out there about five years, and I lost twelve wives in the five years. Well, it was high blood pressure. The climate was so high that the people would take high blood pressure and die right off. . . . Well, I had to do something about it, so I made up a big cage on this little wagon. And I got me two mosquitoes and I put em in this cage. Well, every time I hear of a person with a high blood pressure, I'd take these mosquitoes and I'd go and let 'em suck [his] blood. And these mosquitoes got so big, they had so much trade they got so big that they outgrew the cage. Well, I sold one of these mosquitoes to the sanitarium. They butchered him and drank his blood. Every time a person had to have a blood transfusion they wouldn't have to get out and hunt someone to get their blood. Well, of course the work doubled up on this other mosquito. He outgrew the cage. I had to get a bull ring and put it in his nose and put a chain to it and lead him around. Well, the last man I took him to treat had the T.B. And this mosquito take in the T.B. Well, we had a bad winter that winter and he take in the pneumonia and died.

So after that, then I didn't have no more use for the horse, and I was a-pasturing him. And put him on a dry pasture. And come a real drought that year and he got down so far that he had to be helped up. I thought he was going to die. Well, I traded him to my neighbor for a gallon of buttermilk. Well, this neighbor got him on the mend, got him to where he could get up. So one day he led him out in the popcorn patch and he eat a bite of popcorn and went to sleep. While he was asleep, it got so hot this popcorn popped. And he woke up and he saw this white popcorn, and he thought it had snowed, and he lay down and froze to death. Thank you.

[Laughter and applause]

[S.C. Loop:] That was L.A. Ledford from Tulare. Now we're going to have one by Ernest Arnold and "Lucky Jake."

[Ernest Arnold:] Folks, they all say that they got up here to tell the truth. I'm gonna tell you, I'm gonna tell you a pure, "D" old lie.

One time down in Oklahoma when I was farming, I raised some pumpkins and they was so big, one of em was, I hauled it out and made a house. I hired me three carpenters to put partitions in it, and we made forty-two three-room apartments.

["Lucky Jake":] Well, that ain't nothing, folks. You know, way down in eastern Oklahoma I made a big old steel pot. Twenty-five miles around it, five miles deep.

[Ernest Arnold:] What are you gonna do with a big pot like that?

["Lucky Jake":] I'm gonna cook that pumpkin you raised in it.

[Laughter and applause]

[S.C. Loop:] Last, but not least, Roy Turner from Tulare. Mr. Turner.

[Roy Turner:] Well, never made no pots or raised no pumpkins. My intention was when I got up here to tell about a dear old dog which is gone, but I changed my mind. . . .

A poor old boy from Louisiana . . . was telling me about catching a fish on the Mississippi that [when he] pulled him out, the water went down two foot, from one end of it to the other.

I didn't believe it. But I was down there later, two or three months later, and I seen one of those big turtles walking a-straddle the Mississippi, a-hunting water.

[S.C. Loop:] Now it's up to the judges to find out which [is lying].

137. My Three Favorite Lies

VERNON "SHORTY" ALLEN
Hope, Arkansas, and Shafter,
California
Recorded by Charles Todd and
Robert Sonkin,
Shafter FSA Camp, August 4,
1940

The biblical succession of locusts, floods, and black blizzards visited upon Flora Robertson (story 211) and thousands of other Okies would, it seems, render any freak of nature believable. It is not surprising that the residents of the California migrant camps, having lived through calamities as outrageous as any tall tale scenario, would lighten their loads and pass their unwished-for and too-abundant idle time by trading tall tales. In these short tales told by "Shorty" Allen, nature is a sentient force, benign and laugh-provoking, and not the cruel killer that his audience had come to associate with the Dust Bowl.

Collectors Charles Todd and Robert Sonkin made some written observations about "Shorty." He was a small man with "red-lidded eyes almost always half shut, upper front teeth capped with a kind of tarnished silver metal. One of the camp characters. Known as a teller of tall tales. 'He's told those stories so long, he's come to believe them himself.' Sometimes gets mad if people don't believe him, according to the others. This record is a medley of three of the stories he is proudest of. . . . "Short[y]" always told them with gusto, and they were thoroughly appreciated by the men around."

This is Vernon Allen from the Shafter Camp, and we'll tell you a little fish story one time.

We was going fishing one day, you know, and I thought I was getting about grown, so I carried me a little pint of liquor with me. But by then my dad caught up with me with it, and he'd run out of fish bait. And he says, "Son," said, "if you don't go get me some good fish bait," says, "I'm going to give you a whipping for that liquor." So I go out. And I looked and I hunted and I couldn't find nothing. Finally, I run up on a big rattlesnake. Had a big frog.

So I take out my pint of liquor, poured a little over there in his face so he turned [that frog] loose. And he backed up and he licked his lips, you know. I grabbed up the frog and I carried it down to Dad.

We's sitting there fishing away. Directly felt something behind me sort of knock, and I looked around, and lo and behold there's that rattlesnake with two more frogs.

[Laughter]

So the next morning me and my buddy, we go out a-fishing and carried a old gun along. He had one [that] kicked mighty bad. We go out on a big cypress log, gonna shoot some fish. So we happened to look down there, and there's a great, big moccasin about the size of the bottom of a number three washtub. So he leans way over so the gun wouldn't kick him off in the water, and when he pulled the trigger the gun said *snap* and . . . and he went right in the middle of that moccasin, and I don't know which of em got away the fastest [chuckles].

So then we decided we'd go on out a-duck hunting. We went down there. He was awful good, my buddy was, on killing quails. But you know he missed every duck he shot at. He's coming on back and a great big greenhead [mallard duck] lit on his gun barrel. And he had a double barrel gun, of course. Got to fishing in the end of the barrel. He thought to hisself, "Now I know I'm going to get me one greenhead duck," and when he pulled the trigger he pulled the wrong one—he missed him. So he said, "Well," he said, "I can't kill that duck. I'll have to take him on a quail hunt."

[Interviewer: That's true stories, are they?]

Yeah, that's all but one. [Laughter]

[Interviewer: Which one isn't true?]

That one about the duck. [Laughter]

[Now, where'd you say that happened?]

Down in Arkansas. Down on Clear Lake.

138. The Peach Tree Deer

BILL ROBINSON
Atoka, Oklahoma, and Visalia, California
Recorded by Charles Todd and Robert Sonkin,
Visalia FSA Camp, August 30, 1941

Master of Ceremonies: Ladies and gentlemen, I'm introducing to you one of the biggest liars that ever came from Oklahoma. This is Sleepy Bill from Atoka, Oklahoma, who's now going to tell you a big lie.]

When I lived in eastern Oklahoma, I went a-hunting down in the . . . mountains, and I got over between the river and the mountain, and I saw a deer coming. I had my gun loaded with a peach seed, so I shot this deer with this peach seed. Well, I looked around, and it kept a-getting colder and coming up a cloudy and kept a-getting colder and colder and I built up a fire. So my fire went up about twenty feet and froze. I walked off.

And the next spring I was back down there, and I saw a peach . . . tree coming up through the woods and a bunch of hogs was following it a-squealing. And I discovered it was the same peach seed I had shot the deer with, that growed to a peach tree, and the hogs were following the deer, picking up those peaches.

Well, I went on up where they were a feller cutting logs. I helped him cut down a tree and before we got it down, it busted up, hit him in the stomach, knocked him over the mountain two miles. So I put out to hunt him. Well, I got over there. He had fell in a pool of water. Took me three days to find him, and still he was swimming around. [Laughter]

139. Cornered by a Polar Bear

MICHAEL BRUICK
Visalia, California
Recorded by Charles Todd and
Robert Sonkin,
Tulare FSA Camp, August 30,
1941

Master of Ceremonies: Now, ladies and gentlemen, it gives me great pleasure to introduce our worthy Tulare Farmworkers Community manager, Mr. Michael P. Bruick, who says he's a truthful man. Mr. Bruick.]

One summer on a hunting expedition up in the north country my party and myself were out camping, and that day I'd been out hunting all day long and exhausted all my ammunition. I'd started the homeward trek and walked along, walked along. And turned a corner around an iceberg, and just as I turned the corner I came face to face with a large polar bear. There I was with a rifle in my hand, no ammunition, and a large polar bear in front of me. Well, I, of course, started to back up, and the polar bear after me. I kept backing up and backing up and the first thing you know, he had me up against that iceberg. Well, sir, that bear came after me, and there I was, no ammunition, a rifle,

Charles Todd and Robert Sonkin record Will Neal playing the fiddle at the Shafter Camp, 1940. (Library of Congress, photo by Robert Hemmig)

and I saw that my end had come. So I started thinking back, back to my home country and family and folks, and I started to cry. Well, those tears rolled down my cheek and it was so cold that the tears froze in large balls of ice on my cheek. Well, sir, an idea struck me then and I took those tears as they rolled off my cheek and loaded em into my muzzle. And I leveled that rifle at the bear and fired. The heat of the rifle fire mellowed those . . . tears and shot out a stream of water and that water going through that cold atmosphere mellowed into an icicle. I caught that bear right between the eyes and pierced his brain. And that icicle melted, and believe it or not that bear died of water on the brain.

[Master of Ceremonies: I thought you was a truthful man.]

140. A Land-loving Catfish

DOC MCCONNELL
Tucker's Knob, Tennessee
Recorded at the National
Storytelling Festival,
Jonesborough, Tennessee, October
1986

The tall tale's traditional role as a genre easily adapted to the stage has served it well in recent years, as storytelling has become a major public pastime. Since 1973, the most important public venue for storytelling has been the National Storytelling Festival, which takes place annually in October in Jonesborough, Tennessee. Founded and lovingly maintained by Jimmy Neil Smith, who now serves as director of the International Storytelling Center, the festival is noted as a place where traditional folk culture and contemporary, media-influenced performances thrive side by side. The great traditional narrator Ray Hicks (see stories 28–32) has been the most often featured storyteller at Jonesborough, but other visitors include the professional actor, monologist, and film star Spaulding Gray. Doc McConnell blends both extremes: he is both a traditional front-porch yarn spinner and an irrepressible showman. Born in a log cabin in the tiny Appalachian community of Tucker's Nob, Doc grew up listening to many of the same tales he retells at storytelling festivals today. But he has always felt the pull of the stage.

Doc's love of both the fireside and the limelight found a perfect vehicle in 1971. Jimmy Neil Smith has written of the transformative moment when Doc visited the Folklife Festival of the Smokies in Cosby, Tennessee: "One night, around a campfire, the conversation turned to medicine shows, and those gathered there bemoaned their passing into American history. Intrigued, Doc thought back to the old medicine shows he'd seen as a child, and he returned home and went to work. Over the next few months, he borrowed an old wagon, unearthed a checkered vest, a long black coat with tails, and a top hat, brewed sassafras roots for tonic, and began rehearsing the banter he'd heard while growing up." For the next three decades, "Doc McConnell's Medicine Show" would tour the country, gaining popularity along its unending trail.

In 1974, Doc was asked to perform at the second annual National Storytelling Festival in Jonesborough, where in subsequent decades he has become one of the most popular performers.

You see up there on Tucker's Knob, we pass the time of day a lot of ways. We hung around John Mauk's country store, and I had to do chores a-hoeing corn, and chopping wood, and doing all of them other things. But a lot of times I got to go fishing. Now, one time I went down there to John Mauk's mill pond, down the road there, about three quarters of a mile, I guess. And I was just fishing with . . . a piece of wrapping thread and a cane pole, if you've ever fished that way. And I had a good old red worm on that thing. And if you're careful, you can catch a fish like that, jerk him out, shake your pole real good, and on the same worm catch another one.

And I started catching em more like that and throwing em over here in the field. I must have caught about nine or thirteen in a row. Boy. Wham, wham, you know. When all of a sudden, they stopped biting, just as suddenly. And I sat there and held my pole and held it and held it and—*total silence*, you know.

And I got tired of fishing and I started, I just believe I'll get my fish and go to the house. Already been in the hot sun for about two hours and I turned around and looked, and there was all them old fish laying out there I'd pitched over there behind me. All of them had died and got stiff, and turned up on their ends like boomerangs, you know, and I just started loading em up on my arm like stovewood to carry em in the house, and I looked down there, and there laid a fish, just wiggled his tail just a little bit. And I looked at him again, and he was going *ppsshh-oh, ppsshh.* Breathing. I couldn't believe that that fish was still alive, laying there in that hot sun for two hours, and I just dipped him down in the water a couple times, and let him up on my pile of fish and put my arm around this way and went carrying the fish on home.

Got on at the house and I just dumped em out there in the backyard and I didn't have no heart to clean that fish that was still alive. I just started cleaning all them fish and left that'n laying out there in the backyard and I got carried away frying them fish that night and went on to bed. And the first thing come to my mind the next morning: "I left that live fish laying out there in the backyard. I better get out there before the cats get to him. I tell you." [Laughing] And I run out the backdoor and out there, and there lay that old catfish still alive laying in that grass in the backyard, living off what little bit of moisture and dew that had collected on the grass all night long. I couldn't believe that that fish could live on such a small amount of water. And I thought upon a idea: Wouldn't it be great if I could learn that fish to stay out of the water all the time?

And I started working with that old fish, and I kept him out of the water about four hours a day, and about eight hours the next day, and about sixteen hours the next day, and about thirty-two hours the next day [laughter]. And it wasn't no time at all until I done learn that old fish just to stay out of the water all the time. You never seen nothing to beat it. There, he just lay out there and breathe human air, you know, like everybody else, you know. [Laughter]

And one day I even tied a string to him and started pulling him along, and he got up on them two front fins, and started paddling hisself along there [laughter], you know. And he was doing, doing quite good, and I just took the string off, and then you ought to have seen him, just following me around the house, everywhere I went. Thought it was his momma, I reckon. And that old catfish there, and I started teaching him—I named him Homer—and I said, "Homer, roll over." And, boy, that old fish'd just do a flip there [laughter] like that, you know.

One day, my momma come out the backdoor with the butcher knife, going to the smokehouse to cut a piece of meat, and that old fish, Old Homer, raised up, seen Mama with that butcher knife coming out through there toward him. He thought that he was gonna be for supper and he [laughing]—you ought to have seen him. He raised up and laid that tail kind of over to the side. Lifted up on them two fins, and started propelling himself sideways. You ought to see him hopping down through there on his tail and them two front fins. Beat everything I ever seen. And I had me a walking catfish. [Laughter] Nobody had ever seen a fish that could walk and stay out of the water. Why, they was a man from the biology department of University of Tennessee come up there one day. And he said, "Hey, I heard you got a fish up here that can stay out of the water."

And I said, "Yeah. I done learn him to stay out of the water. He stay out of the water all the time. He never goes. He just lives in what little bit of water is in the dew."

And he said, "How long have you been working with him?"

And I said, "About two weeks."

He said, "You know this is evolution, don't you?"

And I said, "What?"

And he said, "Evolution. This was taken—should have taken two million years for this member of the aquatic family to adapt itself to the human atmosphere. But here you've done it in two weeks." And he said, "I'd like to have that to take back to the university," he said.

I said, "Nah, I couldn't part with Old Homer."

And he . . . took pictures, and wrote a whole bunch of stuff about that fish, you know. They was a carnival come through one time. They wanted to buy him off of me, wanted to put him in a sideshow and charge a nickel a look or something, you know. I wouldn't part with Old Homer. Boy, he was something. Everywhere I went, Old Homer followed me. He'd go down to the country store, you know, and them old loafers sitting around down there, they'd catch them flies like that, you know, and reach in there and get em and hold em, and he'd reach up there and grab them flies quicker than anything you ever seen.

Boy, he liked M&M's too [laughter]. Boy, he'd eat them things. He loved them M&M's. And boy we had more fun with that old fish, boy, and he never did go near the water. Never did. And boy, I got kind of attached to him, you know, and everywhere I went he was following me right along, just wiggling and kicking himself along. And it come kind of down in the fall of the year and about time for books to take up, and I was going to have to go to school.

And Mama told me I was gonna have to do something with that old pet catfish cause she didn't want him around the house under her feet all day long.

And I knowed I couldn't take him to school, cause you all know what trouble Mary had with the lamb she took that time [laughter], and so I just decided to run off and leave that fish at the house, and I started off down the road, and I looked over my shoulder, and that old fish was just troggling down the road walking right behind me, you know, and then he—I looked again. He was right behind me, and I walked, I guess, a half a mile, and he was scooting and a-pulling and tugging and jumping down the road there, following me to school.

Well, I had to cross this old wooden bridge before I went up there to the schoolhouse and Old Homer, my pet catfish, was right back there, just minutes before, and I looked back there and he wasn't back there nowhere. I went back there and called him, and hollered out for him, and I didn't see him nowhere, and I walked out on that bridge that I had just crossed. And one of the wooden boards on that bridge had rotted and fallen away and left a great big old gaping hole right in the middle of that bridge. And I walked out on to that bridge and looked down through that hole, and down there in the water laid Old Homer, drowned. [Laughter]

And that's the end of that story.

141. The Biggest Liar in the State

TILLMAN CADLE
Pineville, Kentucky
Recorded by Mary Elizabeth Barnicle,
January 1938

A native of Massachusetts, privileged in her education and the breadth of her travels, Mary Elizabeth Barnicle (1891–1978) ended her life married to a coal miner in the Tennessee mountains. Barnicle and her husband, Tillman Cadle (1902–1994), had little common background, but they shared an all-consuming passion for social justice. As Barnicle was performing graduate work at Bryn Mawr College and teaching in England, she involved herself heavily in organizations struggling to obtain women's rights, African American rights, and workers' rights; as Cadle worked the coal mines of eastern Kentucky, he became an organizer for the United Mine Workers of America, then embattled in an uphill battle against the mine owners for decent pay and safe working conditions.

In 1935 Cadle received an injury while working in the mines, and unable to find medical treatment in Kentucky, he traveled to New York City to join his friend and fellow mineworker John Garland, brother of the singer-storyteller Aunt Molly Jackson (see stories 102–110). At that time, Barnicle was teaching folklore at New York University, and she came in contact with Garland, Jackson, and Cadle through their mutual interests in traditional culture and the cause of the mineworkers.

Cadle and Barnicle married about 1936 and remained a couple until Barnicle's death forty-two years later. In the following performance, the husband recounts for his wife a tale that was popular in the hills when he was a child.

Once upon a time, down in the mountains of Kentucky, they was two fellows . . . , the biggest liars in the state. They come together to see which could tell the biggest lie. And one of these fellows, he begin telling his story, and he begin with a story of his experience as a hunter. And he told about being out in the mountains and—with an old hog rifle. And he saw seven turkeys and they were all sitting on a limb. And he never could figure how he would be able to kill all seven of the turkeys. So he walked up under the tree, and he shot through the limb and split the limb, and it closed up on all of the turkeys' feet. In this way, he got the seven turkeys.

Mary Elizabeth Barnicle, collector of story 141, during the Georgia, Florida, and Bahamas expedition with Alan Lomax and Zora Neale Hurston, 1935 (see also stories 169–171). (Library of Congress)

So then he begin going on in his way, and he saw three deers. But he never could get all these deers in line to kill all three at once. So he finally decided that he would kill two and let one get away. And, when he shot and killed . . . two, why then the other one loped off. And he loaded his gun and then as he walked along his way, why, he heard a noise behind the hill. And he went around to see what it was, and as he begin to feel for the hammer of his gun, the hammer was gone. And then he went along and discovered this hammer was gone, and he kept hearing this noise, and when he went around the hill, why, he discovered, the hammer had the deer backed up in a fence corner beating its brains out.

And then one day he was going a-hunting. He had a dog that he never was able to fool. All he had to do to let the dog know what he wanted to do was to get his sack, and the dog wouldn't do anything but tree possums. All he had to do . . . to let the dog know what he wanted to do, was to take his ax, and he wouldn't do anything but tree coons. And all that he had to do to get the dog to tree squirrels was take his rifle. So one day he said, "I will fool the dog. I'll start a-hunting and I'll go a-fishing." So he got his gun, and he started, and the dog loped off and then he run back in the house, and put up his gun, and got his fishing pole, and when he got out on the other side of the house, the dog was digging bait.

Well, then he said, "Well, I will fool him." So he went on a-fishing . . . and he said, "Then I'll fish and let the dog hunt and tree a squirrel." The dog treed up the river and when he went to him, why, behold, he had a catfish up the holler in a sycamore tree. So he was never able to fool the dog.

142. Swinging Pigs

LEE WEBB
Newport, Tennessee
Recorded by Joseph S. Hall,
Newport, Tennessee, ca. 1956

This Smoky Mountain tale relies in part on knowledge of old-time farming practices in steep topography. A five-rail fence (that is, a fence with five horizontal bars, spaced at intervals of about a foot) was considered tall enough to keep cattle out of a cornfield. An eight-rail fence would be completely unnecessary unless the ground on one side was steep enough to give the animal several feet's worth of advantage in leaping the fence.

There was an old man who lived out in Cosby and he owned a mountain farm up there, and he said he cleared him a newground and planted it with corn. He put a fence around it, eight-rail fence, and the upper side of it was sort of steep ground. . . . And when he cleared him his corn, he cut a lot of grapevines off and let em die to keep the shade off [his crops].

And his hogs went to getting in the corn. . . . And he went round the fence a lot of times and stopped every hole he could find, but the hogs just kept getting in. So he put em up one night and next morning he turned em out and watched em. And they was going up on that mountain and they was getting over in those grapevines [and taking them] in their mouths, and they'd swing up over the fence and then drop off into the corn. And then when one'd get on that grapevine and swing back, another'n'd get it. And they kept going till they all got in it. So he went and cut the grapevine off where they couldn't reach it and that stopped the hogs from eating his corn.

143. The Roguish Cow

GAINES KILGORE
Wise, Virginia
Recorded by Richard Chase,
Wise County, Virginia, 1950

Richard Chase is famous today for producing the best-selling American folktale collection of all time, *The Jack Tales* (1943), in which he retold the tales of the Hicks-Harmon family of Watauga County, North Carolina (see stories 1–32). Chase's book was celebrated when it first appeared, but over the years he attracted criticism for substantially changing the family's tales, for promising the tellers money that they never received, and for attempting to own the tales by copyrighting them and demanding money from people who wished to retell them. In recent years, members of the Hicks-Harmon family have come forward to express their dissatisfaction with Chase and his methods.

Chase is most famous for the Jack Tales that he reworked, but some of the greatest storytellers that he met were residents of Wise County, Virginia. Gaines Kilgore was well known in the county for his skills as a narrator. Chase had adapted one Kilgore story, "Soldier Jack and the Magic Sack," for inclusion in the Jack Tales, but he found Kilgore's jokes and tall tales equally appealing.

In this performance, recorded by Chase five years after the end of World War II, Kilgore updates his old tale to include a reference to the war.

Well, that was a great cow—
[Richard Chase: It was roguish, huh?]
—roguish cow that we had in our part of the country. The owner of this cow died. And then left this cow in the hands of two girls. One of em married and moved the cow to her house. She had lost her home, I reckon, and she just almost made a wild cow. Outlaw cow. It's all I could tell you. They didn't feed her, and she went to *anybody*, just any place, where she could find her food, she would get it and eat it. Anywhere she could climb or go.

So, she had been a-bothering us there at home. Terribly much. This is a fact now. She ate up our corn crops and everything, destroyed em almost. And everyone in the country would shoot at the old cow, and bang around on her, and I did quite a bit of it myself. Of course. So, I had two oat stacks. I built a fence around them, about ten feet high at the start, and she would jump in there and back out. Eat what she wanted and back out. Never a rail knocked down nor nothing.

Finally at last, I built the pen high as the oatstacks was. She still went in and out.

So I would foller and shoot her just as long as I could run my horse. Till . . . I couldn't get any farther.

And finally, one morning, one day, I got up and went down to the barn and to my surprise I was going up the ladder, and something jumped out—I didn't know what it was. Landed on the ground. It excited me for just a minute. I turned and looked and now, then, I saw it was the old cow. And she had a ladder around her neck.

I wondered, "You old devil, you, have you been a-carrying a ladder to get up in the barn loft with?" [Laughter] I still couldn't size her out.

Well, I'd done my feeding, and went to the house and told my brothers about it. And we decided we'd give her another little chase. We followed her over through the farm quite a bit, and down by the side of an old rock fence, one on one side a-shooting at her, and one on the other one. And we ran her out of the farm. Except she got into the woods again.

Well, she came back again a few nights later. We was listening for her. She had a bell on her. And she came in, around home there, and we got to firing some shots at her and she went over to Edna Bates's. They had a hundred-pound bag of [feed] a-laying in the garage door. She got it and eat it up and went on out to Delmar Moffat and he had about two acres of corn out there, and she ate it. [Laughter] Came on back and got in my barn loft again. I ran her out that time, and follered her, and done some shooting.

She still had the old ladder around her neck and she must have kindly got hung up in the woods somewhere, between Albert Mullins's and Bob Mullins's— that was the old Howay place. . . . So Albert was in the woods a-hunting, and he ran on her a-grazing in the woods with the ladder around her neck. And he tried his best to drive her in. He wanted to take her in. And he seen it was such a slow job that it wasn't worthwhile for him to try it. So she finally went and grazed herself, or waded through somehow, and managed to get through. Got this old ladder up against Bob Mullins's (he married the girl that, I was telling you, their mother died, and left the old cow a widow or something, whatever-much you might call her). [Laughter] So she would climb up in the barn loft and eat what she wanted and come back down and hide out, and go back the next night until she eat all his feed up, he had in the barn. Like to have starved his horse to death.

And after that, I bought the old cow off of him. To get rid of her in the country. And killed her. I sold her hide to Walter Kennedy. Do you know him? Wise. And he shipped the hide to up in Tennessee. And they got enough lead and the most of the fuel out of her—well anyhow, they got enough lead to win the Second World War. And the fuel out of her, I just imagined just now that they presented some of the atomic bomb [laughter] that they dropped on JAY-pan.

144. The Night the Lamp Flame Froze

MARY CELESTIA PARLER
Wedgefield, South Carolina, and
Fayetteville, Arkansas
Recorded by Miles L. Hanley,
American Dialect Society,
Providence, Rhode Island,
August 22, 1934

In the headnote to story 181, I discuss the career of the great Arkansas folklorist Mary Celestia Parler. She was a composed and fearless raconteuse. In her time, it was not characteristic for women to tell tall tales in public venues, but Mrs. Parler did not shrink from so doing. Here, the celebrated linguist Miles L. Hanley of the American Dialect Society serves as her straightman.

In the winter of 1917, which was the coldest winter in the history of our country, I went up to bed one night, and in those days we had acetylene lights in our house. I went up to bed and I lighted the light and got undressed and got ready to go to bed, and when I started to turn out the light, I turned the little—screw that was supposed to turn out the light, and nothing happened. Thought that was strange, so I tried to blow it out. I blew and I blew. And the light didn't even flicker—and, lo and behold, when I came to investigate, it was frozen, so I didn't want to sleep in a brilliantly lighted room all night, so I reached up, snapped off the light, and went to the window, and threw it out in the yard.

The next morning, one of our old hens thought that was a particularly nice-looking grain of corn, so she swallowed it. Ever since then, until our old hen died, we had hard-boiled eggs for breakfast every morning.

[Interviewer: You have to be careful; somebody might dispute that story.]

Well, I don't think anyone who knows me would doubt my truthfulness [laughing], because my reputation is always one for veracity.

145. The Gun Ain't Loaded

FRANK MAHAFFEY
Maggie, North Carolina
Recorded by Joseph S. Hall,
ca. 1940

As Joseph Hall noted in his references to the tale, this story has the flavor of a medieval fabliau: risqué situations, multiple sexual partners, unrestrained lust. Nevertheless, Frank Mahaffey presents the tale as an actual incident from his own life and narrates it in the straightforward, low-key, mock-sincere tones for which the tall tale is famous.

Early in his tale, Mahaffey refers to "two o'clock in the evening," a phrase that reflects his Appalachian background: in the mountains in the early twentieth century, the hours immediately following noon were typically referred to as "evening," rather than "afternoon," hours.

Back in nineteen and thirteen me and my brother coonhunted lots in the Smokies. We had a dog named Track. He was a good'un. We went to Flat Creek one evening, built up a campfire, and stayed till two o'clock next morning. We left and went in on Stillwell and Old Track, he struck. Right up Stillwell he went and us right after. About ten o'clock in the day it begin snowing. We followed Old Track about an hour and the snow was about twenty-two inches deep. We turned back to the camp. About two o'clock in the evening Old Track come back. And we had a big campfire. Chunks'd roll down and Old Track come in and set down by the fire—and directly he stretched down and got a chunk of fire in his mouth and right out the door he went. We was right out after him. Went back in on Stillwell and he was a-tracking him. He'd went off and left us. Right up Stillwell he went and us right after him and about a mile above where we'd turned back, why, we found Old Track at a big cliff. He took this chunk of fire and he treed the coons in a cliff and stuck the fire under it and set the leaves afire. Smoked the coons out and had three big'uns a-lying there dead.

I give em to my brother and told him to come back the nigh way and I'd go up to Balsam Corner, see if I could locate some bear sign, and I didn't take anything to eat with me. Went up there and the fog come in and I got lost and got in on Tennessee. Getting about dark, and I traveled all night, next day and late next evening. Hadn't had a bite to eat. Come to a little log cabin . . . somewhere. I called and someone come to the door, and I asked her about staying all night. I told her I'd starved and froze and give out.

She said she guessed she could keep me. So I went in and she said there wasn't no man of the house. Time for bed, she made four pallets. There was her and two daughters. Made a pallet in each corner of the room. Went to lay down, she got a big pistol and laid it on the fireboard, and she said, "You see this gun. If anything takes place here tonight," says, "I'll use that gun on you." So I just tumbled down in the pallet and was give out and just in a few minutes I was about asleep.

The old lady she begin to snore [imitates snoring noises]. She said, "The gun ain't loaded [snoring sound] The gun ain't loaded [snoring sound]"

I took it for granted that she wanted me to crawl over to her pallet, and I crawled over and laid with her awhile and then went back to my pallet. I just plunked down on it, just—three days' walk and no sleep and nothing to eat and—directly the middle-aged girl says [high-pitched, soft voice], "My turn next. My turn next. My turn next."

I decided that one more piece wouldn't kill me and [laughter] I crawled over to her pallet and lay awhile and I just barely could crawl when I left there and just about halfway over to my pallet, this little girl over in the other corner, with this little tiny [finer] voice, says [whispering, high-pitched voice], "Don't forget me. Don't forget me."

I was about dying, I knew that this was a new job, but I crawled over and had at it.

I got over and stayed with her for a while and just started back to my pallet and fell over it, and just as I went out I hear the old woman say, "I'm ready again. Ready again."

And I said, "The gun ain't loaded."

After about three days, my brother found me there unconscious.

[Laughter]

10

JOKES

---

146. Dividing the Dead

ELLIS OGLE
Pigeon Forge, Tennessee
Recorded by Joseph S. Hall,
Gatlinburg, Tennessee, August 4,
1956

The four legends told by Ellis Ogle in this anthology (stories 118–121) bespeak a man intrigued and often terrified by the prospect of encountering ghosts or the devil. As a young man, Ogle sometimes mistook natural landmarks for supernatural beings. It thus seems apt that the one joke that Ogle shared with collector Joseph S. Hall features a case of mistaken identity in which two ordinary people are mistaken for God and the devil.

The following tale is one of the most popular in American tradition.

Well, I heared this. Why, the devil and God is on the inside of the fence, and this Irishman had to go along the outside and by a little by-trail. And he, he heared a noise. And he stopped.

And one was saying, "You can take this'un; I'll take that'un." "And you can have this'un and I'll take that'un." And he broke and run off to his brother's. And this brother had his legs off.

And he says, "Brother, I heared God and the devil dividing the dead up there up yonder tonight."

Well, his brother says, "If that be the case, if you'd carry me up there, I'd like to hear some of that too." And he took his brother up there, and they's still busy, saying, "You can have this'un, and I'll take that'un," and "You can have this'un, and I'll take that'un."

And when they got down to *two* last ones, they said, "They're two on the outside." Says, "You can have one of them and I'll take the other'un."

And these two men that's listening on the outside, they thought they were the two that they was aiming to take. And, he throwed his brother down—with his legs off—and he run off. And he said that feller came crawling down through there on his hands and dragging his body, run over him, knocked him down. He decided that none of them was going to get him. And he didn't know which one was going to get him.

He come to find out that it was some Irishmen dividing walnuts, and that two fell on the outside. They'd shook a walnut tree. [Laughter]

147. Two at the Gate

SON HOUSE
Mississippi and Syracuse,
New York
Recorded by Harry Oster,
Iowa City, Iowa, April 24, 1965

Like so many other great bluesmen, Eddie James "Son" House (1902–1988) was as much a master storyteller as a master singer. His rich vocals propelled him to fame, but his storytelling remained at home, a private pastime. He recorded his first blues records in 1930 for a commercial audience; it was thirty-five years later, in a private interview with folklorist Harry Oster, that Son recorded the tales he had learned as a child from his father.

Son House's fame seldom brought him very close to fortune. His early records gained him little money. After his first recordings failed to net him adequate money to make a living, he dropped out of the limelight and returned to the Delta country in Mississippi, where he was "discovered" a second time, this time by folklorist Alan Lomax. Again, Lomax's recordings allowed many the privilege to hear a blues master at the height of his form, but they did not suffice to pay Son's bills. Once more, he left the blues behind until "discovered" a third time in the mid-1960s, about the time that Harry Oster recorded this and the following four tales.

Harry Oster (1923–2001) conducted groundbreaking fieldwork in folk music—blues, Cajun, and zydeco—as well as in folk festivals—primarily, the Cajun Mardi Gras. He is less known for his folktale studies, but one of his most important works, "Negro Humor: John and Old Marster" (1968), is a study of such Master-Slave tales as those he learned from Son House.

Son House, teller of stories 147–151. (Jeff Titon/Son House Collection)

Son described for Oster the typical occasions on which such stories were shared when he was a boy: "Well, sometimes they would just get to sitting round, telling jokes, but most times that I would hear jokes like that, be from my father and his friends, and they would get together and get to drinking and telling funny stories and things like that. And I would listen, and I could remember a lot of em." Son also offered a perceptive analysis of the dynamics of these jokes, in which wealthy whites and poor blacks engaged in wars of wits. "The other man, this Boss, was always the smartest and had the best education and learning, and [the black man,] he didn't. But . . . he'd work himself out of something he got into, without education, but it would be just smartness, to try to fool the Boss Man."

The following tale shares the same general plot as Ellis Ogle's "Dividing the Dead" (story 146), but, true to form, the African American version elaborates upon the joke by introducing a master-servant relationship.

Yeah. One I can remember, my father used to tell me about a lot of times, when I was quite young in those days. He would sit down and tell me what his father used to tell him and *his* father told him. So these old stories had kept a-going. And so he told me this one about one of the slaves, how he tricked his—in a way—tricked his master into something that he wasn't expecting. So, he, his master couldn't walk. So he had this guy, his slave to roll him around in a wheelchair. And so, that night, he let him off, and so this guy, this colored guy, he goes to see his girlfriend. In the night.

So when the moon was shining. The weather was good. So he goes to see his girlfriend. And, at the same time, it was two more Negroes, they went out stealing one night. Stealing chickens. And so they had these gunny sacks with em, to put the chickens in, that they was stealing. They'd steal the chicken. Then they would tie their legs together, so in case that one would get loose, he couldn't get very far. They could catch him easy.

So anyway, they stoled the chickens, and they put em in the sacks. And so, when walking along, going back home, one says to the other one, "Say, listen. We got to divide these chickens. And *whereabouts*? We don't want to sit alongside the road to do it. Somebody may come along and see us with the chickens. Say, I wonder where could we *go*?"

Then the other guy says, "I tell you a good place where we won't be bothered with nobody. Nobody passin'. There sure ain't nobody coming there."

He says, "Where is that?"

He says, "Let's stop in the cemetery." Said, "Nobody . . . , not at night especially."

"That's right. That is a good place."

So they stopped at the cemetery, and going in the gate, two of the old hens got out of the bag, and the other one stopped to try to get em. He said, "No, that's alright. Let's go in there, and we can get these two when we're coming out." Say, "They can't get far. They have their legs tied."

The other one, "Yeah, that's right."

So they went on into the cemetery. And neither one of em didn't have any kind of education. They didn't know how to count good. So, he says, "I'll tell you the way we'll do it, since you and I don't know to count." Say, "Get one chicken out. And say, 'That one yours.' And the next one, I say, 'This is mine.' See, we can divide em up like that."

He says, "Yeah, that's a good idea."

So they was doing that, and this guy, he was coming from his girlfriend's. It was getting kind of late. And the road went right by the cemetery. So he got along there and he heard em counting: one saying, "This is mine" and "This is yours." Well, he knows this is the cemetery. He says, "Oh, my God." Said, "It must be Judgment Day. God and the devil dividing souls." [Laughs]

So, he took out and run home. He got home, pounding on the door. "Wake up, Old Master. Wake up!"

He says, "What's the matter with you?"

"Wake up! It's Judgment Day!"

He says, "You crazy?"

He says, "No, I'm not crazy. God and the devil is down there in the cemetery, dividing souls right now. If you don't believe it, get up and get in your chair. And I'll roll you down there, and let you hear em yourself."

Says, "Alright. I'm going, and I'm going to take my shotgun with me. And if you fool me, and they ain't there, I'm gonna shoot you."

Say, "Well, okay, you welcome, boss. Get in your chair."

So they roll down there to the gate, near the gate.

He say, "Now you listen." Said, ". . . Listen."

Well, after awhile he got the last chicken and the other one remembered, he said, "At the gate."

And the Old Master thought he was talking about him and the guy he had hired to wheel him.

He said, "He said there's two at the gate."

And the Negro says, "Yes, say old Boss, two at the gate. He's talking about us."

And so . . . Master jumped out of the wheelchair he had and walked out. Jumped out of the wheelchair and said, "You can bring the chair on with you."

[Laughs] That's the first time he walked in years. He thought it was Judgment Day too. He fooled him.

That was just one of the old stories.

148. Possums and Pigs

SON HOUSE
Mississippi and Syracuse,
New York
Recorded by Harry Oster,
Iowa City, Iowa, April 24, 1965

One time, that was another time, a guy was working on the plantation for this particular Old Boss, and he, he had a knack of stealing pigs. But he would pretend that he would go coon hunting and possum hunting every night. (That's when you usually hunt em.) And so he had a hunting sack, just a regular old hunting sack. But he wasn't going coon hunting. He'd wait till late to go, and then he would steal some of the white man's pigs.

So, Old Master, he kept missing his pigs. Said, an old sow would come up short every morning, and he'd say, "There was six yesterday. Now there ain't but five." And like that, it kept degenerating. He said, "Oh, oh. Somebody must be stealing my pigs. So then he thought about this guy, goes coon hunting every night."

He says, "That guy, I believe he's doing that, stealing my pigs." He says, "I'm going to check on him in the morning, . . . it almost be's daylight when he come back."

So in the morning, he come by the lot where the mules and everybody catching out their team and going to the field. And about sunup, he'd be along there.

And so that particular morning, Old Master, he told his wife, he said, "I'm going to meet old John this morning, coming from coon hunting. I'm going to find out what's in the sacks he has."

So he got along there, and, sure enough, Old Master's standing out there waiting on him.

"Well, John, good morning."

So he says, "Good morning, good morning, Old Boss."

He says, "Well, did you have any luck last night?"

He says, "Well, say, no. Old Master, I didn't have much in this sack. I have one little old possum."

"You have one little old possum. Why, John, my wife have never saw a possum before." Says, "I'm going to call her, and you let her see what a possum looks like."

Oh, no, he know he have a pig in the sack. Now, he don't want to come up with this possum.

He says, "Oh, Old Master. Old Missus don't want to see this old possum. He's all nasty and muddy and like that." Said, "I—in the morning I'll come by and I'll show her another one. See, he look awful. He too muddy and nasty."

He says, "Oh, John. My wife got to see that possum. She long wanted to see a possum."

And so he kept on trying to argue with him, and after a while, Old Master got mad. He says, "Listen. You going to empty that possum out there. Come here, honey, and see a possum."

And so she come running out.

He says, "All right. Empty that possum out there so my wife can see him."

He knowed he had to do something then. He said, "Well, Old Master, all right. I'll empty him out." Said, "I put him in here as a possum, but he's liable to be a little old pig now." [Laughs]

So, Old Master caught up with him that time.

149. The Biggest Liar in the State

SON HOUSE
Mississippi and Syracuse,
New York
Recorded by Harry Oster,
Iowa City, Iowa,
April 24, 1965

And so, another one. Another guy. . . . Deer season was out. And he wasn't supposed to kill deers after the season. And so, this guy—he was hungry, his food was low. He didn't have no meat, or nothing like that. . . . He didn't pay no attention about when the time was out of season, like that, and so he happened to see some deers come to the edge of the woods, and then they'd look at him and they'd run back up in the woods. So he run back in the house, and he got his gun. Told his wife, said, "I seed a couple of deers come to the edge of the wood," say, "I'm going to go out there and kill one of em. We'll have plenty meat then." So he got his gun, and he run back out in the woods, and he tipped and tipped, till he tipped up close enough to see one of the deers. And he shot, and he killed the deer.

So, well, he struggled with him till he got him to the house. And it was a doe. The doe is the female deer. So he killed the doe.

And so, the next day, he decided he would go up in the woods again and look around and see could he see some deer tracks, and figure he could find some of em, where they ranged at. And then, being out there, he didn't take his gun with him. So finally the game warden—he was, he was a white boy—he walked up on him in the woods.

He says, "Good morning. How you doing?"

[Nervously:] "Oh, alright. How you doing, captain?"

And he says, "All right. Well, what are you looking for?"

Say, "Well, uh—" (he didn't have sense enough to know that deer season was out). He says, "I was just looking for a few deer signs?"

He says, "Yeah. Deer signs, eh?"

Yeah, this time. "Yeah, yeah. Yes, sir. Yes, sir."

He says, "When was the last time that you ever killed a deer?"

He says, "Oh, yes, sir. I killed one just yesterday."

He says, "Yesterday?"

"Yes, sir. I killed a big, big doe yesterday."

"No kidding?"

"Yes, sir. I sure did."

He says, "Well, . . . all right then. Now, look." Said, "Do you realize who you talking to?"

Says, "No, sir, captain. I sure don't."

He said, "Well, I am the game warden."

"*Game warden?*"

"Yes."

He says, "Well," he say, "captain, you know who you're talking to?"

Says, "No, I don't know, and I don't care. But I know you violated the law."

He says, "Captain, well I'll tell you who you're talking to." Says, "You is talking to one of the biggest liars in the state." [Laughs]

He got away with it.

150. He'll Have to Swim

SON HOUSE
Mississippi and Syracuse,
New York
Recorded by Harry Oster,
Iowa City, Iowa, April 24, 1965

This particular guy, he got away with his Old Master. And his master was a undertaker. Well, back in those days, when somebody died, the undertaker, they would just lay em out on something they called a cooling board.

And they would [wake] them at home, where they'd pick em up at, and rush em up to the graveyard and bury em. So, this particular day, Old Master let one of his right-hand men off, give him a off day, to have a little pleasure. So he suddenly had a funeral occasion. Somebody died, and they come for him. They come to pick him up, take him to the undertaker. His man was off. He couldn't find him. And so this other guy, he went and got him.

He says, "I know him, he's around. I'll pick him up to go and help me with this, with this burial."

So he went to this guy and called him. Just says, "I want you to help me today." (It's on Sunday.) "See, I've got a funeral occasion." Say, "I want you to help me."

"Yes, sir. All right, sir. I'll go. I ain't got nothing else to do. My work is all done."

He says, "All right, come on. Come on. Let's go."

So they gets they horse. They had two horses then, to put to the old, hearse, they called em, hearses. So they gets the horse, and they went to this particular house, and so he gets the dead man out and then lays him up on the cooling board, they call it. So he puts clothes on him. And then they lift him off, and put him down in the coffin, what they called it at the time. The wooden box. And they put him down in there, and so he thought of something else that he was supposed to do, because he didn't do that much and he had a man hired to do it. He didn't understand too much about it, but he remembered how the other guy did it.

He says, "Oh," say, "wait a minute. There's something else you're supposed to do."

He run his hand in his side pocket, and he just got out a handful of silver money, and he dropped it over in the casket. And this guy, this colored guy, Negro, he watched. He looked at the money.

And so, then . . . he thought of something else he was supposed to get. . . .

So he says, "Oh, wait a minute. I know what it is now, in the kitchen."

So, while he was going to the kitchen, this guy, he looks down on the silver money, on the dead man. He says, "Aw." He gets the silver money and puts it in *his* pocket.

And so, when Old Master come back, he just took the top and put it over, and then he went to screwing the lids down on him, and things, and didn't pay attention—hadn't *missed* the money. He was in such a hurry. So then he said, "Old Master, what is the idea of putting the silver money in the coffin?"

He says, "Aw, I don't know. It's just an old custom going around. They believe that that will pay the fare over the River of Jordan."

He says, "Well, well, well, well."

He says, "Now, what's the matter with you?"

He says, "Well, . . . damn. . . . He'll have to swim, Old Master, cause I got the silver." [Laughs]

. . . Dead man don't need nothing. When you're dead, you're gone.

151. Cold as Hell

SON HOUSE
Mississippi and Syracuse,
New York
Recorded by Harry Oster,
Iowa City, Iowa, April 24, 1965

There's a lot of stories on the preacher. Here's another one about the preacher. He—every time he come to his church—it'd be practically on a Sunday all the time, because, Monday, you know, he have to go to the field and work, you know. And you have to do all of what you're going to do Saturday night and Sunday. And Monday, you have to be in the cotton field. So, in this particular time, this old preacher, he had a certain place with one of the deacons, see, separate deacons to the church, but this particular deacon, he didn't like to stay nowhere at night, but at his house. So he, he stayed all night, that Sunday night. So this is on a Monday morning. And, I imagine, the way it was told, it looked just like it look now. Cloudy and rainy and kind of—well it was colder than it is now. The way it was told.

So this deacon's calves got out, and so they went a-wandering all across the fields, away different places, and so the old man couldn't find the calves. And he says, "Oh, I'm gonna make that boy go and hunt them calves."

So this preacher, at that time, they had the old-time fireplaces, we used to call it. It just consisted about that wide. You put wood on it. So this old preacher got up and had his breakfast and everything. And he was sitting, like this, at the fireplace, sitting all wide-legged, you know, enjoying the fire.

So this boy, this little boy, his daddy told him, he said, "You go and find the calves and don't you come back here until you find em."

[Whispering] It was cold. Boy [bobbing?] across the fields in places, looking to see could he see the calves. So his hands commence aching, they got so cold. Boy give up and got mad too.

Said, "I'm going back home. I don't care what Daddy say." And he went on back home.

The old preacher, he's still sitting at the fire. Warm.

So the boy had to get over in the corner, rubbing his little hands [makes shivering, rubbing sounds], trying to squeeze in, warm his hands.

The old preacher looked up at him. "Son," says, "what's the matter?"

Made the boy mad. [The preacher] *knowed* what was the matter. He could see his hand was aching. Asked him what the matter.

The boy was so mad, he said, "I'm cold as hell. [Laughing] That's what the matter."

[Whispering] Oh, the preacher jumped. "Why, son. You should be shamed of yourself. What do you know about hell? Using that kind of language. You don't know nothing about hell. What do you know about hell [to make] you call this hell?"

He say, "I know plenty about it."

He say, "Well, tell *me* something about it, then, since you know so much, smartie."

He said, "It's just like it is here."

"Well, how is that?"

"You can't get to the fire for the god damn preachers."

[Laughs long and loud]

152. The Preacher and the Bully

LULA DAVIS
Fayetteville, Arkansas
Recorded by Sandy Paton,
Fayetteville, Arkansas, November
1962

This is a story I learned from my husband. He's a Tennessean, so I supposed he learned it up in Tennessee. It's about a . . . corn milling. You know, where you grind corn, and you take your corn to mill. Everybody used to take, on Saturday, a turn of corn to mill. And that was really a meeting place for neighborhood gossips and swapping of tales and telling of stories, and having fights, and everything that's imaginable for the community. It was a community meeting place on Saturday, all day. And there's a new preacher in this community, and he came to mill to get amongst his congregation and talk and visit, and there was a bully that always came every Saturday, always finding someone that he could fight or bully. And he specially had it in for the preachers.

So he walked up to this preacher and said he was going to just beat him up. And the preacher said, "All right," but said, "before I have a fight, I always get down and pray to God. So if you'll excuse me just a moment, I'll pray, and then I'll fight you."

So he got down on his knees and he said, "Lord," says, "you know, the last fight I had, I had to kill the man because he was going to kill men. It was his life or mine. And that Bill Jones, that I had a fight with—that I had to take his life—Lord, I know you understand. And that Sam White, and those other guys over in the other neighborhood, that I had to take their lives. And now, Lord, I'm about to have to take the life of another man, and I want you to forgive me, because it's either him or me."

And when he went to raising up from his prayer, he pulled a long knife—pulled a long knife out of his pocket. . . .

When he went to raise up from the prayer, he pulled a long knife from his pocket, and began singing this song:

> Hark, from the tomb a doleful sound;
> Mine ears attend the cry.
> Ye living men come view the ground
> Where you shall shortly lie.

And when he turned around to see the bully, he only saw a little blot of dust down the road. He was running.

153. Baptists and Presbyterians

JOAN MOSER
Asheville, North Carolina
Recorded by Benjamin A. Botkin,
Battery Park Hotel, Asheville,
North Carolina, January 1949

Like their famous neighbor, Bascom Lamar Lunsford (see story number 179), Artus and Joan Moser were both practitioners and students of the traditional arts of the Appalachians. Artus (1894–1992) was born on the Biltmore estate near Asheville, North Carolina, where his father worked as a forester for the enormously wealthy out-of-state owners, the Vanderbilts of New York. After a youth saturated in the traditional culture of the Appalachians, he began to study and collect the lore of his neighbors, and it has been asserted that he was the first native of the Appalachians to audio-record Appalachian lore. Artus took great interest in fiddle music and folk-tales alike. Although he is best known for his work with folk music, his contributions to folktale research have been substantial; for example, he was the first person to record the Jack Tales of Maud Long (see stories 13–23).

When Benjamin Botkin, then director of the Archive of American Folk Song, visited North Carolina in 1949 to record local traditions for airing on the radio, he interviewed Artus and his 11-year-old daughter Joan.

For her first two jokes, Joan drew upon a topic from which many of her elders would have shied away: the traditional rivalry of the region's Baptists and Presbyterians. The subject has given rise to a great deal of local humor, but in 1949 such jokes were far more typically found in front-porch cir-culation than on radio broadcasts. Joan's brief jokes are told with adult poise and style, although her delivery is a bit more demonstrative and a bit less dry than the typical style of her elders in Buncombe County, North Carolina.

This story is used to illustrate the Presbyterians and, well it goes, once there was a man that went toward this town and went over, asked this man if there's any Presbyterians living around there.

"Well," this man says, "there's an old man living up there on the ridge that sets out traps, and he traps everything that comes around. He gets all those varmints that come around anywhere. And he has all this collection," he says, "back on the back of his barn." He says, "You go back there and look on the back of that barn. If there's any Presbyterians around, their hides'll be in back there, tanning." [Laughter]

Well, this is to illustrate just how holy the Presbyterians are. They're known to be a very holy sect, and this illustrates it. Once there was a farmer, just a common hand. And he went to this church where all these high-hatted, sophis-ticated Presbyterians were. And he went up to the clergyman and preacher and asked him if he couldn't join the church.

"Well," the preacher says, "you go back home next week, and you get down on your knees and you pray, and you ask the Lord if it'd be all right. And you ask him what he thinks of it."

And so the man went home, and he came back next Sunday, and the next Sunday the preacher said, "Well," he says, "did you speak to the Lord about it? What did he say?"

The man said, "Well, the Lord said, if I could get in, I'd be lucky, because He's been trying to get in there for twenty years, and He hasn't gotten in yet."

154. The Devilists' Revival

JOAN MOSER
Asheville, North Carolina
Recorded by Benjamin A. Botkin,
Battery Park Hotel, Asheville,
North Carolina, January 1949

This is a story of the devilists' revival. Now these two white boys thought they'd have a lot of fun, so they went to this Negro revival and they sat there one night and listened to the preacher preaching along, and the preacher kept telling these people, he says, "Now, I wonder how many of you would just stand up to the devil and dare say, 'I am not afraid.' " And he says, "Now, I just wonder how many of you"—and he preached on that the whole night.

And so these two boys went home the next evening, and they got these devil's costumes. And they got up there before the preaching, and went up behind the pulpit, climbed up in the loft in these devil costumes, and got ready to wait till the preacher came in.

Well, here came the preacher, and he started talking on the same topic. He says, "Now, I'll bet you, there's not one out of a hundred of you that'd stand up to the devil, right up to him, and say, 'I am not afraid.' "

And just about that time, these two boys climbed out of the back of this loft, from behind the pulpit and—the preacher couldn't see it, but the people could. The Negro people could, and they were the first one out the door. And here came the preacher, right along behind em, just as fast as he could go, too. And they turned around to him, and one of em said, "Well, I thought you wasn't scared of the devil?"

And the preacher says, "Oh, I ain't a bit scared. I'm just too good to associate with him." [Laughter]

155. Jamie the Mountain Lion

MARGARET CHASE
Orono, Maine
Recorded by Marguerite Chapallaz,
American Dialect Society,
Providence, Rhode Island,
June 26, 1934

Margaret Chase was a young linguistics student when she began working on the American Dialect Society project to sound-record the traditional speech of the northeastern United States. Rather than being turned loose in the field without prior experience, the participants spent time making test recordings in order to get to know and use the equipment properly. Some of the American Folklife Center's most interesting narratives (including those of Mary Celestia Parler [stories 144 and 181]) emerged from these trial sessions.

For her trial interview, Margaret Chase was paired with Margarite Chapallaz, the Breton English woman who would go on to demonstrate her genius for fieldwork through her interviews with Joshua Alley (see stories 62–70).

Mlle. Chapallaz asked Margaret Chase, "On what occasions do you generally tell that story?" Margaret's answer reveals much about the folkways of a small New England college town in the early decades of the twentieth century: "Oh, I haven't told that story for quite a long time now. It was first told to me by a Latin professor on a Sunday school picnic a good many years ago. . . . Sunday school picnics used to be a lot of fun, but I'm not sure they would be now or not, because we used to have races and all sorts of games, and then we'd have a meal, mostly baked beans and ice cream cones, as many ice cream cones as you could eat. All the children in the town went to them, went up on the Standpipe Hill as we called it, out on the woods, . . . back of the town hall."

Margaret Chase affects a baritone voice and a broad New England accent when she impersonates the farmer. Her delivery throughout is appropriately dry and deadpan; once or twice, she seems to be struggling to suppress a laugh.

Seems that a zoo lost its lion, so the manager of the zoo was around going through the countryside, stopping at all the farm houses where he thought it might be likely they might keep a pet lion to try to find one to take the place of the one he had lost. So he heard about an old farmer who had a pet lion named Jamie, and he thought he'd call on this farmer and see if he could buy the lion.

So he knocked at the door and the farmer came, and he said, "I hear you have a lion, and I thought perhaps I might buy it for my zoo."

The farmer said, "Well, stranger, you come in and sit down and we'll talk it over. I'll tell you how it is. I found this lion roaming around, and I took him in. He looked as if he didn't have any home, so I said, 'Jamie, you can live with us for a while.'

"The next day, my son little Paul came to bring me my lunch. I'd been working out in the fields. It came time for little Paul to bring me my lunch, and little Paul didn't come, little Paul didn't come. Finally, I went up to the house and, stranger, Jamie had et little Paul. I was so mad I took my trusty gun, and I says, 'No, I can't kill Jamie, even though he has et little Paul.'

"Next day, stranger, I was working in the fields, and it came time for little John to bring me my lunch. Little John didn't come, and little John didn't come. Finally, I went up to the house, and, stranger, Jamie had et little John. I was so mad, I took my trusty gun and I says, 'No, I can't kill Jamie, even if he *has* et little Paul and little John.'

"The next day, stranger, I was working in the fields, and it came time for little Mary to bring me my lunch, and little Mary didn't come, and little Mary didn't come. Finally, I went up to the house and, stranger, Jamie *had et* little Mary, and I was so mad, I took my trusty gun, and I said, 'No, I can't kill Jamie, even if he has et little Paul and little John and little Mary.'

"Next day, stranger, I was working in the field and it came time for my wife to bring me my lunch. My wife didn't come and my wife didn't come. Finally, stranger, I went up to the house, and *Jamie* had et my wife. I was so mad, I took my trusty gun, and I said, 'No, I can't kill Jamie, even though he has et little Paul and little John, little Mary, and my wife.'

"So you see, stranger, I can't let Jamie go. He's sort of et his way into the family."

Well, I was afraid I wasn't going to be able to remember that story.

156. Pedro de Urdemalas and the Plums

ARTHUR L. CAMPA
El Paso, Texas, and Denver, Colorado
Recorded by Benjamin A. Botkin, Denver, Colorado, July 25, 1950

The following seven tales were collected by Benjamin A. Botkin from two Colorado academics with deep traditional roots. Arthur L. Campa was a professor in the Modern Language Department of the University of Denver when Botkin interviewed him. Campa said that his "interest in folklore [had] led him into the Southwest and into Denver eventually." But the Southwest was also the precise site of Campa's earliest folkloric memories, as he explains in introducing the following tale.

Well, back about the time of the First World War, when I was living on my grandmother's ranch, below El Paso, at harvest time, and during the alfalfa season, there was a lot of men used to come down to work. A lot of em were from Mexico or from the surrounding farms. And I usually was sent out by my uncle to work with one of the groups, so that they wouldn't loaf too much, and these fellows would sometimes get the best of me by means of flattery.

The two things they wanted to do was to get under a cottonwood tree and rest, and, secondly, they wanted to eat the watermelons. We had, in those days, a great deal of watermelons. So, they'd call me over and they'd say, "Look here, *padroncito*, if you want a real story, we'll tell you one, but my throat's awfully dry. Why don't you get a watermelon and we'll get underneath that cottonwood tree, and I'll tell you a story."

Well, I immediately made a beeline for the patch and picked me out a nice, ripe watermelon, and bring it in. One of the men would start cutting it lengthwise, the way they cut em in the patch, and we'd start out. Well, that's how I got a lot of these stories about Pedro de Urdemalas, the Trickster.

Well, the stories were of the variety that sometimes a young boy shouldn't have been listening to, but for the most part they were picaresque stories. And it was there that I first came across Pedro de Urdemalas.

Pedro, on one occasion, was supposed to be sent by his master to the orchard to pick a particular type of fruit that he was very fond of. The plum. And so his master told him, "Now take this dish and there must be a few at least that are ripe."

So Pedro went back there. He looked around on the ground and on the tree.

All he could find was about a dozen or so. So on the way back he looked at em, so nice and luscious, and he goes, "He won't miss one," so he'd reach over and eat one. Throw away the seed. And he kept eating one after another, and when he got past the first eight, why, he says, "Well, I'll have to do something when I get there, so I better eat most of em." He ate em all but one.

He got up to the door, and knocked. The fellow said, "Come in."

"Why," he says, "here are the plums."

He looked at the one plum in the dish, and he said, "How many plums were there?"

"Well, there were fifteen," he said.

"Well, what happened to the other fourteen?"

He says, "Well, I ate em."

"How?"

"Oh, this way?" he says. He picked up the last one and he ate it.

157. Pedro de Urdemalas and the Pigs

ARTHUR L. CAMPA
El Paso, Texas, and Denver, Colorado
Recorded by Benjamin A. Botkin, Denver, Colorado, July 25, 1950

Another time he was sent out to take care of some pigs. And there's one thing that Pedro never liked to do, was to work. In particular to take care of pigs. So when he got out into the forest where the pigs were supposed to be eating acorns and whatnot, invariably the pigs would get into a slough and he'd have to pull em out.

So one day on his way home, he stopped at the slaughterhouse. He picked up a lot of ears and tails. He went back to the slough and he said, "Well, now, I can get rid of this, and at the same time, I can make a little money."

So he went around, and he would stick two ears and a tail at the proportionate distance, and the last tail he took some wire and he wired it down to a root.

Just about that time the welfare man of the county was coming by, and he was supposed to be an avaricious sort of a fellow, so he looked over and he saw Pedro in the middle of the slough trying to pull a pig up by the tail.

So went over and he says, "What are you doing, Pedro?"

He says, "I'm trying to pull this blankety-blank pig—they always get into

Folklorist Benjamin Botkin (head of the Archive of American Folk Song, 1942–1945, and collector of stories 153, 154, 156–162, and 179) tending his Victory Garden, Washington, D.C., June 1943. (Photo by Joseph A. Horne, Library of Congress)

the slough, and I can't get em out. For a nickel, I'd sell em, get rid of the whole batch."

This man thought it over and he says, "Pedro, How much would you take for those pigs?"

"If anyone would take em just the way they are now, I'd sell em for a dollar apiece."

The man said, "Alright." He took out his pocket book and says, "How many are there?"

"Well, just count em."

He counted ten pigs and [Pedro] says, "You can have em."

The man handed him a ten-dollar bill.

Pedro said, "Alright. I wash my hands of the whole batch of em. You can have em."

So he left him with his pigs in the slough. And when he pulled the first one, he pulled on the wrong tail, and he sat down in the mud.

158. The *Indito* and His Wives

ARTHUR L. CAMPA
El Paso, Texas, and Denver, Colorado
Recorded by Benjamin A. Botkin, Denver, Colorado, July 25, 1950

Pedro de Urdemalas is a sort of every-*campesino*, a little guy whose mental quickness and resourcefulness allow him to hold his own against the powerful people who try to take advantage of him. Another, not entirely unrelated focal figure in the Spanish-language jokes of the U.S.-Mexican border was the *indito,* the "little Indian." Like Pedro, the *indito* represents the underdog, and, like Pedro, he tends to triumph over his more powerful foes. But in contrast to Pedro's, many of the *indito*'s victories are the simple result of his insisting on adhering to the rules and understandings his own Native American culture, even when those rules seem senseless to the powerful. One can read into the *indito*'s "accidental" victories an implicit critique of the dominant Anglo-American culture. If the *indito*'s codes of behavior are silly and inferior, why does he make the Anglos look silly in these jokes?

Well these Mexicans, as you know, are quite fond of using the diminutive. Some say that it's because of the preponderance of Andalusians that came to Mexico. The fact of the matter is that the Mexicans use the "*ito*," or diminutive ending, to most anything. For a wait—*un gratito*, "a little while." They eat a *bocacito*, "a mouthful." And everything is *ito*. And whenever they wish to refer to any foreigner, whom they particularly like, and call them, they have some sort of a nickname like they used to have for the Americans in the days of "lesser relations"—they referred to them as *gringos*. Today it's typical to see a couple of Mexicans standing on the corner watching a good-looking American girl who probably is taller than they are, and they refer to her as *una gringita*, and they will do the same thing with the Indians. If they tell a story about an Indian, it's not just an *indio*, because *un indio* would be a type of Indian that you would find in a story about war and massacre and so on. Usually it's *un indito*. . . . Then you know the story's going to be about a friendly Indian.

Well these Indian stories are all over the Southwest. And particularly in northern Mexico. Well, in New Mexico, where they follow the same practice in Spanish, they tell the story about *un indito* on the reservation. Apparently this one was a Navajo. And in the usual custom of the Navajo, this fellow called Hosteen had taken on a second wife when the first one got a little older.

So the agent came over and he says, "Look here, Hosteen, you can't do this sort of thing anymore. See, the Great White Father up in Washington doesn't approve of such practices. You take one wife and stay with her until either one of you two dies. And that's the way you should do it. One wife to do the cooking for you, take care of the sheep, shear them, so on."

Well, Hosteen sat there and listened very attentively to what the agent had to say. Never disagreed with him. Every now and then he would grunt and say, "Oof," meaning "yes, yes." Finally, when he came to the end, he said, well, the agent thought he had convinced Hosteen that he was going to mend his ways now.

When he got through, however, Hosteen simply looked at him and he said, "You tell her."

159. The *Indito* and the Banker

ARTHUR L. CAMPA
El Paso, Texas, and Denver, Colorado
Recorded by Benjamin A. Botkin, Denver, Colorado, July 25, 1950

There was another story that was sometimes attributed to the former chief of the Navajo (it's another Navajo story) . . . and, oh, a number of others. It's pretty widespread now.

It seems that this *indito* went to borrow money at one of the local banks, and when he got there, they told him, yes, that was the right place. He could borrow money. He'd heard that you could go to the bank and get money.

He spoke to one of em, and "One of the things you need to do," he says, "is put up a little collateral."

Well, that was a new thing for him. "Collateral. What's that?" he said.

"Well," he says, "you take some property that you own and you put it over here, and then we give you this money, and then in case you can't pay this money, well, this collateral here answers for the money you borrowed."

Well, that made sense to the *indito*, so he said, "All right."

"What kind of property do you have?" the clerk said.

"Well," he says, "I got horses."

"Well, how many horses have you got?"

"Well," he says, "I've got five hundred, six hundred."

"Well, that's good. What can we say? Oh, let's say ten dollars a horse, huh? We'll put aside so many horses."

So he did, and he put up the necessary number of horses to borrow the money. So they gave him some money, which he wanted in silver. He went away. . . . And a year later he come back, and he had two bags of money. In one, he had counted out the money he had borrowed from the bank. He counted it out. Sure enough, everything was there, including the interest.

"Well, that's fine," he says. "Very fine. Glad to see, to do business with such an honest man."

Well, the Indian never said anything. He started out, picked up his other bag. The man said, "Well, now, what do you have in that other bag there?"

"Okay, that's some more money. I sold the wool of my sheep."

"Well, look," he said, "why don't you leave the money here? You won't have to be carrying it around. You might lose it. Somebody might steal it. Leave her here, and if you need it, you come out and take out a little at a time. That'd be safe and it'd be much more convenient for you."

Well, that again sounded very logical to him, so he took his bag and put it on the counter, and before the man could reach over to grab it, he said, "You got horses too?"

160. Unwatering the Mine

LEVETTE JAY DAVIDSON
Denver, Colorado
Recorded by Benjamin A. Botkin,
Denver, Colorado, July 25, 1950

Like Arthur L. Campa (teller of stories 156–159), Levette Jay Davidson was both a practitioner and a student of folk culture. In the following three tales, Davidson shares western hard-rock mining lore with folklorist Benjamin A. Botkin.

There are lots of stories in the mining regions of Colorado about the early days when of course metal mining was the best occupation to follow. There were a number of local characters concerning whom these stories were told. One of them was Gassy Thompson, up around Empire. He also was known in Central City and Black Hawk and over at Georgetown. One of the stories I like best about Gassy is the one telling how he a unwatered a mine.

If a mining shaft is left unworked for a while, very likely water will accumulate for maybe several hundred feet. And if the mine is to be operated again, then it has to be pumped out. If done by hand, this of course takes quite a long time and needs a lot of backbreaking work.

Gassy took a contract to unwater this particular mine shaft, and then regretted that he had signed up for so much work. He had a look over the place, found that there was a lot of water in the mine, so he sat down to think. Noticed a stray dog running along. He hurled a rock at it, knocked it over, went over and killed the dog. Then, with a brilliant idea back of his actions, he dragged it to the mouth of the shaft, found an old hat and coat that had been abandoned nearby, and daubed it over with some of the dog's blood. Then he tied a rock around the dog's neck and dropped it in and heard it hit the water and splash and go to the bottom.

His next step was to go down to Central City and sort of circulate through the bars, spreading word that he suspected foul play up at that mine, that there was evidence that there had been a struggle, and blood was around there. He didn't know just what had happened. It looked bad to him.

Before long the boys went up to investigate. And they found, sure enough, evidences that aroused their suspicions. So they went back down to the town and got the sheriff. He in turn organized a posse and they borrowed some pumps from the county commissioners, and they went up to that mine. The boys set to it . . . and before long they had pumped the shaft dry. Sure enough, they found the body. But it was of the dog.

Meantime, Gassy of course had skipped the country. He did come back a little later to collect the wages from the owners of the shaft for the quickest and most efficient job of unwatering a mine that had been done for some time.

Well, I guess he had a reputation based on this and other tricky deeds, so that before long no one would trust him. But he managed to get along by his wit and by his cleverness.

161. Tom the Burro

LEVETTE JAY DAVIDSON
Denver, Colorado
Recorded by Benjamin A. Botkin,
Denver, Colorado, July 25, 1950

Another body of Rocky Mountain stories is that great body of them concerned with burros. The Rocky Mountain burro—or as he's sometimes called, because of his musical voice, Rocky Mountain canary—was an essential feature of the early days in prospecting, also in working mines, even after the mines had gone underground.

Many stories are told of the burros that were stubborn or the burros that were faithful, or the burros that were intelligent. One I like is concerning a well-trained burro called Old Tom, that one prospector trusted implicitly. He used to ride along through the gulches, a-going from one good prospect hole to another, to work. One day he went to sleep because it was a warm afternoon. Seemed the burro was dozing off too. The burro kept on trotting along the path until it came to the edge of a great precipice, and the rocks weakening, the burro went over—and, of course, the prospector on top.

As they fell, both came to, and the prospector was quick enough to realize that if they landed, they'd both be dead. As they were falling—one hundred, two hundred, three hundred, four hundred feet—the prospector had a little chance to think it over, and so he—when they got about fifty feet from the ground—called, "Whoa!" And Old Tom, just too good trained, didn't do a thing but stop. Short. And then the prospector just kind of eased himself off and lowered down and finally he and Old Tom both were there, unhurt, on the bottom of the canyon. All he had to do then was to mount Old Tom. The two of them proceeded on their way. All because the prospector properly trained his burro to obey.

162. Burros and Beechnut

LEVETTE JAY DAVIDSON
Denver, Colorado
Recorded by Benjamin A. Botkin,
Denver, Colorado, July 25, 1950

Course, not all burros are that well trained. Some of em are stubborn. In one of the mines, there was a trammer who found a new burro [balking]. Wouldn't pull the ore cars. So, wondering what he'd do next, he reached in his pocket and pulled out a package of chawing tobacco. And after taking a chaw himself, he noticed that his burro wrinkled up its nose and seemed interested. He reached out the package of Beechnut to his burro. Burro took him about twenty cents worth in one big chew and with a smile on its face set out off to work and worked the day uncomplaining.

So this trammer had to buy a lot of chawing tobacco, but he never had any trouble getting work out of that burro.

One time, though, this trammer decided to change jobs. He went over to a new mine and was getting along fine when along came the boss from the old mine. Said, "Look here. You've got a right to change your job if you want to. But you haven't earned the right to take away your tramming tricks. How on earth did you get that burro to work?"

And, of course, the trammer said, "Well, I'll tell you. It ain't no secret now. But I want to advise you: that burro will do anything you ask if you just give him chawing tobacco. But be sure and get Beechnut. It ain't Horseshoe, and it ain't Star, it's Beechnut that does it."

163. Willie and the Devil

GAINES KILGORE
Wise, Virginia
Recorded by Richard Chase,
Wise County, Virginia, January
28, 1950

In the following two tales, Blue Ridge mountaineer Gaines Kilgore entertains Richard Chase (both are introduced in the headnote to story 143). Kilgore had learned "Willie and the Devil," an account of a young man who outsmarts a dull-witted Satan, from his father. Chase, who had earlier published one of Kilgore's tales in a collection titled *The Jack Tales* (1943), was particularly interested in a boy-hero named Jack and he had apparently begun to think that Jack should be the generic name for all Appalachian folktale heroes. Chase wondered why the hero of Kilgore's tale was named Willie instead of Jack. Chase asked Kilgore, "What was your father's name?" Kilgore answered, "William, 'Little William.' There was three [Williams] right around here, and he always called himself Little William." Chase then asked, "Is that why he named [the hero] Willie instead of Jack?" Kilgore answered in an indifferent tone, "I guess it was."

Well, the devil tried so hard. They'd been into so many things together to outdo Willie.

[Richard Chase: Well, the first time was it—?]

Well, there were plenty of different times that he had tried to outdo Willie. He never could outdo him in any way. He decided that they would start farming. Maybe he could outdo him there.

So, the first year, they put out potatoes. Fifty-fifty with em. And at the end of the potato crop, the devil came to Willie and said, "Now, what are you going to take? The tops or what grows in the ground?"

Willie said, "Well, I'll take what grows in the ground. You can have the tops."

So Willie got all the potatoes. And the devil got the tops. Barely anything, you know. . . . [Laughter]

Well, it went on till next year. The devil said, "We're not planting any more potatoes. I got beat so bad on that crop. We'll plant corn this year."

Law, they just put acres and acres of corn out, you know.

The devil said, "Well, I'll take my choice this year. I'll take what grows under the ground." So he's taken the corn roots, and Will got to take all the corn. . . . So [the devil] got beat again.

"Well," he said, "I'm tired of that foolishness. I'm not farming any more. I know what I'll do from now on." He said, "We'll start raising hogs. And I know we can have a nice crop."

So they bought a good many root hogs, you know. They had quite a few of em. And they had so many, and neither one of em couldn't count, when they got ready to divide em up. Neither one couldn't count to one hundred, even. They'd never been to school any, no nothing like that. Hadn't any education. And they drave em all in to a big field. Big boundary. The devil figured that he was so much bigger man than Willie that he knowed he'd take all advantage of him there. He said, "Ah, we'll get over in there, and throw the hogs out, and ever which one catches the most and throws em out, why, can have em."

So Willie agreed to that, you know. Right quick.

"All right," he said, "Devil. Let's get over in the field and start throwing em out." There's a big old high fence they had to throw em up over. They got in there, and the old devil, he was a-putting about four and five out to Willie's one. Willie seen that he was taking all the advantage on earth of his [size]. And he wasn't that strong. Couldn't throw so many out.

So after they got all the hogs throwed out—they'd throwed the last one over—the devil came to Willie and says, "Willie," he says, "how many did you throw out?"

"Well," he said, "I don't know exactly how many. How many did you?"

He said, "I don't know either."

Willie said, "One little thing I noticed. That every hog I threw out, I give its tail a little twirl." And they got to looking at all the hogs, and they all had their tails twirled, so Willie got the hogs." [Laughter]

That was the end of that.

164. Old One-Eye

GAINES KILGORE
Wise, Virginia
Recorded by Richard Chase,
Wise County, Virginia, 1950

Richard Chase: Was it "Old One-Eye" you said you knew?]
[Laughing] Oh, yeah. The "Old One-Eye." I don't know much of that now.

Now, that was an old widow woman just lived out by herself. In a little old log house, with an old chimney built on the outside—an old clay chimney. And she was a great woman to fish. And a river run, ran along close to the house, near the house, and she'd mostly fish for her living. . . .

And so . . . this old lady, she went a-fishing one day, and she happened to catch a fish, and a hook went through its eye and jabbed its eye out. Well, this old lady had quite a bit of money you know, and they was an old one-eyed neighbor, lived right closer. And intended on robbing her that night, and he had slipped and got down the chimney, part of the way, aiming to come on down and rob the old lady. Take what money she had.

She was sitting there. And she'd hang her fish up near the chimney and she happened to be sitting there, looking on at the old fish. And she said, "All right, Old One-Eyed Feller," says, "just hang right there," says, "I'll have you in the morning for breakfast." [Laughter]

And she never heard such scrambling in the world. And the old guy heard her up the chimney, you know, and he got scrambling out of there.

165. J. Golden Kimball in His Native Language

HECTOR LEE
Chico, California
Recorded by Hector Lee,
Chico State College, ca. 1952

These tales are extracted from a public performance presented by folklorist Hector Lee to a highly amused audience. In the course of his talk, Lee told more than thirty anecdotes, all centered on J. Golden Kimball, a greatly esteemed figure in the Mormon community during the early decades of the twentieth century and a comic legend to the present day. As Hector Lee explains in introducing his tales, "In the history of the Church of Jesus Christ of Latter Day Saints, more commonly known as the Mormon Church, one of the most interesting of the early-day characters of the second generation was J. Golden Kimball. He was born in 1853 and died in 1938 at the age of eighty-five. He was the son of . . . one of the twelve apostles and Brigham Young's First Counselor. J. Golden Kimball was six feet, three inches tall . . . and as thin as a toothpick, and he had a high voice to match his figure."

Much of the comic power of Lee's performances comes from his skill in mimicking J. Golden's high, thin, quavering voice. In nearly all the tales, a quotation attributed to J. Golden provides the punchline. The last words of the tale frequently contained oaths that most twenty-first-century readers would consider mild, but that far exceeded the limits of the Mormon Church, which had condemned such speech in an official Manifesto on Swearing. The tension between J. Golden's dignified status in the Church and his pronouncedly earthy vocabulary provides the fuel for humor in these tales. In one of Hector Lee's anecdotes, J. Golden described his penchant for swearing as a holdover from a youth spent on the range: "I never intend to cuss when I get up to speak. . . . But those words just come out. They're left over from my cowboy days. They used to be my native language. I can assure you that they come from a far larger vocabulary."

The first three of the six anecdotes below feature J. Golden's strong language; the second three present his characteristically frank observations on love and sex. In the sixth and longest of the tales, Hector Lee not only mimics the thin, high-pitched voice of the Mormon patriarch but also presents his interpretation of Kimball's idea of a Scandinavian accent, as all of Brother Jorgensen's speeches are delivered in a sing-song lilt.

The stories that I'm going to tell now are being told throughout the Mormon country by those who knew him and loved him. Most of these stories were collected from oral tradition and were told by Ranch Kimball, his nephew, and Attorney Shirley P. Jones and Attorney Jesse Budge, and others. . . .

He was always getting into trouble because of his swearing. And he would refer to it quite often in his sermons. "Once, when we were hauling some of those temple logs to the sawmill, I was driving the oxen. And those oxen, dumb as they were, knew that I was driving them. And they lagged behind. They even turned around and looked at me. I couldn't make em go. Well, I spoke respectable for a time. But that didn't do any good. So I began to cuss. It was after the Manifesto on Swearing, but I was mad, and I had to turn loose. And, boy, how I did cuss. Did them oxen sit up and take notice. They got right down to business. But then, you see, they were church oxen, and they understood the language."

One Sunday evening he was all dressed up, ready to go to church. He had on his finest long black coat and silk shirt and his tall silk hat, and he was very handsome and well dressed. Just as he was about to leave for church, he discovered that someone had not fed the calf. So he took the bucket of fresh, warm milk, the sudsy milk, and, in all his finery, he went out to the corral and fed the calf. And the calf came up and dived into the bucket very hungrily and put its nose clear in under the foam, and got a mouthful. And then the calf raised his head and shook his head, and shook milk foam all over the good brother.

He said, "If I wasn't a member of the church, if I wasn't trying to foreswear swearing, if I wasn't a good [brother] in the priesthood, if I couldn't control my temper, I'd take your *goddamn head and push it through the bottom of this bucket. . . .*"

He was called upon quite often to preach funeral sermons. And one story tells of how he went to Idaho to preach the sermon of a friend of his, a Mr. Johnson who he had been informed had died. And he was a little late arriving on the train. And the service was progressing when he reached the church. So he rushed in the backdoor and went up on the platform among the dignitaries until it was his turn to speak. Then he went down, towered over the pulpit, and looked down over the coffin where the man was laid out below, and he began to tell of the fine character of Brother John, what a fine man he was, and how good he was to his family, and how faithful he was in the church. Then he looked down, and sitting on the fifth row in the audience was the very Brother John he was talking about. Well, he stopped right in the middle of a sentence and he turned around to the bishop, and he said, "Hey, Bishop—who the hell is dead around here, anyway?"

During the course of one of his sermons, he was addressing young people. He said, "I'm reminded that this is the month of June and that's the mating time. Now, I suppose, some of you young folks will be getting hitched up. Well, I just want to warn you not to expect too damn much of each other, and then maybe you won't be disappointed. Now, when I got married, I thought I was marrying an angel. And there are many time since I wish to hell I had."

Another time he was advising em on how to select a bride. He said, "Some select a girl because she has pretty eyes. Some because she has pretty hair. I know a man who chose a girl because she could sing. He married her. And the next morning, when he saw her without any paint or powder on, he saw part of her hair on the dresser, and he looked at her and he said, 'Sing, for hell's sake, sing!'"

A little more on the marriage situation. He happened to be down in Sanpete County, and there was an ecclesiastical court about to be held. One of the good brethren there was accused of adultery. It seemed that he had been a little too friendly with Sister Petersen while Brother Petersen was away on his mission. And the bishop was examining Brother Jorgensen, and trying to get him to confess. This was a very serious offense, and the penalty would be excommunication.

And the bishop said, "Now, Brother Jorgensen, it's been established that you were unduly attentive to Sister Petersen while her husband was away on his mission."

"Ya, Biskop, dat is true dat I have been, but it was on a mission, and I tink it is right for us to take care of the folks at home and I just do my Christian duty. And dat is all right. I do nothing wrong."

"Well," the bishop said, "Brother Jorgensen, it's been shown that you've been seen around her house all hours of the day and night, and even on one occasion you were seen to leave the house at five or six o'clock in the morning. Obviously, you had been there all night. Now, what about that?"

"Vell, now, Biskop, dat's all right too. I do all the things that a good brother should do for a neighbor. And I do the chores, and it takes a long time, some time, to do da chores. And maybe it do take all night. But dat's all right. I have do nothing wrong with dat. I just try to do my duty."

"Well," the bishop said, "you know, it's been testified that you were—somebody was passing by the window and looked in and saw you in bed with Sister Petersen. Now, how do you explain that?"

"Vell, Biskop, now it's like dis. I do not deny that maybe I have been seen in bed with Sister Petersen, but I vant to say right here and now dat I have done nothing wrong, and I am not guilty of the thing which you accuse me of."

And just about then Brother Golden unwrapped his legs and stretched. And he said, "I move that we excommunicate the Brother. It is obvious that he does not have the seed of Israel in him."

166. Counting the Wrong Fish

JOHN PERSONS
Iowa County, Wisconsin
Recorded by Helene Stratman-Thomas,
Madison, Wisconsin, August 2, 1946

Much like most of the collectors whose recordings are featured in this book, Helene Stratman-Thomas (1896–1973) was interested primarily in folksong. Unlike most of the others, however, Stratman-Thomas was interested in collecting not only from Anglo-Americans, but also from the many diverse cultures so richly represented in her native Wisconsin. With German and Cornish family roots, Stratman-Thomas had grown up in the southwestern corner of the state, within easy reach of rich strains of non-Anglo tradition.

After receiving her master's degree in Music from the University of Wisconsin, Stratman-Thomas joined its faculty, and her childhood exposure to folk tradition and her professional skills as a music scholar began to mesh in unexpected ways. Folklorist James P. Leary writes, "In 1939 Professor Leland Coon of the University's music department sought funding from the Library of Congress to document the state's folk music, ultimately tendering the project to Helene Stratman-Thomas. Neither folk nor folklorist, she warmed to the task."

Leary continues: "State and federally sponsored folksong collecting flourished as never before just prior to World War II as fieldworkers labored for the Farm Security Administration, the Works Progress Administration, and the Library of Congress. Guided by tenets of populism and pluralism, these agencies and their workers extended previous documentary emphases on rural English-speaking blacks and whites to include peoples whose first tongue was 'foreign.' And so in the summers of 1940, 1941, and 1942, Helene Stratman-Thomas and a shifting trio of recording engineers visited forty-one counties in Wisconsin where more than 150 individual and group performers—representing over thirty Euro-, Native, and African American traditions in nearly as many languages—regaled them with over seven hundred secular songs, sacred hymns, and instrumental dance tunes. Her efforts placed Wisconsin alongside California, Florida, Michigan, and Texas as the first states to document a broad range of non-Anglophone musical traditions."

Stratman-Thomas was still exercising her commitment to diversity in 1946, when she recorded the following tale from Cornishman John Persons. James P. Leary summarizes our meager knowledge of the performer: "Born in 1859, probably in a heavily Cornish mining community in Iowa County, Wisconsin, Persons contributed a number of Cornish Christmas carols" to Stratman-Thomas's folksong survey. The narrator was thus about 87 years old when he performed his well-crafted tale, which draws upon two traits stereotypically ascribed to Cornish Americans: the name "Jack" (Cornish Americans are often called "Cousin Jacks" in the northern Midwest) and a penchant to feign knowledge rather than admit ignorance.

One of the characteristics of a Cornishman is the fact that he doesn't admit he doesn't know everything that you're talking about and has no knowledge of it, or that he can't understand or figure out anything that you're talking about.

And there was a couple young fellows that were working in the mine that decided they wanted to be captains in the mine. In order to be a captain, you must have a little education, to be able to keep time and figure some small sums.

So they decided to go to night school. And after having attended for some time, they met on the street, and one said to the other, he said, "Jack, how are you coming along with the schooling?"

"Oh, tolerably well, thank you. How are you?"

"Well, pretty well. Only one thing: I can't understand the problems."

"Huh! They're as easy as pie for me."

"Well, then. I'll give you one."

"What is it?"

"Well, here are eleven pounds of mackerel, eleven cents a pound. What'll it come to?"

"Wait a minute, I'll have it for ye." And he takes a little pencil and paper to figure, but he couldn't do it. And he says, "Jack, give me that problem once more, will you?"

"Eleven pounds of mackerel, eleven cents a pound."

"I'll have em in a minute. [Pause.] Now give me that problem exactly right. I want to get em for ye."

"Well," he said, "eleven pound mackerel, eleven cents a pound."

"Mackerel, eh, mackerel? Well, no wonder I couldn't get it right. Here all the time I been figuring eleven pound herring."

167. I Love Ewe

ARCHER GILFILLAN
Mitchell, South Dakota
Recorded by Nicholas Ray,
Mitchell, South Dakota, 1939

Wherever sheep appear in a community's cultural landscape, one of the most widespread themes of jokes is the amorous bond that develops between the herder and his female ovine charges. When interviewed by Nicholas Ray in 1939, Archer Gilfillan had many serious things to say about daily details and harsh conditions of the sheepherder's work, but he also shared numerous jokes, all on the topic of carnal relations between the herder and his ewe.

Gilfillan, an easterner by birth, told Ray, "I started herding as the line of least resistance. I had left school and come out to the West to make my fortune. My father gave me my patrimony, and I invested it all in land and a bunch of sheep. Not knowing anything about the sheep business, I lost every cent of the money. I returned to school again for three years and again quit school and came out to the western country. Since I had to do something, I took the first job that came to hand, . . . sheepherding, and I followed that for seventeen years. . . . For about ten years I worked for sixty dollars a year and board. I started at forty, went to sixty, and for one alarming month, I got one hundred and twenty-five."

When anyone meets a sheepherder for the first time, there is one story that he will inevitably try to tell him. It is the taxidermist story. I managed to laugh the first hundred and fifty times I heard this story, but after that it was more difficult.

A stranger entered a town swinging a dead eagle by the legs. He asked the first man he met where he could find a taxidermist.

The man said, "A taxidermist? What's that?"

"Why," he said, "a man who mounts animals."

"Oh," the native answered, "you mean a sheepherder. There's one of them lives in the next block."

[Laughter]

Another story deals with a herder who took his regular vacation of two weeks as herders are apt to do annually. During this time, of course, a substitute herder had to take over the bunch.

This substitute saw a ewe with a ribbon around her neck. He didn't see any particular use in having the ribbon there, and he kind of thought it spoiled the looks of the bunch, so he caught the ewe and cut the ribbon off. After two weeks, the regular herder returned and took over the bunch. And two weeks later, he met the substitute, and asked him, "Why did you take the ribbon off that ewe?"

"Well," the substitute replied, "I didn't see any particular use in having it there. And I kind of thought it spoiled the looks of the bunch. What about it?"

"Well," the herder answered, "I had to fuck the whole bunch to find that one ewe."

There's another story of a herder—a cowboy rather, who was riding across the prairie, and he was pretty dry, and he stopped at a herder's wagon to get a drink of water. The herder was a middle-aged man and pleasant to talk to, and they got pretty well acquainted. Finally, the cowboy said, "You know, I've heard that when herders have been away from town quite awhile, and the pressure gets a little strong, sometimes they have relations with an old ewe. How bout it?"

The old herder thought a moment, and then he said, "Yes, that occasionally happens."

"Yes," the cowboy answered, "I know it happens, but I never expected to hear a herder admit it."

"Yes," replied the herder, "that occasionally happens, and that's where all these half-assed cowboys come from."

[Laughter]

One time I made a trip to a wool meeting in company with a group of wool growers and wool buyers whom I had met several times previously. And I made the rash statement that I would buy the drinks for anybody who could tell me a sheep story that I hadn't heard. I lost twice.

The first one, story, concerned two herders who were sitting in a show in New York. It was a burlesque show with a strip act. Finally, one herder nudged the other and said, "See. It's in front."

A second story concerned a couple of herders who were entertaining a couple of ewes. One of them looked over to the other and said, "You know, I've heard that they're doing this to women in Boston now."

[Laughter]

168. Sports as Markers

ARCHER GILFILLAN
Mitchell, South Dakota
Recorded by Nicholas Ray,
South Dakota, 1939

"Sport" and "marker" both refer to the rare black sheep found among the prairie herds. Sport (as in "sport of nature") alludes to the genetic fact that black offspring appear unexpectedly in the litters of their white parents. Archer Gilfillan refers, in his characteristically dry way, to a playful explanation for the occurrence of the sports:

"The so-called markers in a bunch of sheep are the black ones that occur as sports in the bunch, on the average of about one to the hundred. There is a tradition in all sheep countries that black lambs are the direct results of the efforts of the herder and if the required number of black lambs doesn't show up in the bunch some spring, the sheepman is apt to accuse the herder of losing his power. One spring it happened that the first lamb that was born had the marks of a perfect pair of glasses on him. I had to stand a good deal of kidding at the ranch and I told them that if the lamb hadn't died naturally I would have killed him anyway."

The black sheep serve a practical purpose as "markers," helping the herder get a rough count of his flock and, in their absence, warning him that part of the bunch has strayed: "If the herder has all his markers present, it still doesn't mean that he has all his sheep present, but that is the only thing that he has to go by. But if one of his markers is missing, he is . . . certain that a small bunch is cut off. . . . The more markers he has in the bunch, the better track he can keep of them. But it works the other way. If he has a great number of markers, they are hard to count and the chances are that he won't get an accurate count. About one to the hundred is the most satisfactory number."

There was a white sheepherder once who went to work for the Emperor of Ethiopia. In due course of time, a white child made its appearance in the harem. The emperor was quite disturbed, and since the sheepherder was the only white man around, he called on him for an explanation. The herder said, "Your majesty, that's just a sport. It happens in any kind of offspring. For instance, you take that black lamb out there."

"Wait a minute," interrupted the Emperor of Ethiopia hastily, "don't say anything about that black lamb and I won't say anything about the white child."

169. John and Old Mistress's Nightgown

JOHN DAVIS
Frederica, Georgia
Recorded by Zora Neale Hurston,
Frederica, Georgia, 1935

Zora Neale Hurston was one of the twentieth century's greatest novelists and one of the century's greatest folklorists as well. Early in life she was captivated both by literary versions of Greek myths and by the oral folktales that circulated on the front porches and courthouse steps of her hometown, Eatonville, Florida. In her twenties, Hurston left her home to pursue a career as a writer, traveling first to Washington, D.C., and then to Harlem. She was beginning to receive success and recognition as a literary figure when she enrolled in Barnard College to study anthropology under the country's greatest living ethnographer, Franz Boas. Hurston discovered in New York that her literary interests and her social science interests were effectively one and the same. She was most interested in telling stories rooted in the traditional culture that had permeated her childhood, and she was interested in studying that culture in such a way that not merely its bare bones but its very soul could be revealed through her observations and her wordcraft.

In 1935, Hurston published her first major book, *Mules and Men*, the perfect combination of her interests and her talents. *Mules and Men* is a slightly fictionalized account of a fieldwork expedition of 1929 in which she returned to her hometown to hear again the tales that had so inspired her as a child. The book is both a literary milestone and a major collection of folklore. More than a description, and more than a loosely assembled bundle of tales, *Mules and Men* is an exploration of why people tell tales and a demonstration of the social arts of narrative. The fictional aspects of *Mules and Men* cannot detract from the profound social and esthetic truths that it imparts. According to folklorist Roger Abrahams, the book is "simply the most exciting book on black folklore and culture I have ever read."

The same year that *Mules and Men* appeared, Hurston embarked on one

Zora Neale Hurston, collector of stories 169–171. This photo was probably taken during the Lomax-Hurston-Barnicle recording expedition to Georgia, Florida, and the Bahamas in 1935. (Library of Congress)

of the Archive of American Folk Song's most ambitious collecting ventures. Teamed with folklorists Alan Lomax (see particularly stories 92–110) and Mary Elizabeth Barnicle (see story 141), she began a three-month fieldwork expedition beginning on her home turf, in Florida and Georgia, and ending in the Bahamas and Haiti. As the three folklorists worked at close quarters, Hurston developed an intense dislike for Barnicle, who seemed to be cultivating an erotic liaison with Lomax. At this time, Barnicle was 44 and Alan was 20; Hurston considered Barnicle's behavior so appalling that she took it upon herself to write to Alan's father, John A. Lomax, to warn him. In writing the elderly Lomax, Hurston displayed her trademark iconoclastic courage; she herself was well aware that she was crossing social boundaries to approach John A. Lomax, as she reveals in a letter to him: "You are a white Southerner and I am a Negro and so I am certain that [Barnicle] feels she could be daring and you would never believe me." Ultimately, John A. Lomax did not take Hurston's advice.

As *Mules and Men* was being prepared for press, the Lohuba expedition (as the collaboration of Lomax, Hurston, and Barnicle has come to be known) stopped in Frederica, Georgia. Hurston was soon to leave the expedition altogether, but her recordings of five remarkable performances by John Davis reveal that she was already going her own way. The expedition was preparing to record a children's choir (ultimately, some thoroughly over-arranged and tepid performances of "Froggy Went A-Courting" and other songs were indeed captured on disk) as Zora enticed Davis to begin telling folktales. Neither Alan Lomax's nor Barnicle's voice can be heard on these pressings, but Zora's laughter, commentary, and encouragement are everywhere apparent.

Because Davis tells his tales in an echoey auditorium, and because his performance is often drowned out by the sound of furniture and risers being rearranged to accommodate the choir, the sound quality of the following three performances is extraordinarily poor. In all, Davis told five tales. Only three of them are sufficiently well recorded to allow reasonably full reconstructions of the tale texts.

Even with all the imperfections of the miking and background noise, the recordings leave no doubt that Davis is a great performer. If many of his words are unintelligible, the brilliant modulations in his tone make it clear that his voice is acting out the stories. Periodically, the sound of his feet stamping on the auditorium floor fills the disks. There can be little doubt that Davis is gesturing dramatically from time to time. Through it all, Hurston laughs uproariously and calls out her encouragement.

Here's another one. And, John, there's another boy named John, he's getting along good. . . . But they was another old guy, Brother [Cap], see, *he* wanted to be the sharp guy. Everything John would do, this fellow would try, you know.

[And John would get mad:] "Hey, don't do it, do it so close to the gopher hole."

John started wanting to get rid of him. . . .

One day, John come along, . . . and see one of mistress's *underthing* hanging on the line, you know. John got there, and come through there, and looked up under there—and went on back to the house.

And [John] said, "Boy, you know what I done today?"

"What's that?"

Said, . . . "I went and looked under the Missus's un*der*skirts."

"You *did*?"

Say, "Yeah!" [Laughter]

Said, "And she didn't done nothing?"

Say, "No."

"I'm going to try it. I'm going down there now."

He got out there and she's standing in the yard. He just went up to her and just pulled up the underskirt and just looked under and she beat him flat as a [driveway]. [Laughter]

He come back. "I thought you said, you could. . . ." "I thought you said that you looked under old Missus's underskirts."

He said, "Oh, that old thing was on the line that I looked under it."

[Laughter]

[But Cap] went right up to the old Mistress and looked under her underskirts.

170. John and the Bear

JOHN DAVIS
Frederica, Georgia
Recorded by Zora Neale Hurston, Frederica, Georgia, 1935

Master, he had him a big corn field, you know. There was a bear in this Master's corn. Master say, "John, could you stop that bear from eating my corn?"

Said, "Master, I don't know that I'm gonna stop him, but I can catch him for you." Said, "I'll do that."

[At midnight] John go down to the . . . field . . . and that [bear], he come through the corn.

"Hey! What are you doing in Master's field?"

Bear wouldn't say nothing.

"Hey, what you doing in Master's field?"

John run up to him and, you know, and hauled off and pop him with ear of the corn, you know, and that made the bear kind of mad, you know.

The bear throw down his arms, come up through the corn and light out behind John. John and that bear ran back [to the corncrib]. The crib door was open, you know. And John run and run and . . . John slip [by] this door, you know, and the bear come in [the pen]. John shut the door. [Went back. Told master.] . . .

Master says, "Did you catch that bear and put him in there, put him in there?"

"Yeah."

"Well, by God," he says, "If you put him in there, I could take him out."

Old Master, he run up to the door, you know, and pull the door open [laughter]. He pull the door and the bear jump right in his face and God Almighty, you know, him and that bear [head back for the swamp]. . . .

"Say, John," he say, "how in the world did you got that bear in that crib?"

John tell him, "See how [you're] walking backward and going in them swamp, that's how I did it." [Laughter]

171. John and the Coon

JOHN DAVIS
Frederica, Georgia
Recorded by Zora Neale Hurston,
Frederica, Georgia, 1935

This is one of the most popular of all the John and Master tales. "Buck Asa" Ulisses Jefferson told a version to Alan Lomax in 1942 (see story 93). Both tales pivot on the word "coon," which can apply either to the raccoon or (as a racial slur) to the slave John. By believing himself caught and calling himself a coon, the slave displays a submissiveness that he hopes will lessen his punishment, and he is the most surprised of all to learn that "coon," his admission of defeat, is actually his ticket to victory. John Davis's performance differs from most other versions of the tale by emphasizing the notion that "John couldn't lose," that he was blessed with an extraordinary luck. Davis's power as a narrator emerges in full force toward the climax of the tale as his voice intensifies the drama unfolding between the frightened slave John and the white man who has bet against John's master. In mimicking the slave's voice, Davis's drops to a slow whisper; then, mimicking the white man's, he begins to bellow in an adept imitation of an Anglo-American accent.

Master kind of take a liking to John. . . . John didn't do nothing at all, but he was taking a liking to John, you know. And John going on [like he knew everything]. But he didn't *know* nothing.

Master got together a party, you know, and they went out hunting that night. So the dogs ain't able to catch but one coon. And when they come back with the coon, come back, nobody know what to think of, they just there messing around and thinking of first one thing and another, you know, coming back off the hunt. And they want to get something to bet on. "Bring the coon back alive. . . . And we going to . . . bet something off of him."

Master [said,] "By God, I don't got an old darkie at home. I bet you he could tell you just what we caught tonight."

"Oh, I gonna bet on that." They're betting [against him] you know. And the money, they couldn't come up with the money, they didn't have enough money. But they had land. Master say, "By God, I'll bet you two or three plantations, a big bet that John gonna tell what they caught that night."

They put [the coon] under a tub, you know.

Next morning, here comes John on up to the house. . . .

"Well, John, I got a big bet on this morning, and don't cause me to lose, now."

"No, Master, I—you can't lose."

Say, "John, well, we want you to tell us what's that under that tub."

[Long pause] "Mm." [Long pause]

[Loudly] "Come on, John."

[Weak voice] "Well. . . ." [Laughter]

That old fellow, he had his bet on, you know [gruff, angry voice], "Well, by God, come on now, and tell us what's under this tub! Quick!" [Laughter]

[Another long pause]

And he said, "Boss, Sir," he said, "the coon has run a long time, but finally you catch him."

Master say [loudly], "By God, I told you that [John could tell] there was a coon under there!" [Laughter]

John didn't know what in the world it was. [Laughter] It was under the tub, you know. John thought they catch *him*. You know, *he* was the coon. . . . [Much laughter]

"But, John, how come you wait so long before you tell em what's there?"

Said, "Master, I don't want you to bet no more." [Laughter]
He didn't know what it was. John thought that they catch *him*, you see.
But he *couldn't lose.*
[Zora Neale Hurston: He must have been telling fortunes before that.]

172. Monkey and Buzzard

CORA JACKSON
Rappahannock County and
Fairfax, Virginia
Recorded by Charles L. Perdue Jr.
and Nancy J. Martin-Perdue,
Philadelphia, Pennsylvania,
November 11, 1967

Cora Jackson was the wife of the celebrated Virginia bluesman John Jackson; the two participated in a marathon storytelling session at the home of their friends Charles L. Perdue Jr. and Nancy J. Martin-Perdue (for two of John's contributions to the evening, see stories 129 and 130). That evening, Cora specialized in jokes. Although she was intimately familiar with the quintessential African American trickster hero, Brer Rabbit, she was often hard on him. In Cora's version of the Tarbaby story (see story 189), Brer Rabbit emerges as a loser. Similarly, in the following animal tale, the rabbit meets an untimely death and it is the monkey who prevails against the murderous buzzard.

There was the old buzzard. He wanted something to eat, and he went, first thing, he asked the old terrapin, said, "You wanna take a ride?"
Said, "Yeah."
He hopped on his back and flied way up in the air, and he dropped him down and he busted him all to pieces, and he eat him up.
Well, next, it was . . . the rabbit or something he picked up. It was the rabbit. He asked him, and he flew way up in the air with him, and he turned him loose, and he dropped him, and he eat him up.
And then he came across a monkey. He flew way up in the air with the old monkey holding on. He said, "Don't go too high. I get the swimming in the head."
"Oh, no, I'm gonna give you a good ride." He went way up in the air with this old monkey, so when he got ready to drop the monkey, that old monkey wrapped his tail around his neck. And he said, "Hey, Mr. Monkey," say, "You choking me."

Cora Jackson (teller of stories 172–175, 189) with her husband, John (teller of stories 129, 130), and their children, Jamie and Cora Bethwas, ca. 1966. (Photo by Carol Bruce)

He said, "Straighten up, damn you, and fly right then."

That broke the buzzard from carrying the monkey up in the air and dropping him on the ground.

173. Twenty-five Roosters and One Hen

CORA JACKSON
Rappahannock County and
Fairfax, Virginia
Recorded by Charles L. Perdue Jr.
and Nancy J. Martin-Perdue,
Philadelphia, Pennsylvania,
November 11, 1967

During the story-swapping session in which Cora Jackson narrated this tale, she and her husband, John, told more than eighty tales, with Cora telling more than twice as many as her husband. In an ongoing study of the evening's storytelling, collector Chuck Perdue has noted that eighteen of Cora's tales "might be classed as obscene. It is interesting to note the part that women play as bearers of obscene materials. John has never told me an obscene joke, either in mixed company or alone. It is Cora who does this. However, John does not mind an obscene joke; in fact, he seems to enjoy them and will go so far as to suggest one to Cora, so she can tell it!"

Most of Cora's tales are tastefully elliptical; she skirts the boundaries of the obscene, suggesting a great deal more than she reveals. The tales often engage a general conflict between the sexes more than they actually touch upon sexual matters.

There was one with the lady married an Irishman. . . . She married an Irishman, so . . . he would thin corn all day or something like that. He give her enough money to get twenty-five hens and one rooster. She goes and gets twenty-five roosters and one hen.

So he said, "Lawd, honey, what have you done? You got twenty-five roosters and one hen."

She said, "Well, I don't want that hen to suffer like I do." [Laughter]

174. Thinning Corn

CORA JACKSON
Rappahannock County and
Fairfax, Virginia
Recorded by Charles L. Perdue Jr.
and Nancy J. Martin-Perdue,
Philadelphia, Pennsylvania,
November 11, 1967

This and the preceding joke feature Irishmen as the lazy husbands. Although Irish settlers arrived in Rappahannock County and elsewhere in the Blue Ridge as early as the eighteenth century, it was the massive mid-nineteenth-century Irish immigrations that spurred the surge in jokes about Irishmen. As the most recent and often the poorest arrivals in the United States, the Irish were singled out for joking ridicule by Appalachian whites and blacks alike. The telling of such jokes remains a popular pastime in the Appalachians, even though by the beginning of the twenty-first century little actual prejudice against the Irish remains. The Appalachian Irishman, like the northern Polack, has become a generic term for numskull.

There was another Irishman. He married a girl so he worked all day. She would have to get up and milk the cow. The old bull would be laying asleep in the barn lot, so every time she'd go down there he'd tell his wife at night, "I thin corn all day. I'm tired."

So she gets up the next morning and the old bull's laying in the barn lot and the cow's a-grazing. She jumps up and kicks the old bull: "Get up from there, you son of a bitch. You been thinning corn all day too." [Laughter]

175. That's the One

CORA JACKSON
Rappahannock County and
Fairfax, Virginia
Recorded by Charles L. Perdue Jr.
and Nancy J. Martin-Perdue,
Philadelphia, Pennsylvania,
November 11, 1967

Then I know another one about three men. Two of em was rich men and one of em was poor man, but he was just helping em. One had a bunch of sheep and one had a bunch of cows.

So it come up a big rain, and so they had to spend the night at this farmer's house and they didn't have but two rooms. There was one bedroom and a kitchen and one daughter, but they didn't have but two beds so they took the daughter out and put her in the bed with them and let these . . . men have the bed. So it kept a-raining and they were sitting there talking and one man said, "Lord, I hope it don't come a flood and wash all my cows away."

The old man said, "Daughter, that's the one for you."

So the other one said, "Well, I hope it just don't wash all my sheeps away."

The old woman said, "Daughter, that's the one for you."

The other one said, "Hey, you get off my string [penis] over there."

Said, "Mama, Mama, that's the one for me."

176. The Cook

PAUL E. YOUNG
Miles City, Montana
Recorded by Paula Johnson and
Barre Toelken,
Miles City, Montana, August 11,
1979

Among the most popular storytelling topics is the practical joke. A memorable practical joke is often celebrated so often and with such verbal artistry that it becomes a major part of a storyteller's repertoire.

The following joke illustrates the length to which tricksters in all-male working communities will go to mount a practical joke. Paul E. Young, a retired cowboy, shared this joke with folklorists Paula Johnson and Barre Toelken, who were interviewing him as part of a statewide survey of Montana folklife.

Young intimated to Johnson and Toelken that "cowboys just loved" to play jokes on each other, and then he launched into the following account of an extraordinarily sustained and elaborate practical joke, one that seemed, at least to its victim, serious enough to be life-threatening.

They hired a new cook, and he was a good cook. But cowboys . . . were great jobbers. They'd job one another every time they got a chance. It's part of their horseplay of entertaining. They had no radios, they had no TV in those days, or anything like that, you know, and it was just part of fun. It started out fun for everybody, you know. And if they had a chance to pull a gag on somebody, they did it.

And the one that I was going out to relieve—Ted Angel was his name. . . . He he lived down by Vidora, and he was in camp all before noon, waiting for that manager . . . for Hutchison to come back from the ranch, with that big old Packard car, haul his saddle and bedroll into Miles City. His folks needed him. They wanted him to come home. . . .

Hutch had already dropped off this new cook. And he was green, right out from the East. And here's this Ted Angel sitting around this camp, waiting for Hutch to come back down from the ranch. He took some groceries and some . . . stuff they needed up there, and he said, "I'll be back down. I'll take you to town. And—but he dropped on down to Terry . . . and got me. He didn't come back till the next day. He'd left this Ted Angel there, with this cook. Well, [Ted] really loaded him.

[The new cook] said, "What do they—I never cooked in a cow camp." He said, "Are they like anybody else I suppose? Just give em regular fare, of course?"

"Oh, yeah," he said. "They're the easiest people in the world to cook for." Says, "You can gave em mulligan."

He says, "And yeah," but he says, "you vary it, of course, don't you? You give em mulligan pretty often, you mean, don't you?"

"You can give em mulligan three times a day," he says.

And so he says, "You mean you give em mulligan for breakfast, at noon and night, and everything?"

"Yeah. Mulligan and cornbread." (See, what'd made [Ted] think of that, that's what they'd just had. Their other cook had quit, and one of the cowboys had cooked, and that's what he had cooked over. They had laid over there and they'd had time to cook up a stew. As a rule they don't have time to cook a stew.)

And so [the new man] said, he couldn't hardly see that.

But, oh yeah, and then [Ted] went around talking about something else, never tried to press the point at all. Just a straight face you know, acted like he wanted to change the subject entirely, you know. But this new cook, he just wanted to know, and he just . . . made him tell him. So, "Yeah," he said, "that's on the square."

And this cook went over and he cut a look at these pans, and sure enough, here was the remains of cornbread . . . over on the stove. (They had little camp stoves that they carried. Before that, they'd used these dutch ovens, you know, that you put the coal on the top . . . , but they'd graduated to these stoves that they carried in a cart behind the chuck wagon. Four holes on top, and four lids. Pretty good stoves, too, they are. And a oven. You can bake bread in there.) So, sure enough, that's what the remains was. That's what made him think—that's what made this Ted Angel think of that.

Well, he started feeding us that. That's the food we got. [Laughter]

And [Ted Angel had] prepared him for griping. He said, "One thing about em," he said, "they're a queer bunch." He said, "They'll gripe about that food. They'll go ask if you can't cook anything else. [Laughter] They'll ask you right out if you can't cook anything else, but you don't dare," he said, "cook anything else. Because they're the [type] that'll start shooting you if you cook anything else."

And [the new man] said, "Now, that's queer." He said, "Now what's this other food in here?"

"Oh," he said, "once in a while, the owners, if they come to the wagon," he said, "you might have to cook up a little something like that," he says, "for *them*. But," he says, "that's the cowboy fare, is mulligan, cornbread, and coffee, of course." So he convinced him.

And he started giving us mulligan three times a day. And cornbread. [Laughter] And I think we had it for three days, and *everybody* was a-kicking, you know, three meals a day, you know, on this mulligan.

[It made no sense to the cook either.] He'd said, "You mean, you cut up good steaks? . . . Meat that would make good steaks, and everything? . . . And quarters of beef hanging there, you know?"

"Yeah, you bet. . . . A cowboy got to have his mulligan."

He said, "Haven't you heard about the good mulligan they cook in the West?"

"Yes, it seem like I . . . have," this cook said.

So there's this fellow that I was telling you about, Prudy Bill. . . . He always wore a gun. (Most of the rest of us, if we had guns, why, we'd carry em in our war bags, get em out if we needed to for something or wanted em for anything special, but we hardly ever wore em.) But he wouldn't go three feet from that camp without a gun buckled on his waist. I guess there was a feud [he was involved in]. But anyway, he told us when we was . . . just coming in, headed for the camp: . . . "If that mulligan pot's on the stove tonight, nobody will cook another bean in it." [Laughter]

And it *was* on. And they had the tent up. Most times, they never put the tent up. But it looked like rain, and somebody was in ahead of us, and stuck up a mess tent. And the stove was in the mess tent, of course. And, sure enough, here was the mulligan pot a-burning, boiling. It was done, you know, and everything. And that poor man didn't know. He thought that's what he had to cook. [Laughter]

And this wagon boss was to blame. He—we would complain to him, you know, some of em did. He said, "Aw," he said, "I think" (he was kind of easygoing), he says, "I think he'll start cooking pretty soon." [Laughter] "Let's give him a little time." And he said, "I'll talk to him after a while."

But anyway, sure enough, here's this big old kettle, big old stew pot, you know, and it was on the stove. Old Prudy, he just pulls out this—he was carrying a .38 on a .44 frame—and he just starts shooting holes in this big kettle. [Laughter] Stew goes squirting out in all directions [laughter]. And . . . a Wyoming boy and I, each of us grabbed a gunnysack so we could grab the—we was afraid it was going to put the fire out. And we was getting hungry for steaks [laughter] and some food. We didn't want . . . to have to make a new fire and everything.

So we each of us grabbed a gunnysack quick, and . . . I told him, "Grab a gunnysack, and we'll get rid of that pot before it puts the fire out." Cause this steaming-hot stew was squirting out, but we grabbed them so that it would hit these sacks, you know. We grabbed it from each side, . . . its handles, carried it out, and dumped it, threw the kettle away.

Oh, yes, we crawled up in the wagon, and there was about a third of a sack of—you know, seamless sacks, of cotton, seamless sacks of cornmeal left. And we camped on the banks of Powder River. And old Prudy, and he poured that out into the Powder River for the fish. And he said, "Nobody cook any of this anymore," and threw the empty sack back up into the wagon.

But the first shock, why the poor cook, he said, "What'd I do wrong? Salt that mulligan too much?" [Laughter] And under that tent he went like a squirrel, you know, like a rabbit, and out across the prairie. [Laughter] We was on a flat, out on the river, you know. And *away* he lit out across the flat there, just as hard as he could run, you know. And . . . he thought maybe he'd salted that stew too much or something.

So Scoggins, this . . . wagon boss, he come riding in just as [the cook] ducked under and started across the flat. He loped out there and headed him off. Oh, a hundred yards he'd got out there, quite a way, before he caught him. And he got off his horse and he sat down, and they had a heart-to-heart talk, while we was cooking us another, a *good* meal, you know. And . . . somebody grabbed a knife and started whittling off steaks, and somebody else dug up some good canned stuff, and we didn't bother to peel potatoes or anything. We dug up some cans, of canned goods, you know, one thing or another, but with some good, thick steaks. And we cooked a good meal, you see.

And he *did* have some good coffee made. He made good coffee. [Laughter]

And so he told this Tom—Tom just had a heart-to-heart talk with him. He said, "Can't you cook anything but stew?"

"Oh, yeah," he says, "I'm a good cook." He says, "I've cooked in restaurants," and he said, "I've cooked in hotels, big hotels," he said, "back to New York." And he says, ". . . it bothered me," he says, "to cut up good meat into stew. But," he said, "Ted Angel said that's all I dared cook for cowboys." [Laughter]

And, well, Tom started laughing. He said, "You've been jobbed," he said. "That's all." He said, "We've all been jobbed," he says. He said, "That isn't your fault." He said, "You come back and just cook," he said. And he said, "If there's things that you're short of," he said, "this outfit eats *good.*" He said, "What you're short of, when we get near the railroad . . . , why, we'll get it for you." And he said, "Just keep track of what you need. . . ."

He says, "Good! I'm glad to hear it." He says, "I'll show you some cooking."
[Laughter]

[Paula Johnson: "Great!"]

And he *cooked!*

177. A Mountain Wedding

UNCLE ALEC DUNFORD
Galax, Virginia
Recorded by Alan Lomax and Pete Seeger,
Galax, Virginia, January 1939

Galax, Virginia, has long been known as a major center of Appalachian fiddling traditions and as the home of the Old Fiddler's Convention, apparently the nation's oldest and certainly one of its most popular fiddling competitions, founded in 1935. Among the chief entertainers at Galax was Uncle Alec (also known as Alex and Eck) Dunford (1878–1953), a consummate fiddler, guitarist, and singer as well as a founding member of the Ballard Branch Bogtrotters. The Bogtrotters, whose other members included the legendary Wade Ward and W.P. Davis, possessed a repertoire of more than 300 songs and instrumental pieces, which they collected and performed "to help preserve the old-time folk music and stories." The story that Uncle Alec tells here is based on his own personal experience in the not terribly distant past.

Folklorist Alan Lomax visited Galax in 1939, accompanied by Pete Seeger. Pete, the son of the famous ethnomusicologist Charles Seeger, grew up in an environment where traditional music was studied, performed, and revered. Well before he achieved fame as one of the nation's best-loved popular folksingers, Pete was steeping himself in the folk music traditions of the Appalachians.

The following tale concerns a wedding that Uncle Alec attended as a young man and that took place on Chestnut Creek, about two miles from Galax. As Alec explained to his interviewers, this account, like many tall tales, contains a kernel of historical truth that the teller has elaborated for effect: "As far as the wedding's concerned, that part is true. And the boy did actually come down on the table, and his coattail did actually land on the joist. And they had to help him down. But, of course, there's a few details put in it to lend color to the tale."

Pete Seeger, collector of story 177, playing the banjo, 1948. (Library of Congress)

Well, folks, I'm going to tell you about an old-fashioned wedding that happened in my neighborhood when I was young. They was some neighbors lived close to me had a girl, and they was thrifty people. They had plenty around em, and they was a young man a-going to see their girl, and they got engaged and was going to marry, and the older people liked the young man, and so they thought they'd fix a pretty good dinner and invite the whole neighborhood in. And so they did, and me and Laverne. And so we all gathered there at the appointed time, and everybody seemed pleased over the wedding except the girl's smallest brother.

His favorite sister was a-going to marry, and he was down and out over it, and wouldn't come in the house. Nor he wouldn't put on his new jean suit of clothes neither. But his father finally told him to go upstairs and put on his new clothes, that the dinner would be ready in a few minutes. And so the boy had a favorite cat that he always carried around to catch rats with, and he had the cat trained till it knowed about as much about the rat-catching as the boy did, when they hunted together. And so he picked up his cat and went upstairs to put his clothes on, and he went over the kitchen in the loft, to dress. And the planks was laid down loose. And the weddingers, they all were set down around the table and was just a-fixing to pass the grub around.

And the boy saw a rat, and he made a jump with his cat, and stepped on the loose plank, and it tilted up, and let the boy down right on the table. Well, the tail of his coat hooked over a spike that was drove in the joist to hand-dry pumpkin on, and the boy's tiptoes just touched the dishes on the table. [Laughter] And one foot was a-sitting on a dish of pie, cobbler pie, and the other foot was a-sitting in a dish of fried ham. And the cat, of course, it come down when he did, and the cat's front feet was in a bowl of chicken gravy, [laughter] and its hind feet was in a dish of turnips, and its tail dropped down in the cream pitcher. [Laughter] Well, . . . everybody of course just sit there, and the boy he was a-scratching to get a toehold, and he'd rake out a rasher of fried ham and throw it in somebody's face with his foot. And then he'd rake with the other foot, and pass a piece of pie out in somebody's face, and the cat all the time, it was a-sitting there, just scared to death. And it'd jerk its tail out of the cream pitcher and give it a switch or two and slap the cream around in all their faces. And after a while, the crowd come to their senses, and some of em jumped up and grabbed the boy, and helped him down, and his father took him out and was going to lick him, but the crowd wouldn't let him. But in the meantime, when they went to help the boy down, somebody turned the coffee pot over and spilled it all over the table and spilled it on about half of the people that was sitting down at the table. And the coffee was hot, and I'll tell you right there, there were some of the fastest moving around that ever [laughs] I saw in my life. [Laughs]

Well, it all went off all right after all. They soon got some more grub on the table, and all set down and cleaned up the tablecloth a little, and all of em set down and eat and had a good time. I wish to goodness I could be at another wedding like that right now.

[Laughter]

11

PASSING IT ON

STORIES FOR CHILDREN

The stories in this section represent some of the earliest narrative memories of their tellers. Here, twelve voices vividly relate the oral entertainments with which their grandparents and parents captured their imaginations. When their voices were recorded by folklorists, all but two of the storytellers were themselves passing these tales on to children and grandchildren.

Not surprisingly, three of the tellers—Barry Jean Ancelet, Bascom Lamar Lunsford, and Mary Celestia Parler—were also folklorists. The childhood sessions from which these tales emerged were part of the fabric of their traditional up-bringing and represented cultural contexts so influential on their subsequent lives that they went on to devote their careers to the study and celebration of the folk cultures that gave them their stories.

Although a great many of the tales in other sections of this book were learned by their tellers at a young age, most of them were also frequently retold among adults. The great majority of the tales in this section, however, were intended exclusively for children and were passed on as special communications between a mature storyteller and a very young auditor. Hence, a pervasive theme in the tales that follow is obedience. "The Girl Who Didn't Mind Her Mother" (story 178), "Show Me Your Paw" (story 183), and "Skullbone" (story 184) were told to the children to reinforce behavior deemed appropriate by adults.

Many of these tales carried very specific meanings for the families that handed them down. The plots of such tales as "Show Me Your Paw" and "Skullbone" are known in many parts of the world, and thousands of narrators have given these plots their own particular nuances and twists of meaning. But when Arthur Anderson told "Skullbone" to his daughter Debra, he always used it to keep her from tattling on her brothers and sisters. Similarly, Caroline Ancelet's mother

Barry Jean and Caroline Ancelet with their son Jean, 1980. Two years later, Barry would tell Jean "Gaillum, Singo, et Moliseau" (story 182) and Caroline would tell him "Show Me Your Paw" (story 183). (Photo by Jim Zeitz)

made "Show Me Your Paw" the basis of a little ritual to ensure that her daughter would not let a stranger enter the house.

Other tales in this section were told more for entertainment than for instruction, and some of them seem to have been told expressly for the purpose of giving their young listeners a good scare. As children and as adults, the storytellers sometimes had opposite reactions to these whimsical tales of terror. Both Bascom Lamar Lunsford and Glen Muncy Anderson frequently heard a tale of a monster stalking a human who had stolen its big toe (stories 179 and 180), a story known to millions of Americans through Mark Twain's closely related telling of "The Golden Arm." Lunsford, and Anderson's brothers, delighted in this story, but it scared Anderson so badly that she never retold it to her own children.

Among the stories elsewhere in this book that were told primarily to young children are Alberta Harmon's "Old Black Dog" (story 12), J.D. Suggs's "Pull Me Up, Simon" (story 60), and Jane Muncy Fugate's "Tailipoe" (stories 84 and 85).

178. The Girl Who Didn't Mind Her Mother

EARTHA M.M. WHITE
Amelia Island and Jacksonville,
Florida
Recorded by Robert Cook and
Stetson Kennedy,
Jacksonville, Florida, January
1940

Eartha White was born into a family of slaves. It was her mother, Clara White, who first told her this tale. Clara had a rich repertoire of stories, and she made them an important tool in her daughter's education. As Eartha explained to collector Stetson Kennedy, Clara "was a slave, and that was the method . . . they had then to make their children go straight."

The interviewers asked Eartha how long ago she had heard this tale. She responded, "I wouldn't mind telling you that I was a very, very small child. Mother used to tell these stories of all kinds. Most every night she had a homemade story to tell. Course, I just realized that after I got larger. I don't mind telling you I was a very small child, but I wouldn't like to tell you how many years ago."

My mother delighted in telling fairy tales or ghost stories that had the moral in it to make a child tell the truth and behave her. This particular story had a wonderful effect upon me.

It was a girl who would not mind her mother, and she was determined to get rides in everything that came along. Riding in buggies and so forth. And this particular day, a man came along with a buggy, and she begged a ride. And when she'd traveled a distance, he said to her, "Do you know where you are now, little girl?"

She said, "I'm in my father's rice field."

He went on. "Do you know where you are now?"

"I'm in my father's watermelon patch."

He went another distance. He said, "Do you know where you are now?"

"I'm in my father's . . . cane field. . . ."

And so he went until [they got to a place where] her father owned nothing.

And then he jumped out of the buggy, and he marched her down into a *great* big hole. And when she got out in this hole, it was a room under the earth. And

Eartha White, whose tales were the first to be recorded by the Florida Writers Project (1937) with the machine on loan from the Library of Congress. The recording took place at her Eartha White Mission in Jacksonville, which provided free meals and lodging for needy persons, including a number of ex-slaves. (Courtesy of Stetson Kennedy)

there he had a *large* pot with fire under it. He began stirring this pot. In a voice he said [threatening, low-pitched whisper], "Why, I'm going to put you in this pot. And I'm going to boil you up, so that you'll know how not to run away."

And she began to scream and cry. And her pet cow came along, and he heard her voice down in this hole. And so he *ran* home, the cow. And the people were attracted by the peculiar motions of the cow, and they followed him back to this dirt hole, and there they heard her crying.

Her father reached down and pulled her out of the hole, and carried her home, and of course naturally she was frightened so that she was put in bed.

The doctor came to quiet her nerves. And that next Sunday, here this strange man drove up to the door with that horse and buggy and inquired how she was. And her mother saw him coming. And she had a kettle of hot water on the fire.

And she ran to the door as he went to come in the house, and she threw the hot water in his face. And you know [high pitched, childish voice], that's why you see horses with white faces. That's the reason why they have white faces.

And from that time on, believe me, that little girl told the truth.

179. The Crooked Old Man

BASCOM LAMAR LUNSFORD
North Carolina
Recorded by Benjamin Botkin,
Asheville, North Carolina, 1942

Like several other storytellers featured in this book, Bascom Lamar Lunsford was both a folklorist and a "folk," a man who grew up to study and perform many of the traditional musical and storytelling arts that made up a substantial part of his own family life. He grew up in the mountains of western North Carolina. Lunsford told this story during an interview conducted with Benjamin Botkin while Botkin was serving as director of the Archive of American Folk Song. Right after the performance, Lunsford explained, "I've heard that story, Dr. Botkin, since I was a child. The age of my little grandson over there, Colonel Lunsford. And they'd tell it to children. Very good bedtime story for a mountain people."

Picture around the big open fire, on a cold, long winter night, a bunch of children. Someone says, "Tell us the story about the crooked old man." All right.

One time there was a crooked old man and a crooked old woman, and they lived together in a crooked old house. And they had a crooked Irish potato patch. And they worked together in that crooked Irish potato patch. Each had a crooked hoe.

So one evening after they'd been working in the potato patch, digging potatoes—each dug a bucketful with the crooked hoe—they dug up a man's toe, a big toe. They looked at it, they thought what they'd do with it: put it in one of the buckets, carry it into the house. They got ready for supper. They raked out some of the coals out of the fire, made a little old cavity, put several of the big potatoes in there, and covered it up first with coals and then with ashes and then they put in the big toe—and roasted it with the potatoes—and sat back there and waited for them to roast.

After the steam began to come through the ashes, they heard a *sound* on the

Bascom Lamar Lunsford playing the fiddle, joined by Mr. and Mrs. Lyda Brooks and Gaither Robertson in a performance of "Doggett's Gap," 1927. (Lunsford Scrapbook, Mars Hill College Archives)

outside of the house. It said [growling whispery voice], "Where's my big toe—o? Where's my big toe?"

"What's that, Ma?"

"What is that, Pa? Go out and see."

"No, you go out."

So the old woman, the crooked old woman, got up and went all around the house. And come back.

Says, "What did you see?"

"I didn't see nothing."

"Didn't you see nothing?"

"No, I never saw nothing."

Sat there and waited a few minutes, and then they heard it come a little closer, and a little louder, "Where's my big toe—o? Where's my big toe—o?"

"Now, you go, Pa."

"No, you go, Ma."

"No, you go, Pa."

So Pa got up. Then he went out, stayed a little while. After a while he come back.

"Well, Pa, did you see anything?"

"No, I didn't, Ma. Didn't see nothing."

Sit back for a little while. After a while they heard it again, *louder than before*. "*Where's my big toe? Where's my big toe?*"

Says, "Let's both go out."

"All right, we'll both go out."

And they got up and they went all around the house and they went around again, and they come to the chimney, and they looked upon the chimney and they saw a great big thing up there. It had big eyes and a big long bushy tail, and claws.

And they said, "What's them big eyes for?"

He said, "To look you through."

"What's that long, bushy tail for?"

"To sweep your grave."

"What's those big claws for?"

"To dig your grave."

"What's them big teeth for?"

"To chew up your bones."

And then they'd all go on up to bed.

180. Grown Toe

GLEN MUNCY ANDERSON
Hyden and Danville, Kentucky
Recorded by Carl Lindahl,
May 4, 1997

"Grown Toe" (sometimes called "Overgrown Toe") is obviously closely related to Bascom Lamar Lunsford's "The Crooked Old Man" (story 179), and Glen Muncy Anderson, like Lunsford, heard it told repeatedly when she was a small child. Unlike Lunsford, who was tickled by the tale, Mrs. Anderson was terrified. She recalled in vivid detail the storytelling ritual played out nightly from at least 1915, when she was a girl of 4, and when her mother told her this tale. "Grown Toe" would "scare me to death. . . . I had a pull-out bed, you know. . . . And I would sleep on that for a while, and then I'd get so scared that I crawled—get up and crawl across the floor and get in the bed with her. I'd get at the foot of the bed. And [my

Glen Muncy Anderson (standing, right) considers herself one of the least accomplished storytellers in her family. Glen's mother, Sydney Farmer Muncy (seated, left), was the family's master narrator, but Glen's half-sister Nora (standing, left), who sometimes told "The Tarnished Star" (story 83), and sister Hope (standing, center), who was fond of telling "The King's Well" (story 80), were also expert storytellers. Seated at right is Glen's brother Mark Muncy, father of Jane Muncy Fugate (teller of stories 76–85). (Courtesy of Bob Jason Fugate)

brothers] Mark and Gill had the bed over. They would get out and they'd come. And Mark and I would be at the foot, and [Mother] would be up there, [sister] Hope would be on one side and Gill was little bitty, he was two. We were two, four, and six, like that. . . .

"I tried to forget em. The stories would scare me. . . . At the time I thought they were real. You know, children think—things are real to them. . . . You have to tell them it's make believe or what. Just like on the, on the television sometimes it gets so graphic that the children will think it's real, and you have to tell them that that's not real—or not let them see it."

Glen grew up to be an avid storyteller, but she did not tell "Grown Toe" to her own children. Instead, she narrated "funny stories or good stories, about what they did, and I'd tell a story and have their names in it, you know. Make up stories."

Elsewhere in this book, Glen's niece, Jane Muncy Fugate, tells a related version of the tale, which she calls "Tailipoe" (stories 84 and 85).

There was an old man and he lived up in a hollow and had a log cabin. And they had one bed—big, high bed—in there. And he had three dogs. A large dog, that was lazy; and a middle-sized dog; and a small dog.

So, he went out in his little garden and he dug up potatoes. And he dug up this big toe. And he brought it in, and the dogs were hungry. And he was too. And he got some of his potatoes, put em in a pot, put that toe in there, and he cooked it all day. And he ate all he could, threw the bones to the dogs, and went to bed.

And he heard something that night, on the door, that said [deep, gruff voice], "I want my big overgrown toe. I want my big overgrown toe." And he opened the door and scooted the little dog out, and said, "Go get it! Go get it!"

So the little dog went out. Never came back.

The next night when he went to bed, he heard a noise at the door, and he said, "Who is it?"

And it said, "I want my big toe. My big overgrown toe."

And he took the middle-sized dog, put him at the door, and said, "Go get him! Go get him!"

Well, he went out. He never came back.

So, the next night, the thing came again, and said, "I want my toe! I want my big overgrown toe!"

And he put the big dog out and said, "Go get it!" The dog never come back at all. And the next night it came, and he didn't have any more dogs, and *he* went to the door.

And the thing came in and said, "I want my toe!" And it ate him. Ate him up. And when it went out, the thing went out the door, saying, "Now, I've got my big toes! I've got my big toes!" It'd eaten the dogs. The three dogs. And it ate him. So it had its big toe.

That was another scary one.

181. The Forty-Mile Jumper

MARY CELESTIA PARLER
Wedgefield, South Carolina, and
Fayetteville, Arkansas
Recorded by Miles L. Hanley,
American Dialect Society,
Providence, Rhode Island,
August 22, 1934

The following two tales, told in two different languages, were performed nearly fifty years and learned 700 miles apart. They are both versions of one of the most popular traditional bedtime stories in the South, in which the supernaturally skilled dogs of a young hero save him from a witch or a monster. The tale is well represented in both African American and European American traditions. In all versions, the hero sings or chants the names of the magic dogs to call them to his rescue. Retelling these tales learned in childhood, adults tend to remember the dog-calling scenes and the strange names of the dogs more vividly than other parts of the tale.

As a child growing up in South Carolina around 1910, Mary Celestia Parler often heard her "Aunt Flora" tell "The Forty-Mile Jumper." Listening to the recording housed in the American Folklife Center, one could easily conclude that Aunt Flora was Parler's blood relation. However, Parler later wrote a description revealing that the storyteller was Flora Smith, "a young Negro woman who lived in the village of Wedgefield in central South Carolina," who "told my brother and me many stories before the First World War. Mam Flora was what would be called a baby-sitter nowadays. Of all the tales she told us, the one we demanded most often was the story of 'The Forty-Mile Jumper.' In 1924, when Mam Flora was 'way up in ninety,' I refreshed my memory by having her tell it to me again."

In 1935, when she recorded the tale for the benefit of the American Dialect Society (ADS), Mary Celestia Parler was a 30-year-old scholar with an advanced degree. The ADS was interested primarily in capturing regional dialects for linguistic study, but Parler was at least as interested in hearing and telling tales. In 1948 she would join the faculty at the University of Arkansas, where she was to teach folklore classes and maintain an archive of recorded folklore that has contributed a rich store of tales to Library of Congress collections. Soon after moving to Arkansas, Mary Celestia Parler met the great Ozark folklorist Vance Randolph. By 1951, she was telling him stories, many of which he published in his various collections of Ozark folktales. The two lovers of tales grew to love each other, and in 1962, at age 57, Mary Celestia Parler married the 72-year-old Randolph. They had been married eighteen years when Randolph died in 1980. Within a year of Randolph's death, Mary also died; she was buried in South Carolina, where she had first heard "The Forty-Mile Jumper."

I'll tell you my Aunt Flora's story about Bah-manecker rody and Kai-anger. I only wish that Aunt Flora were still alive to tell it for you herself.

It seems that once upon a time there was an old witch who kept a hotel out in the country somewhere, and everybody marveled at the fact that although a number of people stopped at that hotel and went in to spend the night, nobody ever left again. One night, two men were traveling along the road, and night caught them just as they were passing this hotel, about which they knew nothing. So they stopped in the hotel and asked if they could spend the night. And the old witch was very pleasant and told them, yes, she'd be very glad to have them spend the night, and furthermore, she'd let them sleep with her two daughters. So the two men went to bed with the two daughters, and they, for some reason, became suspicious of the old witch. And when they noticed that the two daughters slept with peculiar long nightcaps on, they decided that perhaps it would be a good idea . . . after the daughters went to sleep, to put the nightcaps on their own heads, which they did. And they stayed awake and noticed that when the old witch came in in the dark, with a long, gleaming butcher knife in her hand, she felt around in the dark, and she felt around in the dark till she felt the nightcaps, and then she felt the ones that didn't have nightcaps on and slit the throats of her own two daughters.

After she went out of the room, these two men hot-footed it away and they went rushing away and made quite a good distance before the first of day.

When the old witch woke up and went in to see about these two men that she'd killed and hide them in the cellar, there were her two daughters with their throats cut. When she saw that she was so mad, she just was so mad she could *die.* So she ran out in the yard, and she got her forty-mile jumper, and she got on her forty-mile jumper, and she jumped and she jumped until she caught up with the men.

And one of them ran and climbed a tree. And the other man rushed off to call the dogs that they had—for some reason—in the vicinity.

The old witch got a ax and she went at the tree and she'd . . . chop the tree and say,

"Willy, willy, willy, come down."

And the man up the tree'd say,
"Willy, willy, willy, come up."
She'd chop the tree:
"Willy, willy, willy, come down."
The chips'd fall.
The man up the tree'd say,
"Willy, willy, willy, come up."
The chips'd fly back up.
All this time, the other man was calling,
"Bah-manecker rody, Kai-anger."
"Bah-manecker rody, Kai-anger."
And the old witch going,
"Willy, willy, willy, come down."
And the man up the tree going,
"Willy, willy, willy, come up."
Pretty soon the old dogs were coming,
"*Aa-oow, Aa-oow, Aa-oow, Aa-oow.*"

And the old witch, when she saw the dogs coming, she tried to get on her forty-mile jumper, but . . . the dogs got there first and they got her and they caught her, and they caught her by the throat, and killed her.

And the two men got on the forty-mile jumper and they jumped and jumped and jumped till they went back to the hotel and found all the bones of all the people that had been murdered in that inn and, down in the cellar, a *great pile* of treasure.

182. Gaillum, Singo, et Moliseau

BARRY JEAN ANCELET
Ossun, Louisiana
Recorded by Carl Lindahl,
June 23, 1982

Barry Jean Ancelet was brought up in Cajun Louisiana. Cajun French was the first language of his grandparents, but it was so stigmatized by the dominant English-speaking society in the 1950s, when Barry was a small boy, that his parents spoke English at home in order to help their son succeed. But Barry's paternal grandparents never learned English, and when he would visit them on their farm five miles from downtown Lafayette, he absorbed their language and traditions. It was Edouard Dugas, Barry's step-

grandfather, who told him "Gaillum, Singo, et Moliseau." M. Dugas, Barry recalls, "told all kinds of tales, but this is the only one that I remember."

Largely because of the influence of his grandparents, Barry grew up to study traditional Cajun culture. In the early 1970s, he began extensive fieldwork in Cajun-language storytelling traditions. When recording tales, he would ask the narrators if they knew one similar to "Gaillum, Singo, et Moliseau." Nearly twenty years after Barry's search began, Jennifer Ardoin, a student in the French class of Barry's wife, Caroline (see story 183), recorded a Creole version quite similar to his own. "Gaillum, Singo, et Moliseau" may not have been the most popular tale of his grandparents' generation, but it may have been the one, more than any other, that led Barry to the study of folklore.

In the recording that follows, Barry passes the story on to his 2-year-old son Jean and to his maternal grandmother, Ida Mayer. Mme. Mayer had never heard the tale before; she listened to it attentively and responded to it excitedly, interjecting comments as her grandson spoke.

C'était un jeune homme qu'avait trois chiens, trois gros chiens. Et il était beaucoup glorieux de ses chiens, il était fier de ses chiens. Et il avait été pour chercher l'aventure, pour faire une vie, essayer de faire une vie dans le voisinage. Et pis il avait rencontré une belle femme.

Et la femme était un petit brin plus vieille que lui, et il l'avait rencontrée, il avait été faire la chasse avec ses chiens. C'est ça l'affaire. Et quand il a rencontré cette dame, elle venait juste d'arriver avec une nouvelle famille dans le voisinage. Et quand elle l'a rencontré, elle avait peur de ses chiens. Et lui, il trouvait ça drôle. Ses chiens voulaient venir sur elle. Et il trouvait ça drôle parce que ses chiens, ordinairement ses chiens étaient bons pour dire quoi c'est . . . qui qu'était bon et qui qu'était pas bon.

[Ida Mayer: Mais, ouais.]

Mais il la trouvait assez belle que il pouvait pas croire que ses chiens avaient raison. Ça fait, il les a amarrés, puis ils se sont

There was a young man who had three dogs, three big dogs. He was extremely proud, extremely proud of his dogs. And he took off in search of adventure, to make a living, to try to find work in the neighborhood. And then he met a beautiful woman.

And the woman was a little bit older than he was. He met her while hunting with his dogs. That's how it happened. And when he met this woman, she had just arrived in the neighborhood with a new family. And when she met him, she was afraid of his dogs. And he thought there was something funny about that. His dogs wanted to attack her. And he thought that was funny because as a rule his dogs were good for telling who was a good person, and who wasn't.

[Ida Mayer: Yes, indeed.]

But he found the woman so beautiful that he couldn't believe that his dogs were right about her. So he leashed them up,

mis à parler, puis là, plus ça allait, plus ça se rencontrait, et ils ont tombé en amour.

Elle a dit qu'elle l'aurait marié. Il voulait la marier. Elle a dit elle l'aurait marié, mais elle avait une condition. C'est il fallait il se défait de ses chiens. Parce que elle voulait pas . . . elle avait peur des chiens. Elle voulait pas vivre avec les chiens.

[Ida Mayer: Elle voulait pas il go ahead élever les chiens.]

Ça fait, ça le chagrinait un tas parce qu'il aimait ses chiens. Il a venu à la maison, et puis il a tué ses chiens. Il a tué les trois, et il les a enterrés en bas de la maison. Mais il a sauvé le sang dans des seaux. Chacun avait son sang.

(Et ses chiens s'appelait Gaillum, Singo, et Moliseau. Et chaque fois qu'il allait à la chasse, il les appelait comme ça là,

Gaillum—llum—llum,
Gaillum—llum—llum,
Singo, Moliseau.

C'était un chanson qu'il avait pour appeler ses chiens, quand ils etaient après un lapin et des affaires comme ça.)

Et il a dit à sa mère, il dit, "Quand . . . si jamais quelque chose arrive, quelque chose va mal, si j'ai besoin de l'aide, si je suis dedans le tracas, et tu vas entendre cette chanson. Et si jamais tu entends cette chanson, tu vas aller, et tu vas verser le sang dessus les tombes, les fosses des chiens. Ça va prendre en vie. Ça va venir m'aider." Ça fait, elle a dit que elle l'aurait fait.

Ça fait, il a parti. Il s'a marié avec la femme. Mais ca s'adonnait que cette femme était pas bonne. Elle était méchante, mauvaise. Et elle avait juste en idée de le tuer, mais elle pouvait pas avec ses chiens.

Ça fait, une fois elle l'avait tout seul, elle a commencé . . . Elle voulait l'em-

and he and she started to talk together, and then to meet and go out together. And they fell in love.

She told him that she wanted to marry him. He wanted to marry her. She said that she would marry him, but on one condition: he had to kill his dogs. Because she was afraid of dogs. She wouldn't live with those dogs.

[Ida Mayer: She didn't want to go ahead and raise those dogs.]

And this pained him greatly, because he loved his dogs. He went home and then killed his dogs. He killed the three dogs and buried them under the house. But he saved their blood in three buckets, each holding the blood of one of the dogs.

(And his dogs were named Gaillum, Singo, and Moliseau. And each time that he went out hunting, he called them like this [singing]:

Gaillum—llum—llum,
Gaillum—llum—llum,
Singo, Moliseau.

That was his song for calling the dogs when they were chasing rabbits and the like.)

And he said to his mother, he said, "If ever any evil befalls me and I'm in need of help, if I'm in trouble, and you hear this song—if ever you hear this song, go and pour out the buckets of blood over the dogs' graves. Then they'll come to life and come to my aid." And so she said that she would do that.

Then he left home. He married the woman. But it soon became clear that this woman was not good. She was wicked, evil. She just wanted to kill him, but she couldn't do it when his dogs were around.

Then, one time, she had him all

poisonner et elle a essayé de l'em-poisonner, et lui, il était auprès de la morte, en grand danger de mourir, il dit, il s'a mis à chanter cette chanson:

Gaillum—llum—llum,
Gaillum—llum—llum,
Singo, Moliseau.

Et il a chanté ça, et il a chanté ça jusqu'à sa mere a entendu la chanson. Elle s'a rappelé de ça il avait dit, et puis elle a foncé en bas de la maison et puis elle a at-trapé les seaux. Elle a jeté ça dessus les fosses. Et les chiens ont pris . . . et ils ont revenu en vie. Et puis ils ont couru là bas pour trouver leur maître. Et quand ils l'ont trouvé, la femme était juste au moment de le tuer, elle l'avait empoisonné et il était faible, faible, et puis elle était après venir avec un couteau pour le finir.

Et les chiens ont sauté sur elle et puis ils l'ont tuée, et c'est ça qui l'a sauvé la vie.

[Ida Mayer: Elle était maudite!]

[Carl Lindahl: Ouais, au moins.]

Et là, il s'en a retourné à sa maison avec ses chiens pour vivre avec sa mère.

alone. She started—she wanted to poison him, and she tried to poison him, and he was close to death, in great danger of dying. He started to sing this song:

Gaillum—llum—llum,
Gaillum—llum—llum,
Singo, Moliseau.

And he sang it and sang it until his mother heard the song. She remembered what he'd said, and went under the house and got the buckets. She threw the blood over the graves. And the dogs returned to life. And then they ran out to find their master. And when they found him, the woman was just on the verge of killing him. She had poisoned him and he was weak, weak,·and she was coming at him with a knife to finish him off.

And the dogs leapt on her and then they killed her and that's what saved his life.

[Ida Mayer: She was wicked!]

[Carl Lindahl: To say the least.]

And then he went back to his house with his dogs to live with his mother.

183. Show Me Your Paw

CAROLINE SPURLOCK
ANCELET
Shreveport and Ossun, Louisiana
Recorded by Carl Lindahl,
June 23, 1982

On the same afternoon that Barry Ancelet told "Gaillum, Singo, et Moli-seau" (story 182), his wife, Caroline, told this tale to a young boy who was visiting at her house. It was a favorite tale of her maternal grandmother. As a child growing up in Shreveport, Louisiana, in the 1950s, Caroline heard it often, both from her grandmother, Mercedes Supple Postel, and her mother, Caroline Spurlock. "My mother used to always tell us this story, and every time that she and my father would go out, they'd have to show us their 'paw' before we let em in. That's what she'd tell us to do. . . . Even if they had a baby-sitter, my mama and daddy would come home, would knock on the door, and we would say, 'Show us your paw.' And they'd do like this [holding up her hand], and we'd recognize their hands. So we knew it was Mama and Daddy, and we wouldn't let any wolves in."

Once upon a time there was a family of goats, and it was a mama goat and seven baby goats. And they didn't have a daddy. I don't know what happened to the daddy, but he wasn't there with them anymore. I think that the father had been eaten by a wolf that lived nearby.

And so the mother was always afraid of the wolf, and every now and then she would have to leave the children alone, and she would say to them, "When I come home, I will knock on the door. And you must ask—*before you open the door*—for that person to show you their paw. And if it's a white paw like mine, then you can open the door because it's me."

And so the little goats would always say, "Yes, mother." And when she would leave, they'd lock the door, and then they'd start playing all over everywhere and they'd jump on the furniture and frolic all around.

And one day the mother said to the children that she had to go to the store. And she said, "Now, while I'm gone, I want you to lock the door, and if anyone knocks on the door, *don't you* answer it till you ask to see their paw. And you make em show you their paw, and then if it's white like mine, you can open the door."

And she didn't know it, but the wolf was right outside the door listening, and he heard her say that to the children. And when she left, the children locked the door, and then they started playing, and they jumped on top of the cabinets and they jumped from bed to bed and they jumped on the sofa, and they played all around. They were having a wonderful time. And the wolf was just waiting outside. And pretty soon, when he thought the mother had been gone long enough, he knocked on the door, and the goats ran to the door, and they said, "Show us your paw."

And the wolf stuck his paw into some flour. You know, flour is white. And he stuck his hand into some flour that was right next to the door, and then he showed his paw at the window and it was white, so the little goats opened the door and, lo and behold, it was the wolf.

And he started to eat em all up. And they ran and hid in different places. One of em ran into the closet and shut the door. One of em ran under the bed.

One of em got into a barrel. One of them hid in the oven. And he found almost every one of the seven little goats. He ate em up, one by one.

And only one little goat—the little goat that was hiding in the closet—got away. [The wolf] didn't look in the closet. So he had plenty of goats anyway. When he had eaten six of em, that was enough. And he went out to sun himself by the river. He said, "Well, um, I've got to take a nap after that meal."

And the one little goat stayed trembling in the closet, just scared to death. Pretty soon the mother came home and there was the door wide open, and she knew something terrible had happened. The house was a wreck. She could tell that someone had been there, and there were no little goats around, and she started screaming.

And finally the one little goat that was in the closet said, "Mother, Mother."

And she opened the closet. And she said, "Where are the rest of my children?"

And he said, "The wolf came, Mother, the wolf came. And his paw was white, so we opened the door, and he ate everybody up, but he didn't find me."

She said, "Where is he now?"

And the little . . . goat said, "I don't know," but they went to look for him. And they found him down at the river, fast asleep with his stomach poked out here as big as mine, because it was full of baby goats.

And so then, while he was sound asleep and nothing could wake him, the mother went back home and she got her sewing box. She got a needle and thread and scissors and she cut the wolf up—cut open his stomach like that—and she pulled out all of her baby goats and set em all free. And then she filled his stomach with big rocks for each goat, so she put six big rocks in the wolf's stomach. And then she took a needle and thread, and she sewed him back up. And he never woke up. And when she finished sewing, she and all the baby goats rolled him into the river, and he sank. And that's the end of that story.

. . . You know, you got to show your paw.

184. Skullbone

DEBRA ANDERSON
Donaldsonville, Louisiana, and
Houston, Texas
Recorded by Carl Lindahl,
November 13, 1981

This tale, common among rural African Americans at the beginning of the twentieth century, was a staple in the house where Debra Anderson grew up. Her father, Alfred Anderson, was a master narrator who had learned his tales as a child in a farming community near Donaldsonville, Louisiana. Back in the 1930s and 1940s, he said, "there was no TV or radio; this was our best way to pass the time."

As an adult, Alfred Anderson passed quite a lot of time sharing these tales with his daughter Debra and her thirteen brothers and sisters. Debra Anderson, the fifth of Alfred's children, heard "Skullbone" often during her girlhood in the 1960s. In such a large family, conflict and competition among the children was inevitable. Alfred tailored "Skullbone" as a special message to his daughter. When he told the tale, it was always about the negative consequences of tattling, or "telling everything that you hear. Some things you just don't tell everybody . . . , you know, because people won't believe. And this particular thing, you know, [the man in the story] should have kept to himself." The tale had a strong effect on Debra. Of her father's many tales, it is the one that she now remembers best. Now that she is married and a mother, Debra Anderson Fournay retells "Skullbone" to her own children in Houston, Texas. Debra told this version at age 24, before she had her own children to share the tale with.

This man, he works on the farm. And he's out in the pasture and there's this *skeleton head* just lying there. And it talks to him and tell him, "Tongue got *me* here, and it will get *you* here too."

And that man turned around and looks—and no one else is out there but Skullbone. And so he . . . started walking off. And it says, "Tongue got me here, and it will get you here too." And so he realizes that the Skullbone talks.

"Skullbone talked to me." He said, "Wait till I get back and tell everybody about this Skullbone talking."

So he went to his boss and he told the man that a skullbone talked to him. The man said, "Impossible. Skullbone cannot talk."

And he said, "Yes, sir, that Skullbone talked to me—*and he'll talk to you too!*" And he said, "I bet my head on a chopping block Skullbone can talk." So the man took him up on the offer and said, "Okay. If Skullbone doesn't talk, I have your head."

He says, "Skullbone talked. And I know he can talk again."

So the man and his boss and about two other people go out there to where this Skullbone is, just lying here. And so the man say, "Skullbone, talk like you talked to me before." Nothing happens. So he says, "Skullbone, talk to me! You talked to me once; why can't you talk twice?"

So skull says nothing. So now the man, he's begging him, *pleading*, because he bet his head on the *chopping block*. So he's down here, "Skullbone, *please* talk to me! *Please*! You talked once; why can't you talk twice?"

And so he's just begging. And the man says, "I told you, Skullbone cannot talk. Now I have your head."

And he was just still begging: "Skullbone, *please* talk. Why won't you talk?" Ha, ha—and the thing doesn't say anything!

So finally they chop his head off. His head rolls off right next to the Skull-bone head. So they drive off.

So the Skullbone turn around and face the man head, and say, "I told you, tongue got me here and it would get you here too."

185. *La mata de higo*/The Fig Tree

ZIOMARA ANDUX
Ybor City, Tampa, Florida
Recorded by Stetson Kennedy and
Robert Cook,
August 23, 1939

This story comes from the rich Spanish-language tradition of Cuban Americans living in a Tampa neighborhood known as Ybor City, named in honor of cigar maker Vicente Martínez de Ybor. Ybor City was settled in 1886 by cigar company employees who moved from Key West when the owners relocated their factories to avoid the unionization of their workers.

The storyteller, Ziomara Andux, age 13, first summarized this tale in English and then told and sang it in Spanish for collectors Stetson Kennedy and Robert Cook. Below appears the version that she performed in Spanish, alongside Martha Ellen Davis's close English translation of the Spanish-language performance.

Like "Gaillum, Singo, et Moliseau" (story 182), "The Fig Tree" is a *cante-fable*, a tale that is both spoken and sung. Because of their catchy and repetitious musical passages, *cante-fables* are popular vehicles for entertaining children in Spanish-language storytelling traditions.

"*La mata de higo*" is a close relative of "The Juniper Tree," the most controversial of all the tales in the famous collection of the Brothers Grimm. These tales are versions of *My Mother Slew Me, My Father Ate Me* (AT 720), a plot that centers on the brutal murder of a child by her stepmother. Many educators have declared "The Juniper Tree" too gruesome for children and have made efforts to ensure that children will not be exposed to it.

Robert Cook (with camera) and Stetson Kennedy (with recording equipment) recording a performance by Edith Ogden-Aguilar Kennedy, Ybor City, 1939. (Photo by Stetson Kennedy; reproduced with permission)

Nevertheless, Ziomara Andux tells her version of the tale with obvious relish; she is one of the many children worldwide who have found the tale much less upsetting than adults have.

*E*sto era un hombre y su mujer, una madrastra, y tenía cuatro muchachos: dos varones y dos hembras. Y la más chiquitita era a quien siempre le pasaba todo.

Y una vez, ella tenía una mata de higo muy lindo en el fondo. Y no dejaba que nadie cogiera los higos. Y una vez vino un pajarito y le cogió un higo. Y todos dijeron que ellos no habían cogido el higo. Entonces dice: "Parece ser la más chiquitica." Y le preguntó y dijo que no.

Entonces hicieron un hoyo al lado de la misma mata, y le dejó una aguja caer. Y le dijo a chiquita que la pueda coger. Cuando la chiquitita va a coger, que se mete dentro

*O*nce there was a man and his wife, a stepmother, and he had four kids: two boys and two girls. And the littlest girl was the one always getting into trouble.

One time, the mother had a beautiful fig tree in the back of the yard. And she didn't let anybody pick the figs. One day a little bird flew by and plucked a fig. All the kids swore that they hadn't picked the fig. She said, "It must be the littlest girl." So she asked her, and the girl said no.

But the stepmother dug a hole right beside the tree and let a needle fall in. Then she asked the littlest girl to pick it up. When the littlest girl went to get it, she got

558

del hoyo, la tapa de todo, al lado de la misma mata de higo.

Y pasaron los días, y el padre preguntó por su hija. Y dijo que se había ido para la casa de una tía. Pero no era verdad: Que estaba enterrada al lado de la mata de higo.

Entonces pasó dos o tres días. Y se estaba viendo muy linda la mata. Y dijo la hermanita que la dejara coger. Entonces dijo, "Bueno, pues, cógelo." Cuando fueron a buscarlo, oyó una voz que le dijo:

"Hermanita, hermanita,
no me cojas mis higuitos;
porque Mamá me ha enterrado
por un higo que ha faltado."

Y la chiquita se puso que se fue corriendo para donde estaba la madre.
La madre dice, "¿Qué te pasa?"
Dice: "Que oí una voz muy extraña. Me estaba cantando a mí."
"¡Ah! ¡Tú estás oyendo cosas!"
Entonces fue el hermanito; dice, "Entonces, pues, yo voy a oír el canto."
Dice: "Pues, bueno; cógelo."
Cuando fue a buscarlo, dice:

"Hermanito, hermanito,
no me cojas mis higuitos;
porque Mamá me ha enterrado
por un higo que ha faltado."

Y fue cogiendo para la madre otra vez. Y dijo que sí, que había una voz extraña.
Entonces fue el otro hermanito. Y fue para arrancarle un higo.
Y empezó a cantar:

"Hermanito, hermanito,
no me cojas mis higuitos;
porque Mamá me ha enterrado
por un higo que ha faltado."

inside the hole. And the stepmother covered her all up, right beside the fig tree.

Some days went by and the father asked after his daughter. The stepmother replied that she had gone over to an aunt's house. But it was not true: She was buried beside the fig tree.

Two or three more days went by, and the tree was looking very beautiful. Her sister asked permission to pick a fig. The mother said, "Well, all right; go ahead." When the sister went to pick it, she heard a voice which sang:

"Little sister, little sister,
don't pick my figs;
because Mama has buried me
for a missing fig."

The girl went running to the mother.
The mother said, "What's wrong?"
"I heard a very strange voice. It was singing to me."
"Bah! You're hearing things!"
Then one of the brothers said, "Well, I'm going to listen to the song."
The stepmother said, "All right; go pick a fig."
When he went to pick it, the voice sang:

"Little brother, little brother,
don't pick my figs;
because Mama has buried me
for a missing fig."

He went running back to the mother. And he said that, yes, he had heard a strange voice.

Then the other brother went. He pulled off a fig.

And the singing began:

"Little brother, little brother,
don't pick my figs;

Y cogió para la madre y le dijo que sí, que había una voz muy extraña y que les estaba cantando a ellos. "Ustedes están oyendo cosas!"

Entonces fue la madre también a cogerle el higuito.

*"Mamaíta, Mamaíta,
no me cojas mis higuitos;
porque tú me has enterrado
por un higo que ha faltado."*

Entonces ella fue para adentro. Sabía quien era.

Entonces vino el padre y le dijo, "¿Qué pasa?"

Entonces dice: "Ay, no; no sé. Una cosa que hay en la mata."

"¿Qué cosa es?"

Entonces: "Nada; una voz, parece que hay; sí, una voz."

"¿Adónde está mi hija?"

Entonces dice: "Está en la casa de la tía. ¿No te lo dije?"

Entonces fue para donde estaba a cogerle el higo, y oye:

*"Papaíto, Papaíto,
no me cojas mis higuitos;
porque Mamá me ha enterrado
por un higo que ha faltado."*

Entonces dice el hombre, "¡Ah! ¡Porque me ha enterrado a mi hija! Ah, eso porque me dijo que estaba en casa de la tía."

Entonces coge y dice: "Usted me ha enterrado a mi hijita. ¿Por qué?"

Dice ella: "Nada; es que ella me ha robado un higo" y eso.

Y dice: "¡Si es . . . !" Entonces cogió una pala y empezó a sacar y sacar y encontró a la hija. Y la llevaron al hospital y la salvaron.

because Mama has buried me
for a missing fig."

So he went back to the mother and told her that, yes, he too had heard a very strange voice and it was singing to them. "You're hearing things!"

Then the mother herself went to pick a fig.

"Mommy, Mommy,
don't pick my figs;
because you have buried me
for a missing fig."

She went inside the house. She knew who it was.

Then the father came home and asked her, "What's going on?"

She said, "Oh, I don't know. There seems to be something in the tree."

"What is it?"

She said, "Nothing. Well, it seems to be a voice; yes, it's a voice."

"Where is my daughter?"

She said, "She's at an aunt's house. Didn't I tell you?"

Then he went out where she was, to pick a fig, and heard:

"Daddy, Daddy,
don't pick my figs;
because Mama has buried me
for a missing fig."

The man said, "Ah-ha! She has buried my daughter! And she told me she was at an aunt's house!"

So he went and said: "You have buried my little daughter. Why?"

She replied, "It's just because she stole a fig from me."

He said, "Oh, is that so?" He took a

Entonces cogió a la mujer. La mató, y vendió la carne.

Y ahí se acabó el cuento.

shovel and began to dig and to dig and he found his daughter. They took her to the hospital and were able to save her.

Then he grabbed his wife. He killed her and he sold off the meat.

And that's where the story ends.

186. *Señorita Martínez Cucaracha y Señor Ratoncito Pérez*/Miss Martínez Cockroach and Mr. Pérez Mouse

EVELIA ANDUX
Ybor City, Tampa, Florida
Recorded by Stetson Kennedy and Robert Cook,
August 24, 1939

Evelia Andux, age 11, is the younger sister of Ziomara, who narrated "*La mata de higo*" (story 185). Apparently, Evelia's story was a family favorite: Her father, Evilio, also recorded a version of the tale for collectors Stetson Kennedy and Robert Cook (not included here). Evelia was bilingual; responding to her English-speaking interviewers, she began the tale in English, but when they requested her to continue in Spanish, she readily complied. Martha Ellen Davis, who transcribed and translated this tale, remarks on its difficulty. The narration was "sometimes confused," perhaps in part because of the teller's bilingual approach; furthermore, the performance is very difficult to follow "due to recording distortion." Yet Evelia shows talent as a narrator, particularly in her rendition of "superb true-to-life animal sounds."

*L*a cucaracharita *Martínez* goes and buys some powder and. . . . She sits in the window and puts the powder on. . . . She gets "*elegante*" and begins to. . . . *Entonces coge la guitarra, se pone en la ventana, así, a tocar la guitarra.*

Después pasa un chivo. Y entonces dice, "Chivito, ¿te quieres casar conmigo?" Dice: "¡Ay, sí!" Dice: "¿Y cómo es que tú haces con la voz?" Dice: "¡Baaaaaaa!" Dice: "¡Ay, no, no! ¡Que me asustas!"

Entonces pasa una vaca. Dice: "Vaquita, ¿te quieres casar conmigo?" Dice: "Sí"

*M*iss Martínez Cockroach goes and buys some powder. . . . She sits in the window and puts the powder on. . . . She gets elegant, picks up her guitar, sits in the window and begins to play.

Then a goat passes by. And she asks, "Little Goat, do you want to marry me?" He says, "Yes, I do!" She asks, "But what sound do you make?" He says: "Baaaaaa!" She cries, "Oh, no, no! You frighten me!"

Then a bull passes by. She asks, "Little bull, do you want to marry me?" He says, "Yes!" She asks, "But what sound do

Dice: "¿Cómo tú haces con la voz?" Dice: "¡Muuuuu!" "¡Ay, no, no! ¡Que me asustas!"

Entonces hace así y pasa un perro. Dice, "Perrito, ¿te quieres casar conmigo?" Dice: "Sí" "¿Cómo tú haces con la voz?" "¡Bow-wow!" "¡Ay, no, no! ¡Que me asustas!"

Entonces pasa un gallo. Dice, "Gallito, ¿te quieres casar conmigo?" Dice: "Sí" "¿Cómo es tú haces con la voz?" "¡Aaa—a-a-aaa!" [kikirikí] " "¡Ay, no, no! ¡Que me asustas!"

Entonces pasa un ratón. Dice: "Ratoncito, ¿te quieres casar conmigo?" Dice, "Sí." Dice: "¿Cómo tú haces con la voz?" Dice: "¡Wi-wi-wi-wi-wi!" Dice: "All right."

Entonces se casaron. Entonces era un domingo y ella fue y se metió en la "Chochi" [church]. Entonces ella dejó la olla en la candela. Y le dijo que no cogiera la [cuchara] chiquitica, que cogiera la grande [a menear la olla]. Entonces el ratoncito se cansa y se manda a la olla[?]. Y el ratoncito se le olvidó sobre la cuchara chiquitica. No cogió la grande; y se cayó [dentro] del otro lado de la olla.

Entonces viene ella. Dice: "¡Ratoncito Pérez! ¡Ratoncito Pérez!" "Eres muy mal parado[?]; estás comiendo de mi . . . , estás comiendo de mi—"

Entonces dice: "¡Ay! ¡Se me está quemando la olla!" Entonces . . . se va al otro [lado] y encontró al ratoncito.

Entonces se puso el [polvo] blanco y cogió la guitarra y se sentó en la ventana, dice:

"Ratoncito Pérez
Cayó en la olla
Por la gelocina
De una cebolla!"

you make?" He says: "Moooooo!" She cries, "Oh, no, no! You frighten me!"

Then a dog passes by. She asks, "Doggy, do you want to marry me?" He says, "Yes!" "But what sound do you make?" "Bow-wow!" "Oh, no, no! You frighten me!"

Then a rooster passes by. She asks, "Rooster, do you want to marry me?" He says, "Yes!" "But what sound do you make?" "Cock-a-doodle-doo!" "Oh, no, no! You frighten me!"

Then a mouse passed by. She asks, "Little mouse, do you want to marry me?" He says, "Yes!" She asks, "But what sound do you make?" He replies, "Wee-wee-wee-wee-wee!" She says, "All right."

So they were married. One Sunday she went to church. She left the pot on the fire. And she told him not to stir it with the little spoon, to use the big one. The little mouse got tired of waiting and went to the pot. He forgot the warning about the little spoon. He did not use the big one and fell into the far side of the pot.

Then she came back. She called, "Little Mouse Pérez! Little Mouse Pérez!" "You are in trouble! You have been eating my stew!"

Then she cried, "Oh! My pot is burning!" And when she looked on the far side she found the little mouse.

So she put on her white powder, took up the guitar and sat in the window, singing:

"Little Mouse Pérez
Fell into the pot
Because of his craving
For an onion!"

187. *Antonio, cortador de leña/* Antonio the Woodcutter

MARTIN NORIEGA
Ybor City, Tampa, Florida
Recorded by Stetson Kennedy and Robert Cook,
August 23, 1939

Like the previous two tales, this delightfully subversive märchen is told by a Floridian of Cuban descent. Unlike the previous two narrators, however, Martin Noriega was not a child, but a 51-year-old man. His seasoned verbal skills are substantial, and he seems to be tailoring his performance to meet the unreasonable demands of the recording technology available to his interviewers: a twelve-inch aluminum disk that will allow him only about four minutes to tell a relatively complex tale. Folklorist Martha Ellen Davis, who translated this and the preceding tales from Ybor City, noted both the excellence of the narrator and the difficulties he faced recording "Antonio": "It's a great story—though the storyteller was rushing through it, cutting detail, I think to fit it on a record. . . . The storyteller—who is very good— speaks very fast and swallows words." Remarkably, Noriega was able to get all but two sentences of this tale onto one side of one disk.

"Antonio the Woodcutter" builds on one of the most popular themes in European märchen tradition: the magical bond formed between an unassuming child hero and a series of animals that he has saved from death. More specifically, "Antonio" is an example of an international tale type known as *The Magic Ring* (AT 560), which possesses substantial popularity through much of Europe as well as in parts of Hispanic America. Although known in distinctive Caribbean versions in Cuba and Puerto Rico, the tale is rare among Spanish speakers in the United States and rarer still among English speakers. To date, no English-language American version has been reported.

In many versions of *The Magic Ring*, the queen and the hero are happily reunited at the tale's end. But Noriega's tale, which emphasizes the loyalty of the downtrodden animals and the deceptiveness of the queen, ends with the animals and Antonio living alone together. The cat, dog, and boy will be happy together as long as Antonio accepts the pets' demands to "never again marry a queen." This antiroyalist twist seems appropriate from a man whose forebears emigrated from Cuba to Florida when Cuba was a colony of monarchist Spain.

Éste era un muchacho que tenía a la madre que era una viejita. Y él iba al campo a cortar leña para llevarle a la madre dinero para poder comer entre ellos. Y así llevaba un poco de tiempo viviendo, y el muchacho cortando leña.

Pero en eso ese muchacho vio a un hombre que iba con un saco; y llevaba un gato en el saco y lo iba a tirar al agua. Y el muchacho le dijo: "No, señor: no haga usted eso al pobrecito gatico. ¿Por qué lo va a coger y lo va a matar?"

Y dice el hombre: "Bueno, cógeselo. Porque este gato se puede meter con las palomas en casa y no me deja ni una paloma en mi casa."

Dice: "Bueno, démelo. En mi casa no hay palomas. Déjemelo. Déjeme el gatico." Cogió y lo llevó para su casa.

Y entonces la madre que ve que el muchacho viene con un gato y le dice: "Pero, hijo mío, ¿cómo tú traes un gato aquí? Nosotros pasando miseria, que tú tienes que cortar leña y eso."

Y él dice: "No te preocupes, Mamá; yo corto más leña." Entonces fue él y sigió cortando leña.

Pero al poco tiempo él vio que a un hombre que llevaba un perro también en un saco, y lo iba a tirar al mar. Y le dice: "¡Oiga, señor! No sea usted tan malo. No vaya usted a matar al pobre perrito ese. Démelo a mí, que yo lo llevo para mi casa."

Entonces dice: "[Ten cuidado], porque muerde a la gente."

Dice: "No importa; me lo llevo para mi casa. Él no me va a morder." Y cogió y lo llevó para su casa.

Y la madre le arma otra pelota y le dice, "Pero, hijo mío, ¿cómo es que tú traes un perro para acá?"

"Pero no te preocupes, Mamá. Yo sigo cortando leña."

Once there was a boy who had a mother who was very old. He would go to the forest to chop firewood to bring money for his mother to buy food for them both. And that's how they lived for a time, with the boy chopping firewood.

But one day the boy saw a man who was walking along with a sack. He was carrying a cat in the sack and was going to throw it into the water. And the boy said, "No, sir! Don't do that to the poor little cat. Why are you going to take it and kill it?"

And the man replied, "Well, you can have it. This cat can get into my pigeons at home and leave me without a single pigeon."

The boy said, "Give it to me, then. At my house I don't have any pigeons. Give it to me; leave me the cat." And he took it home.

His mother saw that the boy was coming home with a cat and said, "My son, why are you bringing a cat here? We are so poor that you have to chop firewood and such."

And he replied, "Don't worry, Mama; I'll just chop more firewood." And so he went out and continued chopping firewood.

But soon afterward he saw a man who was carrying a dog, also in a sack, and was going to throw him into the sea. The boy said, "Hey, sir! Don't be so so mean. Don't go and kill that poor little dog. Give him to me, and I'll take him home."

The man said, "Be careful! That dog bites people." But the boy replied, "That doesn't matter; I'll take him home anyway. He won't bite me." And he up and took the dog home.

His mother hollered at him again: "My son, why are you bringing a dog here?"

E iba con su perro y su gato todos los días a cortar leña. Y se aparecía en su casa y daba el dinero a su madre. Y la madre muy conforme.

Pues, entonces pasó un tiempo muy malo. Y en eso va al monte a cortar leña, y ve una culebra allí, que un hombre la iba a matar. Y él dice: "No mate a esta culebra, señor"—una culebra de cascabel.

Y él dice, "Bueno, si tú la quieres, cógela." Y él cogió y la puso en el seno.

Y va para donde está la madre y dice: "Mamá: mira lo que iba a hacer un hombre: iba a matar a esa culebrita, y la pobrecita. Mira: yo la tengo aquí."

"Hijo mío, ¿qué vas a hacer con eso? Dios mío, ¡llévatela! ¡Llévatela, que yo no la quiero ésta en mi casa!"

Y el muchacho cogió y la llevó al monte. Y allí le llevaba todos los días de que comer. La culebra se ponía a esperarlo para que la llevara la comida todos los días.

Pero en eso coge el muchacho y se enfermó. Y pasó mucho tiempo. Y el muchacho estaba muy triste porque no veía a su culebrita.

Bueno, entonces cogió y se puso bien. Y siguió cortando leña, pero con el perro y el gato, a cortar leña. Y en eso cogió y fue adonde estaba el nido, y no encontró en el nido a la culebra. Y dijo, "¡Ay, Dios mío! La culebra mía se me murió por no darle de que comer."

Y coge el muchacho y se va para su casa, muy triste, y la madre le dice: "¿Qué te pasa, hijo mío?"

"Mamá, no me pasa nada, no me pasa nada."

Bueno . . . y en eso vino un tiempo muy malo. Y él se fue a cortar leña así y todo. Y se encuentra con una culebra grandísima que se abría la boca y le quería comer. Y le dice: "No me tengas miedo; que en un

"Don't worry, Mama. I'll keep chopping firewood."

And so he went out every day, with his dog and his cat, to chop firewood. And every day he went home and gave the money to his mother. And the mother was very pleased.

But then a stormy time came up. And during that time, he went to the forest to chop firewood and saw a snake that a man was about to kill. He said, "Don't kill that snake, sir!" It was a rattlesnake.

And the man said, "Well if you want it, take it." And the boy took it and put it on his chest.

And he went to his mother saying, "Mama, imagine what a man was going to do! He was going to kill a little snake, the poor little thing. Look! I have it here!"

"My son! What are you doing with that thing! My goodness, take it away! Take it away; I don't want it in my house!"

And the boy took it back to the forest. And every day he carried it some food. The snake waited for him to bring her food every day.

But then the boy got sick. A long time went by, and the boy was very sad because he couldn't see his little snake.

But then he got better. And he returned to chopping firewood, with his dog and his cat. So he went to where the snake's nest was, but the snake was not in her nest. And he said, "Oh, my goodness! My snake has died on me because I didn't feed it." And the boy went home, very sad. His mother asked him, "What's the matter, my son?"

"Nothing, Mama, nothing."

Well, then a big storm came up. But he went to chop firewood anyway. And he comes upon a *huge* snake who opens up

tiempo tú me salvaste a mi la vida y ahora yo te voy a salvar a ti. ¿Tú ves este anillo que tengo yo aquí en el rabo? Tú la coges. Y con este anillo tú pides lo que tú quieras, que Dios te lo da."

Y el muchacho fue muy contento para su casa con el perro y el gato. Dice: "Mamá, ¡ahora es que sí vamos a ser felices!"

Dice: "¿De qué manera dices que tú lo ves?"

"La culebrita aquella que yo salvé aquella vez que la iban a matar, pues, me dio esta sortija; y con esta sortija yo puedo pedir lo que yo quiera."

Y entonces coge y dice el perro: "Pide usted, señor amo, lo que usted quiera."

Y el señor amo dice: "Me quiero casar con una reina." Y en seguida viene un palacio grandísimo—y la riqueza y todo. Vivían más contentos.

Y el perro y el gato estaban comiendo bien, porque el criado le tenía que traer la comida al perro y al gato, sabe?

Entonces . . . la reina no le gustaba el muchacho. Y la reina cogió y le quitó la sortija al muchacho, y dice: "Pásenme para el otro lado del río." Y cogió la reina y se fue para el otro lado del río.

Y entonces la familia se volvió pobre otra vez y pasando miseria. Y el perro y el gato decían, "Chico, si no tenemos de que comer, cómo nos vamos a arreglar ahora? Tan bien que estábamos y ahora con esta cuestión que se llevaron—la sortija—de nuestro amo, estamos pasando miseria. Pues tenemos nosotros que hacer algo por él."

Y entonces coge el perro y el gato y dicen: "Vamos a buscar el modo de ir allá al otro lado para buscar la sortija." Coge el perro y el gato y se van. Y cogen una calabaza y hacen un bote. Y pasan del río al otro lado. Y llegaban allá donde estaba la reina, que estaba en un palacio.

her mouth [as if] to eat him! But instead the snake says, "Don't be afraid of me. Once upon a time you saved my life, and now I am going to save yours. See this ring that I have here on my tail? Take it. With this ring you can ask for whatever you want, and God will grant it."

So the boy went home, very pleased, with his dog and his cat. He said, "Mama, we are going to be happy now!"

She asks, "And how do you know that?"

"The little snake that I saved one time, when they were going to kill her, has given me this ring. And with this ring I can ask for whatever I want."

So the dog said, "Make a wish, master, for whatever you want."

And his master said, "I want to marry a queen!" Right away an enormous castle appeared, with all of its treasure and everything. And there they lived very happily.

The dog and the cat were eating very well, because the servant had to bring food to the dog and the cat, you see.

However, . . . the queen did not like the boy! So she took the ring away from him and said: "Carry me over to the other side of the river." And the queen up and went to the other side of the river.

And then the family fell into poverty again and were having a very hard time. The dog and the cat said to each other, "Hey, pal, we don't have anything to eat. What are we going to do now? We were sure doing well; but now with this thing— that ring—that they took from our master, we are having it real bad. Well, now we have to do something for him!"

And so the dog and the cat said, "Let's figure out how to go over there to the other side and get the ring back." So

Y en eso ve el gato un ratón. Y agarra el ratón, y le dice: "Como tú no hagas lo que yo te digo, yo te voy a comer."

Y entonces el ratón dice: "Lo que tú quieras."

Dice, "Bueno, pues tú me haces esto: tú vas donde está la reina y le quitas la sortija. Y en eso, te doy un queso de bola."

Y sale volado el ratón: ¡Pum! Y le quita la sortija a la reina. Y coge el perro y el gato y se la llevan. Y se van para el otro lado nadando.

Pero en eso coge el perro, y con la ambición de tener la sortija en la mano, se le cae al mar. "¡Ay! ¡Ay, Dios mío!" Y en eso ven que un pescado se la come, y un pescador lo cogió.

Y al coger el pescado, dice el gato: "No te preocupes, que yo se la saco al pescado." Se llevó el pescado, le sacó la sortija a la barriga al pescado y luego se la llevaron allá.

Y entonces le dicen el perro y el gato al amo, dicen: "Mira, señor amo, . . . aquí le traemos la sortija para que usted no se vuelva a casar más con reina, y con eso nosotros vamos a volver a ser felices como antes."

Y ahí se concluyó.

the dog and the cat took a gourd and made a boat, and they crossed the river to the other side. And they arrived at the place where the queen was, in a palace.

And as soon as they got there, the cat saw a mouse. He grabbed the mouse and said, "If you don't do what I say, I'm going to eat you!"

And so the mouse said, "Whatever you want!"

The cat said, "Well, this is what you have to do: You will go to where the queen is and take away the ring. And if you do, I will give you a cheese ball."

And the mouse dashed off. Zap! He takes the ring from the queen. And the dog and the cat get it, and head off for the other side, swimming.

But then the dog, who wants so badly to hold the ring in his paw, drops it into the sea. "Oh, no! Oh, my goodness!" And just then they see a fish that swallows it, and a fisherman who catches the fish.

But when the fish was caught, the cat said, "Don't worry; I'll get it out of the fish." He took the fish away, he removed the ring from the fish's belly, and he took it back home.

And the dog and the cat said to their master, "Look, master, we are bringing back the ring here, but you must never again marry a queen! And with this we are going to be happy like before."

And that's the end.

188. The Fox, the Rabbit, and the Tarbaby

E.L. SMITH
Oglethorpe County, Georgia, and Calvin, Michigan
Collected by Richard M. Dorson, Calvin, Michigan, 1952

The story of Brer Rabbit and the Tarbaby is perhaps the best known of all African American tales. Popular among white readers as well as black storytellers from the time that Georgia journalist Joel Chandler Harris published a version in his *Nights of Uncle Remus* (1880), the tale attained even greater currency through an animated version that appeared in Walt Disney's film *Song of the South* (1946), which focused on Harris's storytelling slave, Uncle Remus. The Disney version also exerted a strong influence on African American narrators, who in the 1940s were unaccustomed to seeing black heroes in feature-length films. Many storytellers who had dropped the tarbaby story from their repertoires began retelling the tale after it had been featured in *Song of the South*.

E.L. Smith was a master narrator who told many family legends dating back to slavery days (see stories 195 and 196). The following version combines the tarbaby tale with another extremely popular African American tale in which Rabbit cheats his animal "friends" by pretending to hear distant voices calling him and begging him to assist at a birth. When safely out of sight, the rabbit steals the food that all the animals had set aside to share among themselves.

There was a rabbit and a fox. They was having what they call a house-raising. And the rabbit was supposed to be a doctor. And they had milk in the spring, and this here Rabbit would, every once in a while he'd work a little bit, and he'd holler, "*Whooo!*"

The fox said, "Who is that?"

"Somebody calling me."

Says, "What they want?"

"Oh, I don't know, and I ain't going to see."

"Oh, yes, sir. You's a doctor. You—better go see."

So he went on down to the spring and got in this milk. And drink some of that. Come on back.

And when he got back, Fox says, "Who is it? What was it?"

Says, "Just Started."

All right. He went on, worked a little bit, and directly he says, "*Whoo-oo-oo!*"

"Who is that now?"

"Somebody else calling me. I ain't going this time."

Fox say, "Yeah, you're going." Says, "You got to go." Says, "You's a doctor."

And he went on down to the spring to drink up this milk, part of it. About half of it. Come back.

Fox says, "What'd you name him?"

"Half Gone." [Laughter]

He went on back and worked a little bit. Directly then, "*Whoo-oo-oo!*"

Says, "What is that now?"

"Somebody else calling me."

"Well, better go see."

"No, I ain't going."

"Yeah, you go ahead."

So he went on down to the spring and drink it *all* up. Filled his jug up with water. Kept on doing that until the fox decided he would see what, who it was. He put him a tarbaby down there.

So, the rabbit he come down there and seen it setting there. Says, "What you doing here?"

Tarbaby didn't say nothing.

He says, "Speak, or I'll knock you over."

Tarbaby just sat there. Didn't say a word.

And he hauled off, slapped him with one foot. When he slapped him, that foot stuck to him. He says, "Now, turn me loose. I've got another one here." Said, "I'll slap you with it."

He slapped him with the other one, and that one stuck.

He said, "Just turn me loose. I got another one here, but I kick you with it. I'll kick you over. So he kicked him with that foot, and that one stuck. He says, "Better turn me loose." Said, "I got another one here," says, "and I'll kick you with it." Says, "I'll kick you clear over." He kicked him with that one and that one stuck.

He says, "Better turn me loose. I got a head yet. I'll butt you to pieces." So he butted him, and his head stuck.

There he was. Couldn't get loose.

Fox, he come down to the spring and, "*Um, hum.* I knowed I get you. I knowed you was the one drinking up my milk."

He turned him and started to the house with him. Says, "I don't know what hardly to do with you," and says, "but I'm going to take you to the house." They got up the road a pretty good piece toward the house. There's a big, thick briar patch there. He says, "I'm of a good mind to throw you out in them briars."

The rabbit says, "*Oh*, Mr. Fox, *please* don't throw me out there in them briars. I'd get all scratched up and all tore up with them briars. *Don't* throw me out there."

"Yes, I aim to. Shut up! I'll throw you right out there in the middle of em." After a while he took the rabbit, you know, and throwed him over in the briar patch.

And the old rabbit kicked up his heels. He says, "*Ohhhooo*, here's where I want to be. Here's where I's bred and born anyhow."

189. The Tarbaby

CORA JACKSON
Rappahannock County, Virginia
Recorded by Charles L. Perdue Jr.
and Nancy J. Martin-Perdue,
Philadelphia, Pennsylvania,
November 11, 1968

Cora Jackson, wife of the great blues singer and guitarist John Jackson, told this story to a gathering of folklorist-folksingers in Philadelphia in 1968. Jackson family friends Chuck and Nan Perdue and folklore student (later AFC archivist) Gerald Parsons were present for the session, as was folksinger Bryan Sutton.

Cora's version of the famous tarbaby story ends with an unexpected twist; the listeners express surprise and ask Cora for explanations.

I know one about the tarbaby.
[Charles Perdue: Well, tell me that one.]

There was this old . . . fox kept on bothering this old rabbit. So [the rabbit] didn't want him to catch him, so . . . the old fox made the tarbaby.

[Bryan Sutton: What's a tarbaby?]

It's a bunch of tar—you make it [to look like] a human being, like a little boy or girl.

Well, this old rabbit goes down to the spring, so he sets this tarbaby down there to catch him.

So the old rabbit come along. He said, "Good morning, Mr. Tarbaby."

He wouldn't say nothing.

He said, "I said, 'Good morning, Mr. Tarbaby.' "

So he would say nothing.

So he said, "I will slap you." So he hauled off and he smacked the old tarbaby, and his hand stuck. And he said, "I have another hand, and I'll smack you again." So he smacked him with his other hand, and both his hands stuck. And he said, "I have a foot. I'll kick you." So he kicked him and he said, "I have another foot." And he kicked him with the other foot so both his feets stuck, and when the fox come along there was the rabbit stuck to the tarbaby.

Old fox said, "Ha, ha, I knowed, Mr. Rabbit, I'd catch you if I put out the tarbaby." So the old fox caught the old rabbit with the tarbaby, and he et him up.

[Nancy Perdue: He ate him?]

[Bryan Sutton: He didn't get away?]

No, he stuck to the tarbaby.

[Nancy Perdue: How'd he get him loose to eat him?]

[Charles Perdue: Cooked him in tar.]

I imagine that's how he get him.

190. Jack and the Beanstalk

WILBUR ROBERTS
Riviera, Florida
Recorded by Stetson Kennedy and
Robert Cook,
Riviera, Florida, January 15, 1940

"Jack and the Beanstalk" is probably the best-known tale in English-language storybook tradition. Nevertheless, folklorists have rarely recorded it in live performance, and it seems to be much more popular in print and cartoon forms than in living folkloric traditions. The only other version I have been able to find in the collections of the American Folklife Center is "The Bean Tree" as told by Samuel Harmon (story 9), which is closer to the storybook tale than is the following version.

Wilbur Roberts, born in 1856, was 84 years old and blind when the following performance was recorded. A native of the Bahamas, Roberts had lived in Florida for nearly four decades when folklorist Stetson Kennedy recorded this tale from him. Roberts had heard the story when he was about 55 years old, from a Puerto Rican immigrant. They were "just sitting down, talking" when the tale emerged from their conversation: "I was in Florida.

He was in Florida too." Thus, "Jack and the Beanstalk" is the only tale in this section of the book that the teller learned after childhood, and it is the only tale that was not passed on within a family tradition. When Kennedy asked Roberts from whom he had learned the tale, Roberts had trouble remembering the teller's name or place of birth; he simply answered that the storyteller had come from a "place up there where the hurricanes always start at."

The following tale bears little resemblance to the version that most Americans know. Note that the hero does not bear the name "Jack," and that the only major plot element shared by this performance and the storybook tale is the fact that the hero climbs a beanstalk. This tale features no giant, no giant's wife, no singing harp, nor golden-egg-laying goose. I think it likely that the familiar title was tacked upon this version by the collectors and not by the storyteller himself.

Well you know, this fella once, he climbed a beanstalk. And he keep a-climbing and climbing and climbed and he climbed up so high till he got up to the [third heaven]. And when he got up there, he could just make to get out and that was all. And when he got up there, he looked around. And he saw, he saw fifty thousand women making clothes for the people. And they turned around and looked at him and asked him what he was doing there, said, "This ain't no place for you to be." In there. Then [they] asked for him to go down. [He] said, well, there was no way for him to get down. Said well, he'd better tear up the linen cloth and knot it together, until he could get, reach down. So they [finally] tied it up and knotted it together, and knotted it together until they just got enough to reach down just about thirty feet from the ground. And he come down by that. First he thought he'd fall feet forward. He doesn't know that if he falls feet forward his legs will go up. . . . Says, "I guess I'll go head forward."

So he went down headfirst, and when he come down headfirst he was buried up to the forehead in the sand till he couldn't get out. And he said, well, he thought he'd go home and get him a hoe and go down and dig hisself out. Well he went home and got him a hoe and . . . went down and dug himself out. And while he was digging, he stuck a corner of that hoe in his eye and it made him slit-eyed. And that's why you see slit-eyed people today.

191. Little Nippy

LEE WALLIN
Sodom, North Carolina
Recorded by Henry Glassie,
Madison County, North Carolina,
June 10, 1963

Whereas Wilbur Roberts's "Jack and the Beanstalk" (story 190) has nothing in common with the English storybook tale except the beanstalk, Lee Wallin's "Little Nippy" lacks the beanstalk but runs closely parallel to the tale in most other ways. Nippy, like Jack, undertakes three journeys to the realm of a giant, but instead of ascending a stalk, Nippy crosses a river. On each of the these journeys, Nippy steals one of the giant's prized possessions: a yoke of oxen, a "half-moon" water pitcher, and an enchanted (or, as Lee Wallin puts it, "chanted") harp that plays any tune that comes to the boy's mind.

Lee Wallin comes from a family noted for the richness of its singing traditions, but as far as I can determine, no one recorded folktales from the family until folklorist Henry Glassie visited in 1963 in the company of collector Richard Chase, who was also present when this tale was recorded. Chase at this time was a seasoned folktale collector (see stories 143, 163, and 164), and twenty years had passed since he had authored *The Jack Tales,* the most popular of all American folktale anthologies. Glassie, on the other hand, was a young man just beginning to make his reputation as a folklorist. In the years to follow, he would write landmark books on folk architecture and folk art, and in another two decades he would publish *Passing the Time in Ballymenone* (1982), an exploration of storytelling traditions in a Northern Irish village and one of the finest studies of folk narrative *in vivo* ever written.

When Glassie and Chase asked him to tell them a tale, Lee Wallin responded eagerly, but with one condition: he would need young children in his audience to tell it right. Accordingly, some neighbor children were rounded up. One of the newcomers was a baby, who can be heard crying loudly in certain sections of the taped performance. The other members of the audience, however, often broke out in hearty laughter to express their appreciation of the storyteller's art.

Wallin's performance is powerful and unique. He speaks in "breath units," beginning his phrases on a loud pitch and gradually softening his voice as he nears the end of the phrase. Wallin's style is much like that of the traditional preachers of the region. His preacher-like tones and rhythms are particularly strong in the call-and-response chants in which the giant and Nippy taunt each other. The giant bellows out, vibrato: "Wel-l-l, Nippy, when are you going to see me again?" And Nippy chants his answer.

Lee Wallin's storytelling vocabulary is rich with phrases and pronunciations that were already archaic when this recording was made. Apparently, he uses the term "pie crusts" to refer to the "sleep," or mucus, that collects overnight in the eyes of sleepers. Seeming to doubt that the collectors will know what a "half moon" is, he explains that it is something "to carry water in." Similarly, when Nippy tells the giant, "I'm so fat I'll *spile* on your hands," Lee clarifies by repeating the phrase with the standard pronunciation, "spoil," and telling his listeners that Nippy spoke the word the way "old people" do.

One time they's three boys, Sam and Nod and Nippy. They started out to seek their fortune. They was a-going to the king's house. And they wanted Nippy to stay there—he weren't too big—feed the calves and things. (I'll tell it a little slower now, okay?) The calves and things. And he follered them anyhow. They got up way up on the hill and they'd see him a-coming. And they'd say [chanting]: "Go, ba-a-ck, Nifty." And he'd run back around the bend and after a while when they got around the bend, he'd run out and overtake em again. [Laughter] And they'd say, "Go back, Nifty." He'd hide again, and he kept on till he got so far-r-r away that they was afraid that he would get lost and couldn't get back. And they asked him, said, "Wel-l-l, Nippy," said, "We'll let you go with us."

He said, "Will you?"

"Will you ask to stay all night, when night comes tonight?"

He said, "Yes, I'll do that." They went on. They traveled and traveled and traveled; now it be getting late and the evening begin to come on. They come up on a big house and it happened to be the giant's house. Nippy says, "What about getting to stay all night with you?"

"Well," he says, "I guess I could keep you." Well, he said, "I'll try to keep you then."

"Well," Nippy told him, said, "they's me and my two brothers."

"Well," he said, "where will you'uns want to sleep at? Sleep downstairs in the cellar with me, or upstairs on the good beds with my three daughters?"

"Well," he said, "we'll just sleep upstairs where you got the beds and . . . your three daughters sleep. [Laughter] . . .

"Wel-l-l," he says, "that's all right then." And he put em up there.

And Nippy looked over and he noticed that the three daughters had golden lockets around their necks: big, fine, golden lockets. He waited till they got asleep a-way in the night and he eased up and he unlatched them lockets and put em on his'n and his two brothers' necks. Well, way in the night, Nippy heard him coming up the stairs a-whetting and a-whetting. He come up a-whetting that knife and he come over and he felt . . . Nippy's and their necks, and they had lockets on em. Well, he thought that was his three daughters. And he went over to t'other bed and he cut his three daughters' necks, cut their throats, you know, and killed em. And Nippy let the boys sleep a little longer and then he said, "Wel-l-l, we'd better get up and get away from here." Said, "The giant's come up and thought he killed us and killed his three daughters." Says, "I took the lockets off their necks and put em on our'n," and says, "we'd better be a-making tracks away from here."

Well, they got out and as they come down the stairs . . . coming on down the stairs, Nippy seed a staff there, there was a chanted staff [that is, an "enchanted staff"] sitting there by the side of the house. He picked it up. Well, he got to the river, and when he got to the river, he looked and seed the giant a-coming. He spread that staff out, and it just made a bridge across the river. They got across and Nippy pulled it across.

He said, "Wel-l-l-l, Nippy, when are you coming back to see me again? You caused me to kill my three daughters, took my three golden lockets and my golden staff, and," he said, "Wel-l-l, Nippy, when you be back and see me again."

He said, "I'll be back to see you again some of these days."

Well, he went on and come to the king's house. He told the king what he had done and the king said, "Well, Nippy. He's got three more things—now if you'll get," he says, "I want you to get for me." Says, "If you'll get what he got," says, "I'll give you my oldest daughter for a wife." And says, "You'll inherit half of my kingdom with my death."

He says, "What is it?"

He says, "It's a big yoke of oxen." Says, "The giant stole em from me a-way back there." And he says, "I want em back." And he goes to the giant's house and he looks around and around and around a-trying to get a chance to steal them oxens. He never get no chance, and he kept laying out a-looking. One day he seed a boy taking em out in the field to plow. He hustled on to that boy, and he said, "Son," he said, "the giant's sick." He said, "Your master's sick and very sick," and said, "for you to come there as quick as you could and bring the doctor for him, and me to plow the oxens till you got back."

[The plowboy] just threw him the lines and made a beeline to the house. When he got there, and he went into the house, the old giant says, "What you come a-staving in here at this time of day for without them oxen?" and he says, "I'll lay-y-y Nippy's about." He made for the river again. By the time he got to the river, Nippy'd stretched out the golden staff across the river and went across and pulled it across.

And he says, "Wel-l-l, when are you coming back to see me again, Nippy?" He said, "You caused me to—you killed my three daughters, took my three golden lockets and my golden staff, and," he said, "now you've took my yoke of oxens. Wel-l-l, when'll you be back to see me again?"

He said, "I'll be back some of these days."

He went on and the [king] told him, he said, "Now, you can have my oldest girl."

He said, "I don't want her myself, but I want her for my oldest brother."

So the oldest brother got that girl.

And he said, "Now, the next—you can have my next oldest daughter if you'll get another thing he's got."

He said, "What's it?"

He said, "It's a half-moon, to carry water in." He said, "He stole it from me a-way back yonder," and said, "my wife wants it back," and said, "I want you to get it for me." And he says, "I don't know what it'll be pretty hard to get."

And [Nippy] says, "I'll do the best I can."

He went and watched and watched and watched, and one day he seed the old woman a-coming toward the spring to get a pitcher of water in that half-moon of a thing. He went down to the spring to her and he says, "Can you travel pretty fast?"

And she told him, "No," said, "I'm getting old. I can't go as fast as I used to."

"Well," he said, "I'll tell you what." Says, "I'll carry that half-moon of water to the house for you and let you go up the nigh way here, and I'll go around the far way, and I'll bet you I can beat you to the house."

She says, "I don't believe you could do that." [Laughter] She reached him that half-moon and when he picked up the half-moon she started up the nigh way and she got out of sight. Nippy threw the water out and he made for the river again.

Just as he got there and sticked that staff out across there, he seed the old giant a-coming over yonder.

And said, "Wel-l-l, Nippy, when are you coming to see me again? You took my three golden lockets, stole my golden staff," and said, "caused me to kill my three daughters, and took my yoke of oxen, and now you've took my half-moon. And when-n-n you coming back to see me again?"

He said, "I'll be back to see you some of these days."

He went on and the king was pleased with the half-moon. He said, "Nippy," said, "he got one more thing I want back that he stole from me." And he says, "You can have my baby girl for your wife, and you'll inherit half of my [realm] at my death," and says, "you and her can live happy here forever."

And he says, "What is it this time?"

He said, "It's a chanted harp. It'll play any song that you think of. Don't differ what it is, if your mind comes on it," says, "it'll go to playing it."

"Well," he says, "that's going to be hard to get to. That's in the house, but," he says, "I'll do my best." Says, "I want your baby girl for me wife."

So he left and he watched and watched and watched and layed out in the woods and he had to watch a long time. One night, there was a meeting. The old woman and the old man started to the meeting. They went, and when they got there, the preacher sent word he wouldn't be there. [The giants] didn't stay as long as Nippy thought [they] would. [The preacher had] sent word he couldn't come that night. He was sick. He'd be there another time. The old woman and the old man a-come back to the house . . . and when they sat down, Nippy he just scooted, he got over behind the bed to get it—it was up hind the bedstead. One of them old-time wooden bedsteads, and he reached up to get it, and he just brought it back down, and he set there a while and then he thought of that tune, "Buttermilk and Brandy" [laughter]—"mind your step and let the girls be handy." And [the harp] went to playing it.

And he said, "Old Woman, have you thought of that buttermilk tune at the end of the meeting tonight, Old Woman?"

And she said, "No, indeed, Old Man, I haven't."

He just said, "I lay-y-y Nippy's about."

He reached over and took him by the top of the head, that-a-way. [Laughter]

"Well, Nippy," he said, "if you'd done me like I have you," he says, "what would you do with me?"

Nippy says, "I believe I'd put you up in a pen and fatten you and kill you and eat you."

He said, "I guess that'd be about as good a thing as I could do with you."

So he put him up in a pen and he fed him eggs and everything good to eat that he needed. And [it] went on and on and on until one day he come down to feed Nippy, a good plate of eating to give him. He give it in to him.

Nippy said, "I guess that I'm about as fat as you're going to get me," he says. "I believe that the best thing you could do," he says, "would be to kill me right now and eat me."

He says, "I guess that'd be the best thing I could do then."

Well, he began to get ready like he was a-going to kill him, and [Nippy] says, "I believe if I was you I'd go out and ask my friends and neighbors to come in and help eat me," he says. "I'm so fat I'll spile on your—spoil on your hands." (He said it like old people), says, "I'm so fat," says, "I'll spoil on your hands."

So he said, "I'd let the old woman kill me," said, "if I was you. And go and ask the men."

He said, "I guess that'd be about the best thing I could do."

So the old woman, she goes down, took a broad ax and went down to kill Nippy. And when she got down, put her on a pot of water to cook some of him in when she got back to the house. When she got down and prized the log out of the pen and got him, he crawled and got out with her, you know, and he layed down on the block for her to cut his head off. As he layed down, why, she made three or four licks. And he'd dodge em. He'd dodge right and he'd dodge left. He says, "Old lady," says, "you got pie crusted in your eyes." [Laughter] Says, "Come lay down on that block," says, "and let me—I can pick them out of your eyes till you see as good as you could when you were sixteen years old." [Laughter]

She said, "The Lor-r-r-d have mercy, I'll certainly be glad for you to do that."

She laid her head down on the block. Nippy, he just reached back like he was looking for pie crusts and got that broad ax. And he come down and hacked her head plumb off. He grabbed it up and made for the house with it. Big, long hair. And when he got there, he just throwed it in that pot of boiling water she'd been planning to cook some of Nippy in. And Nippy, he grabbed in behind the bed and got that harp. He got that chanted harp and made for the river. . . .

The old giant come. The old giant come and looked in that pot. Heared something a-cracking and frying and boiling. He went and looked down in there, and he said,

"Old Woman, Old Woman, your meat's a-burning up
Old Woman, Old Woman, your meat's a-burning up"

He thought it was Nippy a-cooking. And when he looked down in there, he seed that big long hair and he knowed right then: Nippy. He said, "I lay-y-y, I know that Nippy's made his escape." He made to the river. Just as he got to the river, why Nippy pulled that staff across and he couldn't get across.

He said, "Wel-l-l, Nippy, when are you coming back to see me again?" Said, "You caused me to kill my three daughters, took my three golden lockets, took my golden staff, took my yoke of oxen and half-moon," and said, "you took my chanted harp. When-n-n you coming back to see me again?"

He said, "Never, you old pup, you."

He went on and married the king's baby girl and if nothing ain't happened to him, he lives there yet.

[Laughter]

12

VOICING THE PAST

TALES TRACING THE PATHS OF AMERICAN HISTORY

NATIVE AMERICAN VISIONS

The greatest Native American treasures in the American Folklife Center are beyond the scope of this book: for example, one field collection contains 800 Zuni tales, all told in the Zuni language, and all, as far as I can determine, untranslated. It is beyond my linguistic skills to translate them. Thousands of other Indian narratives, rendered in dozens of native languages from all corners of the continent, are similarly available for listening at the AFC reading room, but are not accessible to my understanding. Because these tales have not been translated, they do not appear here. Consequently, most of the tales that make mention of Native Americans in this book are told by European Americans, and most of the European American narrators viewed Indians from a biased perspective.

The following three tales are offered merely to hint at the breadth and power of Native American storytelling traditions. This sample does not begin to do justice to the vast wealth of Indian narrative in the American Folklife Center, but each tale is a strong performance that conveys some idea of the importance of the Library of Congress's collections of the verbal artistry of the descendents of the nation's earliest storytellers.

192. The Old Woman's Vision

AMONEETA SEQUOYAH
Tow Strong Creek, Tennessee
Recorded by Joseph S. Hall,
Qualla Indian Reservation, 1937

The following account comes from the Cherokee culture, which has experienced a long and troubled history with the government of the United States. When European settlers arrived, the Cherokee inhabited much of the southeastern section of the country, including the southern Appalachian Mountains. Individual relationships between European and Indian families could be positive (as illustrated in parts of story 211), but the gross effect of the white settlement was to overpower the Indians, rob them of their land, and force them into exile. In 1838 the Cherokee became the victims of one of the cruelest dislocations in Native American history. Although some groups, such as Amoneeta Sequoyah's Qualla culture, hid in the forests and otherwise managed to maintain their mountain homes, a huge number were forced to traverse a torturous path from the high country of the Southeast to the arid plains of western Oklahoma along a route that came to be known as the Trail of Tears. For 165 years, the Cherokee Nation has thus been divided into two branches: the Western Cherokee of Oklahoma and the Eastern Cherokee of Tennessee and North Carolina.

Amoneeta Sequoyah, son of Mollie Running Wolf, told the following tale to linguist Joseph S. Hall in 1937. Hall had been hired by the U.S. government to participate in a cultural survey of the Great Smoky Mountain region, particularly the area on the Tennessee–North Carolina border that was soon to become the Great Smoky Mountains National Park. In the late 1930s, hundreds of European American families who had made the mountains their home for centuries were forced off their lands (Sam Harmon, narrator of tales 1–12, was one of the people displaced by the government); and many Native Americans, who had inhabited the mountains far longer, were relocated as well.

Amoneeta Sequoyah's tale centers on the coming of the white people, the transformation of the land, the disruption of the natural balance, and the suffering of the native peoples. Such a story would serve as an apt illustration of very nearly any given period in Cherokee–United States relations, but it was particularly appropriate in 1937, when the federal government was once more invading Cherokee ancestral land, this time to convert the mountains into a tourist trap. The following narrative is doubly prophetic: Amoneeta Sequoyah first reports the vision of an old woman, a vision being fulfilled as Sequoyah speaks; he then adds a prophecy of his own about ways in which technology will replace the traditional trails with "great highways" and how "great machines" will drive away the animals that once filled the forests. Many would argue that Sequoyah's predictions were as accurate as those of the old woman, and that the prophecy that ended his tale in 1937 has now come to pass.

This story I'm going to tell you now was told several, several years back, you know, that's back in, as the Indians used to call it, many moons ago, here on, back here on the reservation. There's a woman lived here. A pretty old lady, till she was up in years. And there was several gathered at her house one day. They knew not of her, what she had in mind at the present time. She was sitting in the corner, all humped over. And several people around her was talking of other subjects, and all at once, you know, she raised up her head and begin to call out, and she said, "Children, I'm going to tell you something you don't realize. Which I will never be able to see but you younger people may be able to see and say that I have told you something several years before it happened."

And this is what it is.

The Indians had been troubled quite a bit with the stalking of wild animals of the forest here—which was mostly [because] of the wolves. There were great droves of wolves that roamed the country, and through the forest, and attacked the herds of sheep that used to be here. So the Indians were worrying about how they were going to get rid of all these wolves. So they asked this old lady what was just going to become of their sheep if they didn't get rid of these wolves.

She [stopped to think], and all at once she spoke. She said, "Now, children, I'm going to tell you something that you may never thought of. It's strange, it's something came in my mind just as a dream. Someone has brought this message, this story. I need to tell you younger people that there's a day coming that these wolves will not be bothering you people, or stalk these sheep that you are losing by the hundreds as this great flock of wolves roams through hills and valleys [coming into] your herds of sheep and destroying them. It has been brought to me to tell you, to let you know. . . .

"The great droves of wolves of the forest, not knowing what they had done in the lowlands, will come rushing out of the high, high mountains down to the creeks where this railroad has been laid. It has always been known that the wolves are afraid of steel. And when they come rushing out of the woods down . . . to the river where the railroad is built they will come across this railroad that is built of steel.

"And when he [the wolf] gets down to the railroad—it has a scent that is strong enough to kill—notices the steel that is laid before him and he will come to a dead stop—and upraise his head toward the sky and he will begin to howl that he has run across something, that he dare not to cross—is this steel, iron steel rail—no way for him to make an escape in crossing this railroad.

"So he has nothing else to do but only to turn right around and take to the woods and never be heard again. And after the railroad has been completed and all the work is done, the railroad is taken up and destroyed, and another—something else that will be strange, when our roads are built eighteen or twenty feet wide, there will be something come strolling up this road that has been built, which we do not know what it is, will be a strange sight coming and we will come to learn that it is something sinful to us. Maybe a wagon, some might call, that will bring people in from strange countries that we do not know, strangers to come to see how our people live deep up in the wild woods."

Thirty, forty years after the, this woman had predicted this, this strange thing that was going to happen here, after she had been dead forty years, the strange story that she had told began to happen. At that time part of the land that we owned was sold, which the Indians used to say, to the "paleface." . . . Part of the land that we were holding at that time was sold to the white man, and he began to make plans of building the railroad up into this country, which he did build a railroad up into our country here and also put up a sawmill to saw these big timbers that we have on our, our property. And the land that we have sold to the white man, the white man begin to cut down, into so many wooden links to be made into saw logs. And the railroad was built to complete by this firm, so that they may be able to haul these logs to the mill, as far as the railroad could be built. And they began to cutting this timber down, leaving our forest bare, which at that time was plenty game which we do not have today, which was plentiful of our troublesome wolves who destroyed our flocks of sheep by the hundreds.

After the railroad was built, as this old woman predicted, that'll be the time that you will not be bothered with wolves as you are today. Because the wolf will come out of the forest, and down to the creeks, down to where the railroad is built and he will come down in droves. . . .

Now if you will, you will only stop and take a look around through the country here that you are occupying at this present time. Look, look at the woods of these hills of this fine grass for your sheep to herd in. There's a time a-coming, there's some strange thing going to happen right here amongst us. It may be several years or longer before it happens but—our . . . timber here that is so thick, the great life that we have here for our hunting and our fishing, our clear waters that flows.

The day comes here when, when all these woods will be destroyed and all our little trails that we travel through these woods nowadays will be highways. They will not be just the three-foot trails that we have through these woods today. They will be great highways loaded with great machines that travel over, but we know not where that will come from or who will make all that great increase of our country here. Time will come, when it takes us three or four days to travel to a certain place, they will then be a time come when we can travel that distance in just a few minutes, when these great machines come up in our country to travel over these highways that's going to be built. But they will build a railroad, . . . owned by big companies that will come up here to take away this nice timber. That we have. And make our forest bare. Our hunting will cease also. Will be not so great as it is today. Our wild animals will move away from us and go farther where there is more timber to be found so that they may be able to find their food, which they must. . . .

193. The Blackfish

GEORGE YOUNG (DOCTOR STEPPING FAST)
Nisqually Reservation, Washington
Recorded by Willard Rhodes,
Auburn, Washington
August 8, 1950

This long and complex narrative from the traditions of the Nisqually people of what is now called Washington State centers on struggle. A rivalry between two brothers forces one into exile; while in exile, the younger brother learns the way of the northern peoples and develops close affinities with animals. A seal becomes his "dog," and he himself eventually transforms into a blackfish, or killer whale.

The tale discusses and explains many things. One of its most obvious purposes is to account for the red markings of certain rocks in Puget Sound as the blood shed in a conflict between the killer whale and other fish. "The Blackfish" also offers a lesson in cultural geography: the narrative's opening scenes are set in the present-day home of the Nisqually (a reservation bordering the military base Fort Lewis near the southern shores of

Puget Sound), but subsequent scenes cover a swath of ocean, coasts, and islands extending north well beyond the Sound, into the open sea, and along the coasts of Canada and Alaska. George Young's sure knowledge of this extensive geography illustrates the nautical range of his sea-going ancestors and offers an implicit contrast with their current conditions—these master mariners are now settled on a reservation and confined to a tiny section of coastal Washington. The narrator also introduces details that invite us to consider how scornfully European American culture has treated the Nisqually. For example, the Indians preserved a special stone commemorating the man who had become a killer whale. Near the end of the tale, George Young informs us that it has since been destroyed by European Americans. He then speaks of a special marble plate upon which the Nisqually made special offerings of food to the blackfish: "As a small boy myself, I, George Young, have seen this plate, which in later years [was] destroyed also by the white people."

George Young's first language was Nisqually, and he recorded numerous sacred songs and narratives in Nisqually for collector Willard Rhodes. Thus, the following tale in English cannot begin do justice to the range and depth of Young's oral artistry. The teller's vocabulary and syntax, heavily influenced by Nisqually usage, are difficult to follow. Nevertheless, his English vocabulary is rich and colorful, and his slow, deep-voiced, often rhythmic delivery is powerful.

Ladies and gentlemen, this story starts from Nisqually. The Nisqually Reservation. There were two brothers, the elder and the younger, the younger of the two being a sort of lazy fellow like always—rather fell up [relied] upon his brother. He fell up on his brother for everything might came along.

The biggest object of the story was the brother's wife. The younger man wanted to take the wife. In the meantime, the elder brother surmised the idea. Later on conceived the idea that he would fool the brother by carving a wooden seal. The elder brother carved the wooden seal for three or four days, up until he had perfected the seal. He placed the seal on top of a rock down at the beach. Next to the water line. He commanded the wooden seal to slide off of the rock at a moment's notice. This was done so, up until the work of the elder was perfected. Later on, the wooden seal was placed up on top of a snag projecting from the shore over the water's edge. There he commanded the seal there to fall off from the log. This was done so.

Everything was quite satisfactory then. The kill was about to take place. The elder brother telling the younger brother that the seal had been seen. The elder brother telling the brother, "Brother, you better get your equipment. The seal has been seen out in the front. Get your equipment and take after him." This was done so.

Finally, in the harpooning, the younger brother got the seal. Then the travel was on. The wooden seal dragged the younger brother down the Sound from Nisqually through on to different parts of the Puget Sound.

From this, they passed McNeil's Island, Fox Island, Point-aux-pine, the waterfronts of Tacoma, and across from Tacoma to Browns Point. And on past Robertson Point, from there on into Seattle, different parts of Seattle waters, through on down the Sound.

They come to the Deception Pass. There in the Deception Pass, the seal dove down and became tangled up in, what you might say, was kelp. They become so fastened and tightly in this kelp, that they had to tug and tug and tug. Finally, they made headway by getting the seal up to surface again. Well, in the meantime, this young man with the seal condemned the kelp. . . . He said, say to the kelp, "From today on, you are punished—you are punished people." (And that time, everything was people—even to all the different sorts of vegetation.) "From today on, you will have nine heads. You will be scaly and checkered." That's why, even today, at the Deceptions Pass, you will find kelp of just that sort: nine heads and checker-board-like.

Well, we're all cleared now, we're off again, down again down to the lower parts of the Lower Sound. Passing through George's Strait down in through British Columbia. They pass British Columbia through the Queen Charlotte Sound. From the Queen Charlotte Sound down to Wrangell, Fort Wrangell, Alaska. From there, back, up on the left hand side of the channel, going into Alaska. All this time, he still hung to his seal.

Getting up to Alaska, where the northern parts are—of the frozen Alaska, he'd came to an Eskimo village. At the place, the people somewhat dis-recognized him. Nevertheless, he stayed, he made himself practically at home with the people. He, at the time then, had mastered his seal. His seal became his pet and dog. The seal hunted for him and fished for him and done different sorts of things.

Just about at that time, a war was declared. A war was declared between this Qually man and all the ducks of the North. The ducks used quills and feathers, but different sorts of ammunition. This Qually man had nothing to use but his spear pole. He struck down and batted down the ducks, as they invaded him, with his pole.

He battled them all down up until he just about won the war.

So at this time, he conceived another idea. This time he was going to steal fish. He wanted to steal fish from the Eskimos. A small little Eskimo come out there with a great, big kayak—whatever you might want to call it. A canoe. This little Eskimo got up from the canoe and down to the icy waters he dove. For a small man, every time he came up back to the surface, he came back to his canoe with two halibut, one in each hand. He threw them in his canoe. He'd get up on his canoe again. Look *all* around.

No one had seemed to have seen him. Although this Qually man at all times was watching him from the distance. This little man dove down to the bottom of the sea. He was coming back up four or five times with halibut in each hand. After a while, this Qually man, he got the idea that the little Eskimo was down in the waters long enough for him to get out and steal one or two of the halibut. So out he went. He got two. He got out in plenty of time. Hid himself. In the meantime, the little Eskimo come back up to the surface again. He gets up: "Something is not right. Something is all wrong. Whoever is here, is not *from here.*"

And from nowhere at all, the little Eskimo, he spoke. And where he got the words from, nobody ever did know. But the little Eskimo spoke Kallup or Nis-qually (being that the language is practically the same). The little Eskimo says, "Tw-ack, a goo-so-la-las"—meaning that he had very large eyes all the year around. "Tw-ig sa-lad"—meaning that he had a big nose all the year round. "Twig kwul de a lad"—meaning that he had very large ears. So, from there on, he gets back into the village. This time there were other things that popped out. Popped up to—at the Eskimo village—that he would decide that he would return home now, but before sailing back for home, they had sort of a social gathering, a sort of a get-together supper or dinner. They all eat of ducks and seal. They just had a wonderful time. Up until the one day, here, he decided, "Well, I'm going to sail back home." So he got his canoe and paddle. A long, long paddle, a board-like paddle with a paddle on each end—of a pole, like. He sailed and he sailed and he paddled and he paddled. Come back home from the Squally in Thurston County, just up from Olympia. He sailed and he sailed, and he sailed, using his two paddles for *sails* now. As he sailed, he became to feel himself kind of slipping and feeling funny. He knew there was something going on wrong, but he didn't exactly know what was coming.

At this time, he somewhat evolutionized. He turned into a blackfish. His canoe—and the whole different parts of the contents he had, all turned into this blackfish, the "killer whale," whatever you might call him.

Before he was gone many miles, he was altogether turned into this here blackfish. So from that time, he was a living fish now. He still came home; he was still bound . . . back for the state of Washington.

He came here and he came there, and it seemed, though, that he had already had a different feeding ground. All this here different ground supporting him to a different kind of small fish.

On his way back home, he come to battle with the smaller fish . . . from the different parts of the ocean, back and forth. Adventure on, wherever he might be able to find a livelihood. He cruised around different places, back and forth, with nothing particular in mind with the exception of getting back home to Nisqually, Washington. He couldn't get the idea of fighting out of his mind. He fought his way all the way through. Fought different smaller fish, such as perhaps maybe shark and so forth.

Now, heading into British Columbia waters, roaming around by the British Columbia waters for a while. Then up the straits he came. He came . . . back home by the way of George's Straits. Passed through Bellingham, back into Port Townsend, crossing back into the Deception Pass. Just the way he went.

Now, I might tell you, Deception Pass is a pretty rough piece of water. Very, very swift and fast, and it is just pretty much of a danger and a risk to go through in small boats. All these different smaller and larger fish, of course, ventured through.

Passing the Deception Pass, he came up and through Mukilteo, and from Mukilteo across over on to the Bainbridge Island side. There he got into a battle. He got into a battle with some other fish. Around different parts of the island, there was quite a bloodshed. A lot of blood was spilled. There was blood spilled all over the island there for half a mile or three quarters of a mile.

Right up until today. If you go over to these different islands, you will find those rocks still painted red from what was thought to be blood. Today the place where they had this battle was called Pipidge.

You go to visit these different stretches of beaches, you will find that the beaches are all stained red. Nothing changes them. You go to dig it out and dig it out and dig it out, it'll still be red. That all came from that one-day-and-night's battle. The bloodstains from this here blackfish and whoever the opponents might be, just left em stained . . . and the whole beach was stained.

Well, from there now, we come in to Seattle waters now. They roamed around Seattle waters for two or three days. It's always a rule: a blackfish will stay wherever he get a livelihood, for two or three days before moving on.

While they make the first move, they move into Three Tree Point. There they go and stay and visit for two or three days. From there, up and across the Narrows to Robinson Point. There, at Robinson Point, you will find the waters to be really deep. And there was always a plenty of small fish to feed upon. There they stay two or three days. From Robinson Point, they continue their travel up to Brown's Point. And from Brown's Point they shift on over to Point Defiance. And from Point Defiance over to Gig Harbor way. From there—at that time the Indians, from years before, had a mother made for the blackfish. This mother was a stone. Perhaps twelve, fourteen feet high. This stone in later years was destroyed by the white people that now live in Gig Harbor.

Of course, at the time, Nineteen three or four, perhaps the white people at that [time] had no value of the blackfish mother, the stone. Destroyed it.

And from there, to Point Evans, another mile and a half, the Indians had a white marble plate, which was twelve or fourteen feet long, six or seven inches [thick]. Beautiful white marble. Nobody knows where the Indians ever got the marble from. As a small boy myself, I, George Young, have seen this plate, which in later years had been destroyed also by the white people. Which way the stone had ever moved to, nobody ever knew, but as far as I *do* know myself, it was destroyed by the white people.

This plate was used to feed the blackfish. The Indians at the different times, up until my time, used this plate for putting fish [entrails] and heads and so forth, and all the different wastes for the blackfish to eat. In the early days, the Indians had a belief that these blackfish came up at the high tides, eating all these different waste matters. . . . Myself, I know different. It was the smaller fish, such as dogfish, ate all of that up, and of course, naturally, the older Indians had different beliefs, and their belief was, the blackfish ate all these different waste matters.

From there, we move on. We move on inside, into the smaller parts of the Sound, here now, between Fox Island and Willachit Bay. There the blackfish would visit for two or three days. Still heading for Nisqually. They're rather somewhat confused. I mean, which way, how they gonna get to Nisqually. It's just a matter now of a few miles to get back to Nisqually, to where his starting point started from.

These blackfish would roam around all around each other or different small islands. Different small inlets up until they finally reach around McNeil's Island, Anderson Island. There, they had to go around the islands here now, for a time or so, then eventually they would cross back, back home. They would be back over into Nisqually waters. Just out of the Nisqually place, on the Nisqually reservation itself. There, the blackfish would visit a week or ten days, two weeks.

They had plenty to eat there. In the shallow waters. Then, from there, they would roam and roam and roam. Still continue. They, they're back home. Ladies and gentlemen, that ends my story.

194. How the Terrapin Got Scars on His Shell	**GEORGE GRIFFITH** **Oklahoma and Providence, Rhode Island** **Recorded by Helen Hartness Flanders,** **Providence, Rhode Island** **February 28, 1950**

Helen Hartness Flanders, one of the great New England folksong collectors, visited George Griffith and recorded the following story from him on his one-hundredth birthday. Griffith was the son of a European American father and a half-Osage mother. In his youth, he spent time with a number of native cultures, including the Creek and Kiowa.

Griffith does not identify his source for the following tale: it could have come from any of a number of Native American cultures. "How the Terrapin Got the Scars on His Shell" is typical of many aetiological legends, stories that explain the origin of current natural beings and forces in terms of prehistoric conflicts. In this tale, Terrapin plays the role of the trickster, an animal that relies on the arts of deception to get the better of the other wild creatures. Tricksters are rife in Native American cultures: Coyote is a major deceiver in many narrative traditions stretching from coast to coast, and Raven plays the trickster's role in the tales of many Northwest Coast cultures. But Terrapin and Turtle also appear frequently in trickster narratives from the South and Hispanic Southwest, among other regions. When a slow or small animal—a terrapin or rabbit, for example—is assigned the role of trickster, the storyteller often emphasizes its extreme intelligence, a trait essential to its success in duping faster and larger foes, such as the possum and the wolves in the following story. Underdog tricksters often use reverse psychology to overcome their physical shortcomings. In the following tale, Terrapin—like the famous African American trickster, Brer Rabbit, who pretends to fear the briar patch (see stories 188 and 189)—makes his escape by begging the wolves not to throw him in the water—which is exactly where they do throw him, and exactly where he wants to go.

A terrapin is a small, smaller than the turtle, you know. Well, one time, the terrapin was very hungry, and he couldn't find anything to eat. And he met. What was it he met?

[Woman's voice: A possum.]

He met a possum. And said, "Hello, Possum. I'm awful hungry. Can you tell me where I can get something to eat?"

"Well," said Possum, "come along with me. I know where there's a big tree full of red, ripe plums." So the terrapin went along with the possum and they came to a big tree and red plums. And he said to the terrapin, "Now, Terrapin, you can't climb a tree. But you wait down there, and I'll climb up into this tree and throw down some nice, ripe plums for you to eat." So the terrapin waited and the possum climbed into the tree and [began] to throw the plums down.

And along came an old wolf and ate up all the plums as fast as [Possum] threw them down. The terrapin said, "I'm so hungry, and this old wolf gets all my plums."

"Never mind," said Possum, "here's a great big ripe soft one I'll throw down for you so you can get it." So he threw the big soft plum down, and before it struck the ground, the old wolf jumped up and caught it in his mouth and swallowed it. And he opened his mouth so wide that it went down his throat and choked him to death.

"Now," said Terrapin, . . . "Now that you ate all my plums, I'm going to cut your ears off and take them home and use them for spoons to eat my soup with." So the terrapin cut the wolf's ears off and took them home and [used them] for spoons, and all of the wolves heard about it. And they said, "We got to catch Terrapin, or he'll cut all of our ears off."

So the wolves went out and hunted for Terrapin. Here and there, and here and there. After a while they saw him and they caught him. "Now," they said, "we're gonna—because you cut Wolf's ears off—we're going to put you in the fire and burn you."

"Ha, ha," said the terrapin. "You put me in your big fire and try to burn me, I'll dance on your old fire and put it out."

"Well," they said, . . . "we'll take you to the river and throw you into a deep, deep hole in the river."

"Oh, please don't do that," [he] said.

And that's just what he wanted them to do.

So they dragged Terrapin to the river and threw him in, and he struck a big rock, and . . . broke his shell all to pieces. But he had a good medicine song and he sang that song, "I've sewed myself together. I've sewed myself together."

Now as he sang that song, the pieces of his shell began to come together. They came together and came together until they *all* came together. And Terrapin was just as good as he was before the shell was broken. But the scars where it was broken stayed on his shell. As you can see for yourself. I've got one somewhere.

SLAVERY DAYS AND THE CIVIL WAR

195. Romey Howard: Freedom in the Grave

E.L. SMITH
Oglethorpe County, Georgia, and
Calvin, Michigan
Collected by Richard M. Dorson,
Calvin, Michigan, 1952

An African American born on a Georgia farm in 1886, E.L. Smith joined the Great Northern Migration when an infestation of boll weevils destroyed the local cotton crop. He arrived in Chicago in 1921, and in 1935 he moved to the majority-black rural town of Calvin, Michigan. Smith was 66 years old in 1952, when collector Richard M. Dorson recorded from him the following tales.

Smith's family retained vivid memories of his grandfather Romey Howard, a man of legendary speed, strength, and resourcefulness who outran bloodhounds, hid in graves, wriggled out of the clutches of pursuers, and won a race that ensured him an otherwise unobtainable freedom to travel at night.

Romey Howard grew up in Georgia, but as an adult he was sold to a master in Virginia. His grandson recalls the story as passed down in his family: "They boxed him up, put him on a crate, just as you would a hog or a dog. And put him on a train. . . . They shipped him . . . to Virginia, and he stayed there till freedom. And when freedom come, . . . he come back to Georgia." Howard arrived back at his old master's Georgia plantation on Christmas Eve (probably 1865) and cussed out his former master for selling him and separating him from his family.

The "patterollers" referred to in Smith's story were poor whites hired to hunt down escaped slaves. Their brutal tactics were emphasized in many of the tales told by former slaves to their descendants. Smith's term "one-gallus man" refers to whites so poor that they could afford only one suspender strap to hold their pants up. In the oral historical traditions of slavery, the poorest patterollers tended to be the meanest.

Richard M. Dorson: Mr. Smith, would you tell us about Romey Howard, your grandfather, . . . how he used to get away from the patterollers . . . ?]

He didn't let nobody whip him. And he would run away. Said he didn't let no one-gallus man whip him. . . . So he would run away, and he'd lay out at night, and the patterollers would get after him to catch him to whip him. And he was running with hounds, bloodhounds. And he would run till he run these dogs down. They had rail fences, and the dogs would get so tired that when they'd get to the fence, they wasn't able to get over the fence. And he'd let the fence down, and he'd run all around, about a mile or so, and let these dogs get through. And then he'd come back, put up this fence. Then he'd run em till he'd get tired of fooling with em, and then he'd go to the cemetery. They had these here marble stone slabs, and . . . they'd have a slab over the top. Well, he'd slide that back, and he'd get out in that cemetery, in that grave, and lay down *in* there, and . . . then slide this top back over. And these dogs would come down and scratch and howl, and these paterollers were scared. They said it was a *haint* [ghost], they wouldn't come there. And they'd blow the horns then and call the dogs off, and go on home. Let him alone. Wouldn't bother him.

196. Romey Howard: Fresh Meat Tonight

E.L. SMITH
Oglethorpe County, Georgia, and Calvin, Michigan
Collected by Richard M. Dorson, Calvin, Michigan, 1952

Here, E.L. Smith relates the one occasion on which Romey Howard was caught by the white men. True to form, Romey then gets away twice, once through flight and once in a race that persuades his captors to leave him alone.

Richard M. Dorson: Well, one time they did catch him. Remember?]

Oh, yeah. That was when they caught him and carried him out on that rock. They was going to whip him. And made him strip off all his clothes and they said, "Fresh meat tonight; fresh meat." And he pulling off, got down to his last pieces, wondering how he could get away from em. So when he pulled off the last piece, he slid right down off of this big rock and went to running.

Large group of slaves standing in front of buildings on a southern plantation, Beaufort, South Carolina, 1862. (Library of Congress)

And there was a white fellow there named John. A long, tall fellow. He was a mighty good runner hisself. So he took out after him. Every once and awhile, he got close enough to rake him in the back. And [Romey Howard would] bend over and run out from under him. And about the time he straighten up good, why, [John would] rake him in the back again. You see, he didn't have nothing to catch a hold of, you see. So [Romey Howard] knew where a big gully was. He run on down and went around this gully, and this white fellow didn't know where this gully was, this patteroller. So he come a-running down through there and he run and fell in this gully.

He hollered [high voice], "*Oh, . . . come and get me! This nigger done killed me.*" [Laughter]

Well, [Romey Howard] went on home to his old mistress, see. And she wasn't married. She was a widow. And he just run up to the door and knocked on the door, he was just as naked as he could be. Without clothes on at all. She called him "Romeo." She says to him, "Romeo, where have you been?"

He says, "The patterollers is after me."

So she got him some clothes. He put em on, and about the time he got his clothes on, why, they come. And brought his clothes and told her, asked her was he there? And she told him, "Yeah."

Said, "Well let him come up here to the jailhouse and run back with John." Says, "If he outrun John," says, "when we catch him out, we'll never bother him no more."

So she said, "Well, he can go if he want to. . . ." So he *knowed* he could outrun him, he said. And he went out there, and another fellow went along to judge the race, you see, to start em off.

And when they got up there, they said,

> One to make ready,
> Two to make show,
> And *three to go*.

And when they said *three to go*, he said he made a leap. And when this fellow got around half way, . . . [Romey] was going in the door. Done outrun him.

So they never bothered him any more, then . . . when they catch him out.

197. Remembering Slavery	**LAURA SMALLEY** **Hempstead, Texas** **Recorded by John Henry Faulk,** **Hempstead, Texas, 1941**

Of all the spoken-word recordings housed in the Library of Congress, none are more famous, or more justly famous, than the "ex-slave narratives," interviews conducted with former slaves in the 1930s and early 1940s. Together, these firsthand accounts of a life of extraordinary oppression make one of the most important social documents to be found in any library.

Archive of Folk Song director Benjamin A. Botkin drew extensively upon these recordings to create a major book—*Lay My Burden Down* (1945)— the first comprehensive history of slavery actually narrated by the slaves themselves. Botkin's work has been succeeded by many others. Because the ex-slave narratives have been continually transcribed, published, and re-

John Henry Faulk (left; collector of story 197), with J. Frank Dobie (teller of stories 111–113). Dobie was Faulk's mentor, and Faulk was present when Dobie told the stories printed in this book. Faulk's affection for Dobie was so great that he named his son Frank Dobie Faulk. (Center for American History, University of Texas, Austin)

leased on commercial recordings, only one sample account is included in this book.

The collector of the following narrative was a young Texas folklorist named John Henry Faulk. At this time he was often in the company of the two most influential folklorists of the previous generation, John A. Lomax and J. Frank Dobie (see particularly stories 111–113, performed by Dobie with both Lomax and Faulk present). Faulk went on to become a media personality and enjoyed a successful career until the mid-1950s, when he was accused of "communist" motives by rightwing organizations and fired from his job. Faulk challenged his accusers and was eventually cleared in a court case; his long ordeal is recounted in his book, *Fear on Trial.*

By and large, the ex-slave "narratives" are not narratives in the strictest sense. Most of them follow a question-and-answer interview format in which the speakers reveal important details of daily life during the slavery era. There are relatively few actual stories embedded in the interviews. In the following account, for example, Mrs. Laura Smalley describes the general conditions in which slaves would meet to pray: in the woods, in secret, using a water tub to muffle the sound of their prayers. She then tells one brief story of a slave who would not stop praying even as he was being whipped by his master. The second part of Mrs. Smalley's account as presented here is an autobiographical recollection of her childhood encounters with Indians. These brief vignettes serve equally as damning evidence against slavery and as testimony to the extraordinary moral strength and resourcefulness of Mrs. Smalley.

[John Henry Faulk: Did the slaves have church?]
I never remember no church. Mama said, the only church (I didn't remember that part of it), all the church they would have, be a tub, a tub of water sitting just like this thing is, you know, and that would catch your voice. And they would . . . have church around that tub, all of them get around the tub, get around the tub.

[John Henry Faulk: The old master didn't want them having church?]

Didn't want them having no church. No, they didn't have no church. And old master come along with one of them. One of them was there, having church round the tub, and he was down praying. And said he was down there praying, just a-praying. Old master come in. He just a-praying. He come in, he did, and told him to get up from there. He didn't get up, he just a-praying. And say the old master commence to whipping him. He quit praying and then ask, "The Lord have mercy on old master, the Lord have mercy on old master." Say old master sure would hit him with a bullwhip. He holler after mercy on old master. Until old master whipped him and he kept, wouldn't get up, you know. When a person hit you, you know, you flinch. He just praying for old master.

Old master step back and said, "I'm good mind to kick you naked. I'm good mind to kick you naked." The nigger never did stop praying, you know. He had, he had to go off and leave him praying, he had to go off and leave him praying, because he wouldn't stop. Well, that was through the Lord, you know, that cause that.

[John Henry Faulk: Yeah, the Lord works a lot of things.]

Yes, sir, cause the Lord was—suffered him to stay down there and get that whipping and pray. You know, just keep a-praying. And I think I'd jump up, I don't know. Seem like to me I'd jump up. . . .

Well, I don't know about the church when it first started up, no more than, you know, when I was a child, you know, they used to didn't have no church, you know. In no house, you know. That had it in the trees. . . . And I don't know, you know, the cause of churches and when they started, but I know when Mama and them used to go to church with all the trees, you know. Under the trees. Didn't have no church houses, much then. Just like, you know, you get a big old tree, and clean it all out from one end and make a dry stalk down, you know, and make benches on it, you know. That's where we'd have church.

[John Henry Faulk: What kind of songs did they sing? Do you remember the names—]

No, I couldn't—I can't read. I don't remember the songs. But they didn't sing songs like they sung now, you know. They'd sing them old songs about "Amazing Grace, how sweet the sound," and all like that. But you know, I can't recollect all of them. I can't recollect them since I've been grown.

All the Indians I ever seed it was over—it was here. And they wasn't wild. I used to hear Mama talk about em. When she was a child, she said, that one morning she went out to the old mistress. She was big enough, you know, to handle water. And say when she got to the door to open the door, the stars was falling. Now when stars was falling that morning, and said, she didn't know. Said old mistress looked out and said, "Don't you go out there." She says, "Stars," she said she just went like meat frying you know, the whole earth would just, just lit up you know. Said it was just going like meat frying. *Phhew, phhew, phhew, phhew.* Just before day. . . .

When she went to go to the water, to the spring, after the stars fell—when they quit falling it was daylight—and said she met some angel—Indians—down there. You know, they pack water from a spring, she said. And says she met some wild Indians. And they had—old missus's cook had give her a piece of bread. And they give her the beads, you know, give her some beads, you know, and took the bread. And, yes, and took the bread from her . . . and said every time she'd go step in front or go walking, they'd step in front of her. Every time that she go to walk, they'd step in front of her, and said, finally, at last, they ate the bread up and reached their hands back, you know the, and took, took the beads away from her. And said they was wild. Took it away from her. And said she went back to the house crying, went back to the house crying. She said she told she had met some people and took her bread and give her some beads and then took her beads away from her. . . . I've seed some of them . . . when I was a child. I don't know whether them was the Indians or not then. You see, when I was a child, they'd go in droves. Just in droves. And come in the house and take what they wanted, something to eat like that. They'd never take nothing but something to eat. Like that. And then get out, you know, and make fun of you, and grin, you know, and laugh, you know.

[John Henry Faulk: Oh, is that right?]

Yes sir, laugh. Take . . . go and take it. If they offer their hand, you know, for it, and made the motion, you'd just as well go get it to em. Or let em. Cause they'd go on in there and get that stuff. Mama had her an old chicken once. Great big old chicken. And they didn't have nothing but pots then. Didn't have, didn't have no stoves. Just had pots as I can recollect it, had pots. And had that chicken in that pot. And I don't know what that man said to her, said to her, you know, to the other, now, those. He said some kind of language. We didn't hear it. Here he come in with a bucket and just take that pot and poured all that stuff in that pot, with them feathers in his head—in his hat, you know. Poured all that in it—vittles in that pot. And us little children standing around there hungry.

198. The Sisters and the Renegades	LEE WINNIFORD Cumby and Houston, Texas Recorded by Lee Winniford, Houston, Texas, June 2002

Lee Winniford learned the following two tales as a child growing up in the cotton country of northeast Texas. They were part of a rich narrative heritage, a family saga extending back to the early years of the nineteenth century. In the following performance, she passes the tale on to her granddaughter Bethany, 12 years old, about the same age at which Lee herself first learned the tale.

Like all of the Winniford family legends about the Civil War, this one focuses not on the violence and heroics of the battlefield but on the hard times of the homefront and on the courage and determination required of the women left behind when their husbands went to war.

Following Old Fencelines (1998), Winniford's autobiographical account of storytelling in the 1930s and 1940s in Hopkins County, Texas, prints her brother James Winniford's version of the same tale. In James's telling, only one sister—Becky—is involved in the shooting, and the bodies of the renegades are stuffed in a ditch rather than buried by the well. Lee, of course, prefers her version; she does not find the detail of the ditch sufficiently plausible: "It seems to me that the ditch burial would have struck the two women as a very temporary and, therefore, unworkable way of hiding potentially damning evidence. With the first gully washer, the bodies would have flushed out and started floating toward the creek."

But the major reason why Lee prefers her version to her brother's has to do with her childhood memories of the well: "A well just outside the barnyard of the old Winniford homeplace seemed a mysterious edifice to me during my childhood. Because it was shaded by a clump of chinaberry trees and caught water that rained off the steep roof of the big barn, this well was always full, even during the periodic droughts that plagued northeast Texas. The well was always sparkling clear and cold—a real temptation to children playing hide-and-seek in the haylofts. But my brother and cousins and I were warned never to drink water from this well. The water, we were told, was fit only for cattle and was strictly off-limits to human beings. Not until we appeared convincingly mature and stable were we 'kids' told the family legend that explained the well's strange contamination."

Bethany, I'm going to try to tell you some stories about some of your ancestors. Your great-grandmothers and -grandfathers, and great-great-grandmothers and -grandfathers, and people like that. Old family stories, in other words, that maybe you haven't even heard before. Have you ever heard me talk about my Great-grandma Sarah and Great-aunt Becky?

[Bethany: No.]

Okay, well you're going to this morning. These are my daddy's side of the family, the Winnifords and the Alexanders. And these families came to Texas back in the early part of the nineteenth century, back about 1840, along in there. And the Winnifords came originally from up in Virginia, and the Alexanders came from Illinois. And they wound up settling on some land grants. That was back when people who came to Texas as settlers, frontiersmen, could get these *huge* grants of land, lots of acres. And they had managed to do that. I'm not quite sure whether they settled on adjoining land grants or whether they wound up splitting one land grant. That's not very clear. But they had a lot of land around this little town that at that time was called Blackjack Grove. And it was a very boisterous, very mean little town. It was a little frontier town. But these two families settled there.

And on the Alexander side, there were two older girls. The oldest child in the family was Becky, and then next to her was another girl, Sarah, and Sarah was going to become my great-grandmother. Your great-great-great-grandmother.

And then there were a number of boys, younger than these two girls. Well, it turned out that Sarah married one of the young Winniford men. This man was George Dawson, and he, of course, was my great-grandfather. . . .

And about that time, getting on toward the middle of the nineteenth century—do you remember from history what happened about that time? That was when the Civil War happened. . . . Well, the Civil War broke out. And meanwhile my great-great-grandfather, the father of these two girls, Urbane Alexander, had been killed, and then his wife died the next year. So there really wasn't what you'd call an older generation around. There were just these young people, either married and starting families or, as I said, the older sister, Becky, was engaged to be married.

And then they had, they had these Alexander brothers, and within a short period of time, Sarah had at least one little boy. She had Norve before the war even started, and sometime along in there, she had another little boy named Sam. But the Civil War broke out, and all of the young men in that part of the country joined the Confederate Army. They were fighting for the South. Probably *weren't* fighting for slavery, because none of them had slaves, but probably for states' rights. They had come a long way to have a lot of land, and they didn't want the government stepping in there and interfering. So the men had to go, and they had to leave the women to fend for themselves. And it was very, very hard.

There is a story about Great-grandma Sarah and Great-aunt Becky, that . . . for a period of time at least, they all shared the same house. That would make a certain amount of sense. And they raised horses. And, of course, word of that spread. And so they were there, I think it was, along in the morning. And a couple of men rode up. They were renegades. Probably soldiers from one side or the other, or just plain outlaws, you never could tell. But they rode up and told the two women who were there in the house, my Great-grandma Sarah and Great-aunt Becky, that they had come and they were going to take some fresh horses. They were on a couple of horses themselves, but, of course, these horses had been ridden a great deal and they were worn down, not much good for anything anymore. And the two women knew that they had to be very, very careful, because men like this were dangerous. Had been known to hurt and kill women. So they didn't put up any immediate resistance. They just pointed the way to the barn. A lot of the horses were in the barnyard. And in and around the barn.

And so the two men went into the barnyard. Meanwhile, Great-aunt Becky and Great-grandma Sarah went into the house, and each got a gun. And they decided before they stepped out on the back porch which one of these men each one would take down, so that they wouldn't make any mistakes. And when the men came through the barnyard, leading their fresh horses that they were stealing, well, the two women shot them. They were good shots and they shot them. Well, of course, they couldn't just leave them lying there. [Laughing]

[Bethany: Did the horses—were the horses okay?]

[Laughing] The horses were all right. Yes, they were good shots. They didn't maim or kill a horse. They saved their horses. People back at that time treasured horses, and especially if you raised them, as they did. Yes, they took care of their horses.

But, anyway, they had to bury these guys. And there are different stories of where they buried them. My brother, the way he tells it, the way he heard it was that they took them down in the pasture in back to sort of a ditch, sort of a place where the water had drained off and cut a ditch through the pasture, and that they put them in that ditch and then covered them up. Another story had it that they took them down to an old well in the barnyard, and it was kind of dry weather. It wasn't easy digging in the ground. And so, what they could do, they could draw up a bucket of water, and pour it out on the ground and soften the ground. And that way, they managed to dig a hole deep enough to bury these guys up against the wall of the well.

And so the evidence was hidden.

And they used to tell us—older people in the Winniford family [would tell us], when I was a kid. We were always wanting to go down and play in the hay in the barn. Or run around the barn and play hide-and-seek. And they would tell us, "Now, you mustn't drink water from that well. The water in that well isn't good. We only use that water for horses." Because—supposedly—those two guys were buried right up against that well. And that would, I guess, in their eyes have contaminated that water. But, until we were a lot older, they didn't tell us why it was that they thought the water was no good. They just warned us.

[Bethany: You all lived in the same place they did?]

We came back and visited there. Now, the truth of the matter is that the well that they indicated, that these two guys were buried next to, probably wasn't the well. This wasn't the location where the old homestead would have been. It would have been another barnyard and another well. So—but somehow or other, they told the story about that particular well in the barnyard of the house that was occupied by my grandparents.

So that's one Civil War story. Kind of a gruesome one, isn't it?

199. Great-aunt Becky's Beau

LEE WINNIFORD
Cumby and Houston, Texas
Recorded by Lee Winniford,
Houston, Texas, June 2002

As the preceding tale makes apparent, Lee Winniford's Great-aunt Becky was a family hero, noted for resourcefulness and strength of determination. When her father died in 1853, followed within a year by her mother, she became, at age 24, the head of her family. As Lee Winniford relates in *Following Old Fencelines*, "Great-aunt Becky's responsibilities increased when the war began and most of the able-bodied men left to join in the fighting. As the oldest child in the family Becky was called upon to handle business matters that did not normally fall to women at that time. According to some accounts, for instance, a problem arose about the legality of one of the Alexander land grants, and Becky had to go to the state capital in Austin to settle the matter. Accompanied by a younger brother . . . , Becky traveled on horseback from Hopkins County to Austin, a round trip requiring several days of hard riding through country that was fraught with danger from Indians, outlaws, and renegade soldiers. Great-aunt Becky acquired a reputation for being strong willed and fearless.

"The most widely circulated story about Great-aunt Becky did not, however, have to do with any of her daring exploits. It is for her poignant, tragic love story that she is best remembered." Here is that story, as Lee Winniford passed it on to her granddaughter Bethany more than 170 years after Rebecca Jane Alexander's birth.

Great-aunt Becky, when the war broke out, was engaged to a young man, whose name was C.C. Mount. Kind of a strange name. And he went off to war. As a matter of fact, [C.C. Mount and the young men in Great-aunt Becky's family] were all in the same little unit. They were in the cavalry, which made sense, because they raised horses. It just came naturally for them to fight on horse. And he went off with the young man who would become his brother-in-law, if he married Great-aunt Becky. He went off with George Dawson Winniford, and with a couple of the Alexander Brothers, who were bound to have been no more than in their teens when they went off to war, really *young* men.

And they fought up in Arkansas first, and C.C. Mount was one of the first men from that part of the country who was killed in battle. And so word came back to Blackjack Grove that my great-aunt Becky's fiancé had been killed in battle up there—and, of course, was going to be buried in this strange foreign place. Well, his father—C.C. Mount's father—even though he was getting way on up in years, he just couldn't stand the thought of his son being left up there in that strange country. And so he took, I think he took a train part of the way up. But, of course, he had to bring the body back in a wagon. And he went up to get his son's body and bring it back to Blackjack Grove where it could be buried properly.

Now, the stories vary as to when he did this. The way I oftentimes heard the story told was that the war was still raging, it was, you know, the war was not over when this old man decided to get up to that part of the country where his son had been killed and retrieve his body and bring it home. And that his trip was therefore rather dangerous.

There's some evidence that they waited until after the war was over. And so the story would be a little bit different, depending on when this man made the trip. But in the most gruesome version of the story, the young man's father went up after his body while the war was still in progress—and pretty soon, as a matter of fact, after the young man had been killed. Just as soon as they got word that he was dead, he prepared to go up there and get the body. And so he did, and, of course, he had to drive back then, all the way from up in Arkansas. And even though that's up by northeast Texas and it's not the kind of distance that we would think of it being from here, it's still a long trip to make with a wagon and horses. And naturally Great-aunt Becky was devastated. She—this had been the love of her life, and she was full of grief and sorrow. And so she was waiting for the old man to arrive in the wagon carrying her fiancé's body. And word came to her that the old man had reached the blackjack grove (blackjacks are kind of an oak tree) and that he had pulled in under that blackjack grove to wait until they had a grave, managed to dig a grave for his son. Because, of course, the body was decomposing, and it was in a terrible condition—it was a strong smell.

And so Great-aunt Becky went out to the well and drew a jug of cold, fresh well water, and rode out to that blackjack tree grove, and brought water to the old man, and waited there with him until they were sent word that, yes, the grave had been prepared, and they could bring him on into the cemetery and bury him.

And when they got to the cemetery, the mother also—the boy's mother—was there. And both she and Great-aunt Becky insisted on viewing the body, because they had to know in their heart of hearts that this *was*, you know, the person that they loved. The mother wanted to be sure, yes, we're burying my son. And Great-aunt Becky needed to know that that was indeed the man that she loved and, and he was gone.

And the men urged them *not to* insist on opening up—I think they had put the body in some kind of wooden casket. But they insisted. And they opened the casket. And some of the men fainted, you know, when they saw . . . the sight of the, the gruesome sight of the dead and decomposing body of this young man. But Great-aunt Becky and his mother held up. And they were able to— the mother looked at the hands. And apparently there was something about the color of the hair that reassured them that, yes, this was Mount, this was C.C. Mount.

And so they closed the casket and buried him. And his grave is still there in the Cumby City Cemetery. As a matter of fact, he's buried on one little hill, and then Great-aunt Becky wound up being buried just about, maybe fifty feet away from him, on another little hillock with other members of the Alexander family. She never did marry. As far as anyone knew, never showed any interest in any other man. That was the love of her life, and he was killed in the war, and she remained faithful to him until she died, an old woman.

So that's the sad story of Great-aunt Becky and her Civil War lover.

STRUGGLES WITH NATURE AND NEIGHBORS

200. Dream No More

MAGGIE HAMMONS PARKER
Pocahontas County, West Virginia
Recorded by Dwight Diller,
ca. 1972

In 1970, Alan Jabbour and Carl Fleischhauer of the American Folklife Center began a three-year project to document the musical and narrative traditions a West Virginia family, the Hammonses of Pocahontas County. The family's lore proved so rich and diverse that in 1973, three long-playing records based on Jabbour and Fleischhauer's work were released by the Library of Congress and accompanied by a booklet focusing on the family's traditional history and artistry. Dwight Diller, a native of West Virginia and a master of the traditional banjo, joined with Jabbour and Fleischhauer in recording the family's repertoire of songs and stories. Diller collected the following tale, which may be considered the prologue to the Hammons family saga. Carl Fleischhauer notes, "Although the Hammonses do not do

Kitchen table storytelling at the home of the Hammons family (narrators of stories 122 and 200), Pocahontas County, West Virginia. (Photo by Carl Fleischhauer)

so, the[ir family historical] stories can be arranged in a more or less chronological series." The one account that dates back to the family prehistory, the one account that does not link directly with the other chapters in the family's oral record, is "Dream No More," a story that portrays a complex set of relationships between the Native Americans and the European American settlers. On the one hand, the settlers' close Indian friends give them the know-how and the specific information needed for them to survive; on the other hand, the Indian population as a whole grows resentful of the whites and attempts to exterminate them.

The central episode of Maggie's narrative, the dreaming contest between the Indian and the settler, shares a plot with a complex of legends and jokes reported in many regions of the United States.

Maggie Hammons Parker (1899–1987), an expert singer and compelling raconteur, structures her narrative in such a way as to end by stressing that her ancestors owed their lives to the Indians.

There was just the two, the two families of the white people that lived there and all the others was Indians, and they lived right close to the bunch of

Maggie Hammons Parker, teller of "Dream No More" (story 200), near Marlington, West Virginia, 1973. (Photo by Carl Fleischhauer, 72112/22)

em. And so they was an old Indian, he always come every day. They said after he got acquainted with em, he'd come every day and talk with em and they liked that old Indian. And they liked the others.

They seemed like they was awful good people and good to em. And they had a little boy. He'd come. And so my great-granddaddy, he had a boy just about the same age or size, and he'd come and he'd play with him. And he had a little whistle, the little boy did, and he said he could just call up all kinds of birds with that whistle. And he had a bow and arrow and they said he never missed a shot. And he'd take that boy and go out and get a whole string of birds and he strung em up on a string, and he'd bring em in and they had a fireplace, and he'd just rake a place out in the fireplace and lay all of them birds right in there, feathers and all, and roast em. Roast em in there and then take and pick the meat off of the bones and they'd sit there, him and that little boy would, and eat that, eat them birds. So when he had him out, why they didn't know it, but he had him—he could just swim any way he wanted to—he learnt that little boy of [great-]grandpa's to swim. He could swim any way, dive or anything. They had him trained, that little Indian did.

And so, well, the old man, he'd come every day and he'd talk with em and they'd tell big tales and jokes, and they liked that old man. And so, after a while, one of the Indians come, he told him, he said, "I had a dream last night." And he said, "Always when we dream anything, our dreams has to come true." He said, "Now that's the way it goes with us. When we dream anything, the dream has to come true." So [Great-grandpa] had a gun, he had a gun, a awful nice gun. He wouldn't have took nothing for the gun, he said. And [the Indian] told him he dreamt about owning that gun. And so he couldn't do a thing but let [the Indian] have it, let him take the gun. He was afraid not to, I guess. But anyhow, he took the gun. Well, it pretty nigh killed him because [the Indian had] taken that gun and he didn't know what kind of a plan to fall on to get his gun back.

Finally at last passed on right smart about a couple of weeks or more, and he said he got up and told em, he said, "I had a dream last night," he said. "I dreamt I owned my gun back and one of the ponies." He said to em at home, he said, "I'm a-going to tell em this morning," he said.

So he went, and he went over, he told em that he'd had a dream that night, and he said, "I dreamt about owning my gun back and one of your ponies."

[The Indian] studied a while, he said, before he said anything. At last he said, "Take it, paleface, but dream no more."

And he took the gun and the pony.

And then, he said, a few days after, why that old Indian got to coming and he wouldn't talk. He wouldn't talk, he said, to em, he didn't have nothing to say and they knowed there was something wrong with him. He wouldn't say nothing at—finally at last they went to asking him to tell em and finally at last he told em. He said, "If you people knowed what I did," he said, "you wouldn't be here." He told em, he said, "If they find it out," he said, "they'll kill me sure, as sure as they find it out."

Of course, they promised him to not tell it at all, and he told em they was going to come kill em. Get rid of em a-waiting there. They was going to kill em, the Indians was. He didn't know to do nothing, only to go to the other family and told em. And they just put what they could get on their ponies. They just gathered up and put on their ponies all they could . . . put on em, . . . and started. And they rode and rode and they heard the Indians a-hollering and they followed em till they come to that big river. Now, they said it was the Newcon River; now, that's all I can tell you, that's what they told me it was. And that's as far as they come when they come to Newcon River, why they swum it, the horses did, and they got away from em, and that's the way they got away now from the Indians.

And he said that when they . . . come back they didn't even know it but that little boy could swim any way he wanted to swim. That little Indian boy had learnt him how to swim, dive, and everything. They didn't know, and he could shoot a bow and arrow too. Yes, sir, and that boy, he lived to be, he was an old man, I reckon. And he got drownded, yes, sir, he got drownded.

201. She Saved the Children

MARY EVA BAKER
Springfield, Vermont
Recorded by Helen Hartness Flanders,
Springfield, Vermont, 1943

Mary Eva Baker possessed an enormous store of historical traditions from her native Vermont. Not only could she retell in vivid detail dramatic tales of Indians, sea captains, pirates, Revolutionary War soldiers, and escaped slaves, she could also list genealogies of narrators: who learned the story from whom, from whom, and from whom, tracing a chain of tellers back to the time of the tale's earliest tellings. In Baker's narratives, the Native American chiefs and warriors of the eighteenth and nineteenth centuries often emerge as principled and heroic figures, even when directed to conduct a slaughter of innocent children.

The real hero of this tale, however, is the schoolteacher, whose bravery wins the respect of the warrior sent to kill her. This unnamed woman, like the similarly nameless females who stand alone against Indian invaders in stories 26 and 63, seems hopelessly outnumbered; however, whereas the women in the other tales conceal themselves from the attackers, the Vermont schoolteacher places herself in conspicuous danger and, through her own desperate courage, survives.

Mary Eva Baker's tale was recorded by the great Vermont folksong collector Helen Hartness Flanders (1890–1972), who recorded more than 9,000 folk performances in a career that spanned four decades. Flanders's granddaughter Nancy-Jean Siegel writes, "Helen Hartness Flanders said she was allergic to ballads—that is, whenever she was near them she caught them." In the process, Flanders also caught some remarkable tales (including story 194 in this collection).

In one of the early school districts of Springfield, they cut down a very large tree to make a place to build a schoolhouse, which was a little log schoolhouse. About that time the Indians became especially troublesome and were killing more people than usual. And the teacher [was] with her pupils in the little log schoolhouse.

A man on horseback came to the door and told the teacher she could *not* go home that night, or let any of the scholars, or they'd certainly be massacred. Well, the children were frightened almost to death, and the teacher wasn't much better. But she tried to get the children to lie down on the seats—they stuck planks on blocks around the schoolroom, and she told them to lie down there, but they were so frightened they wouldn't.

So she told them that she would open the schoolhouse door and go out and *stand up* on this place where they cut the tree down to show to them that she was not afraid. And so she opened the door and went out and got up onto this stump of the tree.

And as she did so, on the opposite side, she saw an Indian crouch. And he spoke only a very little English, but he told her that he came there to kill her and the children, but she had been so brave, if she would return to the schoolhouse, he would go away and not molest them. This is a *true* story.

Helen Hartness Flanders, collector of stories 194 and 201. (Photo by Clara Sipprell, Courtesy of Nancy-Jean Siegel)

202. The One-Legged Indian

DOMINICK GALLAGHER
Beaver Island, Michigan
Recorded by Alan Lomax,
Beaver Island, Michigan, 1939

Among the early Library of Congress recordings, the vast majority of the tales told by European Americans about Native Americans feature hostilities between the two groups. The following short narrative, however, was offered by Irish American Dominick Gallagher as a salute to an indomitable Indian neighbor.

High Island, the home of the Indian featured in this account, lies in Lake Michigan about forty miles west of the Straits of Mackinac, in the midst of a watery expanse known for its isolation, harsh winds, and fierce winters. Dominick Gallagher lived on nearby Beaver Island, which is located about twenty miles from the Michigan mainland.

During a lengthy fieldtrip to collect ballads and songs centered on sailing and lumbering—as well as the often neglected musical traditions of northern Midwesterners of Finnish, French, and Polish descent—Alan Lomax visited with Gallagher and some of his friends. After the Beaver Islanders had sung at length, Lomax pumped them for stories about the "little people," the fairies of Irish tradition. No one volunteered a fairy story, but Dominick responded with an account of one man determined enough to endure the ferocity of fate and the elements in an extraordinarily hostile environment.

You know, I can tell you a story about an Indian that chopped his own leg off here. In the woods. A tree bumped him. And he waited till night. And he was about [half] of a mile away from his wigwam—you know, they lived in those little wigwams. And his squaw was in the wigwam when he went out to chop wood. About a half a mile he was, from his house—or wigwam, shanty, or whatever it was. And he [felled] a tree that lodged off the stump, and it caught him below the knee and shoved his leg down on the ground. And he hollered for a long time. He couldn't get out of there, and there was snow on the ground, about a foot of snow. And his squaw couldn't hear him. When he tried to get out, he couldn't.

And about sundown—he could reach where his ax fell down. He caught his ax and he whittled his own leg off below the knee. And then he cut two crutches, and he went through the snow. He wrapped his coat around the stump till he got in [back home]. And then they doctored it. He got all right.

And then he took a small cedar and he cut a kind of duck's nest on the end of it for to put the stump in and put some straps on it, and he got on all right. And a few years afterwards he used to carry the mail on the ice . . . from Cross Village here, you know. And this Indian took the contract to carry the mail. He lived on High Island, that's nine miles from here. And he had a little team of dogs, they didn't have nothing but just a small mail back then, you know. They were only one man, I think, Earl Robie was getting the *Michigan Catholic*. And that was all the newspapers that was going here. So he left High Island at seven o'clock in the morning, came over nine miles, he took the mail from here. The dogs was so small he couldn't ride. He had this wooden leg that he made when he got his leg chopped off. And he took the mail. He went to Cross Village, thirty-three miles, and came back with the mail that night and delivered it at the post office on his wooden leg. Went back and had his supper at home on High Island.

What do you think of that for a story?

[Alan Lomax: He was some man.]

203. Panther Bill

JAKE SUTTON
Cataloochie, North Carolina
Recorded by Joseph S. Hall,
ca. 1956

Stories of resourceful men and women who elude panthers (or, less often, bears) by leaving a distracting trail behind are rife in the United States.

I can tell you a story about a panther running a feller. His name was Bill Campbell. And his brother-in-law . . . lived in what we know as the Hickory Butt, next to Pigeon River. This feller Campbell was fishing on what we call Mt. Sterling Creek, near the mouth of Pigeon River, and he heard something make a noise and he looked around and he saw a large panther laying on a log fixing to jump up on him. And he had a few fish, something like eight or ten. And he jump and broke to run, and the panther took after him. And he still had his fishpole in his hand. And he had a very steep mountain to run up, something like a mile. And this panther followed him. And he looked every minute him to, for it to catch him. So the noise of his fishpole kept the panther—backwards, and it never jumped on him. And directly he throwed his fish. And the panther stopped to eat his fish, and when it'd eat the fish, it continued on after him. And he still held to his pole, it was the only protection that he thought caused the panther to not catch him. So he run up within a hundred yards of the house and jumped the fence and screamed and the panther just run to the fence and stopped. So he's known as Panther Bill.

204. Trying to Mix Liquor and Laughs

JAMES L. HUSKEY
Sugar Lands, Tennessee
Recorded by Joseph S. Hall,
Gatlinburg, Tennessee, August 3,
1956

James L. Huskey was born about six miles outside of Gatlinburg, Tennessee, in a region known locally as the Sugar Lands, on the Little Pigeon River. He was raised in a large, hard-working, poor family: As a young working boy, Huskey, like many of his siblings and neighbors, plowed the fields barefooted. "Never had a pair of Sunday shoes until I was fourteen years old. . . . Had nothing to go to, no amusements of any kind, except Sunday school and church. . . . I'd go to church and Sunday school, and come back home. I'd pull them shoes off, take me a rag, clean all the dust off of em, put em under the bed. I didn't bother em more till next Sunday morning. I thought more of them shoes then than I would, I guess, of a hundred dollars right now. . . . We had it pretty tough. . . . We had fourteen in the family, and we had to make our support mostly. And there was some things that we couldn't make, we had to buy, but my mother has spun cloth, carded it, spun it, wove it, and made a homemade, or hand-built, cloth, and made our clothes. I've wore suits of clothes—pants and coats—made by her own fingers, and the cloth was made by her own fingers. I've wore the handbuilt shoes. Tan the hides. Get that old bark and tan it the old-fashioned way: took three months to tan it. And there's men through the community that made shoes. Fact of the matter, I've made em myself after I got grown. I made myself two pair. . . . Just the curiosity of the thing. I didn't have to do it, but I wanted to do it. But back then, . . . when we didn't make our shoes, my dad would buy us one pair a year . . . and if we wore that shoe out, we went barefooted. Sorry to have to say it, . . . and no reflection on my parents, but I have made tracks in snow—bare-footed tracks—because they wasn't able to buy shoes.

"Then after I got up, grown, a man of my own, . . . I didn't know anything but hard, rough work. And I drank some liquor, but I wasn't bad like some fellows was. . . . I helped make some moonshine, but it was real whiskey, it wasn't poison stuff. Did that a while, then I took off to Public Works, . . . worked on Public Works pretty well till I was up about twenty-four years old. Then the First World War broke out and I went into it. Married about thirty days before I went into the war. Course, . . . I didn't know what married life was, hardly. When I came back, I went to North Carolina, and I joined up with the . . . lumber company. I was working in what they called a 'dry lumber yard' a-shipping dry lumber to Europe, to build up [rebuild] the destruction from the warfares. . . . And then went from there into cabinet work. . . . Then I got in touch with the Pi Phi Settlement School. They had just a-come in to this part of the country at that time, put up a few buildings, and just had started their settlement school. I worked for them about a year. Through them, they helped me get to Berea College in Kentucky. . . . So I taught wood-carving for six years, lacking two months, and also went to school. Then in thirty-two . . . I quit, came back here and bought my property. . . . Built this little shop and got started here a-making novelties, furnitures of different kinds. And I kept that up until my children was pretty well grown. Second World War broke out; we couldn't get materials, they was hard to get. The labor was hard to get. Men that was able to work and also women had to go into defense plants. So I closed my shop up, and as it happened, fortunately or unfortunately, the army got several of my boys. They all passed the examinations, my two sons and the . . . three boys I had a-working with me. Took em all in, left the shop with me. So I closed the doors and I went into the defense plant, worked in a aircraft office as an inspector the duration of the war. Then, after the war, we played around in the woods a couple of years. Didn't have no success with it. . . . Closed out. And I'm working now for a wholesaler . . . making those tomahawks and darts out of those canes, making em pretty good. I'm not making so much money, but it's easy money, and it's funny money. I like it, because it's funny. I meet the public—that's educational. Go all over the country, have a quite a few good stories to tell em and they have quite a few to tell us, different things that we learn from each other. So I love this part of it. Life is easier, as far as the labor part is concerned, NOW. But, otherwise, I like the old life that I lived in the . . . mountains in the Sugar Lands."

I had a uncle by the name of Waley, Joe Waley. And he lived in the Sugar Lands. He married my dad's oldest sister. And we knowed him—most of the people that does know him, knowed him—by the name of Logging Joe. And he was droll of speaking, but he was an honest man, very dependable, truthful. And he was a big farmer, for the mountains. He hired quite a bit of help, cleared land, raised quite a bit of corn.

I remember one time—he had a big, long crib and sometime just along about Christmastimes—he had maybe a couple or three hundred bushel of corn in the crib. And he called in a corn shucking. And in the middle of this corn—it was supposed to have been near the middle—he buried a gallon jug [laughing] of the old-time corn whiskey, double distilled, and the man that found the jug first, got the first drink.

And we had a man . . . known in the community as Tim Williams. A very interesting man to be around, always telling his little, dry jokes. Get quite a laugh out of em, himself. Most of the people that knew him personally, they thought more of his laugh than they did of his jokes. And they'd laugh more at him than they would at his jokes.

Well, Uncle Joe, he was bald-headed, just had a little hair around the back of his head and above his ears. And then Uncle Tim, he kept *ba-ha-ha*-ing, a little bit. After a while, Uncle Joe says, "Timmy," he says, "what is it that's so funny?"

He says, "Well," he says, "I was just thinking about what made you so bald-headed."

Uncle Joe says, "What is it?"

He says, "You walked on your head to keep the devil from tracking you."

Made old Uncle Joe mad. And he [laughs] . . . first told Tim to get out. "Get out." Said, ". . . that liquor, if you find it, I wouldn't let you drink it. . . ." Uncle Tim, he got mad and went home, and the whole crew got busted up. And they never did get to drink their liquor.

205. The Biggest Bear That's Ever Been Killed

JAMES L. HUSKEY
Sugar Lands, Tennessee
Recorded by Joseph S. Hall,
Gatlinburg, Tennessee,
August 3, 1956

During a period of more than two decades recording tales in the Smoky Mountain region, Joseph S. Hall collected dozens of bear tales. Bear hunting was the ultimate macho pastime for mountain men, and stories celebrating the exploits of intrepid bear hunters were rife. The danger and intensity of the hunts were real enough, but the dramatic potential of these fights to the death between men and their largest (and most nearly human-looking) animal competitors naturally encouraged narrative inflation. Thus, "bear story" became a virtual synonym for "tall tale" in many parts of the Appalachians. As North Carolinian Granville Calhoun explained to Hall, "You asked me what a bear tale was. Us fellows at the camps—a fellow would come in, tell a little extra story, and a little out of line, like he had an extra drink or something: we'd call that a bear tale. It meant his story was a little exaggerated in places."

As much as one may expect exaggeration in a bear tale, the following account by James Huskey is told in an almost quiet voice, in a tone of great sincerity, and in such copious detail that it seems almost as matter-of-fact as a newspaper report.

When my dad lived at Magus Mountain, I was a boy of about seven years of age. And if you had quite a few stock in the mountains—sheep, and cattle, hogs—the bears was killing em. Destroying em. And they killed several bears, but this one, that I'm about to tell [of] now, was the biggest bear that's ever been killed in the mountains, so far—as yet know of. It was an old He. And we had a dog, a big dog, unusual size, big size. And he was give up to be the best bear dog in the country. And might near ever[y] man in the community—that is, families—owned that dog at one time. I believe I can truthfully say that. They all liked him. He was so high-prized.

So they took this dog, and some other dogs. And my dad and a neighbor by the name Will Robison, and two colored boys that was raised in the mountains there with em—John Turner and George Turner—they went with em. They got after this bear one afternoon, and they run it all that afternoon, all night, and the next day, up in the day, down just before dark, and the bear had got so stiff he couldn't travel well. And the dogs were pretty well give out. They was *all* pretty well give out.

The old bear backed up agin a poplar tree that was about eight feet in diameter. Started to fight with the dogs. Will Robison, he had ordered him a new Remington shotgun, one of those old side-locks, about the first ones that was put out. He had loaded it with a load of buckshot, not a-knowing the [principles] of the bear, and what the bear might do, not thinking of the danger of it. He was in front of him; he run up and shot that bear in the face with this shotgun. Shot both of his eyes out. The bear couldn't see him, but it could *smell*. It started toward him. He went to backing through the rhododendrons, laurel. Scared. Trying to get another cartridge into his gun. The bear was a-closing up on him pretty fast. And he was trying to back through the laurel and get away from it too.

And this colored boy by the name of John Turner, he had one of those old western saddle guns. Pump gun. (First repeating rifles made by the Winchester company, many years ago.) He dropped down on his knee and begin to pour the lead into that bear, and I believe it was twelve or fourteen shots that he shot it, before it fell. And when it fell, it fell within three feet of Will Robison. If it hadn't a been for [John], no doubt, the bear would have killed him.

So that was the biggest bear that's ever been killed in the mountains. It weighed something near nine hundred pounds.

206. Trials of a Dog Driver

CHARLES CARTER
Juneau, Alaska
Recorded by Amos Burg,
Juneau, Alaska
Summer 1941

Collector Amos Burg left no documentation concerning Charles Carter, but some of his stories can be supplemented in Eva Anderson's book *Dog-Team Doctor* (1940), an account of the life and career of Dr. Romig, the subject of Carter's second tale.

Kind of a peculiar incident happened to me just at the other side of the divide. We expected to get supplies at . . . the head of Nightnik Lake. And that is the dogfeed, anyway. But it had been a tough season for salmon and they hadn't provided anything from the year before. And they had no dogfeed. So we had to go on towards the pass with hungry dogs.

And when we got to the pass we couldn't cross it. The wind sweeps down through a gust that a man just can't stand against it. And I had to—one of those Eskimos won't go over alone with the Cheechako [i.e., "greenhorn"], white man, you know. They think he don't know anything. And so you have to hire two to go with you.

Well, one of them that knew the pass, he says no chance of getting over. And he would, in his guttural way, he'd say, "*A-seet*"—and that means it's very bad, and that we can't cross.

And I thought they were loafing on me, and I'd had a dog, an old dog that had been bitten by a mad dog, and I knew that I'd have to kill him sooner or later, and I told them that if we didn't go over the next day, that we'd kill that dog that had been bitten by the crazy dog and that we'd eat him.

And they have kind of a superstition against eating a dog there. They'll eat rotten fish and everything else, but a good, clean dog, they wouldn't touch at all. It must be superstition.

But anyway, next day, he was very alert, you know, in the morning. He was watching that pass. And long about noon, he says, "*Seeto*," which means that she's good now.

And so we started up the pass. And we got to—oh, got pretty well up the incline on the northern slope. The dog team can pull a sled *up* it all right, enough, but you got to "line down" this side of it: use a long line and drop your sled down on it. Unhitch your dogs and let them go on ahead, and you just drop your sled down, and from place to place, as you can get hold of . . . something to tie to.

Well, we got near the top. And this native, the guide, he couldn't speak any English. But he come back and says it's bad, and it's gonna get worse, and we'd never get across. So I just spoke to my leader, and wheeled him around, and I says. "All right, we'll come back and eat dog." And that native, he dug right in, and up he goes and we got over the pass, and just come down on the Katmai side as it was getting dark.

Well, . . . I could talk to you for hours regarding that trip there and over those trails, but, really, it's something that probably wouldn't be particularly interesting. . . .

There's [someone] in particular I have in mind now. It was Doctor Romig, who was afterwards the surgeon for the Alaska Railway. He was then medical missionary for the Moravian Missions, including Bethel. . . . I never met him after that for almost forty years. And I had quite a talk to him as he was going through on a boat and we got reminiscing. And his wife . . . , she died, and he was married again while he was at Anchorage.

And the doctor and I, we were reminiscing on the natives up there and their customs and so forth. And the fact of them being so lousy. And his wife began scratching, and she said, "I wish you men would talk about something else."

So, but he just continued on talking, and, of course, I couldn't stop the conversation, so she had to get up and leave. The . . . doctor says, "Did you ever see them delousing?"

"Yes," I said, "I've seen them delousing. They just picked em off the parka, you know, and they were too indolent to crack a louse after they had em and they'd just throw em down, and that's where we had to spread our bed at night, and consequently, we got pretty buggy."

"But," he says, "did you ever see them cracking the nits?"

And I said, "No, now that's something I did miss."

"Well," he says, "they just turn the parka inside out, and the nits, they gather along the seam. And they just run them through their teeth and crack em that way." That's what made Mrs. Romig leave the stateroom. But the first Mrs. Romig—when I arrived in Bethel. That was about the tenth of December, nineteen hundred and one. The doctor very graciously come and ask me if I wouldn't be his guest during the time I was in Bethel, and, of course, naturally I accepted. I'd been sleeping out in the tent, or sometimes no tent. And so he brought me into the house, and Mrs. Romig said, "Are you lousy?"

I says, "Yes, ma'am, I sure am."

And "Well," she says, "I have a nice spare bed, but I wouldn't like to get it loused up."

"Well," I says, "if I slept in it, it sure would be. And haven't you got any old shack or anything that I can sleep in?"

"Why," she says, "I have a big bath house up there with four bunks in it, and we'll have the boys put on a fire, and you'll be real comfortable out there, I'm sure. And it don't matter if you mix the breed out there a little bit, it'll be perfectly all right. Now, you don't take any offense at this, because every time the doctor's out on the trail, I meet him just in the entry here, and he's got to strip right as he was born, and then walk in . . . to the tub (galvanized tub, you know). And he's got to take a bath and then I scald those clothes that he's worn. Otherwise, they'd just take us away, you know. Crawl away with us. . . ."

So he became quite famous afterwards. And he has written a book. And it's known as the *Dog-Team Doctor*. Well, you know that, if you go to a new country, it don't matter how much you know about conditions in one part of Alaska, for instance, but if you go to another part, like I was going up there, going through on my first trip, I was a tenderfoot, you see. And he was talking about the, in this book, the *Dog-Team Doctor*, and he said that he was mentioning various times . . . about the profanity used by dog drivers. And I might pause to mention at this time that profanity has an eloquence. Profanity, you know, it might start with muleskinners, bullwhackers, and dog drivers. The dog driver, he rises to heights of profane eloquence never thought of by others. Well, the doctor in his book gave me credit for the most profane person and using the most unique profanity that he had ever heard. And he just shuddered for fear his wife would hear it.

I didn't know I was so close to the mission at the time. There was a cutbank and I was trying to drive a tired dog team up it. And you know how it is, if you got a cutbank, you simply get your lead dog up on top, you know, and haul em up by the line and get another one up probably, you know, and then you go back to boost your sled, and those dogs that are up on top, they lie down and have a nap. And that—I was just talking to em, trying to encourage em to get up and pull the load. And you know, if you talk to a dog and you were to say, "Please, go on now," that wouldn't mean anything to the dog. But they seem to have, they just seem to understand profanity, you know, and it just works magic with them, you know. . . . I've bought dogs that didn't understand the English language, but there's something about profanity that seems to put the spirit into them.

207. I'm Still Here: Healing at Home

VORIES MOREAU
Basile, Louisiana
Recorded by Carl Lindahl,
Opelousas, Louisiana,
January 15, 1997

Born in 1925 on the prairies of southwestern Louisiana, Vories Moreau grew up steeped in the small-farm culture of the prairie Cajuns, a group of French Americans whose ancestors immigrated to the Gulf Coast in the eighteenth century after being forced by the English to leave their lands in Canada. By the time of Vories's birth, his family had lived in Louisiana for more than 150 years, but they still spoke French as their first and only language. The relative isolation of their communities and their intensely close family bonds allowed the Cajuns to maintain much of their musical and linguistic culture even as they interacted increasingly with English-speaking Anglo-Americans and African Americans.

When Vories speaks about home healing on the Louisiana prairies in the 1930s and 1940s, he invokes some cures (such as the use of turpentine, or coal oil, to prevent infection) that were used by most ethnic groups, especially in rural areas, well into the twentieth century. Yet he also speaks about the custom of *traitement* (or "treatment"), a particular type of faith-based healing rooted in the French culture and language. Typically, the patient's plight is brought to the attention of a *traiteur* ("treater"), usually a close neighbor, who then prays for the patient, quietly uttering a rhymed incantation whose words must remain secret for the cure to work. The *traiteur* has learned the words from another *traiteur*, yet has received healing powers from a divine source. *Traiteurs* believe that they are doing God's work, and they do not charge money for their healing rituals. At the dawn of the twenty-first century, *traitement* continues to thrive in Cajun Louisiana.

Many families consult both doctors and *traiteurs* when facing serious medical troubles.

The first tale of healing that Vories narrates is based in pan-ethnic, non-supernatural medical traditions, but all the other stories involve *traitement* to some extent. In the first of the *traitement* tales, the *traiteur* does not seem to help Vories, but in the other narratives, the prayers of the *traiteur* prove effective. The last tale may raise some puzzling questions of faith: if *traitement* is a gift from God, why would God let it be used to stop the bleeding of an animal that has already died?

Vories Moreau told the following tales in his home near Opelousas, Louisiana. The stories were set some forty miles to the west, in the neighborhood of Basile, where Vories was born and lived most of his life.

I don't remember exactly how old I was, but I was a young kid then. You know, we didn't have much to play with. We didn't have much toys to play with when I was a kid.

And they were butchering at my cousin's house—butchering hogs. . . . They'd get up early in the morning, before daylight, and build a fire, and put the water to heat so that they could scald the hogs. Well, they did that.

And I went with my daddy, you know. And so they'd put the water in the pots and they'd build the fire, and then they decided they was going to go in and drink their coffee. And they had sharpened their knives. So, I don't know why my daddy stuck his knife in the ground—by the big pot, you know. Everybody else had put theirs on the table, but Daddy stuck his in the ground. Why I don't know.

And while they were gone to drink coffee, there was three of my cousins there that was big enough to play. So we decided to play "Devil," you know. I was the devil. I started chasing them around the pot, round and round we'd go, you know. And after awhile, man, I passed my toes right on that knife—the knife went between my toes. And, man, I just slashed it.

We didn't go to the doctor's in those days. So they brought me home and my old aunt was there. She got a bucket with some coal oil in it and she soaked my foot in there and then she wrapped it up in some white—piece of sheet I guess. White material. And it grew back together. I still have the scar from it, you know. It was a bad, bad cut. And that's all she'd do: about every two or three hours she'd put my foot in that pan of coal oil and then she'd wrap it up with a white rag. That's it. No doctor, no nothing. That was our doctor. . . .

[Carl Lindahl: How long were you bleeding . . . before . . .]

Before I went home? Oh, a good while, because they had to take me back in a wagon, you know. And it wasn't very, very far from the house . . . but in a *wagon* it's far. It was maybe a couple of miles from our house. But at my cousin's my dad wrapped my foot up in some stuff. And it was bleeding but not gushing. . . .

[Carl Lindahl: How far did the blade go into the skin . . . ?]

Till my toe would hang [off the foot].

[Carl Lindahl: So your aunt just poured the coal oil over that?]

No. She put the coal oil in the pan, and she put my foot in the pan.

[Carl Lindahl: Did that hurt?]

No. . . . It didn't burn or nothing. *Now* it'd probably kill you to put your foot in coal oil [laughter], but in those days it didn't. . . . She did it every three or four hours. She did it for the rest of that day and through the night . . . till the next day, and then we started doing it about three times a day, morning, noon, and night. . . . Three or four days. . . . But I didn't get no infection or nothing.

[Carl Lindahl: Good medicine!]

Nowadays, you'd get an infection right away. You'd have to run to the doctor and get a tetanus shot and all kinds of other shots, you know. But that's the way it was then. . . .

When I was about six years old, one morning I was going with my brother to round up the horses. It was in the woods, kind of in the woods. We were going to round up the horses for Daddy so that he could go to work in the field. And my brother was ahead of me. And, they had an old gallon can or something—that was half rotten, but it was on the ground. So my brother jumped over that, and when I got there I was going to do just like him. I was going to jump over it too.

And when I jumped, there was a little ground rattler, and he got my foot. Well, my brother put me on his back and we started to go home, but before I went to the house, I was throwing up and I was sick.

And when we got home, my mom got me a glass of milk—because I hadn't eaten breakfast. She got me a glass of milk and, not long after that, then I started throwing up *blood*. I don't know why—maybe I was bleeding in my stomach. But I started throwing up blood.

But they didn't take me to the doctor then either. They took me to an old guy that was treating—for snakebite. But he treated me and it didn't get any better. They had another one across the woods that would treat for snakebite and they took me over there. And he treated me, and it didn't do much good either.

So about three days after that, they decided—I was so sick they decided to take me to the doctor. It was Doctor Carlin, in Eunice. They brought me over there. He looked at me and he told Daddy, said, "You better bring him back home. [Chuckling] He's going to die anyway. There's nothing I can do." You know.

So they brought me back home, and that was—about sixty-five years ago, and I'm still here. [Laughter]

But we didn't have no money for the doctor anyway. . . . We was about fifteen miles from the doctor. Either you'd go on horseback or you'd go in the wagon. We didn't have a car. We went in the wagon. It'd take you three hours to get there and three hours to come back. So it's a whole-day *affaire*, you know.

[Carl Lindahl: What did the *traiteurs* do?]

They'd say prayers, you know. That's what they all do.

[Carl Lindahl: Did they put a hand on you anywhere?]

Yeah. You know, around your leg, like this. The snake bit me right here. . . . It didn't work for me. You know, some people it works for. But it didn't work for me.

[Carl Lindahl: But the doctor didn't work either. . . . Do you remember any time that *traitement* worked for you or your family?]

Yeah. [Chuckling] For toothache it worked.

[Carl Lindahl: And how old were you then?]

Eight or nine years old. We had moved from that place where the snake had been and we moved to another place—and I had a toothache. And there was an old man there who would treat for toothache. So Daddy brought me over there and he treated me. And the toothache went away [laughing]. And I don't know if the *traitement* did it or not.

But I'll tell you what I *saw*. We had a mule that got ran over by a plow. And he cut his foot. And it was—I mean, blood was *gushing*. So Daddy told me to run across the field to an old man—his name was Portalise Sonnier. He said, "Run to Noncle Portal and tell him Jerry (that was the name of the mule), tell him Jerry cut his foot and he's bleeding real badly."

So I went to Portal's and I told him. And he didn't even leave the house. He treated from his *house*. And the mule stopped bleeding. . . . Just like that.

[Carl Lindahl: And how far away was his house?]

Oh, maybe a quarter of a mile. Across the field. It wasn't very far. But—the minute he treated the mule, the mule quit bleeding. . . .

And one time [chuckles]—I was married to a Doucette girl, and her daddy treated to stop blood, you know. And I'd laugh at him all the time. I'd tell him (his name was Tony), I'd tell him, "Hey, Tony, you *can't* stop the blood."

"Yeah, I can." He said, "Yeah, I can."

So one day—I was home making gumbo, so I cut a rooster's head off. And you know how the blood *gushes*. I told Tony, I said, "Well, you stop it, man." And he *did*, just like that.

[Carl Lindahl: He said a prayer and stopped the blood?]

He said something, you know. And just as fast as you'd snap your finger, the blood stopped running out of that rooster's neck. Now, he wasn't out of blood. He just quit. . . . So . . . you know, he kind of made a believer out of me. If you see somebody do something and it works, you almost have to believe it. . . . You know, a lot of the *traitement* . . . would *help*. . . . Like I said, we couldn't go to the doctor. There wasn't no going to the doctor. We didn't have the money, to start with. And then, by the time we would have got to the doctor, anyway, we would have been dead anyway, half the time. . . . It was way over there, like fifteen or sixteen miles, and that was a long way in a wagon, you know.

208. I'm a Man Too: Fights Every Night

VORIES MOREAU
Basile, Louisiana
Recorded by Carl Lindahl,
Opelousas, Louisiana,
January 15, 1997

In the course of his life, Vories Moreau held some forty jobs, ranging from the rural crafts of farming and the arts of Cajun music making (he played fiddle in the band of the great accordionist Iry Lejeune) to offshore oil-drilling and repairing voting machines. Among the jobs at which he excelled was dance hall proprietor. During the first half of the twentieth century, the dance hall was a magnet for the most important Saturday-night event, the *fais-do-do*, a communal dance in which people of all ages participated and which served as the principal stage for courtship. Couples would meet and spend their most intimate pre-marriage moments on the dance floor, closely observed by their elders.

But violence was also a dance hall staple. As Barry Jean Ancelet writes, "Dances rarely passed without incident, because making trouble was a traditional form of amusement for some. Stories abound about the neighborhood bully who goes to a dance expressly to test the system. He might walk

Vories Moreau, in white shirt, and his neighbor Mike Broussard during a Cajun Mardi Gras celebration, Basile, Louisiana, 1992. (Photo by Carl Lindahl)

in and yell at the top of his lungs, *'Je suis le meilleur homme dans la place!'* (I'm the best man in the place!)"

Vories Moreau heard and told many such stories because as a dance hall manager, he had to stave off every threat and answer every act of violence that occurred in his club. Sometimes those threats would come from rival dance hall owners, such as Boeuf in the narrative that follows. At other times, it could be a group of soldiers on leave and looking for a good time. One man explained, writes Barry Ancelet, "that men fought 'because they liked it. There was no television . . . in those days. That was their only fun—to see which of them was the best man.' A long-time dance hall owner agreed, adding, 'Sometimes two of those boys would go to a dance together and, hell, if they couldn't' find anyone else to fight with, they fought each other.' "

People killing their own kids, and kids killing their momma and daddy: once in a while you'd hear about that, in the big city—New York and places like that. *Around here*, there wasn't such thing as that. Murders.

. . . But today, it's no big deal. . . . You get sent to the pen, and get out in three years for good behavior, and do the same thing again.

But when I was a kid—when people would go to Angola [the Louisiana State Prison Farm], when they would come back, I promise you, they didn't want to go back no more. But now, oh man, it's second heaven. You go to the pen, you got the exercise room. You got air conditioning. You got food. You got a good place to sleep. But if they don't like it, they're going to fight, man. You got to cook what they want to eat. You can't just feed em anything. And they don't want to work. They don't make em work. That's inhuman, you know, to make a criminal work. [Laughter] It is. And the *lawyers*—if you touch him, he's going to sue you. The guy in the pen can sue you if you touch him. And make you pay for it, for hitting him. And now they have all kinds of rights.

But when I was a young man, when you went to the pen and you come back, you didn't have no rights. Couldn't vote. Couldn't own a home. You couldn't do nothing.

But now, man, they've got all kind of rights. The criminal's got the rights and the people don't have no rights. That can't go on forever. That has to come to an end.

[Carl Lindahl: Why did Boeuf go to Angola? Why was he there? What did he do?]

They went to the other side of Elton, and they had an old couple there that supposedly had money. They got in the house, and the old people wouldn't tell them where the money was. So they tore their fingernails out with pliers, and their toenails, but they never did make them talk. They never did say where the money was. Then they got caught, and he went to the pen.

[Carl Lindahl: That's where somebody like that ought to be.]

Yep. That's a good place for him. But Beouf didn't stay. He swam the Mississippi River. [Laughter] No, *really*. And, *then*, if you could swim the Mississippi from Angola, then you was a free man. Well Beouf was, he was a *man*, he was a real man—a strong, big old man. And he was strong. And they say that there was a jackass there, and he pushed [it] in the river, and hang onto his tail until the jackass drowned, and then he caught himself on a log or something and swam across the river.

And that was it. They never did come get him. He stayed. That was it. That was way, way back . . . sixty-five, seventy years ago.

[Carl Lindahl: But Boeuf was kind of tough . . . and not always fair?]

Yeah, Boeuf was tough. . . . But, you know, he was kindhearted. If you'd go to him with a hard luck story, and you needed a couple of bucks, and he had it, he'd give it to you. But he might stop you down the road and steal it back. [Laughter]

They said during bootleg days that Boeuf would bootleg. He'd serve bootleg. So you'd go to his place. People would go to his place and buy it, and then when you was going back west, at the bayou—Bayou Nez Pique didn't have no bridge then—you'd have to pass in the bayou. And you'd bog down, and all kind of stuff, you know. Well, he'd sell them the booze and then they load up the car. And they'd take off again. And he had three or four guys over at the bayou, so when you'd get to the bayou, they'd stop you and point a gun at you and steal your whiskey and bring it back to Boeuf. And then he'd sell it again. The same whiskey, he'd sell it seven or eight times. . . .

I can't prove that. I didn't see that. But everybody said that, so it must be true.

But, you know, I was in business when Boeuf was in business. Wasn't very far apart—the old Avalon and A.J.'s was maybe a mile and a half apart. And I was at A.J.'s and Beouf was at the Avalon. But we got along. . . .

[Carl Lindahl: But didn't he send some people over to your place one time?]

Yeah. . . . But he was always trying to put the screws to me—like sent those guys over to break up the dance, you know. They made a mess, but they didn't break up the dance, I promise.

[Carl Lindahl: Didn't they come in and try to start a fight with you?]

They didn't just try. We started a fight. . . . I think it was Sunday afternoon. And there was four of em. They had a big red-haired guy. And I was by myself at the bar, and they was sitting in the dance hall. And they'd holler. And I'd go see what they wanted, you know. And they'd holler for something. And every time I'd go to the table, the big old red-haired guy would say, "I hear you're tough. How tough are you?"

I said, "I don't know. The only way you can find that out, you have to try. If you try, you'll find out how tough I am."

Well, they went on like that for a while, and then they left. They went to the Quest Lounge. And the Quest was like that house over there, maybe twenty-five yards from the business I was in, . . . the Rainbow. . . . Well, they went over there and after a while they came out of the Quest Lounge. They made like they was fighting, but they wasn't. That was planned, you know. Boeuf threw em out, and they walked to the Rainbow. And the redhead didn't have no shirt.

So I was watching. And when he got to the door, I said, "Man, you can't come in here like that. Without a shirt, you can't come in here."

"Yeah," he said. "I can come in."

He started pushing me. And . . . the Rainbow was a long dance hall. You know, it was a big place. And he pushed me and pushed me until way in the back. I let him push me till way in the back, to the bandstand. And when my back hit against the bandstand, I said, "Well, it's time to get rid of this boy." [Laughter]

So—I had a blackjack, you know. And I hit him with the blackjack. And I knocked him down. And every time he'd get back up, I'd knock him down again. I pushed him back and back, the way he came from, all down the hall.

So, finally, I said, "Are you going to get out?"

"Yeah," he said. "If you show me the door, I'm going to get out."

So I drug him to the door and I kicked him out. And two of his buddies had sat at a table. And they was sitting there. They wasn't taking part in the fight, you know. But they was sitting there. And I had a big, big fan, you know. One of those big fans . . . in the wall. And it was even with the floor, the bottom of it. And I had, like a screen in front of it. So when I saw them there—I had my pistol in my belt. I took my pistol out and I pointed it at them and I said, "You all want some of this?" [Laughing]

And they didn't say yes or no, man. They ran. They hit that big fan—I thought they were going to take the fan with them to wherever they was going. [Laughter]

[Carl Lindahl: They ran out right through the fan?]

Through the fan. That was the end of that fight.

[Carl Lindahl: So, did Beouf try to mess with you after that?]

Well, he'd try to hire my bands so they wouldn't show up [to play for my customers] and stuff like that, but—no, Beouf never did mess with me, you know, *personally*. He could have slapped me down with one finger because . . . , well, I weighed a hundred and forty-five pounds. He weighed *two hundred and twenty-five* pounds. But if he have tried to slap me, he would have had to kill me. You know. Because I had the difference, and I would have used it. That's the only way I knew how to fight.

You fight to win. If you're going to fight, you fight to win. You know, there's no clean fighting as far as I'm concerned. If I get in a fight, I'm going to kick you, I'm going to bite you, I'm going to dig your eyes out. I'd pull your hair. You know, whatever it takes. That's what I'm going to do [chuckling]. Maybe that's kind of cold-hearted, but if I'm going to fight, I don't want to *lose*.

And I've used, you know, my knife to fight, if that's what it took.

[Carl Lindahl: Was that a sign of respect from Boeuf that he didn't try to fight you personally? Or was that just the way he was? He'd send other people—]

Well, he'd send other people, but he never did come in and start nothing. . . . He knew better. . . . I don't know if you know Cannonball. Me and Cannonball was real good friends. . . . And Beouf told Cannonball (I'm not bragging, I'm just stating what the man told me). Cannonball told me that Boeuf had told him that the only man he was scared of in Basile was me. He said, "That son-of-a-bitch's crazy. He's going to kill you." [Laughter]

And I will, you know. If a man messed with me, I would have killed him. If I had to, I sure would. Some people say, "No use to have a gun," cause if they had to use it, they wouldn't use it. I can use a gun. If I have to use it, I can use it. I wouldn't even hesitate. I wouldn't think about it, you know. Same with a knife. I'd just as soon have a knife as a pistol. A good knife that cuts. You never miss with that baby. With that pistol, you might miss; but with that knife, you don't miss. Whoever you're fighting with ain't going to catch you, cause if they catch you, his hand is going to fall off.

[Carl Lindahl: When you were running the Rainbow, you had a pistol on you all the time?]

All the time.

[Carl Lindahl: And you had a blackjack?]

Um, hum.

[Carl Lindahl: Did you have a knife too?]

Yes. [Laughter] I was well prepared. . . . I didn't have a floor bouncer. *I* was the floor bouncer. . . . One time at a dance, five soldiers come in the bar. And I had a dance that night. And one of them was supposed to be a bully, I guess. I'd never seen him before. He was a big guy and he had four guys with him. They come in the bar. In the lounge. And each had a couple of drinks. And they decided to go in the dance hall.

Well, I had a cover charge for the dance hall. So I had a guy selling tickets. And they just went by him, you know, like they didn't have to pay. So he told them, you know, if they wanted to get in the dance hall, they'd have to pay. So, they said, no, they wasn't going to pay. So, he comes and tells me. And I talk to them. You know, I talked nice to them. I told them, I said, "Look, if you all want to stay in the lounge, it don't cost you nothing but your drinks, you know. But if you want to come on the dance floor, you're going to have a cover charge."

"Oh, okay." So they come back in the lounge.

Well, it wasn't five minutes more—here comes my ticket man again and tells me those five guys went in there again. So I went and I told them, I said, "Now, look, you all can't come in here unless you pay. You can sit in the lounge, like I told you before, but I'm not coming back to tell you again."

"Well, okay." They got out of there and back in the lounge. But another five minutes and they were back in the hall. So when the ticket man come told me—so I went and got the bully. If you get the bully out of the way, there's nothing, you see.

So I told that big guy, I said, "Well, look, I done told you twice. And I don't want you in the lounge, I don't want you here either. You get your butt out."

He said, "Well, who's going to make me get out?"

I said, "I will."

He said, "You will?"

I said, "Yeah. That's right."

So he did like he was going to swing at me. And I always had that little blackjack in my hand, you know, when it was rough. I'd have it in my pocket, you know, but it was wrapped around my hand. So when he tried to swing at me, you know, I whopped him with that blackjack, and on his knees he went. And every time he'd get up, I'd whop it to him again.

So, finally . . . I said, "You're going to get out of here?"

He said, "Yeah, if you show me the door, I'm going to get out."

So I drug him to the door and I threw him out on the gravel and then I told him I didn't want no more of that. And the other four, they never did nothing, you see. They didn't try anything. They just got out. . . .

And then about a week later, some guy from Camp Polk . . . come question me. I believe he was . . .

[Carl Lindahl: MP, like military police, or something like that?]

Something like that. He come to question me about what happened. So I told him what happened.

He said, "Did you have to hit him so hard?"

I said, "I tried not to hit him. I told the man three times. . . ." I said, "He wouldn't listen to me. . . . When I told him to get out, he asked me who was going to make him get out. . . . And I *did* make him get out."

And he says, "Well, I guess you did the right thing. But he thinks he's a bully and—"

I said, "He's not no bully now. There ain't no bullies here." [Laughter]

That's true. There ain't no bullies here. . . . I never saw the man that I couldn't put out of my dance hall. Never. I wasn't big, but I had the guts. I had the guts.

I'm not scared of—a *man*. That's nothing. I'm scared of a dog. I'm scared of a snake. But a man, that's just like *me*. That's just a *man*. And I'm a man too.

DUST BOWL TALES

The Dust Bowl of the Southern Plains remains, to date, the most extensive ecological disaster in the history of the country. Caused most immediately by widespread drought conditions—conditions created in part and greatly intensified by agricultural practices that rendered the land naked and vulnerable—massive dust storms began to sweep the prairies in the 1930s. According to historian Donald Worster, it was the monster storm of May 1934 that announced the onset of "a new dark age": "On 9 May, brown earth from Montana and Wyoming swirled up from the ground, was captured by extremely high level winds, and was blown eastward toward the Dakotas. More dirt was sucked into the airstream until 350 million tons were riding toward urban America." Before the next morning, enough airborne prairie had rained down on Chicago to cover each of its 3,000,000 citizens with four pounds of dirt. The next day, the storm, sometimes reaching the speed of 100 miles per hour, darkened the skies over Buffalo, New York, and by May 11, dust was sweeping the streets of the east coast, from Boston, Massachusetts, to Savannah, Georgia, as well as the decks of ships hundreds of miles offshore in the Atlantic. This was the first of the great storms that came to be known as black blizzards.

In succeeding years, the Southern Plains—especially western Kansas and the Oklahoma and Texas panhandles—increasingly bore the brunt of these storms. The black blizzards of the spring of 1935 created giant, land-bound clouds, reaching as high as 8,000 feet into the air, that piled enough dirt on railroad tracks to derail trains, generated darkness so thick that people standing two feet apart were invisible to each other, and afflicted farmers even inside their own homes. As one west Kansas woman wrote: "All we could do about it was just sit in our dusty chairs, gaze at each other through the fog that filled the room and watch that fog settle slowly and silently, covering everything . . . in a thick, brownish gray blanket. When we opened the door swirling whirlwinds of soil beat against us unmercifully. . . . The door and windows were all shut tightly, yet those tiny particles seemed to seep through the very walls. It got into cupboards and clothes closets; our faces were as dirty as if we had rolled in the dirt; our hair was gray and stiff and we ground dirt between our teeth." Several people suffocated in these storms, and thousands of others developed a more slow working and often fatal condition known as "dust pneumonia": in April 1935, more

Black Sunday: A dust storm hits western Kansas, April 14, 1935. (Kansas State Historical Society)

than half of the hospital patients in Meade County, Kansas, were suffering from acute respiratory ailments, and thirty-three of those patients died.

The most dramatic of all the black blizzards fell on April 14, 1935—Black Sunday. Giant dust clouds formed on the Northern Plains, swelled as they blew south over Kansas and Oklahoma, and churned into Texas. It was "the blackest dust storm that ever filled the sky," as Woody Guthrie remembered it. "Well, the worst'un I ever seen was, was on the fourteenth day of April in nineteen hundred and thirty-five. I was living at that time at about sixty mile north of Amarillo, Texas, up on the plains there: they're thirty-six hundred feet high and just as flat as a floor. A thousand miles wide, and there ain't a thing in the world to stop that wind but just a barbed wire fence about a hundred miles north of there, and it ain't got a barb on it. . . . It looked like a ocean was jumping on a snail. That's just the way the dust storm hit our town."

As the storms became more frequent, reaching a peak of seventy-two "regional storms" and countless smaller "sand blows" in 1937, the human dimensions of this natural disaster became impossible to ignore. Farming on the Southern Plains, always difficult in the past, was now impossible for many. Two and one-half million of the region's inhabitants left their farms during the 1930s.

Most of these people had been afflicted by crop failures and the concurrent Great Depression even before the dust storms delivered the final blow, and many now had no place to go. By the late 1930s, hundreds of thousands were on their way to California. Lured by handbills that promised decent work and decent pay, the "Dust Bowl refugees" flooded California, and they soon found that if any work at all awaited them, it would be for microscopic wages. Many of those who had come to work were driven out of the state; others lived hand-to-mouth and day-to-day, sleeping outside, wandering from house to house and farm to farm, offering to work for food on those too-rare occasions when they could find either work or food. Tens of thousands of "Okies," migrants from Oklahoma, were settled into government camps, often living in tents and denied even the most basic daily comforts—running water, for example.

Even in the context of the hardships of the Great Depression, the Dust Bowl and the fate of its "refugees" appalled the nation. The sufferings of the Okies and the dignity with which they bore their adversity inspired artists to fashion notable works of social protest with rich folkloric content: John Steinbeck's *Grapes of Wrath* (1939), John Ford's film adaptation of Steinbeck's book (1940), the photography of Dorothea Lange, and the Dust Bowl Ballads of Woody Guthrie.

209. Dust Bowl Refugees

WOODY GUTHRIE
Okemah, Oklahoma
Recorded by Alan and Elizabeth Littleton Lomax,
Washington, D.C., March 27, 1940

Woodrow Wilson Guthrie, most famous as the composer of "This Land Is Your Land," "Pastures of Plenty," "Deportee," and dozens of other songs of national celebration and social protest, was also a wordsmith in prose, both a talented author and an effective storyteller. Born a farmer's son in Okemah, Oklahoma, Guthrie experienced a childhood constantly visited by natural and social upheavals: drought, hunger, cyclones, house fires, his mother's mental illness, widespread unemployment, the barroom fights that accompanied oil booms, and the deepening poverty that accompanied oil-field busts. Okemah's farms and businesses had largely dried up before the black blizzards rolled in, and Woody was living in the Texas panhandle town of Pampa when the most powerful storms swept the plains. Both the town he left behind and the town to which he moved were darkened by dusters repeatedly from 1935 to 1940.

In *Bound for Glory* (1943), the remarkable book that describes his childhood and coming of age, Guthrie relates so many intense hardships that the Dust Bowl seems no more notable than most. He portrays the experience not as a cataclysm of black blizzards but, rather, as the slow, steady strangulation of an already troubled landscape: "The dust crawled down from the north and the banks pushed the farmers off their land. The big flat lakes dried away and left hollow places across the plains full of this hard, dry, crackled gumbo mud. There isn't a healthier country than West Texas when it wants to be, but when the dust kept whistling down the line blacker and more of it, there was plenty of everything sick, and mad, and mean, and worried." Yet for all the disasters that Guthrie portrays in *Bound for Glory*, he continually looks beyond the hardships suffered by his family and neighbors, to make his book a quiet celebration of their strength of character and the stoic and unaccountably good-humored ways in which they endured their afflictions.

Woody Guthrie's storytelling style is as understated as his writing. Even when narrating the most outrageous natural calamities and social wrongs, he speaks in an effective deadpan. Instead of raising his voice to emphasize a phrase or situation, he repeats certain words or phrases and runs off lists of examples until the sheer length of his sentences and weight of their detail impress the listener with the dimensions of the tragedies he describes. As one example, Guthrie embeds the following list inside what would otherwise be a short and simple sentence: "They was hundreds and hundreds and hundreds and hundreds of thousands of families of people living around under railroad bridges, down along the river bottoms, and in old cardboard houses, and in old rusty, beat-up houses that they'd made up out of tote sacks and old dirty rags and corrugated iron that they got out of the dumps and old tin cans flattened out, and old orange crates. . . ."

To intensify his descriptions, Guthrie speaks slowly, drawing out his words, and using pauses for emphasis. When narrating tragic situations, he often laughs softly or lowers his voice to a whisper. The effect is considerable. Guthrie's oral style is the verbal equivalent of the stoic, proud, unpretentious lifestyle of the Okie community into which he was born, and it is the ideal vehicle for conveying the acts and words of the characters that populate his tales.

The following "tale" is really more a series of meditations than a continuous narrative. Alan Lomax and his wife, Elizabeth, were interviewing Woody in Washington, D.C., just as his songs were beginning to attract national attention. Woody's answers and observations were interspersed with songs. Joe Klein, Guthrie's biographer, remarks of the session, "Even though he was being recorded seriously for the first time in his life, Woody didn't seem at all nervous. In fact, with his smooth, soft mesmerizing voice and nimble mind, he dominated the proceedings."

Elizabeth Lomax: Tell me Woody, what was these people thinking about all this time?]

[Laughing:] What was they thinking about?

[Elizabeth Lomax: What were they talking about?]

Well, we used to, all of us would get together, in the little old shacks and houses there in the Dust Bowl, and we'd talk about some place to go to and some place to move to, and some place to pick up and go to, where maybe we could get a hold of a piece of land or a little farm of some kind and get out of all that dust, and all that dust pneumonia, and all of that wind that was up there on the Texas plains. And people talked about going everywheres in the world. Once in a while you'd hear a feller say something about going to Arkansas to get him a little farm, once in a while you'd hear somebody talking about going down on the Gulf of Mexico to get him a little farm, and once in a while you'd hear somebody talking about going down to the Rio Grande Valley to get him a little farm and to start raising some kind of fruit or vegetables or watermelons or apples or orchards or something that would be useful, you know, to where they could do honest work and make an honest living. But most of em, most of the people in the Dust Bowl talked about California. The reason they talked about California was that they'd seen all the pretty pictures about California and they'd heard all the pretty songs about California, and they had read all the handbills about coming to California and picking fruit. And these people naturally said, "Well, if this dust keeps on blowing the way it is, we're gonna have to go somewhere." And most of em, I'll dare say seventy-five percent of em, was in favor of going to California because they had heard about the climate there. You could sleep outdoors at night, and any kind of seed that you put down in the ground, why, it'd grow back out again. And all such things as that, made all these people want to go to California. . . .

A little song that I remember . . . attracted several hundred thousand families—it helped, I'll say—to go from the Dust Bowl to California, and the name of this one is the "California Blues" . . . an old song that Jimmie Rodgers sung and he put it on a . . . phonograph record. And that phonograph record went all down through Oklahoma. . . . I have stood around in lots and lots of towns, and I've seen in them days, the electric phonograph was quite an attraction. And I've seen hundreds and hundreds of people gang up around an electronic phonograph and listen to Jimmie Rodgers sing that song about going to California:

> . . . gonna sleep out every night,
> Because the Oklahoma women just naturally ain't treating me right. . . .
> California waters taste like cherry wine,
> But Georgia waters taste like turpentine.

And it seemed awful funny to me that all these verses and all that was said in this song . . . had a big effect on all these people all over that country, because I've stood around in different towns, and heard big crowds of people gather around all of these electric phonographs and listen to that "California Blues" and they'd [laughing] punch each other in the ribs with their elbows and they'd say, "Boy, there's a place to go. That old boy's singing the truth. Listen to him sing. I'm telling you, that makes me just want to pick up right now. . . ." Anyway, there was thousands and thousands and thousands more of em, fact there was about three or four hundred thousand of em, that got up out of these states and started off down that Sixty-six highway, and they didn't know where they was going or when they was coming back. All they knew was that they was going somewhere where they could maybe get a job that'd be of some use to somebody.

[Elizabeth Lomax: Well, Woody, did these people really pack up their duds and leave, or were they just joking around?]

Well, they [laughing], they wasn't joking. Cause there was several hundred thousand of em. Not just several hundred thousand *people*, but they was that many families that, right about that same time, they just woke up one bright clear morning and they found theirselves walking down the road. Wives, kids, fathers, and everybody else that you could think of.

And they heard that there was some kind of work out west in California. And so, these people had been workers all their lives, that's all they'd ever knowed how to do, was just a-work. That's what they liked to do. They got as much kick out of a hard day's work as a lot of people would out of a hard day's drunk. But anyway, they traveled fifteen hundred or two thousand miles in these old, broke-down jalopies, and they went to California. And I was one of the first ones just to go to California, cause some people started talking—where I'm always kind of a dad-gum feller that jumps up and takes off, right while they're talking about it.

Anyway, when I got to California, I seen things out there that I wouldn't believe. If people'd sit and tell me—that they was hundreds and hundreds and hundreds and hundreds of thousands of families of people living around under railroad bridges, down along the river bottoms, and in old cardboard houses, and in old rusty, beat-up houses that they'd made up out of tote sacks and old dirty rags and corrugated iron that they got out of the dumps and old tin cans flattened out, and old orange crates that they'd been able to tear up and get boards out of it—I wouldn't believe it. Cause all these people didn't go out there to loaf around. They didn't go out there to have a good time. They went out there for one reason, and absolutely one reason, and that was because they thought that they could get some work there. . . .

[Woody describes the conditions awaiting the families that arrived in California.]

Camping around, three or four families on a hillside, and three or four families on another hillside, they had a little old spring of water running around there somewhere, and they'd use this little spring of water, or little hole of water to do their washing in, to shave in, to take a drink of water out of, to wash their teeth in. They used that spring of water as sewage disposal. They used it for everything in the world. And [laughing] a lot of times I've seen three or four hundreds of families of people a-trying to get along on a stream of water that wasn't any bigger than the stream of water that comes from your faucet when you go into the kitchen and turn the faucet on. These mountain springs wasn't any stronger than that one faucet, and yet three or four hundred families of people found theirselves trying to sanitary on that amount of water.

[Elizabeth Lomax: What did the Californians think about this? How did they react? What did they call these people? What did they say to them? Have you got any little songs made up about that?]

Well I got [a song] here that tells about a brand new name that people made up for us. Something we've never been called before in our whole lives. They called us Dust Bowl refugees, all the newspaper headlines was full of stuff about "Dust Bowl refugees." Refugees here, refugees yonder, refugees everywhere that you looked. They called us Dust Bowl refugees, but then there's more than one kind of a refugee. There's refugees that take refuge under railroad bridges, and there's refugees that take . . . refuge in public office, but when we was out in California, all the native sons and daughters called us, was just "Dust Bowl refugees."

Well, when we got to that country, and they got to calling us Dust Bowl refugees, why, a lot of people from Oklahoma that had worked hard all their lives, had split white oak staves and made walnut timber and split up walnut timber, a lot of em had made moonshine liquor and a lot of em had drilled oil wells, a lot of em picked that cotton, a lot of em had had little farms around over that they raised different crops on—and when they got out to California, several hundred thousand of em, and heard everybody calling em "just a Dust Bowl refugee," why they didn't know exactly what to think about it, didn't know exactly how to take it. Didn't know exactly what people meant when they called somebody else [laughing] a refugee. But anyway, they traveled fifteen hundred or two thousand miles afoot. They walked down the highways with blistered feet, carried their shoes in their hands and walked across the desert with blisters all over their feet, fifteen hundred or two thousand miles, trying to find a job of work. And they had already gone past, they'd already outgrown any little old kind of a word like a Dust Bowl refugee that fellers would call em.

[Elizabeth Lomax: Well, Woody, these Californians sort of looked down on you all, and maybe they had a right to, but how did you feel about all this? What did you do? What did you have to fall back on to kind of keep your pride up all this time?]

Well, we'd always been taught to believe that these forty-eight states that's called the United States was absolutely free country, and that anytime anybody took a notion to get up and go anywhere in these forty-eight states, then nobody else in these forty-eight states would proceed to ask him a whole bunch of questions, or to try to keep him from going where he started out to go.

Well, the native California sons and daughters I'll admit had a lot to be proud of. They had their ancestors [laughing] there that came in on the old covered wagons, a long time ago, and they discovered oil, they discovered gold, they discovered silver, they discovered all kinds of mines in California, and they had built up, in California, quite a wonderful [sarcastic tone] *empire*. But then, they hadn't built up quite a wonderful enough empire. What they needed in California was more and more people to pick their fruit: to gather in their peaches, their extra select and their select apricots, and their prunes, and to gather in their grapes, and they admitted *theirselves*, these people that was born and raised in California, that they needed people to do that, but at the same time they looked down, for some reason or other, on the people that come in there from other states to do that kind of work.

And I don't know why it was—a big long story behind it. Something about the Japs, the Chinese, the Filipinos, and the Mexicans—had had in there before.

But all of these: the Japs, they formed them an organization. They unionized. The Japs. And the Chinese. The Chinese done the same thing. They kind of unionized. And the Filipinos, they finally got to where they had a little better jobs than getting out [and] rooting in . . . all this hard work. They finally got to where they was taking care of the apartment- and rooming-houses and the buildings of that kind over in California. And so there was just, just one bunch left. And that was what you called Okies, that fell into that country.

And they had a lot of things to be proud of out there in California, I admit that. I admit California's one of the most wonderful states that I ever seen in my life.

But Oklahoma didn't just draw a blank. We've got in Oklahoma, a lot of things to be proud of, some of the biggest oil fields in the world that we developed. We drilled em, we [tooled] em, we roustabouted. We done everything in the world in Oklahoma. And a lot of things we got down there to be proud about. In the first place, we—some of the greatest movie stars in the world come from the state of Oklahoma. . . . Hollywood thinks, for some strange reason, that all these people didn't come from anywhere. But they did. They had to come from somewhere.

And just to go a little bit further, I think Oklahoma claims the greatest and the best-known and the best-loved, the best-liked movie star that ever lived on this earth. I think that Oklahoma can claim that we have got the second-most famous man that ever lived on the face of the earth. I was looking at a book here a while back, and it was giving all the most famous men in the world. The first-most famous man on the face of the earth that ever lived, was Jesus Christ. The second-most famous man that ever lived on the face of this earth was Will Rogers. Will Rogers come from Oklahoma. And that Sixty-six highway that runs from New York City down through Oklahoma and out to Los Angeles, California is named the Will Rogers Highway.

[Elizabeth Lomax: And can't you tell a little more about this?]

The reason why Oklahoma's got something to be proud of is that Will Rogers never got proud . . . of all that money that he was making. All that he wanted to do was just sort of help somebody out. And there's lots and lots of times that he'd be going down the road, talking to some big guy that had a million dollars, and he'd meet an old boy on the street that wasn't worth a nickel. He'd take a five-dollar bill out of his hand, and he'd fold it up in his hand to where he couldn't hardly tell what it was. He'd keep on a talking to this big rich feller while he was walking down the street. At the same time he'd find some way to hand this five-dollar bill to the poor old boy that was walking up the street. Will

Rogers had a reputation that—and Oklahoma as a whole state has got a reputation of that kind, and I think you'll find more of that same spirit down in that country that *anywhere* back in the fast and nervous, overworked and overrun and overindulgent East, or North, or New York, or anywhere else. Down in Oklahoma we take it just a little bit easier, do things a little bit slower. We might not get as many dates covered every day, or as many telephone calls put it, or as many bus rides, but we'll do just as much on one bus ride and on one phone call, on one meeting as a lot of people do on a dozen.

210. The Man on the Road

WOODY GUTHRIE
Okemah, Oklahoma
Recorded by Alan and Elizabeth
Littleton Lomax,
Washington, D.C., March 27,
1940

In soliciting the following story, Alan Lomax made the mistake of asking Woody to tell it "briefly" so that it would fit on the side of the record that was being recorded at the time. Woody, whose style lay largely in his pauses, repetitions, and slow, drawn-out phrases (and whose sense of identity lay largely in not doing what other people told him to do), responded by running out the side of the record that was currently recording and talking on until he filled up an additional side.

In "The Man on the Road," Woody draws attention to certain words by stressing syllables that are not normally stressed, as when saying "IMportant" or "Los Ange-LEES." Like most of Woody's tales, this is one in which little happens, but much is said. A hitchhiker joins another hitchhiker in the back of a truck, and together they speak volumes about hopeless working conditions and indestructible hopes.

Alan Lomax: Woody, you told me a story that I'd like you to put on the record, about the old man that you met in Oklahoma when you came back from California to Oklahoma the last time?]

Oh, yeah.

[Alan Lomax: Could you tell that kind of briefly so we can get it on the rest of this record?]

Well . . . I guess you know about the handbill situation . . . where they handed out all the handbills, you know, all through down that country, telling

Woody Guthrie using his guitar as a weapon against the Nazis, 1943. (World Telegram photo by Al Aumuller, Library of Congress)

that there was good work, good pay in California. Plenty of cotton needed picking: "EIGHT HUNDRED PEOPLE WANTED, COME ON OUT, GET EM WHILE THEY'RE HOT." So [laughing] they got about eight—well they got about pretty near three hundred thousand out there. That was just one successful advertising campaign.

Anyway, a lot of people wondering how that same condition is today, if there's anything like that still taking place.

Well, the latest trick [laughing] that I found, and one of the worst, one of the stinkingest things that I ever run on to, was down in Oklahoma about a month ago. I was hoboing it down the road and I caught a ride on a truck. And I was sitting on the back of the truck with my feet hanging off, just a-going and a-blowing right on down the road, just skipping through the dew, and making about fifty miles an hour. All at once the truck driver stopped, throwed on the brakes, and I looked back down the road there, and there was an old man. He was a—well, he . . . was a little feller. He was about five feet, five or six inches tall, and he looked like he was about fifty-five or sixty years old, and had a big, heavy suitcase. *Great* big pair of tough shoes on, and he needed about seven shaves. And he's a-coming right on down the road. And when that truck stopped, why he [laughs], he jumped in there like a jackrabbit. He made about three hops and he was in.

Anyway, he had a big, heavy suitcase, and I helped him get that up in back of the truck. And then I said, "Where are you going?"

"Oh," he says, "I'm a-going up here to the next town." He said, "I got to meet a feller there on some business."

I says, "Whereabouts do you live?"

"Oh, I live back down here now at this next town. It's called Cornivall. That's where I live. But, then, I'm going to work. Been looking for a job now for about ten years [laughs], and I finally found one."

I says, "Whereabouts did you find the job?"

"Oh," he says, "I'm going to California to do the work. CAL-ifornia." Said, "I know a feller out there. He's a contractor." He said, "I got acquainted with him last week and he's taking me on."

I said, "What did you say that man was?"

And he said, "A CON-tractor."

Well, we drove along, and I says, "A contractor, huh?" . . .

He says, "Yeah, the way he works, he goes to California and he contracts several thousand acres of land, and orchards and he guarantees that he'll furnish the men to pick the peaches and oranges and apricots and gather in all the stuff they grow—grapes and so forth."

He says, "I'll make about five dollars a day out there. I sure can use it too." He says, "I'm not going to work very hard either, they tell me. Get out there, pick a little fruit, five dollars, every day. Going to set up my wife too, quick as I can get a few days in. She wants to see California. Sunshine. Take her down to the ocean. She always wondered what . . . the ocean was. What it looked like." So he was going to write for her.

And I said, "What part of California are you going to?"

He said, "Well, I'm going to a town." He said, "I don't know just where it is, but it's a little town out there called, uh, eh, uh, Los Ange-LEES."

And I said, "Yes." I said [punning on "Loss" Angeles], "you'll lose worse than that." [Laughter]

And . . . I said, "Who's going to take you out there? How are you going to get out there?"

"Well," he said, "this contractor feller's gonna take me."

I said, "Sure enough? What's . . . got him to be so interested in you?"

"Oh," he says, "I pay him ten dollars to land me in to Los Ange-LEES," and he said, "there's six of us gonna ride with him this trip," [laughing] and he said, "ten dollars apiece. We're going into Los Ange-LEES. And then he's gonna give us the name and address of this here feller that's a-going to pay us the five dollars a day. And then we'll pick some fruit, a little fruit. . . . [And it'll be] fine to have a job," he said.

[Laughing] And I said, "Well, friend, I don't want to discourage you none, but," I said, "I just been out to California. And I've slept under every IM-portant bridge there" [laughter]. And I said, "I just wanted you to know that—I don't want to . . . try to be a prophet or nothing, but," I said, "I'm gonna tell you exactly what you'll do when you get to California."

I said, "You'll go out to California. And he'll give you this card with this name and address on it. And you'll go meet this here feller, whoever it is, Tom Jones, or whoever it is—Bill Brown or Pete Smith, or Cy Jackson, or whoever the name is, and you'll go out to his place. And he'll say, 'Damn, I've never seen nothing like it before. That fruit's in awful shape. It ain't gonna be worth nothing this year. I doubt if it's worth picking, the price they're paying. Think I'm gonna just let it rot. But, of course, if you boys *want* to pick it, just naturally haven't got no job or nothing to do, why, you can pitch in there and pick it if you want to, and when you pick and pack and *carry* and *load* one ton of peaches, why, I'll give you a dollar."

And I says, "You're not gonna see a five-dollar bill while you're in California. I don't care how long you stay there—unless you just go visiting somewheres, just curiosity, a bank or somewhere. And just stand there and look."

[Laughing] And he said, "Well, now," he said, "I've heard that story. . . . You're not the first to tell it to me. But," he says, "here in Oklahoma. Starving. Ain't got nothing. Lost everything I ever had, worked for fifty or sixty years, right here. I was born and raised right here, and my wife was too. Got seven or eight kids, and they're all chasing around like a bunch of wild horses down here somewheres. Never see em. But," he says, "nothing here for me." And he says, "I've heard about the business out there, but," he says, "it's a chance. It's a promise," and he said [voice dropping to a whisper], "I'm anxious to work, and I'm going to take it."

211. Indians, Locusts, Floods, and Dust: An Okie Family Saga

FLORA ROBERTSON
Oklahoma and Shafter, California
Recorded by Charles Todd and
Robert Sonkin,
Shafter FSA Camp,
August 5, 1940

If Woody Guthrie had little positive to say about the way that Californians treated the Dust Bowl refugees, at least one migrant camp resident strongly disagreed. Although "heartsick" for a home of her own, Mrs. Flora Robertson felt so well treated by her hosts in California that she celebrated them in poetry.

Mrs. Robertson was living in the Shafter FSA Camp in the summer of 1940 when she captured the attention of two men who were touring the camps to record the music of migrant workers. Charles Todd and Robert Sonkin soon discovered that Mrs. Robertson possessed an extraordinary family story stretching back to the early decades of the nineteenth century.

Like most of the camp's residents, Mrs. Robertson had arrived in California with almost nothing to her name. Yet, zealous to preserve her family history, she had brought with her a photograph of her old family home and a couple of pages she had copied from documents bearing on her family history. She shared with the interviewers some of this written information, including the war record of her grandfather, who had fought in Texas when it was still part of Mexico: "My mother's father was named John Smith, and . . . went to, let's see, I believe it was Bexter, Texas. He fought there in the services. A long time ago. Before, before the Civil War. . . . I believe I've got his record here. Some of it, anyhow. . . . 'He [participated] in the battle of Bexter in San Antonio between the fifth and the tenth of December, eighteen and thirty-five. Was also in the service in the Army of Texas from December the second, eighteen and thirty-five to March the sixth, eighteen and thirty-six.' " Neither Mrs. Robertson nor her interviewers seemed aware that March 6, 1836, was the date of the fall of the Mission of San Antonio de Bexar, better known as the Alamo, and that Mrs. Robertson's ancestor died in that battle.

After reading from her history, Mrs. Robertson said of her family, "I like to keep a record and kind of keep up with my people. I'm kind of proud of them. We was always poor, but always had a good name. And I like to keep it up."

Another way in which Flora Robertson kept up with her people was by composing poems about her family's hardships. She had written down many of these poems back in Oklahoma, and she continued writing them while living in the California camp; she read a few to Todd and Sonkin.

Mrs. Robertson and her family moved from Fort Smith, Arkansas, to the Indian Territory about 1904 and settled northwest of Ada, near the Canadian River. The settlers' relationships with the Indians were mixed. There were episodes of great violence as well as some peaceful exchanges.]

Whenever . . . any of our stock would get killed, on the road, or lots of times [some of em] would die, why those Indians'd come down. They'd always ask us for them. Whatever it was, why, they would ask for the yearling or the cow, and then they would take it and have a great feast. They still do that. They just eat that. They'll kill the yearling, or they take the yearling and they'll cut it up and divide it among the tribe there, and they still eat that raw meat. . . .

[We lived] . . . when we first went there, in a little log cabin. And in those days, why, we would start our crop and sometimes, why, the horse thieves would come through. They did pretty bad then. There was a lot of horse thieves, and we had to watch for the Indians. And sometimes our crop would be about half done, and we'd wake up some morning and we wouldn't have a horse or a mule on the place.

And so the neighbor men, they would all go together. Now, they'd get on their horses and go back from house to house and call the other men, and they would try to trail those horse thieves, and if they could catch em, why they always hung em on [a tree near the house that the family built while living in their cabin]. . . . And we built the house and never thought about the hangings in our yard until after we built the house [laughing].

[Interviewer: Scare you a little?]

Yes, sometimes it did, but we didn't pay very much attention. . . .

. . . It was Indian Territory days. We came there in a covered wagon. I remember what a wonderful time we had. We'd camp on the creeks, but we were still afraid of the Indians. And we would have to watch for them. And they would get angry sometimes, and now and then, you see, they was several of the white women killed while we lived there, and by the Indians . . . around us. And some was cut up pretty bad. I know there at home, why, there was a woman killed down there close to Ada, and then the white men, they gathered up, and found them two Indians, and they sure burnt them. Tied them to a stake too. They tried their own medicine on them. [Laughs]

[Later, the family moved to the western part of Oklahoma, near the Washita River, where they developed a friendly relationship with members of the Cheyenne Nation. There, Mrs. Robertson learned the story of the Washita Massacre (November 1868), in which George Armstrong Custer attacked and killed Chief Black Kettle and hundreds of his people. More than sixty-five years after the massacre, Mrs. Robertson's Cheyenne neighbors predicted a calamitous flood. In April 1934, a flood did indeed sweep the Washita valley, washing up the bones of Black Kettle and drowning people and livestock throughout the region. Mrs. Robertson's narrative makes a close connection between the Black Kettle's nineteenth-century prophecy of the Washita Massacre and her Cheyenne friends' prediction of the flood of 1934.]

[Black Kettle] dreamed that a wolf come into the camp, and that it had a white cloth on its head, and a lot of spots of blood on it. And he told his people, says, "Black Kettle will stay with his people, but the enemy will come and many squaw and papoose will be killed. But Black Kettle will stay with his people." And he sent his squaw out and his children.

[In the flood of 1934, Black Kettle's body was washed out of his grave.] And see, his nephews and part of his children identified his bones and his body by the ornaments that they found with it and part of his teeth. Whenever he was dug up—or washed up rather, from the river.

[Interviewer: When his body got washed up on the flood—when was this, do you think, about?]

Nineteen and thirty-four. Fourth day of April was when the flood come. . . .

[Interviewer: Do you think he prophesied the flood?]

Well, he just meant that something terrible would happen, and you know the white people was doing him wrong, you see. Was going to do him wrong. And he said the Great Spirit had warned him of this, and then, of course, the Indians warned us the flood was coming and they moved out of the camp. . . .

[Interviewer: And they warned the white people that the flood was coming?]

And we wouldn't move out. We didn't pay them any attention. And the wealthiest land- and cattlemen, you see, there is, they have their big ranches up and down this Washita River . . . by [the town of] Cheyenne. And it was them that suffered the most because the river overflowed and it was, well, it was terrible, the amount of cattle that was killed there, was drownded.

And not only cattle. There was a lot of the *people* that was washed away and killed. One of my neighbors, Mr. Adams, lost his wife and five daughters in the flood. It washed their home away.

And it just seemed to me like, that if we had paid attention to those Indians, why it might have helped us out a little. They was close to kin, after all.

[1934 was an apocalyptic year for the farmers of western Oklahoma. A plague of locusts preceded the great flood. Then the black blizzards of the Dust Bowl raked the prairies.]

Why, we lived in the western part [of Oklahoma], when the floods got so bad. And first, it was the grasshoppers. And we was doing pretty well and had most anything that we wanted. Just farm, ordinary farm living, you know. We had our cars and we was making pretty good, and could buy everything, nearly, we needed [in] town.

[But not long after the flood, the sky grew dark.]

We looked in the north and we thought it was a Blue Norther a-coming, such a huge black cloud, just looked like smoke out of a train stack or something.

[Interviewer: This was about what time?]

About four o'clock. Nineteen and thirty-four. And, why, it just come a-rolling over, and when it got near to the house, we was all afraid, and we ran into the storm house, because we thought it was a storm. And we lit the lamp, and it was just so dark in there that we couldn't see one another . . . even with the lamp lit. And we just choked and smothered. And my husband was out, after the cows. And he stumbled up against the barbed wire fence, and he followed the fence till he come to the house—is the way he was able to get to the house.

And we had to tie wet rags over our mouths . . . just to keep from smothering. We dipped cloths in buckets of water and tied over our mouths down in the cellar. And that one lasted, so fierce, for about two hours. And then we took courage and seed it wasn't going to blow away, and then we went in the house. And we wet blankets and hung over the windows.

And then, after the first one, of course, we were scared awfully bad. And the old-timers said they'd never seen *nothing* like that. [The dust] seemed *so* fine. Our house was sealed, but that dust came through, somehow. Even those stucco houses—why, all around the doors and the windows. The dust'd be all piled so high and you just had to mop real good when it was over to get it out. You just couldn't get it out no other way.

[Interviewer: How long did it last?]

Well, sometimes, a real bad one would last for a half a day. Sometimes it would be a week before we would see the sun. It was just darkened. And sometimes the cloud would look black, sometimes they would look red. It was according to which a-way the wind come, whether it was the red dirt that was blowing over, or the black dirt, or according to the way that the storm was coming.

And we had cattle. We had cows that we gave sixty dollars [for] and some ninety dollars, in pure old money. And . . . it killed them. They was out in that. And we would cut their lungs open and it looked just like a mud pack of some kind. It just really showed it was the mud.

[Interviewer: So first you had the flood and then the grasshoppers and then the dust storm?]

Yes. And we waited. It was about five years before we just really give up. But every year, we'd begin going back . . . in debt so much we thought we never could get out [laughing].

[Interviewer: You'd think you would want to come to California.]

Well, you'd get afraid of staying there. There was too many had dust pneumonia and died. And it gives too many people T.B.

[Interviewer: Well, that's when you wrote that little poem about the dust storm?]

Yes.

[Interviewer: Could we hear that? Would you mind reading it to us?]

Well, I'll try, but I don't know how good I'll do.

I came to Oklahoma before it was a state.
Among the Cheyenne Indians I roamed from [morn] till late.
We were happy, healthy people
Proud to live in that state.

One dark lonely day a sight did we see:
A thick, smothering dust cloud spread over the prairie,
Killed many people, and [al]most smothered me.

We waited in hope almost five years through.
More people and cattle died, more dust storms came too.
Then we decided something that we had better do:
We loaded a few things into an old car
Hoping west to go very far.

We landed at the government camp on a flat tire [laughing],
So tired and hungry, heartsick and dirty too.
Here we found food and shelter too.
The California people sure are good to you. . . .

In tents we are camped like Abraham of old.
Thank God for a country and a land that's free.
We're so glad that our flag's the red, white, and blue.

I don't know how I messed it up so bad at the last, but I just did.
[Interviewer: How long did it take you to get to California?]
Oh, my, that would be terrible. We had breakdowns and everything else [laughs], and we were so tired I don't know. But we came out. . . . And we got work in Arizona and we worked there for a while, and we just gradually worked our way through. We finally got here. We heared that there was work here . . . and so far, why, we've had quite a bit of work. Anyhow, we have much more help than we ever had in Oklahoma.

[Interviewer: It's not like farming back there, though, is it?]
No. I get so heartsick and homesick for a little home of my own, that I don't know what to do. But, anyhow, I'm going to make the best of it.

[Interviewer: What was the other little poem that you had, Mrs. Robertson? . . .]
My little short one?
[Interviewer: Yes.]
About California. Oh, here it is. . . .

   "Why We Go to California"
Here comes the dust storm. Watch the sky turn blue.

You'd better get out, or it'll smother you.
Here is the grasshopper, he comes a-jumpin high.
He jumps across the state and never bats an eye.

Here comes the river. It surely knows its stuff.
It takes home and cattle and leaves the people feeling tough.
Californy, Californy here I come too.
With a coffee pot and skillet, I'm coming to you.

Nothing's left in Oklahoma for us to eat or do.
There's apples, nuts, and oranges, and Santa Claus is real.
Come on out to California, eat and eat till you're filled.

[Interviewer: When did you write that one?]

I wrote it here sometime back. I've wrote things this way ever since I was about eight year old. I have a number of just little things. I've always wished I could have went on to school, because I believe I could have done something if I'd a . . . had an education. Anyhow, my mind always runs silly, and I write those things [laughing].

13

FOLKTALES IN THE MAKING

THE SEPTEMBER 11 PROJECT

On September 11, 2001, two passenger jets hijacked by terrorists crashed into the twin towers of the World Trade Center, causing the buildings to collapse, thousands to lose their lives, and millions around the world to experience feelings of grief and shock so profound that for the rest of their lives they will be recalling and retelling the ways in which they personally experienced, from whatever distance, the events of that day.

The staff of the American Folklife Center had a front-row seat from which to view many of the most alarming developments of September 11. The Center's main offices are located in the Jefferson building of the Library of Congress, two miles from the Pentagon, which erupted in flames when struck by the third terrorist-guided jet, and just one block from the U.S. Capitol building, which many believe was the intended target of the fourth airliner, which crashed in an isolated section of Pennsylvania after passengers struggled with terrorists for control of the plane. Within sight of a possible third Ground Zero, AFC folklorists would soon have their own stories to tell.

Ten months after the event, folklife specialist Ann Hoog recounted her experience of September 11. She was at her desk when she received a phone call from her fiancé, Scott. They were in the midst of wedding preparations, and she assumed that his call had to do with the wedding. Ann recalled, "He said, 'Two planes just hit the World Trade Center.' And I said, 'You're kidding. . . . Was it an accident or terrorism?' . . . I was thinking, well, one plane maybe was an accident, and I was sort of hoping it was an accident in a way, but, you know, this chill sort of went through my mind. . . . And I was just like, 'Oh, my God. Oh, my God.'"

Ann walked down the hall to an AFC office equipped with a television. "I

September 11 memorial of lit candles and flag, Brooklyn, New York. (© SETBOUN/CORBIS)

came in and there were already about four people from our staff around this tiny, . . . black and white television and . . . the helicopters were flying over New York, and so the film shots were all from above, and so we were just like, ' . . . This is an image we'll never forget': the smoke billowing over New York City. . . . I think we sat around the television for about fifteen, twenty minutes or so and it was just sort of the same information over and over again. And we were all like, 'Well, let's just go back to work. You know, this is just going to go on like this all day.' . . . I was just sort of trying to pick up where I had left off.

"And then . . . our administrative assistant, Doris, called me and said . . . , 'The Pentagon just got hit.' And . . . I didn't believe it for some reason. I was like, 'No, . . . there must be so many rumors floating around that . . . this couldn't possibly be true.' And then all of a sudden my phone rang and it was Scott . . . , calling and saying: 'The Pentagon just got hit!' And I was like, 'Well, that's two people who just told me that. It must be true.' . . . He said, 'I want you to go home. I think you should leave.' And I was like, 'But we haven't been evacuated yet.' [Laughing] . . . You know: just wanting to do what you should do and not wanting to blow it out of proportion and trying to . . . maintain control over your emotions. . . .

"And then . . . one of my coworkers came in, . . . and she said that the South Tower just collapsed.' . . . It was unbelievable. I said, 'What do you mean?' 'It's gone.' And . . . her eyes were welling up. 'I can't believe it's just gone. It's gone.'

"And at that point . . . we all just decided to go home. And so we left. Made sure everybody had the information, . . . and we all walked out of the Library. Everybody was very calm. And it was just . . . , 'Well, see you later. . . . Gee, I wonder when we're going to see each other again.' "

In a strangely silent mass migration, thousands of federal employees stepped from their offices and into the sunlit streets to find their ways home. No one spoke; the only sound came from the open windows of passing cars: the unintelligible voices of newscasters broadcast from a dozen stations and blaring cacophonously from car radios. To Ann Hoog, the pervasive silence of the walkers called up images of war refugees: "It was almost like I was observing the events, and like I wasn't really a part of what was going on. I was sort of in this haze. . . . I'm not even sure it had sunk in. . . . You didn't really know how to greet people on the street. . . . You couldn't say 'How's it going?' . . . You know, the way we greet people is so shallow. And . . . it was hard to look at people. Because you didn't know how to react. There's no social graces that you've learned . . . to ever be able to handle that situation. . . ."

Ann continues her narrative: "And it was strange walking outside of the Library because it was such a beautiful, beautiful day . . . : eighty degrees, clear sky. And everybody was very calm outside and walking. And there were some planes that were flying overhead. I think that Andrews Air Force Base had shot off some military planes that started flying overhead. . . . There was this strange sense . . . when you were walking out and everybody was looking up at the sky, and it was like, 'Oh, my God, everybody's looking up at the sky. Is another plane coming?' Because there was all this news that planes . . . were still coming in. There was one headed for the Capitol, we had heard. And I know that some people in our office had the experience about when they left on the other side of the building there were security officers out there that were saying, 'Get out of here fast! There's another plane headed for the Capitol!' I hadn't heard that at the time, but . . . amazingly people were not panicking and running through the streets. It was just this mass of people just walking, just walking and walking and walking. . . . And it was bumper-to-bumper traffic. . . . I sort of had to weave my way in between the cars. And yet it was just such a beautiful day. It was amazing. But all you could hear were car radios: . . . this hum of NPR news stations, . . . these voices, just this rumble of news, you know, underneath it all. It was very strange. And there was nobody in the park, except people just walking home. Everybody in their suits, with their little federal [security] badges around their necks—that they hadn't taken off yet and everybody just sort of walking home. And, then, when I got close to home, there was a woman sitting on her front porch just bawling, just crying and crying and crying. And . . . that's when reality sort of hit me."

But on September 12, 2001, the American Folklife Center decided that it was their responsibility to tell not only their own but also the nation's stories. AFC director Peggy Bulger called a staff meeting with no other missions in mind than to check on how Center staff members were dealing with the tragedy and to determine how they as a group could deal with it better. Like millions of others across the country, the AFC staff discovered quickly that the best way to fend off emotional paralysis was to respond directly to the disaster by doing something that might make a difference. Staff members Thea Austen and Ann Hoog recalled that Library of Congress folklorists had recorded eyewitness accounts of earlier national traumas. On December 8, 1941, the day after the bombing of Pearl Harbor, Alan Lomax (then assistant in charge of the Archive of American Folk Song) had sent out telegrams to colleagues across the country to abandon their plans for that day, carry audio recording machines into the streets, and interview the "man on the street" to discover the reactions of everyday people to an earlier national tragedy. Ann Hoog proposed a September 11 project similar to Lomax's early Pearl Harbor Project. The Center contacted folklorists, anthropologists, historians, and teachers of all kinds across the country and lodged an open invitation to conduct interviews and then send the recordings of those interviews to Washington. By the spring of 2002, thousands of interviews, drawings, and other spoken and pictorial memorabilia had found their way to the Library of Congress.

Many of the people who lived through both December 7, 1941, and September 11, 2001, were even more shocked by the second event than by the first because in 1941 much of the rest of the world had already been at war for more than two years and there was a general sense throughout the nation that American involvement was imminent, whereas in 2001, the great majority of Americans had never suspected that such a massive terrorist attack would ever happen. Most of the "men on the street" interviewed after Pearl Harbor indicated that although the form of the aggression was surprising, they were not surprised to find their country swiftly swept into the world conflict. Therefore, responses to Pearl Harbor reflected the fact that many citizens had already been prepared for the catastrophic news. But on September 11, in Washington, D.C.—as throughout the country—there was a pervasive sense of bewilderment and shock.

For generations after December 7, Americans would pass on stories relating where they were and how they reacted when they first heard the news of Pearl Harbor, but on December 8–10, when the Library of Congress interviews were collected, the speakers were not yet telling these stories; rather, they were responding emotionally and often philosophically to the disaster. Therein lies the greatest difference between the Pearl Harbor and the September 11 collections. In 2001, as in 1941, the call from the Library of Congress was issued the day after the attack, but in 2001 the American Folklife Center did not send interviewers out on the streets to records ordinary citizens' visceral reactions as Lomax had in 1941. (After all, on September 11, 2001, the radio, television, and Internet were already broadcasting such responses.) Rather, the original e-mail request of 2001 asked public folklorists to organize and conduct interviews without any specified timeline. Thus, most of the interviews were conducted a month or more after the event, time enough for the narrators to have retold many times the stories of what they were doing on the day of the attacks. The respondents had begun to shape their memories and impressions into narratives that, as Lillie Haws (teller of tales 213–215) says, "we will all tell our children." It would be valuable for folklorists to revisit the same narrators in twenty or thirty years to discover the ways in which their stories have changed and taken on new perspectives with the passage of time.

If not already folktales, the following stories are certainly folktales in the making. The narrators have already told their September 11 experiences many times and will almost certainly continue to retell them for the rest of their lives, just as their parents and grandparents continually retold the stories of where they were, what they did, and what they were feeling when the news of Pearl Harbor broke.

September 11 Project director Ann Hoog recommended the following tales for inclusion in this book. The two narrators represent something of the vast range of individual response to the terrorist attacks. Janet Freeman, alone in her home in Iowa City, had only her television for company when the disaster occurred. Lillie Hawes, on a pier in Brooklyn, shared her grief with many people (including some of the firefighters who were closest to its center) and got close enough to the towers to catch a piece of airborne debris in her hand as it fell from the sky. Yet in some ways these two women responded similarly: intensely, immediately, and actively, if not yet fully conscious of their actions; in both women's stories, the unadorned description of simple gestures effectively conveys an otherwise indescribable horror.

212. September 11 in Iowa City, Iowa

JANET FREEMAN
Iowa City, Iowa
Recorded in the Iowa City Public Library,
November 10, 2001

This tape is being made for the Library of Congress's 9/11 Project. My name is Janet Freeman. I live in Iowa City. And today's date is 10 November 2001. I want to tell about that day for me because I've thought about it a lot since. Well, not a lot, but enough.

I got up at eight o'clock or eight fifteen in the morning, and after a while I turned on the radio, and Bob Edwards said there'd been an attack on the World Trade Center, so I went into the kitchen, where I was going to fix my breakfast, and I turned on CNN, on a little television set mounted under my kitchen cabinet.

And had it on in time to watch the second plane hit the other tower. And I was in my bare feet and my pajamas at that time, and what I did was start cleaning my kitchen. I took the screens down off the windows, washed the windows, washed the window sills, cleaned out the sink, cleaned out the cupboard, took everything out of the cupboard under the sink. Scrubbed the surface of the stove. Removed everything from the oven and cleaned out the oven. Washed the floor. Polished the countertops. Cleaned the windowsill over my kitchen sink. Took all the pictures off it. Cleaned it up. Straightened the drawer that all the, the knives and imple—various implements are to be found. I cleaned off the surface of the microwave oven, so the spots were just wiped away.

About three o'clock in the afternoon, I realized that my pajamas were filthy, my hands were all cut up, my fingernails were quite vile. This says something about the state of my kitchen before I got started working.

But my kitchen was cleaner than it had been in a long time.

I was watching CNN that whole time.
Thanks.

213. September 11 in Red Hook, Brooklyn

LILLIE HAWS
Brooklyn, New York
Recorded by Sarah Philipson,
Brooklyn, New York
November 14, 2001

I happened to be a guest at a friend's house in the neighborhood of Red Hook, Brooklyn. And I'd been sleeping on her couch. And she'd left for work. Then she came running in the house telling me the twin towers were on fire.

So my initial thing was that this was a dream, because I was barely awake. And then she told me—grabbed my hand and told me to come with her—we had to go to the pier to see this. So I did. . . . I put on my shoes, I ran out the door with her, and we started running for the piers, because Red Hook . . . has . . . piers right on the water, overlooking New York harbor, and you get a view of the twin towers.

But by the time we ran to the bagel shop to get a coffee and to hear the radio, by that time the second plane had hit, and then that's when the word "terrorism" started to appear. So we left the bagel shop and we started running to the pier, and all it was, was smoke. There were things flying in the air. I ended up catching a piece of fiberglass insulation. There were plane tickets, everything was falling from the sky. And before we even made it down to the main pier, the buildings had started to collapse. . . .

I dropped to the ground. I started crying. . . . You know, it was just disbelief. It was like I was still asleep on her couch, and this was all a nightmare. People were sobbing openly. And so . . . after we spent some time on the pier, I went . . . to my place. . . . I have a bar, a saloon, in Red Hook, called Lillie's. And went back and started . . . immediately calling my friends, to invite them over.

We couldn't get reception on the television, so we took it to the garden, turned on the news, and by that time fifteen people were in my garden. Still in disbelief, of course. We just watched TV all day. So, as night fell, I decided to close the bar, cause I couldn't really, you know, entertain people too well. And then, about twelve midnight, the backdoor started opening and people started flooding in the bar. We had about fifty people in the bar.

And then the firemen came in. From our local ladder companies. We have two houses here, and collectively, you know, they'd been coming to the bar before, so I knew a good many of them, and they started coming in the door. And the smells that were on their bodies—the soot, you know, the burning smell—and their ears were blackened, and they had burns.

They came in, and they asked me how *I* was. Which I thought was just phenomenal, you know, being as they had just been in the midst of a catastrophe that we've never known in our history in this country. Especially in New York.

So they began popping open beers, and we gave em buckets of beers in the garden, and my friends started circling around them, and everybody just wanted to be with them. And that was the closest that, really, anybody that was here had gotten to this disaster. And so we decided, you know, let's just give it a go, let's just all just be together. Stay close together.

They cried. They laughed. They mostly laughed, which I couldn't believe, because they really just tried . . . to find some kind of comfort, you know, in laughter. And we rang in the night, probably all night, you know, and took care of them. And I'll never forget that day, and those guys' faces. And I *looked*—I looked at guys coming in, and I kept looking for certain guys, and—and I didn't see their faces, and then of course I assumed the worst.

And I asked the other fireman, like, "Where's Christian?" "Where's Sol?" You know. Where's these guys? And they were among the missing.

And that was my day—September 11, 2001.

214. Heaven in the Middle of Hell

LILLIE HAWS
Brooklyn, New York
Recorded by Sarah Philipson,
Brooklyn, New York
November 12, 2001

The firemen told me that everybody in the neighborhood was cooking them food. They had too much food. Their fridges wouldn't shut. They had socks. They probably had twenty thousand pairs of socks in the firehouse by the weekend. It was just immense, the [number] of donations that were occurring.

And they had the vigil, which basically met at the VFW, and walked to each firehouse. And that's how the neighborhood came together. And they felt they could do their part. And with candlelights going, we walked to each of the firehouses, and the firemen came out, and they hugged everybody. And the police were there. And they asked what they could do. . . .

During the weeks following this tragedy, the firemen would come in[to Lillie's bar] and they would tell their stories. Do you know what I mean? They started telling *stories*. And I started listening to all of the stories about how one guy jumped out of a window fifteen floors up and survived, you know, and then they were laughing. . . .

And then, basically, I became a bed and breakfast for these firemen, for, like, a couple weeks straight. Because they weren't working, you know. They were taking time . . . and they wasn't working as much as they did later. . . . I mean, there was one point I probably had fifteen firefighters asleep on my banquettes, at nine in the morning. I would bring em coffee, cook em scrambled eggs, you know, and feed them. And just take care of them. I felt like a mother. I really did. *To these children.* . . .

Bars *around* Manhattan and Brooklyn and everywhere else were definitely places where these firemen [stayed]. They would not sleep in the firehouse, some of them. They stayed out. They needed to be with people. They needed to be together. And they . . . , you know, didn't need to see the empty bunks. . . .

And one fireman in particular quoted me, as I'm sure all the other places that helped out, it was like: "You're a piece of heaven in the middle of hell." And I'll never forget that.

215. Christian Regenhard

LILLIE HAWS
Brooklyn, New York
Recorded by Sarah Philipson,
Brooklyn, New York
November 12, 2001

. . . And one gentleman in particular, who I looked for that night—who I did not see his face come through the door—was Christian Regenhard.

And Christian was . . . how shall I say it—a light-toned person—and he came into the room beaming. But he was . . . very, very sweet, and came in . . . to my bar, a few times, and I never even knew that he was a fireman. Ever. He never . . . was the kind of guy who . . . would brag about who he was. . . .

He came in one day looking for a job because he needed some extra money on the side. I told him it was a new business. And that's when he told me he was a fireman. "I'm a fireman. I'm in the house . . . called the Happy Hookers" . . . Ladder Number 101.

I told him, "Oh, I'd love to hire you right now, but" . . . you know, I wasn't making a lot of money. I told him by the end of September we'd have a lot of work, and I would be honored to have a Happy Hooker bartending in my bar. And so that was probably a couple weeks before this happened.

And I didn't see him that night, and so I asked the other firemen, "Where's Christian?" And they said, "Lillie, I don't know." And they didn't want to tell me because they knew, you know, they knew how I felt about him. So I then asked another fireman, "Where's Christian?"

He's like, "Lillie, he's missing, and we presume him to be gone." . . .

And then I burst into tears, and I realized that this is only the beginning of a great person being taken away.

And then I processed this information, and I started to feel like I honestly, I really lost a friend, and I lost a potential team-member in my business that I would have been incredibly honored to have. And still now, I have a big void in here. . . . I have a huge spot in my heart, and I look around, and I still see places where he was sitting or standing, and I smile, you know, or I cry. And it just doesn't leave me. You know, he became part of my place.

And part of me.

I will say one thing, as crazy as this may sound. I was crying on the telephone to a friend of mine one day, and I was like, "Please, just tell me that he didn't suffer—that he went quickly. And with the rest of the people who died, that they're on the other side, in a good place."

And just at that moment I noticed something falling from the sky. In my bar. I had the doors closed, the fans were off. There was nothing; no fabric in my bar. Nothing. And I looked up, and it was dwindling down like a leaf does when it falls, swaggers back and forth, and I held out my hand and it was a white feather. It was a white feather.

And I do have Cherokee blood in me. And I took that as a sign. I took that as a sign that he *flew*, he *did* make it. He did make it. . . .

NOTES ON THE TALES

The Lomaxes. John Lomax's autobiography, *Adventures of a Ballad Hunter* (1947), as well as Nolan Porterfield's biography, *Last Cavalier* (1996), which is also the source of the headnote quotations on the Lomaxes' contract with the Library of Congress (p. 306) and the value of *American Ballads and Folksongs* (p. 337), supply copious documentation on the life of the father, but his son Alan awaits a full-length biography. Discussions of the Lomaxes' difficulties with recording machines are found in Porterfield (1996: 292–96, 400–402) and in Brady (1999: 26, 40), the latter of whom devotes much of her book to exploring ways in which early sound recording influenced the performance of folklore. The reference to Alan concealing his machine and himself under a load of sugar cane was reported to me personally by folklorist Barry Jean Ancelet, who had heard Alan's account of the experience.

86. *I Don't Know How to Run* [AFS 5669A]. Lomax describes his romance with and adventures in cowboy and cattle country in his autobiography *Adventures of a Ballad Hunter* (1947).

87. *You Can Cook Breakfast, Too* [AFS 5681A-5682B].

88. *My Brother's Last Ride* [AFS 5678A,B].

89. *Getting Stuck on a Pony* [AFS 5671].

90. *Shooting a Wife* [AFS 5671 A,B].

91. *Hard Times in the Toyah Country* [AFS 6953A].

92. *John Loses the Race* [AFS 6627A1]. H1594, "Foot-racing contest." I have found no other African American versions of this tale. Among the tales in the John and Old Marster joke cycle are numerous examples in which John, the weaker man and underdog, is pitted against a much stronger rival; see, for example, the note to story 152 in this collection and Dorson 1967: nos. 37–40.

93. *Jack Guesses What Is Under the Pot* [AFS 6627A2, 6628]. This is an example of AT 1641, *Dr. Know-All,* in a special African American form that Richard Dorson has labeled the "best known of all Old Marster stories" (1967: 126) There are many international parallels, but none have the specific resonance for black Americans as this tale, which is most often identified by folklorists as "The Coon in the Box." International variants rest on a lucky pun through which the trickster identifies an animal concealed in a box or under a pot. When the trickster, who bears the name of Crab or Cricket (or that of another animal), cannot guess what is under the box, he sighs in desperation, "Crab is caught," only to emerge successful when it is revealed that a crab is indeed hidden in the box. In the African American versions, however, the desperate trickster announces his defeat with a racial slur: "You've got the old coon at last," and then he

discovers to his great relief that the concealed animal is indeed a raccoon. The fact that the hero is a slave or sharecropper who has been put up to the contest by a white master lends particular poignancy to the black man's lucky words. Only by denigrating himself and assuming the posture of a broken fieldhand can the protagonist find success (see Lindahl 1982).

In an incisive study of sixteen Caribbean and thirty-seven North American versions of AT 1641, John Minton and David Evans established that the popular African American form was derived from European versions but took on its special American coloring in the American South in the nineteenth century (Minton and Evans 2001). The authors state that the reference to "coon" was probably not a racial epithet before the time that the earliest texts emerged; rather, "coon" was a synonym for "sly" or "clever" before it took on racial connotations in the second half of the nineteenth century. The authors suggest the possibility that "the story was created with *both* meanings in mind" (2001: 63). Of the fifty-three New World versions studied by Minton and Evans, thirty-two fall into the pattern of "The Coon in the Box" tale similar to the text collected by Alan Lomax and published herein. Some of the oldest versions (including Hyatt 1970–1978: 1: 236 and Perdue, Barden, and Philips 1980: 312–13) were learned during slavery days and collected by folklorists in the 1930s. All but one are told by African Americans, and the great majority come from the American South. One of the narrators cited by Minton and Evans is J.D. Suggs, teller of stories 47–61 in the present collection; another is Debra Anderson, who tells story 184. In addition to the texts cited in the Minton-Evans study, see two tales collected by Zora Neale Hurston in Georgia: one from John Davis in 1935 (story 171 in this collection) and another from Larkins White (Hurston 2001: 85–86).

94. *The Preacher and His Hogs* [AFS 6627 A4, B1]. AT 1735A, *The Bribed Boy Sings the Wrong Song*. K1631. American versions of this tale date back at least to 1810, when a version similar to Ulisses Jefferson's was printed in Isaiah Thomas's *Almanack* (see Botkin 1959: 235–36); a closely related text was printed in England by S.O. Addy (1895: 18). Aarne and Thompson report only a smattering of examples of this tale type in Europe, but Baughman found a significant number in the United States, including three collected by Herbert Halpert: two in New Jersey and one in Indiana. Abrahams republishes Addy's English text alongside an African American version circulating among teenagers in Philadelphia and analyzes the two comparatively (1970: 183–86).

95. *The Preacher Who Could Always Be Trapped by Women* [AFS 6627B3]. Q243.2.1, "Attempted seduction punished"; cf. K1321.3, "Man disguised as woman courted (married) by another man." Folktales worldwide are rife with situations in which a man disguises himself as a woman in order to seduce a woman, but they are silent on the situation represented in this tale: that of a man who assumes the identity of his wife in order to catch her would-be seducer. Hoffman (1973) adds a motif that would apply to this tale: K1697, "Would-be seducer (seducers) tricked by virtuous wife and her husband." X749.12.1[H], "Man disguised as woman."

96. *The Woman Who Couldn't Count* [AFS 6627B4]. J2030, "Absurd inability to count"; X732, "Humor concerning sexual intercourse." Abrahams (1970: 230–31) prints a joke turning on a similar situation of a woman with three daughters who exchange sex for money, but I have found no exact published parallel to this joke.

97. *The Lady and Her Three Daughters* [AFS 6627B5]. D1610, "Magic speaking objects"; D1610.6.1, "Speaking vulva; man has power to make vulvas speak. This is used as a chastity test"; H400, "Chastity test"; cf. H412.1, "Chastity test: passing under magic rod"; H461, "Talking private parts betray unchastity"; D1610.6.3, "Speaking buttocks."

98. *Watermelon Story* [AFS 197]. J1763, "Person thought to be an object." Apparently, Mose Platt went by many nicknames. In addition to Clear Rock and Wyandotte, he also identified himself as Big Foot Rock; this information comes from the Lomaxes' *American Ballads and Folk*

Songs (1934: 66), which contains Mose's song "Ol' Rattler." In a sound recording preserved in the American Folklife Center, John Lomax gives a general account of his fieldwork with African American prisoners (AFS 24506).

99. *Cat Story* [AFS 2645A2]. B181.1, "Magic cat"; B211.1.8, "Speaking cat." Beliefs concerning the negative supernatural influences of cats are rife in American—as well as in European—folk traditions, as evidenced in such notions that cats are beasts of ill omen (motif B147.1.2.2), confederates of the devil (G303.3.3.1.2), breath-stealing killers of human children (B766.2), and the transformed spirits of dead people (E423.1.2). A Similar, sinister talking cat (in this case, a transformed witch) appears in story 31 in this volume. Both tales converge on motif H1417, "Fear test: night watch with magic cats." John Lomax retells an earlier performance of the same tales by Clear Rock (1947: 184–85). For another African American tale featuring a ghostly cat (which in this case turns out to be the spirit of a dead child), see story 130 in this volume.

100. *Music for Me to Run By* [AFS 2645A]. Cf. J1769.2, "Dead man is thought to be alive"; J1495, "Person runs from actual or supposed ghost." Although Alan Lomax in his notes gave this tale the title "ghost story," the figure here is a revenant, an animated corpse. Mose's story is one of a host of "cooling board" tales, told widely both to frighten and to amuse. John Lomax repeats Mose's story in *Adventures of a Ballad Hunter* (1947: 182–84). Dorson presents a parallel and two other cooling board tales (1967: no. 197).

A huge number and variety of African American jokes and playful legends feature brief humorous dialogs between a supernatural being (or a person thought to be a supernatural being) and an ordinary, terrified mortal. Among the most distinctive of these is AT 1676A, *Big 'Fraid and Little 'Fraid*, a uniquely African American tale perceptively analyzed by John Minton (1993); see story 50 in this volume and note.

101. *The Leaky House* [AFS 2645B]. AT 81, *Too Cold for Hare to Build House in Winter.* This is one of the most frequently collected brief American tales, as well known among European Americans as among African Americans. European American versions tend to cast the lazy central character as a human rather than a buzzard, and it is the lazy human who figures as the protagonist when the tale is incorporated into the stage dialogue of "The Arkansas Traveler." African American versions are very similar to the tale told here by Mose Platt. J.D. Suggs, narrator of stories 47–61 in this volume, recorded an unpublished version (AFS 10987). Dorson published a different version by Suggs (1967: no. 29), and Hurston collected a version from Georgian Armetta Jones (Hurston 2001: 236).

Aunt Molly Jackson. Molly (1880–1960) wanted to write her own life's story, but she never completed the undertaking. She produced several unpublished drafts, "The Story of Aunt Molly Jackson, Herself: Chapter One," and other autobiographical sketches that are now to be found in the various collections, notably the Barnicle-Cadle Papers, Schlesinger Library, Radcliffe College, Cambridge, Massachusetts. Significant portions of Molly's writings are reprinted in Shelly Romalis, *Pistol Packin' Mama* (1999), the only full-length biography of Molly Jackson. Most of Romalis's book focuses on Molly's experience after leaving Appalachia and on her impact on the wider world, but chapters 1–3 offer an excellent summary of Molly's life in Appalachia. Romalis quotes not only from Molly's autobiography but also from interviews conducted by folklorists Mary Elizabeth Barnicle, John Greenway, Archie Green, and Ellen Stekert. Romalis does not, however, draw upon the stories recorded by Lomax and reprinted here.

American Folklife Center documentation lists May 1939 as the month during which Aunt Molly recorded these tales for Lomax. Apparently, the two had met for at least one earlier session, for Romalis (1999: 103) states that a 19-year-old Alan, in the company of Mary Elizabeth

Barnicle, visited Molly and recorded her repertoire in 1935. After her death, Alan Lomax recorded a personal "Appreciation" of Molly in the *Kentucky Folklore Record* (Lomax 1961).

Readers wishing to hear Aunt Molly's tales can find them on two old recordings: *Aunt Molly Jackson*, recorded by Alan Lomax for the Library of Congress (Jackson 1972); and John Greenway's *The Songs and Stories of Aunt Molly Jackson* (1961).

102. *My First Dance* [AFS 2563 B]. (Lomax titles the tale "Skip to My Lou.") Molly relates another version of this story in her unpublished reminiscence, "By Aunt Molly" (see Romalis 1999: 68). This, like many other of Molly's tales, centers on singing: the repeated line from "Skip to My Lou" holds the tale together.

After a slow start, Molly became an accomplished dancer, as she explained to Alan Lomax: "I didn't even know how to dance, learn how to dance till after I was married, and then when Jim Stewart—which was my husband—and I was married, they always attended every barn dance and everything, and at first, when I begin to go with them to dances, just to keep from staying at home by myself, I would just be what they called a wallflower. I would watch the rest dance, but I wouldn't dance because it was agin my father's will, and I was afraid he'd find it out, and I knowed that he'd always said if he'd find out a child of his was going to a dance, that he'd, if they was married and was forty years old, he'd whip em the same. And so—but then I delighted in it, and . . . after awhile I began to take chances. And I learned to dance, and Jim Stewart and my [present] husband and myself, after that, why, we'd win lots of prizes dancing. Fifty and twenty-five-dollar prizes, a-dancing." (AFS 2565A; cf. Romalis 1999: 73). Aunt Molly recorded other narratives on dancing for Alan Lomax (AFS 3338A,B).

103. *How We Entertained Ourselves: Song, Rhymes, Toasts* [AFS 2571B-2572A1]. Romalis (1999: 62–65) prints Molly's sorrowful account of her response to her mother's death as well as the song that Molly composed at age 7 in memory of her mother. Molly concludes with an account of a provocative rhyme composed by her half-brother Jim Garland. Molly and Jim did not always get along, but they shared an intense interest in unions and workers' rights. In 1931, Jim accompanied Molly when she left Kentucky for New York, and the two worked as labor activists to advertise the plight of the Appalachian coal mining community. Like Molly, Jim wrote accounts of his life in Kentucky, and his autobiography, like Molly's, remained incomplete at the time of his death, but it was published posthumously as *Welcome the Traveler Home* (Garland 1983).

104. *An Unreasonable Lie: The Land of the Yeahoes* [AFS 2565B]. Readers versed in eighteenth-century fiction may sense a connection between the Jim Garland's Yeahoes and the Yahoos that appear in Jonathan Swift's *Gulliver's Travels* (1726), a work that was enjoying widespread popularity in Great Britain and Ireland during the first major wave of English, Scotch Irish, and Irish migrations into the Appalachians. Whatever its origin, Yeahoe, or Yahoo, seems to have been a rather common term for a hybrid being, half human and half animal. See, for example, Buna Hicks's account of an encounter with a terrifying "Yape" (story 27 in this volume). Of the various recorded versions known to me, only Aunt Molly Jackson's features a headless Yeahoe; in all other versions, the Yeahoe is a hairy, apelike creature.

In eastern Kentucky in the mid-twentieth century, Leonard Roberts collected three Yeahoe stories, one of which he reprints in *South from Hell-fer-Sartin* (1955: 79; another is found in Roberts 1957); the other two were later printed and discussed by Archer Taylor in *Western Folklore* (1957: 48). A fourth tale, following the same plot as Roberts's but much more elaborate, was told to James Taylor Adams during his boyhood in the late nineteenth century; he retells the story of "The Hairy Woman" (without using the term "Yeahoe") in *Grandpap Told Me Tales* (1993: 19–32). Richard Dorson has printed and discussed a fifth version, from Machias, Maine (Dorson 1959: 329–31; Dorson 1975: 485–86).

In all the recorded tales except Hicks's, the land of the Yeahoes is across the sea. In Adams's,

Roberts's (1955), and Aunt Molly Jackson's tales, the Yeahoe is a female; in all other texts it is male. In all the tales except Buna Hicks's, the Yeahoe mates with the human and a child is born. In all the texts that mention a child, the child dies. In five of the versions, the child dies at the end of the tale as the human traveler leaves the foreign land, abandoning the Yeahoe and the child. In grief the Yeahoe tears the infant in half and throws half of the body into the boat on which the traveler is escaping.

Aside from the tale of the marriage of human and Yeahoe, there are many briefer accounts of Yeahoe sightings, similar to the tales that revolve around Bigfoot or Sasquatch in the American Northwest. Maggie Hammons Parker, teller of story 200 in this book, presents a Yeahoe-sighting tale from her West Virginia family tradition (Jabbour and Fleischhauer 1998: 27–28), and Burton and Manning report similar stories from eastern Tennessee (1966: 11).

Molly attributes this story to her half-brother and fellow activist Jim Garland. Jim labels his tale "an unreasonable lie," a wonderful local term for tall tale. This is the only Yeahoe story of which I am aware that is told as a tall tale; the others possess the properties of legends, and some, such as Dorson's, are clearly believed by the tellers.

Relevant motifs include F112.0.1.1, "Island inhabited by one woman"; *F511.0.1 "Headless person." Near the end of the story, in narrating an escape effected by hanging onto a bear's tail, Aunt Molly incorporates the well-known tall tale type AT 1900, *How the Man Came out of the Tree Stump.* For another example of the bear-tail escape story, see Maud Long's "Jack and One of His Hunting Trips," story 20 in this collection.

105. *Courting Hungry* [AFS 2564A]. Like all tall tales, this one is offered straight-faced as a true account. This seems to be a popular tale in the Appalachians; Jimmy Neil Smith recorded a very similar version from Ray Hicks (narrator of stories 28–32 in this book), who presented it as an autobiographical account (J.N. Smith 1988: 5–6).

106. *Churning Up the Devil* [AFS 2564B]. This anecdote relies on two types of traditional understandings: the widespread folk belief that working on Sunday will conjure up the devil, and a plethora of anecdotes featuring people who are mistaken for the devil. Motifs: C631, "Not to work on Sunday"; J1786, "Man thought to be devil." The plot is closely related to K1554.1(a), "Lorenzo Dow sets fire to barrel of tow in which paramour is hidden" and K1555.2, "The devil in the barrel. The naked lover hides himself in a sooty barrel. The former has been reported in Missouri, New York, and New Jersey. Both tales differ from Molly's in depicting a situation of adultery rather than courtship. See Randolph 1955: 109–10, 207.

107. *Becoming a Witch and Undoing Spells* [AFS 2566B]. Motifs D1385.4, "Silver bullet protects against giants, ghosts, and witches"; G263.5, "Witch revives dead"; G265.4, "Witch causes disease or death of animals"; G271.4, "Exorcism by injuring image of witch"; D2063.1.1, "Tormenting by sympathetic magic; . . . witch tormented by abusing an animal or object." For an audio recording, see Jackson 1972. In this recording, the last name of the person identified as a witch has been deleted to avoid offending any living relatives.

108. *The Witch and the Witch Doctor* [AFS 2566A]. Molly's account stops abruptly as the disk reaches its end. Her recorded words refer to a cure found often in European and American witch traditions: that if one sets out the milk that the witch has spoiled, the witch will be lured to the milk and made vulnerable to capture. Motifs D1745, "Magic power rendered ineffective"; D2083.2.2, "Witch curdles milk"; G274.1, "Witch snared by setting out milk"; G269.10, "Witch punishes person who incurs her ill will." Audio recordings of some of Aunt Molly Jackson's witchcraft tales have been commercially released (Jackson 1972). As in the previous tale, the last name of the person identified as a witch has been deleted to avoid offending any living relatives.

109. *Ridden by a Witch* [AFS 2565]. G241.2, "Witch rides on person"; G263.4, "Witch causes illness"; G273, "Witch rendered powerless"; M429.6, "Coin in churn releases curse";

G241.2.1, "Witch transforms man to horse and rides him." The belief in witch riding, once pervasive in Europe, is still reported frequently in the United States, particularly from African American communities. Among the numerous published texts from Molly's region are one from Kentucky (Roberts 1955: no. 37), four from North Carolina (Thompson 1952: 649–50), and one from Virginia (Barden 1991: no. 33). Dorson (1967: no. 120) presents an African American text from Michigan and numerous parallels; note also McNeil's Alabama text (1985: no. 72). Accounts of witch riding often closely parallel classic nightmare tales; Rickels (1961) makes some explicit comparisons. See also story 129 in this collection, an African American nightmare legend, as well as the notes to that story.

110. *Living in a Haunted House* [AFS 2565]. E281, "Ghosts Haunt House"; H1411, "Fear test: staying in haunted house." Although told as a personal experience, this narrative closely follows the plot of the most popular of Appalachian folktales, AT 326, *The Youth Who Wanted to Learn What Fear Is.* Spending the night in a haunted house is one of the most common themes in American narrative, both legendary and fictional. See the notes on stories 44, 117, and 130 in this book.

111. *My Father Prays* [AFS 5621A,B]. Major sources for Dobie's life (1888–1964) and scholarship include his autobiography, *Some Part of Myself* (1980), and treatments by James McNutt (1982), José Limón (1994), and Lon Tinkle (1978). Nolan Porterfield's biography of Lomax (1996) devotes considerable attention to the interrelationships of Lomax and Dobie. The Dobie quotation on being shamed by his father's humility is found in Tinkle 1978: 8.

112. *Hilo!* [AFS 5619B]. The quotation in the headnote is from Dobie's *Tongues of the Monte* (1935: vii).

113. *Beef and Tallow* [AFS 5621B]. Goodwyn's account of the recording session is summarized in Porterfield 1996: 442.

114. *The Wolf Boy* [AFS 14208A]. B535, "Animal nurse; animal nourishes abandoned child." B453.3, "Helpful wolf"; cf. A511.2.2.1, "Culture hero suckled by wolf."

115. *The Orphan Girl That Died* [AFS 14208A]. N694.1, "Apparently dead woman revives as she is being prepared for burial"; cf. S123, "Burial alive." In a similar Florida tale, for which Reaver suggests the new motif F1088.5*, "Happy escape from being buried alive," a girl is discovered to be alive just before the casket is closed (Reaver 1987: 69). Most stories in which the living are mistaken for the dead end tragically, as the "corpse" is buried, and it is only after the buried person has died trying to claw her way out that the error of the survivors is discovered. In one dramatic Florida version, the mistake is discovered when the casket is opened at the gravesite during the burial service, but the buried girl has already died (Reaver 1987: no. 67; see also no. 68 in his collection and Lindahl, Owens, and Harvison 1997: no. 22). On the fear of premature burial as expressed in tales and other forms of shared behavior, see Winniford 1998: 178–82. For a tale based on the opposite situation, in which a dead person is thought to be alive, see story 100 in this collection.

116. *The Child and the Snake* [AFS 14208A]. AT 285, *The Child and the Snake* (B765.6). This is one of the most extensively reported belief legends in North America, especially in African American communities. But the tale is also popular among European Americans, as Lula Davis's version helps demonstrate. J.D. Suggs, teller of stories 47–61 in this collection, told a version of this tale, which Dorson has published along with two others (1967: no. 145). The fifteen versions listed by Baughman are distributed nearly equally between black and white narrators; to that list, add Barden (1991: no. 2), who reported thirteen versions in the Virginia WPA files alone, and Adams (1987: 14). For international versions of this tale, see the Grimms (1987: no. 105), Waugh (1959), and Lindahl (1984). In addition to this legend and the two that follow, Lula Davis narrates "The Preacher and the Bully," story 152 in this volume; in a separate

recording session, in April 1962, Mrs. Davis narrated five additional tales, including jokes, a legend, and a tall tale (AFS 13136A18-A21, A23).

117. *A Haunted House* [AFS 11426A]. AT 326, *The Youth Who Wanted to Learn What Fear Is*. This is one of the most widespread tales in American tradition. Sometimes, as in Sara Cleveland's version (see story 44 herein), the story is told fictionally and for comic effect; yet the great majority of stories of this type in the Appalachians are told for true. For a fictional version of AT 326, see story 44 in this book; for further discussion, consult the notes to story 44.

The haunted house is one of the most common themes in American legendry. For representative parallels, see the eleven Indiana haunted house legends published by Baker (1982: nos. 79–89), the nine published by Barden from Virginia (1991: nos. 52–60, including no. 57, which replicates the motif of the jingling chains), and the eighteen from Alabama, Arkansas, Kentucky, Tennessee, Texas, and Virginia published by McNeil (1985: nos. 1–18); see also Browne (1977) 220–23 et passim. Salient motifs include H1411, "Fear test: staying in haunted house"; E231, "Return from the dead to reveal murder"; E281, "Ghosts haunt house"; E545.12, "Ghost directs man to hidden treasure"; cf. E402.1.4, "Invisible ghost jingles chains." See also stories 44, 110, and 130 in this book as well as their respective notes.

118. *Lights That Listen* [AFS 11426B]. E280, "Ghosts haunt buildings"; E421.3, "Luminous ghosts"; E491, "Will o' the Wisp"; E421.3.4, "Ghost as fiery ball."

119. *Sounds That Listen* [AFS 11426B]. E280, "Ghosts haunt buildings"; E402.1.5, "Invisible ghost makes rapping or knocking noise." Cf. E402.1.8(g), "Ghost uses hammer, saw, plane in woodworking shop." For a parallel from Louisiana, see Lindahl, Owens, and Harvison (1997: no. 180).

120. *Natural Haints* [AFS 11426B]. J1760, "Animal or person mistaken for something else"; J1784, "Things thought to be spirits"; J1785, "Animals thought to be the devils or ghosts." Personal anecdotes concerning such mistaken identities are extremely common in oral tradition, but they are published much less frequently than other kinds of ghost stories; one exception is the story-stock of Native American Bel Abbey, of the Koasati culture of Louisiana, who often told such stories about himself (Lindahl, Owens, and Harvison 1997: nos. 40–41).

121. *The Scarecrow Dream* [AFS 11426B]. D1812.3.3, "Future revealed in dream"; J1784, "Things thought to be spirits"; E421.3.4, "Ghost as fiery ball."

122. *The Yankee and Marcum* [AFS 14724A2]. D1721.1, "Magic power from devil"; D1777, "Magic results from power of thought"; D2074, "Attracting by magic"; D2074.1, "Animals magically called"; D2197, "Magic dominance over animals"; G224.4, "Person sells soul to devil in exchange for witch powers"; G278, "Death of witch"; G303.9.1, "The devil as a builder"; G303.9.1.3, "Devil as builder of mill"; M211, "Man sells soul to devil"; M211.2, "Man sells soul to devil in return for devil's building house." This tale is available on CD (Jabbour and Fleischhauer 1998).

Jabbour and Fleischhauer recorded many narratives from the Hammons that were not released on CD (see AFS 14460–67; 14722–33; 15551–63; 15566–70); for an example of one of these unreleased tales, see story 200 in this collection.

123. *The Thing on the Bridge* [AFS 17441]. E332.1(a), "Ghost appears at bridge." This and other Newton Downey tales appear in Gorsuch (1973).

124. *The Vanishing Hitchhiker* [AFS 17441]. E332.3.3.1, "The Vanishing Hitchhiker"; E272, "Road ghost"; E422.4(a), "Female revenant in white clothing." This is one of the most popular of contemporary American legends, as evidenced by the fact that it supplied the title for the best selling of all American legend collections (Brunvand 1981). Because modern U.S. versions of the story invariably feature automobiles, many interpreters of "The Vanishing Hitchhiker" tend to see it as a creation of the modern industrial world. Yet the same plot circulated before cars

were invented: one version of the story dates from 1870. Among the most extensive early treatments of the U.S. distribution of the legend are those by Beardsley and Hankey (1942; 1943), who analyzed seventy-five variants, and Louis C. Jones (1959: 161–84, 196–97). McNeil presents and analyzes six southern versions (1987: 106–11, 188–93). The legend appears in myriad cultures worldwide; among the more interesting examinations of its permutations is Keith Cunningham's presentation and analysis of Navajo versions (1992: 88–98). Bennett (1998) notes that more than 400 versions had been published by the end of the twentieth century. She presents a summary of the scholarship on the legend and an engaging reading of its themes: the most recent versions of the Vanishing Hitchhiker focus on a ghost that wishes to return to life; the legend, like much of twentieth-century American culture, views death not from a religious, but from a secular perspective. Death is not the door to another world but a "deprivation, and [the hitchhiking ghosts] refuse to submit to it" (Bennett 1998: 12). The ghost is most often a young girl killed senselessly at the moment when her life showed most promise, and she wants desperately to resume that life; nothing on the "other side" is nearly as attractive as the life she left behind.

125. *The Three Knocks*; *A Grandmother's Ghost* [AFC 2003/001]. E338.1(aa), "Ghosts knock on door"; E402.1.5, "Invisible ghost makes knocking or rapping noise"; D1812.5.1.12.1, "Howling of dog as bad omen" (for a parallel from Virginia, see Barden 1991: no. 110); E422.4.3, "Ghost in white"; E279.2, "Ghost disturbs sleeping person"; cf. E443.2, "Ghost laid by prayer."

126. *The Visions of Lloyd Chandler* [AFC 2003/001]. The quoted materials on Sharp's visit to the Appalachians come from Sharp himself (Campbell and Sharp 1917) and from Wellman (2001: 151, 159); in the quoted reference to Lloyd Chandler, Wellman writes "Floyd" instead of "Lloyd," but an inspection of Sharp's handwritten diaries indicates that the name is as likely to be Lloyd. The number of songs collected by Sharp and the number of singers from whom he collected in Madison County—numbers that vary from source to source—are here take from Yates (2002b). The account of Lloyd Chandler's recorded performance of "Conversation with Death" is found in "High Atmosphere" (1995: [16]). The quote from Reverend James Beaver comes from an interview conducted with Beaver by Garrett Chandler, Carl Lindahl, Johnny Ray, and Jan Sohayda August 16, 2002. The words of the song "Conversation with Death" are printed with the permission of the Garrett Chandler and his family who, with the assistance of copyright specialist Jan Sohayda, finally secured a copyright for Lloyd's song in 2003, eighty-seven years after he composed it.

127. *Witches* [AFS 21592; BR 8-PM-R43]. Patrick B. Mullen, who collected these tales from Quincy Higgins, has published a lengthy study of Higgins's personal narratives (1992: 157–93). Mullen's remarks about Higgins in the headnote to this tale come from page 158 of that book. The quotation by Higgins's daughter Mary Holecheck comes from a letter written to Carl Lindahl on September 25, 2003. D2083.1, "Cows magically made dry"; G271.6, "Exorcism of witch by counter-charm"; G271.4.1(i), "Breaking a spell on cow by boiling her milk with needles." The most commonly reported crimes of witches in American folk tradition are against cows and other farm animals. In the communities where such tales were often told, the health of one farm animal could make a huge difference in the family economy, even sometimes a life-or-death difference. In certain cases, as in this tale, to cure the afflicted animal would be to harm or kill the witch. The witch's health would improve only if she could borrow food from the house of the person who had laid a counterspell on her. See stories 107 and 108 in this book for related accounts of witches torturing animals and spoiling milk. Dorson presents representative related texts from Anglo Americans in Maine and German Americans in Pennsylvania and Illinois (1964: 55–56, 114–15, 314–15). The use of heated metal to exorcise a witch is often mentioned in American legends. Sometimes one uses pins, sometimes needles, sometimes iron

or even a plowshare. In certain tales the metal is placed over a fire or submerged in water or heated red-hot and then submerged in a butter churn. Baughman could not find the needle ritual in the United States, but he did find two occurrences in English legendry. Barden (1991: 38) publishes a legend from Virginia in which cold water poured over a red-hot plowshare kills a witch.

Quincy Higgins's second witch tale, concerning the flying panther witch, contains motifs D1385.4, "Silver bullet protects against giants, ghosts, and witches"; G211.4, "Witch in form of wild bird"; G242, "Witch flies through air"; G249.2, "Witches scream."

128. *The Spider Witch* [AFS 10896A]. G241.2, "Witch rides on person"; G272.6, "Sieve as protection against witches"; G273, "Witch rendered powerless." In the *Motif-Index*, witches possess spider familiars (G225.1), and the devil can take the form of a spider (G303.3.3.17), but there is no motif assigned for a spider witch. Dorson (1952) discusses the recording session during which this performance occurred. A significantly different version of this same tale is transcribed in Dorson 1956b: 142–44.

129. *Nightmare Ridden* [AFS 17611]. The quotations in which Charles L. Perdue Jr. describes his relationship with John Jackson are taken from a paper (Perdue 1996). In a single storytelling session, Perdue and his wife, Nancy J. Martin-Perdue, collected more than eighty tales from John Jackson and his wife, Cora. The majority of the tales are published, together with analysis and annotations, in Perdue 1969. In addition to the performances featured in this book (all of which are found on AFS tapes 17611 and 19612), the Perdues made many other recordings featuring the songs and stories of John Jackson and his family; these too are housed in the American Folklife Center (AFS 14590–600; 17051–52; 17610; 17613–20).

In Perdue's published collection, the current tale bears the title "John and the Nightmare" (Perdue 1969: no. 70). F471.1, "Nightmare presses person in dream"; F535, "Pygmy. Remarkably small man." See the notes on story 109 in this book; also see the related motif G241.2, "Witch rides on person." The belief in the nightmare as a spirit being or witch that tortures sleepers by pressing down on them is extremely widespread and takes numerous forms. In Scandinavian tradition, where the belief has been reported since the Middle Ages, the nightmare, true to its name, takes the form of a horse that rides upon the sleeper. In the great majority of American accounts, however, the oppressive being takes a human or humanoid form, quite often that of an old hag. Hufford (1982) has studied this phenomenon in relation to health issues and suggests that the nightmare is often used as a way of explaining sleep apnea and other conditions in which people lying prone experience paralysis, chest pains, and difficulty in breathing. Rickels (1961) points out many similarities between witch riding legends and nightmare accounts. On witch riding, see story 109 in this book and its note.

130. *The Preachers and the Spooks* [AFS 17611]. E281, "Ghosts haunt house"; E423.1.2, "Revenant as cat"; E423.1.1, "Revenant as dog"; E545.19.2(c), "Proper means of addressing ghost. Person must ask, 'In the name of the Lord, why troublest thou me?' "; H1411, "Fear test: staying in haunted house"; E231, "Return from the dead to reveal murder." This legendary account closely parallels the popular märchen AT 326, *The Youth Who Wanted to Learn What Fear Is*. On haunted houses, see stories 44 and 110 herein; for another, though much different ghostly cat, see Mose Platt's "Cat Story" (story 99 in this book).

131. *Fairy Forms* [AFS 3748A]. F321.1, "Changeling"; F321, "Fairy steals child from cradle"; F321.1.2.1, "Changeling has abnormal features or growth"; F321.1.2.3, "Changeling is sickly." Margaret Sullivan's comments on her love of ballads and early life in Ireland were recorded earlier the same day (AFS 3746B5).

132. *Banshees and Ghosts* [AFS 20450]. J1765, "Animals thought to be spirits or ghosts"; M301.6.1, "Banshees as portents of misfortune." Although still a common figure of belief nar-

ratives in Ireland, the banshee is rarely recorded in American lore; for some exceptions, see McNeil 1985: no. 64. On contemporary Irish beliefs in banshees, see Lysaght's excellent study (1986).

Father O'Sullivan's stories and remarks on Irish American culture in Butte fill five tapes (AFS 20450–54). On the Irish in Butte, see Emmons 1989; the author, who interviewed the narrator, refers to the O'Sullivan family history.

133. *Raising the Dead; The Nephite on the Road* [AFS 8638B]. Q45.1.1, "Three Nephites give blessings as reward for hospitality." The quotation is from Dorson 1959: 115. The first brief tale echoes motif E121.5.2, "Resuscitation through prayers of holy man." The three Nephites are said to have gained a nearly immortal status from Christ himself at the time of his resurrection (D1856.2). This brief Nephite tale possesses a parallel in V231.6, "Angel in the form of an old man." Austin Fife, collector of these two brief tales, has written extensively on Mormon legendry in general (Fife 1950) and on legends of the Three Nephites in particular (Fife 1940). Austin Fife collected many other Nephite tales now on deposit in the AFC (e.g., AFS 8685A2; 8685A3; 8685B1).

134. *Paul Bunyan on Round River* [AFS 2264B]. The fakelore references come from Dorson 1971: 6 and 7; a discussion of W.B. Laughead and the inflation of the Bunyan stories is found in Dorson 1959: 216–26; the most thorough documentation is found in Dorson 1956c; a summary of the Paul Bunyan tradition is found in Lindahl 2000. Stith Thompson recounts his experiences with Paul Bunyan stories in *A Folklorist's Progress* (1996: 44). E.C. Beck provides a substantial source for Michigan lumberjack folklife in *They Knew Paul Bunyan* (1956), as well as a book (1942) and an LP (1960) both titled *Songs of the Michigan Lumberjacks*. Beck knew Perry well and wrote about him affectionately; the quotations in the headnote are drawn from Beck 1942: 6–7 (see also page 286) and Beck 1956: 21. A photograph of Allen appears as the frontispiece to Beck 1942. Beck's career as a folklorist among Michigan lumberjacks is documented in Kozma 1991.

X1547.1, "Round River"; X1547.1.1*, "Logging crew of Paul Bunyan drives logs down a river; they pass a deserted camp several times and finally realize that it is their own camp which they had left several days before. They discover that they are in a round river with no outlet." Baughman lists seven versions from Wisconsin, Michigan, and the Northwest. Hoffman (1950: 308) discusses this Perry Allen performance as part of a stylistic and source study of Paul Bunyan traditions.

135. *Paul Bunyan Moves in Circles Again* [AFS 2259A-2260A1]. X1547.1, "Round River"; X1547.1.1*. Bill McBride possessed a rich repertoire of traditional lumberjack songs; three of these, recorded by Alan Lomax on the same fieldtrip that yielded this tall tale, appear on a commercially released Library of Congress recording, *Songs of the Michigan Lumberjacks* (Beck 1960). The account of McBride and his memory featured in the headnote is taken from Beck 1942: 6–7. See notes on story 134 in this book.

136. *A Liars' Contest* [AFS 5139A1; audio available at http://memory.loc.gov/ammem/afctshtml/toddbibperfindex.html and search by narrator's name]. Jerry Philips's tale possesses parallels in X1314*(a), "Fisherman dips his minnow into bottle of moonshine; he draws in great sea bass which the minnow catches by the throat"; Baughman cites nine versions.

Ledford's inventive and complex account artfully interweaves some of the most common American tall tale motifs: X1733.4*, "Stories of sinking into rock or earth"; X1286, "Lies about mosquitoes"; X1286.1, "Lie: the large mosquito"; X1633.1, "Heat causes corn to pop in crib or infield. Animals think the popping corn is snow, freeze to death." This final motif has been reported from Maine to the Northwest among the northern states and often from the South as well. Baughman cites twenty-one versions. Among the many versions printed since Baughman's index was published are examples from Kansas and Nebraska (Welsch 1972: 31).

The dialogue between Ernest Arnold and Lucky Jake is a dramatized version of AT 1920, *Contest in Lying*, and also incorporates AT 1960D, *The Great Vegetable*, and AT 1960F, *The Great Kettle*. Bascom Lamar Lunsford, teller of story 179 in this collection, narrated a version for Benjamin Botkin (transcribed in Loyal Jones 2002: 187); for related versions, see Ancelet 1994: nos. 65 and 64; Burrison 1991: 174–75.

Roy Turner's giant catfish tale is a variant of X1301.5*(c), "Fish is so big that water level of the streams falls two feet when the fish is pulled out"; Baughman reports five versions, including tales from Arkansas, Indiana, and Missouri.

137. *My Three Favorite Lies* [AFS 4112A1; digital id. AFCTS 4112a1; audio available at http://memory.loc.gov/ammem/afctshtml/toddbibperfindex.html and search by narrator's name]. The first of Shorty Allen's tales falls under the heading X1321.4.4.2*, "Fisherman takes frog or worm away from snake, gives snake a swallow of liquor to compensate for its loss. In a few minutes the snake returns, taps fisherman on leg, offers him another frog." See also X1318*, "Minnow fed liquor brings large fish in its mouth to fisherman." Baughman lists twenty-four variants, ranging from Alberta to Texas in the West and Maine to Florida in the East, including a Michigan variant in which Paul Bunyan is the fisherman.

138. *The Peach Tree Deer* [AFS 5135A2; digital id. AFCTS 5135a2; audio available at http://memory.loc.gov/ammem/afctshtml/toddbibperfindex.html and search by narrator's name]. AT 1889C, *Fruit Tree Grows from Head of Deer Shot with Fruit Pits*. X1130.2, "Fruit tree grows from head of deer shot with pit or pits of fruit by hunter who has no regular bullets." This tale circulated widely in Europe in the many printed versions of the adventures of Baron Münchausen. Yet Aarne and Thompson reported more versions in the United States than in the rest of the world combined. Baughman mentions numerous versions from all over the eastern half of the United States, as well as from central and eastern Canada. More recent references include a Florida version from Reaver (1987: 81) and a Louisiana version from Lindahl, Owens, and Harvison (1997: no. 134).

139. *Cornered by a Polar Bear* [AFS 5136A3; digital id. AFCTS 5136a3; audio available at http://memory.loc.gov/ammem/afctshtml/toddbibperfindex.html and search by narrator's name]. X1122.4.2*(c), "Hunter meets bear, cries when he thinks of mother's grief at his imminent death; the tears freeze and he shoots bear with tears." Journalist Lowell Thomas reported a version of this tale from Pennsylvania (1931: 103); otherwise, I find it rare in U.S. collections.

140. *A Land-loving Catfish* [AFC 2001/008]. Jimmy Neil Smith's quotation in the headnote is drawn from his collection, *Homespun* (1988: 73–77); Doc McConnell is also discussed and quoted in Sobol 1999: 91–98. X1305*, "Fish lives on dry land"; X1306.3*, "Tragic end of tame fish. Tame fish falls into water, usually while crossing footbridge, drowns." A widespread tale, for which Baughman reports sixteen versions spread all over the United States. In addition to Baughman's listings, Baker (1986: nos. 51, 52) reports two from Indiana, Burrison has one from Georgia (1991: 197–99), and Welsch (1972: 98) reprints a Nebraska newspaper version from 1925.

141. *The Biggest Liar in the State* [AFS 2025A]. Tillman Cadle begins his tale with the theme of a contest in lying (AT 1920), but he never returns to the contest. Instead, the first character narrates a series of escalating improbabilities centered on hunting. The first episode is an example of AT 1890A, *Shot Splits Tree Limb*, also identified as motif X1124.3.1, "Gunshot splits limb and catches feet of birds." Baughman lists two dozen variants from the United States and Canada, including an African American telling. The episode of the gun hammer running down the deer falls under the general category X1121.7*, "Lie: marvelous gun" (cf. X1122.5*). The episode of

the versatile hunting dog is motif X1215(ab), "Dog hunts various game according to equipment master carries: if master carries shotgun, dog hunts rabbits; if he takes rifle, dog hunts deer; if he takes fishing rod, dog digs worms." Baughman reports eleven variants, one associated with Paul Bunyan. I could find no precise motif for the final lie, featuring the dog treeing the fish, but it is roughly parallel to a number of motifs classified under X 1215.8(ai), "Dog fishes."

Mary Elizabeth Barnicle's adventures and accomplishments as a folklore collector are summarized by Willie Smyth (1986a; 1986b), who also discusses the role of Barnicle's husband Tillman Cadle in their mutual fieldwork enterprises. See also the headnote to story 169 in this collection for a reference to Barnicle's dealings with Zora Neale Hurston and Alan Lomax.

142. *Swinging Pigs* [AFS 11419]. Other tales by Lee Webb are published in Hall 1978.

143. *The Roguish Cow* [AFS 19080B]. B871.1.1, "Giant cow." Chase (1956: 103–4) prints an earlier version from Gaines Kilgore, although he does mention that Kilgore had begun telling an updated version with references to World Ward II.

144. *The Night the Lamp Flame Froze* [AFS 2599]. This amusing tale is represented by two redundant motifs in Baughman's index: X1203(de), "Hens eat frozen flames which man throws out window; they lay hard-boiled eggs"; X1623.3.3.1*, "Man feeds frozen flames to hens; they lay hard-boiled eggs." The storyteller, Mary Celestia Parler [ADS 1179A], is also the narrator of story 181 in this collection. McNeil (1989: no. 33) reports a version from Arkansas; Lowell Thomas (1931: 193) summarizes versions from Michigan and Florida.

145. *The Gun Ain't Loaded* [AFS 11414B, recording 103A]. Typed by Hoffman (1973) as X735.9.1, "My gun ain't loaded." In an Ozark parallel (Randolph 1976: 58), a man spends the night with a pair of sisters who keep guns under their pillows. They entice him into intercourse by telling him that their guns aren't loaded; after they've worn him out, one of the women asks for him again and reminds him that her gun isn't loaded; he responds that his isn't either. Collector Joseph S. Hall called this a "humorous (and uninhibited) story of a trip to Tennessee," and he noted its fabliau quality; apparently, he considered it too risqué to print in either of his collections of Smoky Mountain folklore. Another U.S. parallel is cited in Lockridge (1947: 111) and a more distant analog, collected in Washington, D.C., in the 1940s, is found in Legman 1968: 354.

146. *Dividing the Dead* [AFS 11426B]. AT 1791, *The Sexton Carries the Parson.* Stith Thompson has remarked bemusedly, "For some reason" this tale type "is about the best known of all anecdotes collected in America" (1946: 214). Why did this relatively simple joke find such a wide and appreciative American audience? Perhaps in part because the story hinges on two themes pervasive in American humor, mistaken identity and unknowing deception. The tale's gullible dupe, caught off guard by overheard voices emanating from the cemetery, concocts a superhuman explanation for a nonsupernatural event. The dual view of the supernatural provides another reason for the tale's popularity: this joke both displays and undercuts supernatural beliefs in a manner reminiscent of many oft-told American legends, such as the tale of the man whose coat catches on a gravestone and who, believing that a ghost is pulling at his coattails, dies of fright. Another instance of mistaken identity in the graveyard occurs in story 132 in this collection.

Baughman identified fifteen versions of this popular tale, but Halpert and Widdowson were able to find more than thirty additional published texts and dozens of additional archival variants; Halpert collected thirty-four versions from one group alone: his college students and their informants in eastern Kentucky (1996: nos. 121, 122). In addition to the tales listed by Halpert and Widdowson, see Burrison 1991: 54–55, 71–72, 147–48; Hurston 1935: 86–87; and Hurston 2001: 171–72; McNeil presents a version (1989: no. 201) and a discussion (1989: 199–200). For another version, see story 147 in this book.

147. *Two at the Gate* [AFS 15585]. AT 1791, *The Sexton Carries the Parson.* J1786.10.2,

"One for you and one for me." Two boys are heard dividing nuts (or fish or fruit) in the graveyard, saying, "One for you and one for me" (or "You take this one, I'll take that one"). Oster's own transcription of this tale (1968: 47–48; rpt. in Georges and Jones 1995: 75) differs slightly from mine.

Son House's version of the story closely follows the plot of this tale as most often told in Europe: the crippled master asks the gullible servant or slave to take him to the graveyard. This version is longer and more complex than the great majority of American versions, which involve, not two, but just one trip by the graveyard and one dupe who is fooled by the voices in the cemetery; see, for example, story 146 in this collection. See also the notes for story 146.

148. *Possums and Pigs* [AFS 15585]. J1391, "Thief makes lame excuse." Son House's pig and possum tale is related to a popular and widespread complex of African American jokes. Dorson collected four parallel texts from African Americans and identified four published variants (1967: 137). In a version collected by Hurston (2001: 174–75) from Florida-born Louise Noble, the protagonist is tricked by men who actually tamper with his sack and substitute a possum for his pig.

Much more often researched than the present narrative are the tales in which John takes the pig or sheep back to his house and swaddles it like a baby; when the master asks to see the baby, John often responds with a similar lame excuse: "I put dat in dere uh baby, I don't give a damn what it done turnt to" (Hurston 2001: 115). Such stories are usually classified as AT 1525M, *Mak and the Sheep*; motif K406.2, "Stolen sheep dressed as baby in cradle." Baughman lists seven additional versions, of which only two are African American; Halpert and Randolph discuss these texts (Randolph 1955: 173–74); and Dorson (1967: no. 41) prints a tale from E.L. Smith, the narrator of stories 188, 195, and 196 in this book. Son House, originally of Mississippi, recorded this tale when he lived in Rochester, New York.

149. *The Biggest Liar in the State* [AFS 15585]. J1155.1.1*(b), "Hunter (or fisherman) meets stranger, tells him about all the animals, birds, or fish he has caught that day. The numbers are all above bag limits, or else the game is out of season. Finally the stranger asks, 'Do you know who I am?' 'No.' 'Well, I'm the game warden.' 'Do you know who I am?' 'No.' 'I'm the biggest liar in this county.' " Baughman cites six versions, including two African American tales from Texas and Alabama and European American texts from Arizona, Indiana, Kentucky, and New York. Baker (1986: nos. 42–44) prints three versions from Indiana, and Leary adds one from Wisconsin (2001: 172).

150. *He'll Have to Swim* [AFS 15585]. Cf.E489.3, "Forgetting Charon's fee." The custom of leaving money with the dead is quite old, and in different traditions it serves different purposes: for example, in parts of India the belief has circulated that money left in the mouths of the dead will prevent their return as revenants (E431.11). Closer to the tradition cited in this joke is an ancient custom that Charon, the ferryman of the dead, exacts a fee from souls to cross the river Styx (A672.1.1; P613). In one centuries-old Italian joke, a dead man arrives before Charon without the requisite coin in his mouth. Charon asks the man, "Don't you know the custom?" "Yes, but I couldn't put off dying for a quarter," the man responds. I have not been able to locate American parallels for this joke.

151. *Cold as Hell* [AFS 15585]. When told about parsons or priests, this tale is often associated with AT 1738, *Dream: All Parsons in Hell*; in 1966, Baughman could identify only one English version of the tale, which he typed AT 1738*, and for which he assigned the motif X459(d). He could not locate an American parallel, but African American versions have surfaced in Virginia (Dance 1978: no. 63), Georgia (Hurston 2001: 34–37), and Texas (Brewer 1953: 90–92). McNeil (1989: no. 154) publishes an Ozarks version, and I have located an Appalachian variant in Shackelford and Weinberg (1977: 46); Jones and Wheeler (1987: 41) print a distant

variant from West Virginia. Halpert and Widdowson (1996) found two versions in Newfoundland (nos. 119, 120). The joke is often told about groups other than parsons, including lawyers and West Virginians. Halpert and Widdowson list a total of ten American versions; the joke is doubtless more popular than has been reported, as is clear in the work of J. Frank Dobie (1953), who identified six versions in Texas alone. McNeil (1989: 187–88) traces a rich strand of published tales in which Abraham Lincoln and (less often Ulysses S. Grant) are given credit for telling the lawyer version of the tale.

152. *The Preacher and the Bully* [AFS 14221]. In 1962, Lula Davis recorded a second version of this story; in the notes accompanying that recording, Lula's husband, her source for the narrative, is named T.M. Davis [AFS 13136]. K1700, "Deception through bluffing"; related to K1766, "Trickster's boasting scares his powerful opponent from contest." The tale of the preacher and the bully does not possess an exact parallel among the tales I have examined, but it belongs to a massive constellation of narratives in which the hero uses clever tactics in order to win a contest by default. In some African American tales that turn on this theme, the protagonist averts the fight by asking if his opponent's grave has been dug yet and then yelling into the sky, "St. Peter, move over" because his enemy will soon be flung into the clouds (Dorson 1967: 38a). In a popular series of more distantly related tales, a tiny mortal is pitted against a giant to see who can throw an anvil the farthest; the hero frightens the giant by calling out to people in distant lands to watch their heads (AT, 1063A, *Throwing Contest: Trickster Shouts*; for an example, see story 14 in this collection. In another variant, popular in African American tradition, the smaller man arrives early at the site of the fight, chops a hole in a tree, and then covers the hole with bark; later, when his opponent arrives, he returns and readies for the fight by punching his arm through the tree where he has already drilled the hole; his opponent forfeits the match (AT 1085, *Pushing a Hole into a Tree*). John Davis, teller of stories 169–171 in this collection, narrates an as yet untranscribed version of this tale (AFS 348A1, "John Whips the Giant").

153. *Baptists and Presbyterians* [AFS 14084A]. Joan Moser appears on this tape with her celebrated father, folklorist Artus Moser, who also contributes a tale; during these same sessions, Botkin recorded Artus Moser's accounts of "collecting folklore among the mountain people" (AFS 14083A; see also 14220B). Parishioners throughout the country engage in similar denominational jokes. Perhaps the most popular in the South are jokes pitting Baptists against Methodists against Presbyterians. They are popular among African Americans (e.g., Brewer 1953: 64–66, 68–69; Dorson 1956b: 174; Dorson 1967: nos. 239, 240; Hurston 2001: 17–43) and European Americans (Jones 1989: 21, 24, 33, 37, 53; Jones and Wheeler 1987: 32–33; Jones and Wheeler 1995: 118–19, 120–21, 124; McNeil 1989: no. 159); all of these cited examples involve at least two of the three denominations.

154. *The Devilists' Revival* [AFS 14084A]. J1786.1, "Man costumed as demon thought to be devil."

155. *Jamie the Mountain Lion* [AFS 25588]. J1900, "Absurd disregard or ignorance of animal's nature or habits"; K2295, "Treacherous animals"; U120, "Nature will show itself."

156. *Pedro de Urdemalas and the Plums* [AFS 14221A]. Pedro de Urdemalas is the generic name for a trickster well known in Spain and throughout the Spanish-speaking New World. The figure of Pedro was already long known in the seventeenth century when the great comic author Miguel de Cervantes referred to him in *Don Quixote*. Aurelio Espinosa (1946–47, 3: 127–29) views Pedro de Urdemalas as an embodiment of social protest themes. Pedro de Urdemalas surfaces in tales told throughout Mexico (see, for example, Paredes 1970: nos. 53–56) and all along the U.S.–Mexico border, including Los Angeles (Miller 1973: no. 82). For further evidence of the richness of the tradition along the border, see note 157.

157. *Pedro de Urdemalas and the Pigs* [AFS 14221A]. K404.1, "Tails in ground. Thief steals

animals and sticks severed tails into the ground, claiming that animals have escaped underground." Thompson's *Motif-Index* lists many more New World than Old World forms of the story. From the time of its printed appearance in the first Uncle Remus book (Harris 1880: no. 20), it has been collected extensively from African Americans in the Caribbean and the American South as well as by French speakers, both black and white, in Louisiana and in Missouri. This tale forms episode I of the tale type AT 1004, *Hogs in the Mud; Sheep in the Air*. This particular episode is often strung together with several other short trickster tales to create a long humorous narrative. The popularity of the pig-tail plot is evidenced by the fact that it is often the episode that narrators along the Texas Mexican border choose to open their stories; see, for example, the collections of Aiken (1935: 49–55) and Whatley (1944: 45–49). The quotation in the headnote is from Aiken (1935: 49). For other U.S. versions in Spanish, see Espinosa 1914: nos. 13, 14 (New Mexico); Mason 1934 (Puerto Rico); Miller 1973: no. 81 (California); and Rael 1942: no. 288 (Colorado).

158. *The* Indito *and His Wives* [AFS 14221A]. T145, "Polygamous marriages."

159. *The* Indito *and the Banker* [AFS 14221A]. Surveying a large body of jokes concerning Indians, Dorson noted that "most frequently the anecdote literature depicted not a credulous booby but a sagacious and cunning rascal, quick to adopt to the business ethics of his conquerors" (1946: 123). This Texas anecdote certainly shows the Indian's abilities to understand and adapt, although it does not, to my mind, show him to be a rascal.

160. *Unwatering the Mine* [AFS 14221A]. The performer of this tale, Levette Jay Davidson, got it from Jim Garrett of Silver Plume, Colorado. In a folklore study, Davidson (1946) retells this tale along with several others devoted to "Gassy Thompson," some circulating from old newspaper columns and some, such as the present tale, circulating from oral tradition.

161. *Tom the Burro* [AFS 14221A]. This tale is quite close to Baughman's motif X1741.7*(d), "Man and horse jump off canyon rim; near the bottom the man calls out *whoa* and the horse stops three feet from floor of canyon. The man climbs off unhurt." Baughman reports one version, from Arizona.

162. *Burros and Beechnut* [AFS 14221A]. Tales concerning remarkably stubborn and otherwise remarkable burros and mules abound in the American West; Beckham (1974: 107–12) presents six such tales, none of which is parallel to this.

163. *Willie and the Devil* [AFS 19080B2]. AT 1030, *Crop Division*; K171.1, "Deceptive crop division: above the ground, below the ground." Chase (1948: no. 9) prints a version he claims he got from Gaines Kilgore and James Taylor Adams, with some additions from another source. James Taylor Adams himself records a version he collected from Gaines Kilgore in 1941 (Perdue 1987: no. 51); curiously, the Adams version is titled "Jack and the Devil," rather than "Willie and the Devil," tempting one to conclude the Adams or one of his fellow collectors changed the title, for Kilgore was adamant in designating his protagonist as "Willie." One of the most widespread traditional American narratives, this joke has been reported from New England and New Jersey and throughout the Appalachians and the Lowland South. Baughman lists fifteen North American versions, divided pretty evenly between versions in which the protagonists are animals (most often a rabbit and a fox) and those in which the protagonists are a devil and a man. Generally, the animal tales are told by African Americans and the devil tales by European Americans, but there are notable exceptions and also cases of tales featuring an animal and the devil (see, for example, Dance 1978: no. 351, an African American narrative).

164. *Old One-Eye.* [AFS 19080]. Chase (1948: no. 23) prints a North Carolina version. N612, "Numskull talks to himself and frightens robbers away"; cf. X111.7, "Misunderstood words lead to comic results."

165. *J. Golden Kimball in His Native Language* [AFS 10490]. Hector Lee collected, presented,

and recorded his J. Golden Kimball tales in many venues. At least two commercially released recordings feature these tales (see particularly Lee 1964b). Lee was also known for his research on Nephite legends (Lee 1949; see story 133 for a representative example) and other aspects of Mormon folk culture. Other writings on J. Golden Kimball (1853–1938) and his humor include Cheney 1973, Fife 1956, and Wilson 1985. One of the passages from the headnote and the joke about feeding the calf appear transcribed in Dorson 1964: 513–14. Austin Fife collected several J. Golden Kimball "yarns" from Professor B.F. Cummings in Provo, Utah in 1946; these are now on deposit in the AFC (AFS 8724A2).

The final joke plays upon stereotypes of the Danes who inhabited Sanpete County, Utah. Brother Petersen and Sister Petersen are staple characters in many of the jokes recorded by Lee himself and transcribed by Dorson (1964: 515–20), but I cannot determine if these are supposed to be perceived as the same Brother Petersen and Sister Petersen who appear in the J. Golden Kimball joke printed here. The exact date of the Lee recordings is unknown, but materials on file in the American Folklife Center state that they were made "prior to June, 1952."

166. *Counting the Wrong Fish* [AFS 8378B1]. Transcribed, introduced, and annotated by James P. Leary in his *So Ole Says to Lena* (2001: 133–34, 221). Leary titles the joke "The Would-be Captain." Here, I modify his transcription slightly to accord with the style rules of this collection. The headnote quotation on the career on Helene Stratman-Thomas is also provided by Leary (1998: 19).

167. *I Love Ewe* [AFS 3677A]. T465, "Bestiality." Archer B. Gilfillan published his reminiscences in a book titled *Sheep* (1928). The book is heavy on humor, but it does not engage the taboo topic of bestiality to the extent found in this tale or story 168 in this book.

168. *Sports as Markers* [AFS 3677B]. T465, "Bestiality." Cf. motif T465.4, which refers to the notion that traces of bestiality can be found in the human offspring.

169. *John and Old Mistress's Nightgown* [AFS 347A]. Hurston's letter to John A. Lomax is quoted from Porterfield 1996: 370. John Davis's animated performance of the nightgown tale is repeatedly interrupted by shouts: "Our chorus, our chorus!" Apparently, others in the room are attempting to stop Davis's narration so that the children's choir may begin singing. Other background noises interfere with the sound quality of this recording; apparently, furniture is being moved to accommodate the choir. The nightgown story is a widely reported African American narrative, anthologized in Botkin (1945: 9). Hurston published two other versions, one in her famous *Mules and Men* (1935: 107–9) and the second in a posthumously published manuscript (2001: 111–13, attributed to Clifford Ulmer). Darryl Dance collected a version in Virginia in the 1970s (1978: no. 189) that is significantly more risqué; than the earlier versions, as the dupe does not merely look up; rather, he runs his hand up his mistress's dress while the mistress is wearing it.

170. *John and the Bear* [AFS 348A,B]. *Mules and Men* contains a similar tale, attributed to Gene Oliver (Hurston 1935: 78–80); Brewer (1946: 92–93) publishes another African American version from the South; Dorson prints a more distantly related text (1967: no. 61). The theme of the "sham warrior" (motif K1951)—in which an underdog uses his wits to scare an opponent of superior strength or, in this case, chooses his words to transform a defeat into a perceived victory—is pervasive in the U.S.; for further references, see the notes to story 152 in this book.

171. *John and the Coon* [AFS 348B]. AT 1641, *Dr. Know-All*. See the notes to story 95 in this book. Hurston collected another Georgia version from Larkins White (Hurston 2001: 85–86).

172. *Monkey and Buzzard* [17611]. Cf. AT 225A, *Tortoise Lets Self Be Carried by Eagle*. In the tale type index, the tortoise is "dropped and eaten." Similarly here, the tortoise and rabbit both die before the monkey gets the better of the buzzard. In Michigan, Dorson (1967: no. 30)

collected a similar tale that ends with the same punchline, "straighten up and fly." The narrator, John Blackamore, explained to Dorson, "Do you know where the title of the song 'Straighten Up and Fly' comes from—that song by Nat King Cole?"

173. *Twenty-five Roosters and One Hen* [AFS 17612]. AT 1487*, *Guarding against Neglect*; X621*, "Jokes about the Irish." Thompson's description of the tale runs, "The old maid has eleven cocks and one hen, so that hen will not be neglected as she has been." The type index locates the tale only in French Canada, and Baughman does not list a single English or North American version. The quotation from Perdue that appears in the headnote is taken from his study (1969: 49); in the course of his research on the Jackson family tales, Perdue has changed his count of the total number of tales told by John and Cora, as well as the number told by Cora that might be considered obscene. Here, I have quoted Perdue's earlier perceptions, but I have changed the count of John's and Cora's tales to occur with Perdue's latest estimates. In a recent communication to me, Perdue stated, "It is sometimes difficult to know just what part of the transcription to designate a tale. The difference between conversation, discussion of a traditional belief, [commentary] added as a result of probing by various people present, and an obviously coherent narrative is not always perfectly clear."

174. *Thinning Corn* [AFS 17612]. X621*, "Jokes about the Irish." As stated in note 46, "Pat and Mike" jokes and other jokes about the Irish enjoyed great currency both in Appalachia and among African Americans from the mid-nineteenth to the mid-twentieth centuries (Roberts 1955: nos. 40–55; Dorson 1967: nos. 241–44). Cora Jackson, whose home lay on the skirts of the Blue Ridge Mountains and whose culture was African American, was understandably exposed to a number of such jokes, of which this and story 173 in this book are typical. Charles Perdue Jr., who collected these tales, notes, "It is interesting (if not meaningful) that [Cora's recorded] jokes about Irishmen all deal with an Irishman's inability to fulfill his family responsibilities and keep his wife happy in bed" (Perdue 1969: 42). See story 46 herein for an example of a tale told about the Irish by an Irish American woman; this tale predictably shows the Irishman getting the better of his English and Scottish rivals. Leary (1984: 4) presents a story from Polish-American Max Trzebiatowski that similarly relates "sex denied" in the evening followed by "scathing commentary in the morning"; Hoffmann (1973) classifies similar tales as AT 1443, *The Pillow Too High*.

175. *That's the One* [AFS 17612]. F547.3.1, "Long penis." Hoffmann (1973) assigns this tale motif F547.3.1.1, "Girl prefers boy with long penis for husband rather than rich men." Vance Randolph (1976: no. 25) prints a very similar version from a man who had heard it in Arkansas in 1917. Other versions include a text from Washington, D.C. (Legman 1968: 328) and a Polish American performance from Wisconsin (Leary 1984); see also Mortimer Hall 1927: no. 282.

176. *The Cook* [AFS 20374]. Narratives about practical jokes are among the most common in American storytelling tradition, yet they seldom surface in folktale collections. Dorson (1964: 67–69) presents a cluster of anecdotes told near Jonesport, Maine, about a local trickster named Art Church who made much trouble for others through his cleverly deceitful use of words. Certain tale types, such as *I Have Not Time to Lie* (AT 1920B), concern verbal tricks; these are often told as true accounts illustrating the cleverness of a local practical joker who is frequently a tall tale teller as well. Much work remains to be done before the narrative afterlives of practical jokes have received adequate treatment.

177. *A Mountain Wedding* [AFS 3766A]. John Lomax's words on Uncle Alex Dunford are taken from his *Adventures of a Ballad Hunter* (1947: 298–99).

178. *The Girl Who Didn't Mind Her Mother* [AFS 3522; audio available at http://memory. loc.gov/ammem/flwpahtml/flwpabibaudiindex.html and search by title]. This brief, effective little

tale does not possess a type number, and it could well have been invented by Eartha White's mother, but it is rife with the characters, situations, and scenery of the magic tale. The tale contains elements commonly found in several tale types (including AT 327G [related to "Hansel and Gretel"], AT 333B [related to "Little Red Riding Hood"], and AT 334). G440, "Ogre abducts person"; F771.3.5, "Underground house"; G312, "Cannibal ogre"; B411, "Helpful cow"; A2330, "Origin of animal characteristics: face."

179. *The Crooked Old Man* [AFS 14084]. AT 366, *The Man from the Gallows*. This and the following tale represent one of the most popular of all American "scare tales." Mark Twain celebrated this plot in his humorous essay "How to Tell a Story." Many narratives and interviews recorded from Bascom Lamar Lunsford are available in AFC collections, including an interview with Duncan Emrich (AFS 9901). Jones transcribes this tale in an appendix to his biography of Lunsford (Loyal Jones 1984: 183). Among the numerous U.S. examples of this tale, I find the Texas performance of Emeline Russell (Dobie 1954: 73–74) the closest to Lunsford's. For further examples of this widespread tale, see the versions of Glen Muncy Anderson (story 180 herein) and her niece, Jane (stories 84, 85 herein).

180. *Grown Toe* [AFC 2003/001]. AT 366, *The Man from the Gallows*. Here is the fourth version of this popular American tale presented in this collection. Although Glen Muncy Anderson's version runs closely parallel to Bascom Lamar Lunsford's (story 179 herein), the teller herself is far more closely related to Jane Muncy Fugate, her niece, who tells two far more distant variants in this book (stories 84, 85 herein).

181. *The Forty-Mile Jumper* [AFS 25590; a second recording of the same tale by Mary Celestia Parler is found on AFS 10811A]. AT 303, *The Twins or Blood Brothers*; AT 315A, *The Cannibal Sister*; AT 1119, *The Ogre Kills His Own Children*; motif B524.1.3, "Dogs rescue master from tree refuge"; D1521, "Miraculous speed from magic object"; cf. D1521.1, "Seven-league boots." When Baughman (1966) classified two Kentucky tales closely related to the present tale text, he designated them as examples of AT 303, one of the most complex of European magic tales; indeed, the Grimms' version of AT 303, "The Two Brothers" (1987: no. 60), is by far the longest of the 200 tales in their famous collection. There are no significant parallels between the first four episodes of AT 303 and the tale at hand; only in the fifth episode does AT 303 present a few threads linking it to this tale. Yet all of the close North American analogs to "The Forty-Mile Jumper" are very brief and consist of just two principal actions: the first in which a witch or ogre threatens and attempts to kill the hero, and the second in which the hero's faithful dogs save him in the nick of time. Therefore, scholars who see a direct historical reaction between AT 303 and the American tales must assume that the American versions are greatly reduced fragments of their European antecedents (see, for example, Lindahl, Owens, and Harvison 1997: 9).

Yet, most of the American tales, however simple, are clearly developed; they stand well on their own and seldom suggest the possibility of derivation from a longer narrative. The American tales are told mainly to children, and much of the zest of their telling—and the most likely reason for their popularity—lies in the curious names of the dogs and the tune or chanting tone in which their endangered master summons them. Among the many sets of dog names noted by Dorson (1967: no. 125) are Take um, Cut-Throat, and Suck-Blood; You-Know, I-Know, and God-Knows; and Wham, Jam, and Jenny-Mo-Wham; the memorably named dogs of Mary Celestia Parler's tale (as well as the dogs that give their names to the title of story 182 in this book) continue this long tradition.

However long the distant antecedents of the present tale may be, the U.S. versions are overwhelmingly African American in their immediate origin. Such a huge number of African, African American, and African Caribbean versions has been collected that William Bascom conducted research suggesting that the American tale is not a descendent of AT 303 but a tale type in its own right (1992: 155–200). Bascom noted the similarities between the African American versions and the fourth episode of AT 315, *The Cannibal Sister*; hence, I have put both numbers at the beginning of this note to designate this tale, although it seems that the time has come to designate the North American version with a subtype number of its own.

Bascom attempted to demonstrate an African origin for this tale. Although many were persuaded, Goldberg (1998) has since enumerated a number of closely related Asian and Eastern European texts to challenge Bascom's conclusions. Regardless of its ultimate origins, however, the North American tradition represented by stories 181 and 182 in this collection merits recognition as an established type. Of the thirty-one North American versions analyzed by Halpert and Widdowson (1996), only two appear in conjunction with other types (and neither of these appears in conjunction with either AT 303 or AT 315). Nineteen of the thirty-one texts were told by African Americans, including four narrators each from Massachusetts, North Carolina, and South Carolina; two from Alabama; and one each from Georgia, Michigan, New Jersey, Tennessee, and the District of Columbia.

Popular as the tale is among African Americans, it possesses significant currency among European American communities, especially in the South: Halpert and Widdowson (1996: no. 14) identify seven such tales, three from Kentucky, two from Texas, and one each from Missouri (in French), North Carolina, and Tennessee. Finally, there are four native American texts, one (Creek) from the southeast of the continent, and three from the Northwest coastal cultures of Washington (Skagit and Skykomish) and British Columbia (Thompson River).

The best general introduction to the English-language tradition of this tale is by Halpert and Widdowson (1996: no. 14). In addition to the sources listed by Halpert and supplemented by Goldberg, add three Louisiana texts (Ancelet 1994: no. 19; and Lindahl, Owens, and Harvison 1997: nos. 56, 210), one from Florida (Reaver 1987: no. 81), and two African American versions collected in the South by Hurston from a Georgia-born and a Caribbean-born narrator (Hurston 2001: 204–5).

182. *Gaillum, Singo, et Moliseau* [AFC 2003/001]. AT 303, *The Twins or Blood Brothers*; AT 315A, *The Cannibal Sister*. See Lindahl, Owens, and Harvison (1997: no. 210) for another performance of this tale by the same teller. See also the notes for story 181 in this book.

183. *Show Me Your Paw* [AFC 2003/001]. AT 123, *The Wolf and the Kids*. See the notes for story 78 in this book.

184. *Skullbone* [AFC 2003/001]. B210.2, "Talking animal or object refuses to talk on demand." This tale enjoys great popularity in the African American South. Thompson's *Motif-Index* mentions references only for the United States; Baughman's U.S. index mentions five African American texts and one European American tale from Arkansas (Randolph 1958: 3–5, 179–80). In the past four decades, numerous additional African American examples have surfaced (Dorson 1967: nos. 49–52; Dance 1978: no. 150; Fauset 1927: 277, 536–37; Hurston 1935: 219–20; Lindahl 1982; Lindahl, Owens, and Harvison 1997: nos. 61, 208; Percy 1941: 294–96). A tale with a different plot but a similar moral is found in Hurston 2001: 113–14.

Most of the African American folktales in this book have numerous antecedents in both African and European traditions, a fact that has led many to speculate about the ultimate origins of these narratives. Had the process of slavery decimated the narrative stock of Africans Americans, causing them to rely upon European tales in the New World, as Richard Dorson claimed, or did the Africans indeed bring their African tales with them to the United States, as William Bascom maintained? Dundes (1992) has admirably summarized this debate, which has dragged on for decades. Debates over the origins of tales are usually futile, but this particular controversy has sparked some substantial scholarship, including major works by Crowley (1977), Minton (1993), and Minton and Evans (2001).

"Talking Skull Refuses to Talk," as Bascom titled this tale type, is the one tale that Dorson admitted to be African in origin. In a thorough study of antecedents, Bascom (1992: 17–39) identified twenty-four African versions, eighteen American versions (the great majority of which were African American), and none from Europe.

185. *La mata de higo / The Fig Tree* [AFS 3533A4; available at http://memory.loc.gov/ammem/ flwpahtml/flwpabibaudiindex.html and search by title]. AT 720, *The Juniper Tree*. This tale, often judged inappropriately gruesome by parents and educators, has nevertheless maintained great popularity among children. Children often laugh at the most grotesque episodes, such as a passage in a Louisiana version in which a woman tries to get her dogs to disgorge the flesh of a murdered human (Lindahl, Owens, and Harvison 1997: no. 58). The tale is widespread among English-speakers, African Americans in particular. Baughman identified nineteen English-language versions, half of which were African American, and only one in Spanish. Hansen (1957), however, located four in Puerto Rico.

186. *Señorita Martínez Cucaracha y Señor Ratoncito Pérez / Miss Martínez Cockroach and Mr. Pérez Mouse* [AFS 3530A3; available at http://memory.loc.gov/ammem/flwpahtml/flwpabib audiindex.html and search by title]. AT 2023, *Little Ant Finds a Penny, Buys New Clothes with It, and Sits in Her Doorway*. This tale can be accessed in audio form through the American Folklife Center's American Memory Project. This tale has particularly strong affinities in Spanish-language traditions. Aarne and Thompson identified more versions in Spain than in the rest of Europe combined. In the New World, it has been collected solely in Spanish and found to be especially popular in Puerto Rico and Cuba. Ratoncito Pérez is a stock character in Hispanic children's folktales. In a Texas variant of this tale, Ratoncito Pérez marries an ant instead of a cockroach, but otherwise he succumbs to the same fate in a pot of boiling soup (Pérez 1951: 80–84).

187. *Antonio, cortador de leña / Antonio the Woodcutter* [AFS 3524B2–3535A1; available at http://memory.loc.gov/ammem/flwpahtml/flwpabibaudiindex.html and search by title]. AT 560, *The Magic Ring*. The figure of the grateful animal (B360) is one of the most enduring in European folktale tradition, but the major tales based on this figure appear never to have been common in the English-language oral tradition in the New World. For example, neither Baughman's North American index nor the massive Halpert and Widdowson Newfoundland collection identifies a single English-language version of AT 560 or its close relative AT 554, *The Grateful Animals*, in North America. Yet Mexican and New Mexican versions of AT 560 exist (see Paredes 1970: no. 36 and note). Hansen (1957) found significant Spanish-language variants of both tales in the Caribbean, particularly in Puerto Rico and Cuba, and it is from Cuban (or Cuban American) tradition that Martin Noriega (resident of a Cuban enclave in Florida) almost certainly got this tale.

188. *The Fox, the Rabbit, and the Tarbaby* [AFS 10896A]. AT 175, *The Tarbaby and the Rabbit*, prefaced by AT 15, *The Theft of Butter by Playing Godfather*. K581.2, "Briar patch punishment for rabbit." Rarely reported among African Americans in Canada (Fauset 1931: vii–viii, 45–46), the Tarbaby tale is most widely reported among African Americans in the English- and French-speaking Caribbean (Parsons 1943: nos. 24, 25, cites 25 texts from the Antilles) as well as the Spanish-speaking New World (Espinosa 1930). Nevertheless, the tale has become emblematic of the American South. In 1880, when the Tarbaby tale appeared in the first Uncle Remus book (Harris 1880: no. 4), the tale of Brer Rabbit's narrow escape began its rise toward prominence. Tarbaby's popularity was intensified in 1946 when it was featured in Walt Disney's animated feature film *Song of the South*. The transformation of an old-time African American

tale into a major popular culture phenomenon deeply affected many narrators, including Creole storyteller Enola Matthews (Lindahl, Owens, and Harvison 1997: 335), and moved them to return to storytelling.

Curiously, Dorson's exhaustive collecting of African American tales yielded only two versions of the Tarbaby tale, one from Michigan and one from Arkansas (Dorson 1967: no. 3). Parsons published three South Carolina versions (1923: nos. 13–15); Lindahl, Owens, and Harvison printed four Louisiana versions (1 Creole, 1 African American, and 2 Cajun; 1997: nos. 33, 49, 190, 200). Other published versions include African American texts collected by Burrison 1991: 227–28; Fauset 1927: 228–31; Charles Jones 1925: no. 4; and Reaver 1987: no. 6; as well as a Cherokee text collected by Mooney (1900: no. 21). The great proportion of Gulf Coast and Sea Islands versions among these texts argues for the Caribbean, rather than the United States, as the principal home of the Tarbaby tale. Significant African versions have been collected and studied (Baer 1980: 29–32).

In *Negro Folktales in Michigan* (1956b: 56–57, 85–86, 139–42, 165), Dorson published four of E.L. Smith's stories, including a slightly different transcription of the Tarbaby tale. The present collection includes two other E.L. Smith tales (195, 196) and one from his wife, Leozie (128).

189. *The Tarbaby* [AFS 17612]. AT 175, *The Tarbaby and the Rabbit*. Cora Jackson's radical ending, in which Brer Rabbit meets a rare defeat, is not unique in folk tradition. In a worldwide study of 152 variants of the Tarbaby tale, Aurelio Espinosa showed that European and Asian versions end in the trickster's death about 50 percent of the time, in contrast to the 19 percent of African tales and the 3 percent of African American tales that have such an ending (Espinosa 1930, summarized in Perdue 1969). One possible conclusion from this data is that European and Asian versions emphasize the negative aspects and motives of the trickster, in contrast to the African American tales, in which Brer Rabbit tends to be regarded as the underdog hero embodying the aspirations of the slaves and sharecroppers who relished his stories. As Michèle Simonsen (2002: 1009) has said about another trickster tale, the protagonist is treated differently when he is a "trickster by vocation" rather than a "trickster in self-defense." When Brer Rabbit appears to be besting his equals rather than outsmarting his oppressors, he is treated unsympathetically and sometimes loses in the end. For another instance of a Tarbaby tale ending in the rabbit's defeat, see Ben Guiné's Lousiana Creole version (Lindahl, Owens, and Harvison 1997: no. 33); the narrator ends his tale, "It was high time to catch Lapin [i.e., "Rabbit"], you understand? It was past time." For other versions of the Tarbaby tale, see story 188 in this book and accompanying notes.

190. *Jack and the Beanstalk* [AFS 3380A3; audio available at http://memory.loc.gov/ammem/flwpahtml/flwpabibaudiindex.html and search by title]. This is obviously not the same tale known to millions of readers of storybooks. The present performance begins much as the famous fairy tale does, with the hero ascending into the clouds by climbing a giant beanstalk. The title was probably supplied by the collectors on the basis of this similarity. Once in the clouds, however, this story sets out on a path that causes it to diverge remarkably from fairy tale to enter the realm of jokes and tall tales. The closing episode belongs to AT 1882, *The Man Who Fell Out of a Balloon*; also motif X1731.2.1, "Man falls and is buried in earth (rocks). Goes for spade and digs himself out." Leonard Roberts collected two very different Kentucky versions (1955: 56, 78) of this motif. Baughman finds an African American version in Florida and two European American versions in New York. Aarne and Thompson report Old World versions from France, Germany, the Low Countries, Hungary, and Russia, but none from Spain or from the Caribbean.

191. *Little Nippy* [AFS 19717]. AT 327, *The Children and the Ogre*; combined with AT 328, *The Boy Steals the Giant's Treasure*; and incorporating AT 1119, *The Ogre Kills His Own Children*.

Motif G512.3.2.1, "Ogre's wife (daughter) burned in his own oven." This brilliantly told tale belongs to a constellation of stories told primarily in the Appalachians. Given the popularity of tales featuring Jack in this region, it is of some interest to note that the tales belonging to this type give the hero a different name. Leonard Roberts collected two eastern Kentucky parallels under the titles "Nippy" (1955: no. 10) and "Nippy and the Yankee Doodle" (1969: no. 19); both closely resemble Lee Wallin's "Little Nippy." Ethel Birchfield's CD performance of "Granster and Nippy"—recorded in Roan Mountain, Tennessee in 1983 (Yates 2002a: track 24)—also runs parallel to Wallin's. Other Appalachian versions feature a female protagonist, who is given a similarly unique name: Muncimeg (Roberts 1974: no. 111), for example, or Mutsmag (Chase 1948: no. 4). Halpert and Widdowson (1996: nos. 17–18) have found two Newfoundland texts of the female version of this tale, which they link to similar tales known in Scotland and Ireland. The female protagonist, relatively rare in worldwide tradition, is otherwise reported only in Norway and Hungary (cf. Dégh 1989: 293; Dégh 1995: no. 2). For a parallel tale in this collection and further references, see story 77 in this book and its note.

192. *The Old Woman's Vision* [AFS 11412B]. M300, "Prophecies"; M301.2, "Old woman as prophet." In the late nineteenth century, the great ethnographer James Mooney recorded several Cherokee traditions regarding the coming of the white man (Mooney 1995: 350–51), but among them there is no tale closely parallel to this, nor have I found it among recent collections (Duncan 1998). Yet the basic subject is common enough in Native American narration. See, for example, the Interior Salish tale concerning a chief's wife who emerged from a four-day trance to prophesy the coming of the Europeans and their technology, specifically trains and airplanes (Hanna and Henry 1995: 123; see also Clark 1953: 204–5). In the story presented in this book, the old woman is slumped over as if in a dream or trance just before she rises to make her prophecy; if I am correct in my reading, then motif D1812.3.3 also applies, "Future revealed in dream."

193. *The Blackfish* [AFS 10090]. Cf. A2101, "Fish made from wood." D435.1, "Image comes to life"; K922, "Artificial whale made as stratagem." For the last of these three motifs, Thompson provides sixteen references, all Northwest native cultures (Thompson 1929: no. 33 and note 101), but from the Skagit culture there is a significant group of tales in which a seal, rather than a fish, appears (Hilbert 1985: 73–85). Other applicable motifs include D170, "Transformation: man to fish" (although the blackfish, or killer whale, is technically speaking a mammal); D2121, "Magic journey"; A2720, "Plant characteristics as punishment"; E422.1.11.5.1, "Ineradicable bloodstain after bloody tragedy." The intense currents of Deception Pass have been the subject of many tales by Native American cultures in the region, including a Samish narrative that features a sea maiden who guides boats safely through the pass (Clark 1953: 199–201).

194. *How the Terrapin Got Scars on His Shell* [AFS 19270]. A2312.1.1, "Origin of cracks in tortoise's shell"; S168, "Mutilation: Tearing off ears." George Griffith's tale possesses a close parallel in an Eastern Cherokee narrative collected by Mooney (1900: no. 31). Mooney cited parallel texts among the Western Cherokee, a group that lived much closer to the Kiowa lands where Griffith spent much of his life, and also from the Cheyenne and Omaha cultures.

195. *Romey Howard: Freedom in the Grave* [AFS 10896A]. The story in the headnote is taken from the same tape. Among the folk histories of slavery, one of the first and best compilations is Botkin's *Lay My Burden Down* (1945), based on Library of Congress recordings; many of these recordings are painstakingly transcribed in Bailey, Maynor, and Cukor-Avila 1991. Dorson (1956a: 85, 217) prints a different text of this tale and refers to two other accounts in which slaves used their arts and trickery to evade the wrath of the patterolls. For other narratives by E.L. Smith, see stories 188 and 196 in this book.

196. *Romey Howard: Fresh Meat Tonight* [AFS 10896A]. See the note to story 195 in this book. Dorson (1956b: 85–86) prints a significantly different version of this same story.

197. *Remembering Slavery* [AFS 5496B-5497A]. Smalley's entire interview is found on AFS 5496A-5498B. Bailey, Maynor, and Cukor-Avila (1991: 61–78) transcribe most of Faulk's lengthy interview with Smalley, but for unexplained reasons they do not transcribe 5497A or 5497B, the source of the Indian narrative. Mrs. Smalley's opening description of slaves gathering around a tub and praying into it to mute their voices and evade the master's wrath is one of the most frequently reported memories among ex-slaves. Rawick (1972: 39–45) studies the custom; Minton and Evans (2001: 94) illustrate its pervasiveness by locating eleven examples in the one Virginia ex-slave narrative collection alone (Perdue, Barden, and Philips 1976).

The ex-slave narratives have been so frequently listened to and studied that the American Folklife Center has arranged them together as a set for ease in access and listening (AFS 14415–14418).

198. *The Sisters and the Renegades* [AFC 2003/001]. Lee Winniford's brother James's telling of the same tale appears in Winniford 1998: 122–23. The same two pages are the sources for the quotations by Lee Winniford that appear in the headnote.

199. *Great-aunt Becky's Beau* [AFC 2003/001]. Winniford retells a version of this tale in 1998: 118–19. The quotations from the headnote come from the same book (1998: 117–18).

200. *Dream No More* [AFS 15561–15563]. I am not certain that Dwight Diller is the person who recorded this tale; the information at my disposal identifies the tapes as having been recorded by Dwight Diller and Carl Fleischhauer. K66(a), "Dream contest between Indian and white man." The punchline—"Dream no more," "Don't have any more dreams," "Let's not dream anymore," and the like—occurs in many versions of the tale, be they told as true stories or jokes. Four versions are reported from New York State alone, with three contributed by Harold Thompson (1940: 177–78). In addition to the five texts reported by Baughman, Ancelet provides a Cajun example (1994: no. 47). A similar anecdote, centering on a dream contest between a black slave and a white master, motif K66(b), is reported from Texas. Maggie Hammons Parker's narrative is transcribed and analyzed by Carl Fleischhauer (Jabbour and Fleischhauer 1998: 8–9). The text in this book is adapted from the Fleischhauer transcription. See also story 122 in this book, told by Maggie's brother Burl, and its note.

201. *She Saved the Children*. The quotation in the headnote is from Siegel 2001: 15. Mary Eva Baker recorded many other local legends and historical traditions, principally from the area immediately surrounding Springfield. None of these recently accessioned tales has yet received a number.

202. *The One-Legged Indian* [AFS 2270A]. Dominick Gallagher, teller of this tale, also recorded a number of sea songs and ballads for Alan Lomax.

203. *Panther Bill* [AFS 11419A]. Tales of eluding a predator by throwing behind meat to divert it are widespread in the United States; Dorson (1949) retells a version in which the pursued man throws fish behind; in Virginia (Barden 1991: no. 6), Kentucky (Roberts 1955: no. 88), and Florida and Georgia variants (Burrison 1991: 342, 377), the human uses meat rather than fish to divert a panther. Perhaps more common than those tales in which food stalls the animal are those in which girls or women leave pieces of their clothing behind them. The clothes tale was told as a true account in the Gentry-Long family: Nora, Emily, and Maggie Gentry (aunts of Maud Long, narrator of stories 13–23 herein), pursued by a panther, managed to outrun it by discarding clothes that the beast stopped to sniff; it followed them all the way to their uncle's house, where Uncle Doc shot it and "the girls dropped exhausted on the porch" (Betty Smith 1997: 38). Lee Winniford, teller of stories 198 and 199 in this book, has published a version of this tale from her own family tradition (Winniford 1998: 185–86). The motif is given a cinematic treatment in the film *Songcatcher* (Greenwald 2000). See also Barden 1991: no. 6; Burrison 1991: 342, 377; and for two more distantly related texts, Randolph 1955: 11–13, 139–40.

204. *Trying to Mix Liquor and Laughs* [AFS 11426A].

205. *The Biggest Bear That's Ever Been Killed* [AFS 11426A]. The definition of "bear tale" [AFS 11423A] was recorded by Hall from Granville Calhoun in August 1953.

206. *Trials of a Dog Driver* [AFS 6336, 6338]. The Dr. Romig to whom the narrator refers arrived Alaska in 1896 and practiced medicine primarily among the Yupik people inhabiting the territory around the Kuskokwim River, in southwestern Alaska. The book *Dog-Team Doctor* was actually authored by Eva Anderson (1940) one year before the interview from which this recording was taken.

207. *I'm Still Here: Healing at Home* [AFC 2003/001]. Vories Moreau (1925–2002) was best known in his native Basile as a great participant in the annual Cajun country Mardi Gras, and several studies of his role have appeared (Lindahl and Ware 1997; Lindahl 1998; Lindahl 2003); one of those studies (Lindahl 1996) devotes considerable attention to his storytelling. Vories's stories about the customs and rituals surrounding healing are typical demonstrations of his verbal powers as well as illustrations of *traitement* ("treatment"), a complex of supernatural healing practices rooted in folk Catholicism. Early studies of *traitement* tended to be superficial (e.g., Brandon 1964); the best work (David 2000; Saylors 1993) is recent and yet to be published in easily accessible form. For a cognate to the tale of the *traiteur* who stopped the bleeding of a headless chicken, see Ancelet 1994: no. 120; the tale is told by the mother of Barry Ancelet, narrator of story 182 in this book, and centers on the trickster activities of Barry's grandfather, Valery Mayer.

208. *I'm a Man Too: Fights Every Night* [AFC 2003/001]. Fight stories form an integral part of the narrative repertoire of older Cajuns. Ancelet (1994: nos. 109–13) prints a number of fight stories, and reports the conviction of narrator Stanislaus Faul that such stories are no longer as vivid as they once were: "You should have heard the old people talk of fights. . . . Now, it's no longer the same. This is true. People are getting along better and they're not as wild as they used to be" (Ancelet 1994: no. 109). In this narrative "Beouf" is a pseudonym.

Dust Bowl Tales. The quoted descriptions are from Worster (1979: 22–24, 38).

209. *Dust Bowl Refugees* [3420B-3421B3422A]. The quotation from *Bound for Glory* is Guthrie 1943: 179; Joe Klein's quotation comes from *Woody Guthrie: A Life* (Klein 1980: 153). Parts of Woody's performance can be heard on the cuts "California Blues" and "Dust Bowl Refugees" on a commercial sound recording made of the Guthrie-Lomax sessions (Guthrie 1988).

210. *The Man on the Road* [AFS 3418B-19A].

211. *Indians, Locusts, Floods, and Dust: An Okie Family Saga* [AFS 4119B, 4120B, 4119B–4120A; audio available at http://memory.loc.gov/ammem/afctshtml/toddbibperfindex.html and search by narrator's name]. Evidently, much of what Mrs. Robertson had to tell her interviewers was not recorded; in addition, the interviewer jumps from point to point, continually redirecting the flow of Mrs. Robertson's story. For these reasons, I have broken Mrs. Robertson's account into three sections and added background material that will, I hope, make it easier to follow.

Folktales in the Making: The September 11 Project. The Pearl Harbor project referred to in the notes can be found online through the American Folklife Center's Web site: http://www.loc.gov/folklife/pearlharbor/. Ann Hoog's narrative on September 11 in the American Folklife Center was recorded by Carl Lindahl in Washington, D.C., on July 12, 2002.

212. *September 11 in Iowa City, Iowa* [AFC 2001/015].

213. *September 11 in Red Hook, Brooklyn* [AFC 2001/015].

214. *Heaven in the Middle of Hell* [AFC 2001/015].

215. *Christian Regenhard* [AFC 2001/015].

BIBLIOGRAPHY

Aarne, Antti, and Stith Thompson. *The Types of the Folktale: A Classification and Bibliography.* 3d ed. Folklore Fellows Communications 184. Helsinki: Suomalainen Tiedeakatemia, 1961.

Abrahams, Roger D. *Deep Down in the Jungle: Negro Narrative from the Streets of Philadelphia.* 2d ed. Chicago: Aldine, 1970.

————, ed. *Afro-American Folktales: Stories from the Black Traditions in the New World.* New York: Pantheon, 1985.

Adams, Edward C.L. *Tales of the Congaree.* Ed. with an introduction by Robert G. O'Meally. Chapel Hill: University of North Carolina Press, 1987.

Adams, James Taylor. *Grandpap Told Me Tales: Memories of an Appalachian Childhood.* Big Stone Gap, VA: Fletcher Dean, 1993.

Addy, Sidney O., ed. *Household Tales with Other Traditional Remains.* London: David Nutt, 1895.

Aiken, Riley. "A Packload of Mexican Tales." In *Puro Mexicano*, ed. J. Frank Dobie. Publications of the Texas Folklore Society 12. Austin: Texas Folklore Society, 1935.

Almqvist, Bo, Séamas Ó Catháin, and Pádraig Ó Héalai, eds. *Fiannaíocht: Essays on the Fenian Tradition of Ireland and Scotland.* Dublin: An Cumann le Béaloideas Éireann/Folklore of Ireland Society, 1987.

Ancelet, Barry Jean, ed. *Cajun and Creole Folktales: The French Oral Tradition of South Louisiana.* World Folktale Library 1. New York: Garland, 1994.

Ancelet, Barry Jean, Jay Edwards, and Glen Pitre. *Cajun Country.* Jackson: University Press of Mississippi, 1991.

Anderson, Eva. *Dog-Team Doctor: The Story of Dr. Romig.* Caldwell, ID: Caxton, 1940.

Anderson, Gillian B. "Putting the Experience of the World at the Nation's Command: Music at the Library of Congress, 1800–1917." *Journal of the American Musicological Society* 42: 1 (1989): 108–49.

Baer, Florence C. *Sources and Analogues of the Uncle Remus Tales.* Folklore Fellows Communications 228. Helsinki: Suomalainen Tiedeakatemia, 1980.

Bailey, Guy, Natalie Maynor, and Patricia Cukor-Avila. *The Emergence of Black English.* Amsterdam and Philadelphia: John Benjamins, 1991.

Baker, Ronald L., ed. *Hoosier Folk Legends.* Bloomington: Indiana University Press, 1982.

————, ed. *Jokelore: Humorous Folktales from Indiana.* Bloomington: Indiana University Press, 1986.

Barden, Thomas E., ed. *Virginia Folk Legends.* Charlottesville and London: University of Virginia Press, 1991.

Barret, Elizabeth, director. *Fixin' to Tell about Jack.* 28 min. videocassette. Whitesburg, KY: Appalshop, 1975.

Bartis, Peter Thomas. "A History of the Archive of Folk Song at the Library of Congress: The First Fifty Years." Ph.D. diss., University of Pennsylvania, 1982.

Bascom, William. *African Folktales in the New World.* Bloomington and Indianapolis: Indiana University Press, 1992.

Baughman, Ernest W. *Type and Motif-Index of the Folktales of England and North America.* Indiana University Folklore Series 20. The Hague: Mouton, 1966.

Beardsley, Richard K., and Rosalie Hankey. "The Vanishing Hitchhiker." *California Folklore Quarterly* 1 (1942): 303–35.

———. "A History of the Vanishing Hitchhiker." *California Folklore Quarterly* 2 (1943): 13–26.

Beck, Earl Clifton, ed. *Songs of the Michigan Lumberjacks.* Ann Arbor: University of Michigan Press, 1942.

———. *They Knew Paul Bunyan.* Ann Arbor: University of Michigan Press, 1956.

———, ed. *Songs of the Michigan Lumberjacks.* LP record AAFS L56. Washington, D.C.: Library of Congress, 1960.

Beckham, Stephen Dow. *Tall Tales from Rogue River: The Yarns of Hathaway Jones.* Bloomington: Indiana University Press, 1974.

Beckwith, Martha W., ed. "Jamaican Anansi Stories." *Memoirs of the American Folklore Society* 17 (1924).

Bennett, Gillian. "The Vanishing Hitchhiker at Fifty-Five." *Western Folklore* 57 (1998): 1–17.

Black History Museum Committee, eds. *Sterling Brown: A UMUM Tribute.* Philadelphia: Black History Museum UMUM, 1976.

Botkin, Benjamin A., ed. *A Treasury of American Folklore: Stories, Ballads, and Traditions of the People.* New York: Crown, 1944.

———. *Lay My Burden Down: A Folk History of Slavery.* Chicago: University of Chicago Press, 1945.

———. *A Treasury of Southern Folklore: Stories, Ballads, Traditions, and Folkways of the People of the South.* New York: Bonanza Books, 1949.

———. *A Treasury of American Anecdotes.* New York: Random House, 1959.

Bourke, Angela. *The Burning of Bridget Cleary.* New York: Penguin, 1999.

Boyd, Valerie. *Wrapped in Rainbows: The Life of Zora Neale Hurston.* New York: Scribner, 2002.

Brady, Erika. *A Spiral Way: How the Phonograph Changed Ethnography.* Jackson: University Press of Mississippi, 1999.

Brandon, Elizabeth. " 'Traiteurs' or Folk Doctors in Southwest Louisiana." In *Buying the Wind: Regional Folklore in the United States,* ed. Richard M. Dorson, pp. 261–66. Chicago: University of Chicago Press, 1964.

Brewer, J. Mason. "John Tales." In *Mexican Border Ballads and Other Lore,* ed. Mody C. Boatright, pp. 81–104. Publications of the Texas Folklore Society 21. Dallas: Southern Methodists University Press, 1946.

———. *The Word on the Brazos: Negro Preacher Tales from the Brazos Bottoms of Texas.* Austin: University of Texas Press, 1953.

———. *Dog Ghosts and Other Texas Negro Folktales.* Austin: University of Texas Press, 1958.

Bronson, Bertrand H., ed. *Child Ballads Traditional in the United States (I) from the Archive of Folk Song.* LP record. AAFS L57. Washington, D.C.: Library of Congress, [1960].

Brown, Mary Ellen, ed. "Issues in Collaboration and Representation." Special double issue of the *Journal of Folklore Research* 37:2/3 (2000).

Brown, Sterling A. *The Collected Poems of Sterling A. Brown.* Edited by Michael S. Harper. New York: Harper & Row, 1980.

Browne, Ray B. *"A Night with the Hants" and Other Alabama Folk Experiences.* Bowling Green, OH: Popular, 1977.

Brunvand, Jan H. *The Vanishing Hitchhiker: American Urban Legends and Their Meanings.* New York: W.W. Norton, 1981.

Bucavalas, Tina, Peggy A. Bulger, and Stetson Kennedy. *South Florida Folklife.* Jackson: University Press of Mississippi, 1994.

Burrison, John A., ed. *Storytellers: Folktales and Legends from the South.* Paperback ed. Athens: University Press of Georgia, 1991.

Burton, Thomas G., and Ambrose N. Manning, eds. *A Collection of Folklore by Undergraduate Students of East Tennessee State University.* Institute of Regional Studies, Monograph 3. Johnson City: East Tennessee State University, 1966.

Campa, Arthur L. "Spanish Traditional Tales in the Southwest." *Western Folklore* 6 (1947): 322–34.

Campbell, Marie, ed. *Tales from the Cloud-Walking Country.* Bloomington: Indiana University Press, 1958.

Campbell, Olive, and Cecil Sharp. *English Folk Songs from the Southern Appalachians.* New York: G.P. Putnam, 1917.

Camper, Joyce A. "Sterling Brown: Maker of Community in Academia." *African American Review* 31:3 (1997): 437–43.

Carter, Isabel Gordon. "Mountain White Folk-Lore: Tales from the Southern Blue Ridge." *Journal of American Folklore* 38 (1925): 340–74.

Chambers, Robert. *Popular Rhymes of Scotland.* Edinburgh, 1826.

Chase, Richard, ed. *The Jack Tales: Told by R.M. Ward and His Kindred in the Beech Mountain Section of Western North Carolina and by Other Descendants of Council Harmon (1803–1896) Elsewhere in the Southern Mountains; with Three Tales from Wise County, Virginia. Appendix and Parallels by Herbert Halpert.* Boston: Houghton Mifflin, 1943.

———, ed. *Grandfather Tales.* Boston: Houghton Mifflin, 1948.

———. *Jack and the Three Sillies.* Boston: Houghton Mifflin, 1950.

———, ed. *American Folk Tales and Songs, and Other Examples of English-American Tradition as Preserved in the Appalachian Mountains and Elsewhere in the United States.* New York: New American Library, 1956.

Cheney, Thomas E. *Golden Legacy: A Folk History of J. Golden Kimball.* Layton, UT: Gibbs Smith, 1973.

Clark, Ella E., ed. *Indian Legends of the Pacific Northwest.* Berkeley and Los Angeles: University of California Press, 1953.

Claudel, Calvin. "A Study of Two French Tales from Louisiana." *Southern Folklore Quarterly* 7 (1943): 223–31.

Cleveland Family. *Treasures from the Attic: Ballads and Songs in the Adirondacks.* Brant Lake, NY: Dark Horse Productions, 2002.

Cleveland, Sara. *Ballads and Songs of the Upper Hudson Valley, Sung by Sara Cleveland of Brant Lake, New York.* LP record. Folk-Legacy FSA-33, 1968.

Cochran, Robert. *Vance Randolph: An Ozark Life.* Urbana and Chicago: University of Illinois Press, 1985.

Cox, John Harrington. "Negro Tales from West Virginia." *Journal of American Folklore* 47 (1934): 341–57.

Cox, Marian Roalfe. *Cinderella: Three Hundred and Forty-five Variants of Cinderella, Catskin, and Cap O' Rushes.* PFLS no. 31. London: David Nutt, 1893.

Crowley, Daniel J., ed. *African Folklore in the New World.* New York: Basic Books, 1977.

Cunningham, Keith, ed. *American Indians' Kitchen-Table Stories: Contemporary Conversations with Cherokee, Sioux, Hopi, Osage, Navajo, Zuni, and Members of Other Nations.* Little Rock, AK: August House, 1992.

Dance, Daryl Cumber, ed. *Shuckin' and Jivin': Folklore from Contemporary Black Americans.* Bloomington: Indiana University Press, 1978.

David, Dana Ann. "Parole, pratique et pouvoir: le rôle des traiteurs dans la société cadienne." Ph.D. diss., Lafayette: University of Louisiana, 2000.

Davidson, Levette Jay. " 'Gassy' Thompson—and Others: Stories of Local Characters." *Western Folklore* 5 (1946): 339–49.

Davies, Christie. *Ethnic Humor around the World: A Comparative Analysis.* Bloomington: Indiana University Press, 1990.

Dégh, Linda. *Folktales and Society: Story-Telling in a Hungarian Peasant Community.* 2d ed. Bloomington and Indianapolis: Indiana University Press, 1989.

———, ed. *Hungarian Folktales: The Art of Zsuzsanna Palkó.* World Folktale Library 2. Jackson: University Press of Mississippi, 1995.

Delcambre, Angie C., et al., eds. "Tales of the Supernatural: A Selected List of Recordings Made in the United States and Placed in the Archive of Folk Culture." LC Folk Archive Finding Aid 13. Series ed. Joseph C. Hickerson. Washington, D.C.: Archive of Folk Culture, American Folklife Center, Library of Congress, 1995.

Dobie, Bertha McKee. "From a Texas Household: Mrs. Russell's Stories." In *Texas Folk and Folklore,* ed. Mody C. Boatwright, Wilson M. Hudson, and Allen Maxwell, pp. 67–77. Publications of the Texas Folklore Society, 26. Dallas: Southern Methodist University Press, 1954.

Dobie, J. Frank. "The Traveling Anecdote." *Publications of the Texas Folklore Society* 25 (1953): 5–6.

———. *Coronado's Children: Tales of Lost Mines and Buried Treasure of the Southwest.* 1930. Reprint, Austin: University of Texas Press, 1979.

———. *Tongues of the Monte.* 1935. Reprint, Austin: University of Texas Press, 1980.

———. *Some Part of Myself.* 1964. Reprint, Austin: University of Texas Press, 1980.

Dorson, Richard M. "Comic Indian Anecdotes." *Southern Folklore Quarterly* 10 (1946): 113–28.

———. *Jonathan Draws the Long Bow.* Cambridge, MA: Harvard University Press, 1949.

———. "Negro Witch Stories on Tape." *Midwest Folklore* 2 (1952): 229–41.

———. "King Beast of the Forest Meets Man." *Southern Folklore Quarterly* 17 (1953): 118–28.

———. "The Astonishing Repertoire of James Douglas Suggs, a Michigan Negro Storyteller." *Michigan History* 40 (1956a): 152–66.

———, ed. *Negro Folktales in Michigan.* Cambridge, MA: Harvard University Press, 1956b.

———. "Paul Bunyan in the News, 1939–1941." *Western Folklore* 15 (1956c): 26–39, 179–93, 247–61.

———. "Collecting Folklore in Jonesport, Maine." *Proceedings of the American Philosophical Society* 101 (1957): 270–89.

———. *American Folklore.* Chicago: University of Chicago Press, 1959.

———, ed. *Buying the Wind: Regional Folklore in the United States.* Chicago: University of Chicago Press, 1964.

————, ed. *American Negro Folktales.* Greenwich, CT: Fawcett, 1967.

————. *American Folklore and the Historian.* Chicago: University of Chicago Press, 1971.

————, ed. *Folktales Told around the World.* Chicago: University of Chicago Press, 1975.

Duncan, Barbara R., ed. *Living Stories of the Cherokee.* Chapel Hill: University of North Carolina Press, 1998.

Dundes, Alan, ed. *Cinderella: A Folklore Casebook.* Madison: University of Wisconsin Press, 1988.

————. Foreword to *African Folktales in the New World,* by William Bascom. Bloomington and Indianapolis: Indiana University Press, 1992.

Dunn, Durwood. *Cades Cove: The Life and Death of a Southern Appalachian Community, 1818–1937.* Knoxville: University of Tennessee Press, 1988.

Ellis, Bill. "The Gentry-Long Tradition and the Roots of Revivalism: Maud Gentry Long." In *Jack in Two Worlds,* ed. William Bernard McCarthy. Chapel Hill: University of North Carolina Press, 1994.

Emmons, David M. *The Butte Irish: Class and Ethnicity in an American Mining Town, 1875–1925.* Urbana: University of Illinois Press, 1989.

Emrich, Duncan, ed. *Folklore on the American Land.* Boston: Little, Brown, 1972.

Espinosa, Aurelio M. "New-Mexican Spanish Folk-lore." Part 2. *Journal of American Folklore* 24 (1911): 397–444.

————. "Comparative Notes on New-Mexican and Mexican Spanish Folktales." *Journal of American Folklore* 27 (1914): 211–31.

————, ed. *Cuentos populares españoles, recogidos de la tradición oral de España.* 3 vols. Stanford, CA: Stanford University Press, 1923.

————. "Notes on the Origin and History of the Tar-Baby Story." *Journal of American Folklore* 43 (1930): 129–209.

Faulk, John Henry. *Fear on Trial.* New York: Simon and Schuster, 1964.

Fauset, Arthur Huff. "Negro Folk Tales from the South (Alabama, Mississippi, Louisiana)." *Journal of American Folklore* 40 (1927): 213–303.

————, ed. *Folklore from Nova Scotia.* Memoirs of the American Folklore Society 24. New York: G.E. Stechert, 1931.

Fife, Austin E. "The Legend of the Three Nephites among the Mormons." *Journal of American Folklore* 53 (1940): 1–49.

————. "Popular Legends of the Mormons." *Western Folklore* 9 (1950): 105–25.

————. *Saints of Sage and Saddle.* Bloomington: Indiana University Press, 1956.

Fine, Elizabeth C. *The Folklore Text: From Performance to Print.* Bloomington and Indianapolis: Indiana University Press, 1984.

Fortier, Alcée, ed. *Louisiana Folktales in French Dialect and English Translation.* Memoirs of the American Folklore Society 2. Boston: Houghton Mifflin, 1895.

Gardner, Emelyn Elizabeth, ed. *Folklore from the Schoharie Hills, New York.* Ann Arbor: University of Michigan Press, 1937.

Georges, Robert A., and Michael Owen Jones. *Folkloristics: An Introduction.* Bloomington and Indianapolis: Indiana University Press, 1995.

Gilfillan, Archer B. *Sheep.* Boston: Little, Brown, 1928.

Glassie, Henry. "Three Southern Mountain Jack Tales." *Tennessee Folklore Society Bulletin* 30:3 (1964): 78–94.

————. *Passing the Time in Ballymenone: Culture and History of an Ulster Community.* Philadelphia: University of Pennsylvania Press, 1982. Reprint Bloomington: Indiana University Press, 1995.

Goldberg, Christine. " 'Dogs Rescue Master from Tree Refuge': An African Folktale with World-wide Analogs." *Western Folklore* 57 (1998): 41–61.

Goldstein, Diane. E-mail communication to Carl Lindahl on the subject of her memories of Sara Cleveland, 1999.

Goldstein, Kenneth S. Notes. *Ballads and Songs of the Upper Hudson Valley, Sung by Sara Cleveland of Brant Lake, New York.* LP record. Folk-Legacy FSA-33, 1968.

Goldstein, Kenneth S., and Dan Ben-Amos, eds. *Thrice Told Tales: Folktales from Three Continents.* Lock Haven, PA: published privately by Hammermill, 1970.

Goldstein, Rochelle. Telephone conversation with Carl Lindahl on the subject of Sara Cleveland. February 9, 2003.

Gorsuch, Robert Allan. *Folk Tradition in Kent County, Maryland: A Collection of Folk Literature as Told by the Citizens of Kent County, Maryland.* [Cover Title: *Ghosts in Kent County, Maryland.*] Salisbury, MD: Shore Press, 1973.

Green, Archie, guest editor. "Aunt Molly Jackson Memorial Issue." *Kentucky Folklore Record* 7: 4 (1961): 129–75.

Greenwald, Maggie, director. *Songcatcher.* 109 min. motion picture. Lion's Gate Films, 2000.

Greenway, John, ed. *The Songs and Stories of Aunt Molly Jackson.* LP record. Folkways FH 5457, 1961.

Grimm, Jacob, and Wilhelm Grimm. *The Complete Fairy Tales of the Brothers Grimm.* Trans. by Jack Zipes. New York: Bantam, 1987.

Guthrie, Woody. *Bound for Glory.* New York: E.P. Dutton, 1943.

———. *Woody Guthrie: Library of Congress Recordings.* Collected by Alan Lomax. 3 Lps. Rounder 1041-1043. Cambridge, MA: Rounder Records, 1988; released in CD format, Rounder 1041, 1989.

Hadley, Charles, and Jane Hadley, directors. *Ray and Rosa Hicks: The Last of the Old-Time Storytellers.* 58 min. videocassette. Charles and Jane Hadley, 2000.

Hall, J. Mortimer. [Joseph Fiesler]. *Anecdota Americana.* Second series. "Boston" [New York]: Humphrey Adams, 1927.

Hall, Joseph S. *The Phonetics of Smoky Mountain English. American Speech* Reprints and Monographs 4. Morningside, NY: King's Crown, 1942.

———. *Sayings from Old Smoky.* Asheville, NC: Cataloochee, 1972.

———. *Yarns and Tales from the Great Smokies.* Asheville, NC: Cataloochee, 1978.

Hall, Stephanie. "The American Dialect Society Recordings." Unpublished paper, 1999.

Halpert, Herbert. Typewritten notes to the Halpert Collection (AFS 2735–3153). Manuscript copy, American Folklife Center, Library of Congress, 1939.

———. "The Cante Fable in New Jersey." *Journal of American Folklore* 55 (1942a): 133–43.

———. "Indiana Folktales." *Hoosier Folklore Bulletin* 1 (1942b): 3–34.

———. "Indiana Storyteller." *Hoosier Folklore Bulletin* 1 (1942c): 43–61.

———. "Appendix and Parallels" to *The Jack Tales.* Chase (1943): 183–200.

———. "Mosquitoes on the Runway." *Western Folklore* 50 (1991): 145–61.

———. "Coming into Folklore More Than Fifty Years Ago." *Journal of American Folklore* 105 (1992): 442–57.

Halpert, Herbert, and J.D.A. Widdowson, eds. *Folktales of Newfoundland: The Resilience of the Oral Tradition.* 2 vols. World Folktale Library 4. New York: Garland, 1996.

Hand, Wayland D., Anna Casetta, and Sondra B. Thiederman. *Popular Beliefs and Superstitions: A Compendium of American Folklore from the Ohio Collections of Newbell Niles Puckett.* 3 vols. Boston: G.K. Hall, 1981.

Hanna, Darwin, and Mamie Henry, eds. *Our Tellings: Interior Salish Stories of the Nlha7kápmx People.* Victoria: University of British Columbia Press, 1995.

Hansen, Terrence Leslie. *The Types of the Folktale in Cuba, Puerto Rico, the Dominican Republic, and Spanish South America.* University of California Publications, Folklore Studies 8. Berkeley and Los Angeles: University of California Press, 1957.

Harris, Joel Chandler. *Uncle Remus: His Songs and His Sayings.* Ed. Robert Hemenway. 1880. Reprint, New York: Penguin American Library, 1982.

———. *Nights with Uncle Remus: Myths and Legends of the Old Plantation.* Boston: Houghton Mifflin, 1883.

Hartsfield, Mariella Glenn, ed. *Tall Betty and Dunce Baby: South Georgia Folktales.* Athens and London: University of Georgia Press, 1987.

Hemenway, Robert E. *Zora Neale Hurston: A Literary Biography.* Urbana and Chicago: University of Illinois Press, 1977.

———. "Introduction: Author, Teller, and Hero." In *Uncle Remus: His Songs and Stories,* by Joel Chandler Harris. New York: Penguin, 1982.

Henderson, Stephen. "The Heavy Blues of Sterling Brown: A Study of Craft and Tradition." *Black American Literature Forum* 14 (1980): 32–44.

Henry, Mellinger E., ed. *Songs Sung in the Southern Appalachians.* London: Mitre, 1934.

———, ed. *Folk-Songs from the Southern Highlands.* New York: J.J. Augustin, 1938.

Herskovits, Melville J., and Frances S. Herskovits. *Suriname Folk-Lore.* New York: AMS Press, 1936.

Hicks, John Henry, Mattie Hicks, and Barnabus B. Hicks. *The Hicks Family of Western North Carolina (Watauga River Lines).* Boone, NC: Miner's Printing, 1991.

Hicks, Orville. *Carryin' On: Jack Tales for Children of All Ages.* Audio cassette. Whitesburg, KY: June Appal Recordings, 1990.

———. *Mule Egg Seller and Appalachian Storyteller.* CD. Boone, NC: Orville Hicks, 1998.

Hicks, Ray. *Ray Hicks of Beech Mountain, North Carolina Telling Four Traditional "Jack Tales."* LP record. FTA-14. Sharon, CT: Folk Legacy Records, 1963.

———. *Jack Alive!* Audio cassette and CD. Whitesburg, KY: June Appal Recordings, 1989.

Hicks, Ray, and Luke Borrow. *Jack and the Fire Dragon.* 20 min. videocassette. Appalachian Storyteller Ray Hicks Series. Part 3. Derry, NH: Chip Taylor Communications, 1997.

"High Atmosphere: Ballads and Banjo Tunes from Virginia and North Carolina, Collected by John Cohen in November of 1965." Booklet accompanying the CD *High Atmosphere.* Rounder 0028. Cambridge, MA: Rounder Records, 1995.

Hilbert, Vi. *Haboo: Native American Stories from Puget Sound.* Seattle and London: University of Washington Press, 1985.

Hoff, Joan, and Marian Yeates. *The Cooper's Wife Is Missing: The Trials of Bridget Cleary.* New York: Basic Books, 2000.

Hoffman, Dan C. "Folktales of Paul Bunyan: Themes, Structure, Style, Sources." *Western Folklore* 9 (1950): 302–20.

Hoffmann, Frank. *Analytical Survey of Anglo-American Traditional Erotica.* Bowling Green, OH: Bowling Green University Popular, 1973.

Holzer, Hans. *True Ghost Stories.* Englewood Cliffs, NJ: Prentice Hall, 1983.

Hufford, David J. *The Terror That Comes in the Night: An Experience-Centered Study of Supernatural Assault Traditions.* Philadelphia: University of Pennsylvania Press, 1982.

Hurston, Zora Neale. *Mules and Men.* 1935. Reprint, New York: Harper Collins, 1990.

———. *Dust Tracks on a Road.* 1942. Reprint, New York: Harper Collins, 1991.

————. *Every Tongue Got to Confess: Negro Folk-tales from the Gulf States.* Ed. Carla Kaplan. New York: Harper Collins, 2001.

Hyatt, Harry Middleton. *Hoodoo—Conjuration—Witchcraft—Rootwork: Beliefs Accepted by Many Negroes and White Persons, These Being Orally Recorded among Blacks and Whites.* 5 vols. Washington, D.C.: American University Bookstore, 1970–78.

Isbell, Robert. *The Last Chivaree: The Hicks Family of Beech Mountain.* Chapel Hill: University of North Carolina Press, 1996. Reissued under the title *Ray Hicks: Master Storyteller of the Blue Ridge.*

Jabbour, Alan, and Carl Fleischhauer. Booklet accompanying the CDs *The Hammons Family: The Traditions of a West Virginia Family and Their Friends.* Rounder 1504/05. Washington, DC: Library of Congress, Archive of Folk Culture, 1998.

Jackson, Aunt Molly. *Aunt Molly Jackson: Library of Congress Recordings.* Collected by Alan Lomax. LP recording. Cambridge, MA: Rounder Records, [1972].

Jacobs, Joseph, ed. *English Fairy Tales.* 2d ed. New York: G.B. Putnam's Sons, 1893.

Jones, Charles C., Jr. *Negro Myths from the Georgia Coast Told in the Vernacular.* 1888. Reprint, Columbia, SC: State, 1925.

Jones, Louis C. *Things That Go Bump in the Night.* New York: Hill and Wang, 1959.

Jones, Loyal. *Minstrel of the Appalachians: The Story of Bascom Lamar Lunsford.* 1984. Reprint, Lexington: University Press of Kentucky, 2002.

————, ed. *The Preacher Joke Book.* Little Rock, AK: August House, 1989.

Jones, Loyal, and Billy Edd Wheeler, eds. *Laughter in Appalachia.* Little Rock, AK: August House, 1987.

————. *Curing the Cross-Eyed Mule: Appalachian Mountain Humor.* Little Rock, AK: August House, 1989.

————. *More Laughter in Appalachia.* Little Rock, AK: August House, 1995.

Kennedy, Stetson. *Palmetto Country.* New York: Duell, Sloan, and Pierce, 1942.

————. "A Florida Treasure Hunt." *Folklife Center News* 22:4 (2000): 3–8.

Kinkead, Gwen. "An Overgrown Jack." *The New Yorker,* July 18, 1988, 33–41.

Klein, Joe. *Woody Guthrie: A Life.* New York: Alfred A. Knopf, 1980.

Klipple, May Augusta. "African Folktales with Foreign Analogues." Ph.D. diss., Indiana University, 1938.

Kozma, Luanne Gaykowski. "E.C. Beck: Collector of Michigan Lumberjack Lore." *1991 Festival of Michigan Folklife.* East Lansing: Michigan State University Museum, 1991. 30–34.

Leary, James P. "The Favorite Jokes of Max Trzebiatowski." *Western Folklore* 43 (1984): 1–17.

————, ed. *The Wisconsin Patchwork: A Companion to the Radio Programs Based on the Field Recordings of Helene Stratman-Thomas.* Madison: University of Wisconsin Board of Regents, 1987.

————. *Wisconsin Folklore.* Madison: University of Wisconsin Press, 1998.

————. *So Ole Says to Lena: Folk Humor of the Upper Midwest.* 2d ed. Madison: University of Wisconsin Press, 2001.

Lee, Hector. *The Three Nephites: The Substance and Significance of the Legend in Folklore.* Albuquerque: University of New Mexico Press, 1949.

————. "Anecdotes of J. Golden Kimball." In *Buying the Wind: Regional Folklore in the United States,* ed. Richard M. Dorson. Chicago: University of Chicago Press, 1964a.

————. *J. Golden Kimball Stories Together with Brother Petersen Yarns.* Folk Legacy FTA-25. 1964b, LP record.

Legman, Gershon. *Rationale of the Dirty Joke.* New York: Grove Press, 1968.

Limón, José E. *Dancing with the Devil: Society and Cultural Poetics in Mexican-American South Texas.* Madison: University of Wisconsin Press, 1994.

Lindahl, Carl. "Skallbone, the Old Coon, and the Persistence of Specialized Fantasy." *Western Folklore* 41 (1982): 192–204.

———. "Feindschaft zwischen Tieren und Mensch (AaTh 159B, 285D)." In *Enzyklopädie des Märchens.* Berlin: Walter de Gruyter, 1984.

———. "Gevater Stehen (AaTh 15)." In *Enzyklopädie des Märchens.* Berlin: Walter de Gruyter, 1985.

———. "Who Is Jack? A Study in Isolation." *Fabula* 29 (1988): 373–82.

———. "Jack: The Name, the Tales, the American Traditions." In *Jack in Two Worlds: Contemporary North American Jack Tales and Their Tellers,* ed. William Bernard McCarthy et al., pp. xiii–xxxiv. Chapel Hill: University of North Carolina Press, 1994a.

———. "Jack, My Father, and Uncle Ray: Frank Proffitt, Jr." In *Jack in Two Worlds: Contemporary North American Jack Tales and Their Tellers,* ed. William Bernard McCarthy et al., pp 27–33. Chapel Hill: University of North Carolina Press, 1994b.

———. "The Presence of the Past in the Cajun Country Mardi Gras." *Journal of Folklore Research* 33 (1995): 125–53.

———. "One Family's Mardi Gras: The Moreaus of Basile." *Louisiana Cultural Vistas* 9:3 (1998): 46–53.

———. "Jack Tales." In *Traditional Storytelling Today,* ed. Margaret Read McDonald, pp. 394–97. Chicago: Fitzroy Dearborn, 1999.

———. "Paul Bunyan." In *Enzyklopädie des Märchens.* Berlin: Walter de Gruyter, 2000.

———, ed. *Perspectives on the Jack Tales and Other North American Märchen.* Special Publications of the Folklore Institute, Indiana University, no. 6. Bloomington, IN: Folklore Institute, 2001.

———. "Finding the Field through the Discovery of the Self." In *Working the Field: Accounts from French Louisiana,* eds. Jacques Henry and Sara LeMenestrel, pp. 33–50. Westport, CT: Praeger, 2003.

Lindahl, Carl, Maida Owens, and C. Renée Harvison, ed. *Swapping Stories: Folktales from Lousiana.* Jackson: University Press of Mississippi, 1997.

Lindahl, Carl, and Carolyn Ware. *Cajun Mardi Gras Masks.* Jackson: University Press of Mississippi, 1997.

Lockridge, Norman [Samuel Roth], ed. *Waggish Tales of the Czechs.* [New York:] Candide, 1947.

Lomax, Alan, ed. *Mister Jelly Roll.* New York: Duell, Sloan and Pearce, 1950.

———. "Aunt Molly Jackson: An Appreciation." *Kentucky Folklore Record* 7 (1961): 131–32.

———, collector. *Aunt Molly Jackson.* LP of her songs and stories. Rounder 1002. Cambridge, MA: Rounder Records, 1972.

Lomax, John A. *Cowboy Songs and Other Frontier Ballads.* New York: Sturgis and Walton, 1910.

———. *Adventures of a Ballad Hunter.* New York: Macmillan, 1947.

Lomax, John A., and Alan Lomax. *American Ballads and Folk Songs.* New York: Macmillan, 1934.

———. *Negro Folk Songs as Sung by Leadbelly.* New York: Macmillan, 1941.

Long, Maud. *Jack Tales.* LP records AAFS 47 and 48. Washington, D.C.: Library of Congress, 1955.

Lysaght, Patricia. *The Banshee: The Irish Death Messenger.* Dublin: The Glendale Press, 1986.

MacNeil, Joe Neil, and John Shaw. *Tales until Dawn / Sgeul gu Latha: The World of a Cape Breton Gaelic Story-teller.* Kingston and Montreal: McGill–Queen's University Press, 1987.

Mangione, Jerre. *The Dream and the Deal: The Federal Writers' Project, 1935–1953.* Boston: Little, Brown, 1972.

McCarthy, William Bernard, ed. *Jack in Two Worlds: Contemporary North American Jack Tales and Their Tellers.* Tales edited by William Bernard McCarthy, Cheryl Oxford, and Joseph Daniel Sobol. Chapel Hill: University of North Carolina Press, 1994.

McDermitt, Barbara Rice Damran. "A Comparison of a Scottish and American Storyteller and Their Märchen Repertoires." Ph.D. diss., University of Edinburgh, 1986.

McGowen, Thomas, ed. "Four Beech Mountain Jack Tales." *North Carolina Folklore Journal* 26 (1978): 51–84.

McNeil, W.K., ed. *Ghost Stories from the American South.* New York: Dell, 1985.

———, ed. *Ozark Mountain Humor: Jokes on Hunting, Religion, Marriage, and Ozark Ways.* Little Rock, AK: August House, 1989.

McNutt, James Charles. "Beyond Regionalism: Texas Folklorists and the Emergence of a Post-regional Identity." Ph.D. diss., University of Texas, Austin, 1982.

Miller, Elaine K., ed. *Mexican Folk Narrative from the Los Angeles Area.* Publications of the American Folklore Society, Memoir Series, no. 56. Austin: University of Texas Press, 1973.

Minton, John. *"Big 'Fraid and Little 'Fraid": An Afro-American Folktale.* Folklore Fellows Communications 253. Helsinki: Suomalainen Tiedeakatemia, 1993.

Minton, John, and David Evans. *"The Coon in the Box": A Global Folktale in African-American Context.* Folklore Fellows Communications 277. Helsinki: Suomalainen Tiedeakatemia, 2001.

Mooney, James. *Myths of the Cherokee.* 1900. Reprint, New York: Dover, 1995.

Mullen, Patrick B. *Listening to Old Voices: Folklore, Life Stories, and the Elderly.* Urbana and Chicago: University of Illinois Press, 1992.

Murphy, Gerard, ed. *Duanaire Finn.* Part 3. Dublin: Irish Texts Society, 1953.

Nicolaisen, W.F.H. "The Teller and the Tale: Storytelling on Beech Mountain." In *Jack in Two Worlds: Contemporary North American Jack Tales and Their Tellers,* ed. William Bernard McCarthy et al., pp. 123–49. Chapel Hill: University of North Carolina Press, 1994.

Niles, John D. *Homo Narrans: The Poetics and Anthropology of Oral Literature.* Philadelphia: University of Pennsylvania Press, 2000.

North Carolina Folklore Journal. Jack Tales Issue. 26:2 (1978).

Ó hÓgáin, Dáithí. *Fionn Mac Cumhaill: Images of the Gaelic Hero.* Dublin: Gill and Mcmillan, 1988.

Ó Muirithe, Diarmaid, and Deirdre Nuttall. *Folklore of County Wexford.* Dublin: Four Courts, 1999.

Opie, Iona, and Peter Opie, eds. *The Classic Fairy Tales.* Oxford: Oxford University Press, 1974.

Oster, Harry. "Negro Humor: John and Old Marster." *Journal of the Folklore Institute* 5 (1968): 42–57.

O'Sullivan, Sean, ed. *Folktales of Ireland.* Chicago: University of Chicago Press, 1966.

Oxford, Cheryl. " 'They Call Him Lucky Jack': Three Performance-Centered Case Studies of Storytelling in Watauga County, North Carolina." Ph.D. diss., Northwestern University, 1987.

———. "The Storyteller as Craftsman: Stanley Hicks Telling 'Jack and the Bull.' " *North Carolina Folklore Journal* 36 (1989): 72–120.

———. "The Storyteller as Curator: Marshall Ward." In *Jack in Two Worlds: Contemporary North American Jack Tales and Their Tellers,* ed. William Bernard McCarthy et al., pp. 56–69. North Carolina: University of North Carolina Press, 1994.

Painter, Jacqueline Burgin. *The Season of Dorland-Bell: History of an Appalachian Mission School.* Asheville, NC: Biltmore, 1987.

———. *An Appalachian Medley: Hot Springs and the Gentry Family.* Vol. 1. Asheville, NC: Biltmore, 1994.

Paredes, Américo, ed. *Folktales of Mexico.* Chicago: University of Chicago Press, 1970.

Parler, Mary Celestia. "The Forty-Mile Jumper." *Journal of American Folklore* 64 (1951): 422–23.

Parsons, Elsie Clews, ed. *Folk-lore of the Sea Islands, South Carolina.* Memoirs of the American Folklore Society 16. Cambridge, MA: American Folklore Society, 1923.

———, ed. *Folklore of the Antilles, French and English.* Part 3. Memoirs of the American Folklore Society 26. Cambridge, MA: American Folklore Society, 1943.

Perdue, Charles L., Jr. "I Swear to God It's the Truth If I Ever Told It." *Keystone Folklore Quarterly* 14 (1969): 1–54.

———. *Outwitting the Devil: Jack Tales from Wise County, Virginia.* Santa Fe, NM: Ancient City, 1987.

———. "1939 Field Trip to the Southern States: Interview with Herbert Halpert." Transcribed by Nancy J. Martin-Perdue. *Folklore and Folklife in Virginia* 4 (1988): 19–30.

———. "From Traditional Songster to 'American Legend.'" Unpublished paper presented at the annual meeting of the American Folklore Society, Pittsburgh, 1996.

Perdue, Charles L., Jr., Thomas E. Barden, and Robert K. Philips. *Weevils in the Wheat: Interviews with Virginia Ex-Slaves.* Bloomington: Indiana University Press, 1976. Reprint Charlottesville: University Press of Virginia, 1992.

Pérez, Soledad. "Mexican Folklore from Austin, Texas." In *The Healer of Los Olmos,* ed. Mody C. Boatright. Publications of the Texas Folklore Society 24. Dallas: Southern Methodist University Press, 1951.

Porterfield, Nolan. *Last Cavalier: The Life and Times of John A. Lomax.* Urbana and Chicago: University of Illinois Press, 1996.

Preston, Dennis. "'Ritin' Fowklower Daun 'Rong: Folklorists' Failures in Phonology." *Journal of American Folklore* 95 (1982): 304–26.

———. "Mowr Bayud Spellin': A Reply to Fine." *Journal of American Folklore* 96 (1983): 330–39.

Rael, Juan B., ed. "Cuentos españoles de Colorado y de Nuevo Méjico. Part II." *Journal of American Folklore* 55 (1942): 1–93.

Randolph, Vance, ed. *We Always Lie to Strangers: Tall Tales from the Ozarks.* New York: Columbia University Press, 1951.

———, ed. *Who Blowed Up the Church House? and Other Ozark Folktales.* New York: Columbia University Press, 1952.

———, ed. *The Devil's Pretty Daughter and Other Ozark Folktales.* New York: Columbia University Press, 1955.

———, ed. *The Talking Turtle and Other Ozark Folktales.* New York: Columbia University Press, 1958.

———, ed. *Sticks in the Knapsack and Other Ozark Folktales.* New York: Columbia University Press, 1959.

———, ed. *Hot Springs and Hell and Other Folk Jests and Anecdotes from the Ozarks.* Hatboro, PA: Folklore Associates, 1965.

———, ed. *Pissing in the Snow and Other Ozark Folktales.* Urbana and Chicago: University of Illinois Press, 1976.

Rawick, George P. *From Sundown to Sunup: The Making of the Black Community.* The American Slave: A Composite Autobiography, series 1, vol. 1. Westport, CT: Greenwood, 1972.

Reaver, J. Russell, ed. *Florida Folktales.* Gainesville: University of Florida Press, 1987.

Rickels, Patricia. "Some Accounts of Witch Riding." *Louisiana Folklore Miscellany* 2:1 (1961): 1–17.

Robe, Stanley L. *Index of Mexican Folktales: Including Narrative Texts from Mexico, Central America, and the Hispanic United States.* Berkeley and Los Angeles: University of California Press, 1973.

Roberts, Leonard W. *South from Hell-fer-Sartin.* Lexington: University Press of Kentucky, 1955.

———. "Curious Legend of the Kentucky Mountains." *Western Folklore* 16 (1957): 48–51.

———. *Old Greasybeard: Tales from the Cumberland Gap.* Hatville, PA: Folklore Associates, 1969.

———. *Sang Branch Settlers: Folksongs and Tales of a Kentucky Mountain Family.* Memoirs of the American Folklore Society 61. Austin: University of Texas Press, 1974.

Roberts, Warren E. *The Tale of the Kind and Unkind Girls: Aa-Th 480 and Related Tales.* Fabula, Supplemental Series B, vol. 1. Berlin: Walter de Gruyter, 1958.

Robertson, Stanley. "Stanley Robertson." Nine tales with annotations by Barbara McDermitt. *Tocher* 40 (1986): 170–224.

Romalis, Shelly. *Pistol Packin' Mama: Aunt Molly Jackson and the Politics of Folksong.* Urbana and Chicago: University of Illinois Press, 1999.

Rooth, Anna Birgitta. *The Cinderella Cycle.* Lund: C.W.K. Gleerup, 1951.

Saylors, Karen. "Cajun Traitement." M.A. thesis, University of Houston, 1993.

Seeger, Charles. *Versions and Variants of Barbara Allen.* LP phonograph record AAFS L54. Washington, D.C.: Library of Congress, [1964].

Shackelford, Laurel, and Bill Weinberg, eds. *Our Appalachia: An Oral History.* New York: Hill and Wang, 1977.

Shannon, George. *A Knock at the Door.* The Oryx Multicultural Folktale Series. Pheonix, AZ: The Oryx Press, 1992.

Shields, A. Randolph. *The Cades Cove Story.* 2d ed. Gatlinburg, TN: Great Smoky Mountains Natural History Association, 1981.

Siegel, Nancy-Jean Ballard. "Field Days in the Flanders Collection." *Folklife Center News* 23:2 (2001): 13–16.

Simonsen, Michèle. "Unibos [One Ox]." In *Medieval Folklore: An Encyclopedia of Myths, Legends, Tales, Beliefs, and Customs*, ed. Carl Lindahl, John McNamara, and John Lindow, pp. 1008–9. Santa Barbara, CA: ABC-Clio, 2002.

Smith, Betty N. *Jane Hicks Gentry: A Singer among Singers.* Lexington: University of Kentucky Press, 1997.

Smith, Jimmy Neil. *Homespun: Tales from America's Favorite Storytellers.* New York: Avon Books, 1988.

———. *Why the Possum's Tail Is Bare and Other Classic Southern Stories.* New York: Avon Books, 1993.

Smyth, Willie. "The Barnicle-Cadle Recordings: A Preliminary Checklist." *Tennessee Folklore Society Bulletin* 52 (1986a): 46–60.

———. " 'Bearing Up': Mary Elizabeth Barnicle and Folklore Recording." *Tennessee Folklore Society Bulletin* 52 (1986b): 34–45.

Sobol, Joseph Daniel. "Jack in the Raw: Ray Hicks." In *Jack in Two Worlds: Contemporary North*

American Jack Tales and Their Tellers, ed. William Bernard McCarthy et al., pp. 3–9. North Carolina: University of North Carolina Press, 1994.

———. *The Storyteller's Journey: An American Revival.* Urbana and Chicago: University of Illinois Press, 1999.

Spencer, Martha Ann [Suggs]. *Suggs Black Backtracks.* New York: Carlton Press Corporation, 1995.

Stitt, J. Michael, and Robert K. Dodge. *A Tale Type and Motif Index of Early U.S. Almanacs.* Westport, CT: Greenwood Press, 1991.

Taft, Michael. "Herbert Halpert: Folklorist-Fieldworker." *Folklife Center New* 23:2 (2001): 20–21.

Taylor, Archer. "A Long-Sought Parallel Comes to Light." *Western Folklore* 16 (1957): 48.

Tedlock, Dennis. "On the Translation of Style in Oral Narrative." *Journal of American Folklore* 84 (1971): 114–33.

Thomas, Lowell. *Tall Stories: The Rise and Triumph of the Great American Whopper.* New York: Funk & Wagnalls, 1931.

Thompson, Harold W. *Body, Boots and Britches.* Philadelphia: J.B. Lippincott, 1939.

Thompson, James W. "The Origins of the Hicks Family Tradition." *North Carolina Folklore Journal* 34 (1987): 18–28.

Thompson, Stith, ed. *Tales of the North American Indians.* Bloomington: Indiana University Press, 1929.

———. *The Folktale.* New York: Dryden, 1946.

———. "Folktales and Legends." In *The Frank C. Brown Collection of North Carolina Folklore*, gen. ed. Newman Ivey White. Vol. 1. Durham, NC: Duke University Press, 1952. 621–704.

———. *Motif-Index of Folk-Literature: A Classification of Narrative Elements in Folktales, Ballads, Myths, Fables, Mediaeval Romances, Exempla, Fabliaux, Jest-Books, and Local Legends.* 2d ed. 6 vols. Bloomington and Indianapolis: Indiana University Press, 1955–58.

———. *A Folklorist's Progress: Reflections of a Scholar's Life.* Bloomington: Special Publications of the Folklore Institute, Indiana University, 1996.

Tinkle, Lon. *An American Original: The Life of J. Frank Dobie.* Boston: Little, Brown, 1978.

Waugh, Butler Huggins, Jr. " 'The Child and the Snake': Aarne-Thompson 285, 782C, and Related Forms in Europe and America: A Comparative Folktale Study." Ph.D. diss., Folklore, Indiana University, 1959.

Wellman, Manly Wade. *The Kingdom of Madison: A Southern Mountain Fastness and Its People.* Chapel Hill: University of North Carolina Press, 1973. Reprint Alexander, North Carolina: Land of the Sky Books, 2001.

Welsch, Roger. *Shingling the Fog and Other Plains Lies.* Lincoln and London: University of Nebraska Press, 1972.

Whatley, W.A. "Mexican Münchausen." In *From Hell to Breakfast,* ed. Mody C. Boatright, pp. 45–49. Publications of the Texas Folklore Society 19. Dallas: Southern Methodist University Press, 1944.

Williams, Michael Ann. *Great Smoky Mountains Folklife.* Jackson: University Press of Mississippi, 1995.

Wilson, William A. "The Seriousness of Mormon Humor." *Sunstone,* January 1985: 8–13.

Winniford, Lee. *Following Old Fencelines: Tales from East Texas.* College Station: Texas A&M University Press, 1998.

Wolkstein, Diane. *The Magic Orange Tree and Other Haitian Folktales.* New York: Alfred A. Knopf, 1978.

Worster, Donald. *Dust Bowl: The Southern Plains in the 1930s.* New York and London: Oxford University Press, 1979.

Yates, Michael, ed. *Far in the Mountains, Vols. 3 & 4.* CDs MTCD323-4. Stroud, Glouchestershire, UK: Musical Tradition Records, 2002a.

———. "A Nest of Singing Birds." *Musical Traditions Internet Magazine,* March 15, 2002b, article 113.

INDEX OF NARRATORS

Numbers in this index refer to the story numbers listed in the text.

INDEX OF COLLECTORS AND COLLECTIONS

Numbers in this index refer to the story numbers listed in the text.

GEOGRAPHIC INDEX

Here follows a state-by-state list of the places where the narrators featured in this book were born and lived, as well as where their tales were set and where they were performed. In many cases, extant documentary information is insufficient to determine where certain narrators were born or lived, or where a certain stories were told or set. Thus, the following index is incomplete. Yet it does contain information useful for readers interested in reading and comparing tales set in or collected in—or told by narrators who have lived in—a given state or community. Numbers in this index refer to the story numbers in the text.

INDEX OF TALES RELEASED IN AUDIO FORM THROUGH THE AMERICAN FOLKLIFE CENTER

As this book goes to press, only about 10 percent of the tales that appear here have been issued in audio form; and only about 7 percent are generally available at this time. Nevertheless, the number of AFC folk narratives available on Library of Congress Internet sites has increased dramatically in recent years. Here follows a list of tales published in LP and compact disk form as well as those available on the Internet.

In the list that follows, the number and title of the tale as rendered in this book are followed by publication information.

13. *When My Mother Told Jack Tales.* Released as "Introduction" to long-playing record AFS 47, *Jack Tales Told by Mrs. Maud Long of Hot Springs, North Carolina,* vol. 1, cut 1.

14. *Jack and the Giants' Newground.* Released on long-playing record AFS 48, *Jack Tales Told by Mrs. Maud Long of Hot Springs, North Carolina,* vol. 2, cut 1.

15. *Jack and the Drill.* Released on long-playing record AFS 47, *Jack Tales Told by Mrs. Maud Long of Hot Springs, North Carolina,* vol. 1, cut 2.

16. *Jack and the Varmints.* Released on long-playing record AFS 48, *Jack Tales Told by Mrs. Maud Long of Hot Springs, North Carolina,* vol. 2, cut 2.

17. *Jack and the Bull.* Released on long-playing record AFS 47, *Jack Tales Told by Mrs. Maud Long of Hot Springs, North Carolina,* vol. 1, band 4.

99. *Cat Story.* Audio available in digital form at http://memory.loc.gov/cgi-bin/query/S?ammem/lomaxbib:@field(DOCID(@range(11+14))); search under title.

100. *Music for Me to Run By.* Audio available in digital form at http://memory.loc.gov/cgi-bin/query/S?ammem/lomaxbib:@field(DOCID(@range(11+14))); search under the title, "Ghost Story."

101. *The Leaky House.* Audio available in digital form at http://memory.loc.gov/cgi-bin/query/S?ammem/lomaxbib:@field(DOCID(@range(11+14))); search under title.

107–109. Witch Narratives. Released as "Witch Stories," on the LP *Aunt Molly Jackson,* Rounder Records 1002.

122. *The Yankee and Marcum.* Available in CD form on *The Hammons Family: The Traditions*

INDEX OF TALE TYPES

This numerical list is based on Antti Aarne's and Stith Thompson's *The Types of the Folktale* (1961), a systematic classification of internationally distributed fictional narratives from oral tradition. Following the conventions of folklorists, I have used the prefix "AT" (for "Aarne-Thompson") in the introductory matter and in the notes to designate tale types. For example, AT 301 refers to *The Three Stolen Princesses,* one of the most common folktales in U.S. tradition, represented by four different tales in this collection. AT 301A refers to the subtype *Quest for a Vanished Princess,* the most popular American subtype, represented by three of the tales anthologized here. A number followed by an asterisk (for example, 1487*, *Guarding against Neglect*) indicates a tale type with limited distribution.

Although Aarne and Thompson designed their catalogue as a guide to folk fiction, many of their tale types are told as legends and claimed to be true when narrated in the United States. For example, Sara Cleveland's "Shiver and Shake" (story 44) and Laurie Hance's "A Haunted House" (story 117) are very similar in plot, and both are classified as versions of AT 326, *The Youth Who Wanted to Learn What Fear Is,* but Sara Cleveland's tale is told as a fiction and Laurie Hance's as a legend, a story that many believe to be true.

Aarne and Thompson divided their catalogue according to genre and content: for example, the tales assigned numbers 300–749 were classified as "Ordinary Folktales: Tales of Magic." In the list below I employ the Aarne-Thompson classificatory headings.

Animal Tales (AT 1–299)

4. *Carrying the Sham-Sick Trickster.*
15. *The Theft of Butter by Playing Godfather.*
62. *Peace among the Animals.*

72. *Rabbit Rides Fox a-Courting.*
81. *Too Cold for Hare to Build House in Winter.*
123. *The Wolf and the Kids.*

155. *Ungrateful Serpent Returned to Captivity.*
157. *Learning to Fear Man.*
175. *The Tarbaby and the Rabbit.*

53. *Brother Rabbit Rides Brother Bear.*
188. *The Fox, the Rabbit, and the Tarbaby.*
55. *Brother Bear and Brother Deer Hold a Meeting.*
53. *Brother Rabbit Rides Brother Bear.*
101. *The Leaky House.*

78. *One-My-Darling.*
183. *Show Me Your Paw.*
48. *Mr. Snake and the Farmer.*
54. *Brother Bear Meets Man.*
188. *The Fox, the Rabbit, and the Tarbaby.*
189. *The Tarbaby.*

Ordinary Folktales (Märchen, Magic Tales: AT 300–749)

Tales of the Stupid Ogre (AT 1000–1199)

Numskull Stories (AT 1200–1349)

Other Jokes and Anecdotes: (AT 1349–1874)

Tales of Lying (Tall Tales, AT 1875–1999)

Cumulative Tales (AT 2000–2399)

INDEX OF MOTIFS

This catalogue is based on Stith Thompson's six-volume *Motif-Index of Folk-Literature: A Classification of Narrative Elements in Folktales, Ballads, Myths, Fables, Mediaeval Romances, Exempla, Fabliaux, Jest-Books, and Local Legends* (1955–58), a systematic attempt to assemble the narrative material of world folk tradition. According to Thompson, a motif is "the smallest element in a tale having the power to persist in tradition" (Thompson 1946: 415). Thompson divides elements into three general categories. First, a motif may be a character, for example a witch (G200) or a "giant ogre" (G100). The second category comprises "certain items in the background of the action," such as "magic objects" (e.g., D1521.1, "Seven-league boots" in story 77), "unusual customs" (e.g., H400, "Chastity test" in story 97), and "strange beliefs" (e.g., G272.6, "Sieve as protection against witches" in story 128). These few examples make it clear that motifs are more than simply tiny story elements: Thompson emphasized the magical, the unusual, and the strange. In selecting material for his index, he gave preference to extraordinary characters and things. Thus there is a motif assigned to a "speaking cat" (B211.1.8), but none simply to a cat.

The third category category of motifs constitutes "single incidents" (1946: 416). Thus, like tale types, certain motifs serve to identify folktale plots. As Thompson explains, these motifs based on action "can have an independent existence and . . . may therefore serve as true tale-types. By far the largest number of traditional types consist of these single motifs." Thus, a given brief tale in this collection may be classified both as a tale type and as a motif. For example, Sam Harmon's tale "The Great Pumpkin" (story 3) may be classified both as tale type AT 1960D, *The Great Vegetable,* and as motif X1411.2, "Lies about large pumpkins."

Often a motif will exist both as an independent tale and as a brief episode in a longer tale. For example, the motif K1611, "Substituted caps cause ogre to kill his own children," is also classified as tale type AT 1119, *The Ogre Kills His Own Children.* Sometimes this motif exists independently, but all three times that it appears in this collection, it occurs as part of a longer tale: in "Little Nippy" (story 191) for instance, AT 1119 is embedded in a longer plot, AT 328, *The Boy Steals the Giant's Treasure.* Because there is a great deal of redundancy between the tale type index and the motif-index, in cases in which the tale type number and motif number signify identical ideas, I have not always classified a tale both by motif and by tale type. In general, I have given preference to type numbers.

Unlike the tale types, which were designed exclusively to catalog folk fiction, Thompson's motifs may refer to fictional stories, or to belief narratives such as legends, myths, and personal experience stories. Thus, such sacred stories as George Young's "The Blackfish" (story 193) does not have a tale type number, but does possess several motifs from world belief tradition. Thus, the motif index is more comprehensive in its generic scope than is the tale type index.

Furthermore, while the *Types of the Folktale* concentrates on European and European-derived traditions, the *Motif-Index* embraces more material from worldwide traditions. Thus, George Young's tale of "The Blackfish," which comes from the Native American Nisqually culture, contains several motifs that are found in other Native American traditions (e.g., K922, "Artificial whale made as stratagem") but that are not often found among the tales classified in *The Types of the Folktale.*

In Thompson's index, each motif number begins with a letter from the alphabet. Each letter represents a distinct subject category: for example, "A" refers to "Mythological Motifs."

Some of the motifs listed below do not appear in Thompson, but were added by Thompson's student Baughman, who created the most extensive catalogue of motifs based on American material: *Type and Motif Index of the Folktales of England and North America* (1966). Baughman's numbers can be distinguished by their endings. When a number ends with an asterisk (for example, X621*, "Jokes about the Irish") or with a letter in parentheses (for example, X459(d) "Parson arrives late for meeting of ministers. . . ."), it is drawn from Baughman.

A. Mythological Motifs

A511.2.2.1. Culture hero suckled by wolf. — 114. *The Wolf Boy.*

A672.1.1. Charon exacts fee to ferry souls across Styx. — Cf. 150. *He'll Have to Swim.*

A901. Topographical featues caused by experiences of giant hero. — 33. *Finn MacCool and the Rocks.*

A977.1. Giant responsible for certain stones. — 33. *Finn MacCool and the Rocks.*

Cf. A2101. Fish made from wood. — 193. *The Blackfish.*

A2281. Enmity between animals from original quarrel. — 55. *Brother Bear and Brother Deer Hold a Meeting.*

A2312.1.1. Origin of cracks in tortoise's shell. — 194. *How the Terrapin Got the Scars on His Shell.*

A2330. Origin of animal characteristics: face. — 178. *The Girl Who Didn't Mind Her Mother.*

A2494.4.4. Enmity between dog and rabbit. — 55. *Brother Bear and Brother Deer Hold a Meeting.*

A2720. Plant characteristics as punishment. — 193. *The Blackfish.*

B. Animals

B29.9. Man-ape. — 27. *The Yape.*

B147.1.2.2. Cat as beast of ill-omen. — 99. *Cat Story.*

B181.1. Magic cat. — 99. *Cat Story.*

B210.2. Talking animal or object refuses to talk on demand. — 184. *Skullbone.*

B211.1.8. Speaking cat. — 99. *Cat Story.*

B253. Animals perform offices of church. — 55. *Brother Bear and Brother Deer Hold a Meeting.*

B360. Grateful animals. — 187. *Antonio the Woodcutter.*

B411. Helpful cow. — 178. *The Girl Who Didn't Mind Her Mother.*

B435.4. Helpful bear. — 62. *The Bear's Tale.*

B453.3. Helpful wolf. — 114. *The Wolf Boy.*

B524.1.3. Dogs rescue master from tree refuge. — 181. *The Forty-Mile Jumper.*
182. *Gaillum, Singo, et Moliseau.*

B535. Animal nurse; animal nourishes abandoned child. — 114. *The Wolf Boy.*

B562.1. Animal shows man treasure. — 62. *The Bear's Tale.*

B765.6. Snake eats milk and bread with child. — 116. *The Child and the Snake.*

B766.2. Cat sucks sleeping child's breath. — Cf. 99. *Cat Story.*

B871.1.1. Giant cow. — 143. *The Roguish Cow.*

C. Tabu

C631. Not to work on Sunday. — 106. *Churning up the Devil.*

D. Magic

D170. Transformation: man to fish. — 193. *The Blackfish.*

D435.1. Image comes to life. — 193. *The Blackfish.*

D1381. Child divides last loaf with fairy (dwarf). — 81. *Rawhead and Bloodybones.*

D1385.4. Silver bullet protects against giants, ghosts, and witches. — 107. *Becoming a Witch and Undoing Spells.*
127. *Witches.*

D1454.1.1. Gold and silver combed from hair. — 81. *Rawhead and Bloodybones.*

D1521. Miraculous speed from magic object. — 181. *The Forty-Mile Jumper.*

D1521.1. Seven-league boots. — 77. *Merrywise.*
Cf. 181. *The Forty-Mile Jumper.*

D1610.6.1. Speaking vulva; man has power to make vulvas speak . . . as a chastity test. — 97. *The Lady and Her Three Daughters.*

D1610.6.3. Speaking buttocks. — 97. *The Lady and Her Three Daughters.*

D1721.1. Magic power from devil. — 122. *The Yankee and Marcum.*

D1745. Magic power rendered ineffective. — 108. *The Witch and the Witch Doctor*

D1777. Magic results from power of thought. — 122. *The Yankee and Marcum.*

D1810. Magic knowledge. — 35. *Telling Fortunes with Cards.*

D1810.8. Magic knowledge from dream. — 25. *Hooray for Old Sloosha!*

D1810.13. Magic knowledge from the dead. — 36. *Spiritualism and Fortune Telling.*

D1812.3.3. Future revealed in dream. — 121. *The Scarecrow Dream.*
192. *The Old Woman's Vision.*

D1812.3.3.11. Death of another revealed in dream. — 34. *Black Horses.*

D1812.5.1.12.1. Howling of dog as bad omen. — 125. *The Three Knocks; A Grandmother's Ghost.*

D1856.2. Three Nephites are granted quasi-immortal state by Jesus Christ at time of resurrection. — 133. *Raising the Dead; The Nephite on the Road.*

D2063.1.1. Tormenting by sympathetic magic; . . . witch tormented by abusing an animal or object. — 107. *Becoming a Witch and Undoing Spells.*

E. The Dead

F. Marvels

H. Tests

L. Reversal of Fortune

M. Ordaining the Future

N. Chance and Fate

P. Society

Q. Rewards and Punishments

Q2236.3*I. Fish caught on Sunday bursts man open.

60. *Pull Me Up, Simon.*

S. Unnatural Cruelty

S110.5. Murderer kills all who come to certain spot.

68. *The Murderers.*

S123. Burial alive.

S168. Mutilation: tearing off ears.

Cf. 115. *The Orphan Girl That Died.*

80. *The King's Well.*

194. *How the Terrapin Got the Scars on His Shell.*

T. Sex

T145. Polygamous marriages.

T465. Bestiality.

T465.4. Children are spotted like leopards as the result of bestiality.

158. *The* Indito *and His Wives.*

167. *I Love Ewe.*

168. *Sports as Markers.*

Cf. 168. *Sports as Markers.*

U. The Nature of Life

U120. Nature will show itself.

155. *Jamie the Mountain Lion.*

V. Religion

V231.6. Angel in the form of an old man.

133. *Raising the Dead; The Nephite on the Road.*

X. Humor

X111.7. Misunderstood words lead to comic results.

Cf. 164. *Old One-Eye.*

X459(d). Parson arrives late for meeting of ministers. . . .

151. *Cold as Hell.*

X621*. Jokes about the Irish.

46. *One Thing the Devil Can't Do.*

173. *Twenty-Five Roosters and One Hen.*

174. *Thinning Corn.*

X732. Humor concerning sexual intercourse.

96. *The Woman Who Couldn't Count.*

97. *The Lady and Her Three Daughters.*

X735.9.1. "My gun ain't loaded."

145. *The Gun Ain't Loaded.*

X749.12.1. Man disguised as woman.

95. *The Preacher That Could Always Be Trapped by Women.*

X1121.7*. Lie: marvelous gun.

141. *The Biggest Liar in the State.*

X1122.4.2*(c). Hunter . . . shoots bear with tears.

139. *Cornered by a Polar Bear.*

X1741.7*(d). Man and horse jump off canyon   161. *Tom the Burro.*
    rim. . . .

Z. Miscellaneous Groups of Motifs

Z356. Unique survivor.

25. *Hooray for Old Sloosha!* -
26. *Feathers in Her Hair.*
65. *Chute's Wedge Trick.*

Carl Lindahl, Martha Gano Houstoun Research Professor of English at the University of Houston, has authored or edited fifteen books on folklore, including *Perspectives on the Jack Tales* (2001) and *Swapping Stories: Folktales from Louisiana* (1997). He currently serves as series editor for the World Folktale Library.